Thomas F. (Thomas Francis) Bayard, J. (Jacob) Schoenhof

The Economy of High Wages

An iInquiry into the Cause of high Wages and their Effect on Methods and...

Thomas F. (Thomas Francis) Bayard, J. (Jacob) Schoenhof
The Economy of High Wages
An IInquiry into the Cause of high Wages and their Effect on Methods and...

ISBN/EAN: 9783744764926

Printed in Europe, USA, Canada, Australia, Japan

Cover: Foto ©Suzi / pixelio.de

More available books at **www.hansebooks.com**

THE

Economy of High Wages

AN INQUIRY INTO THE CAUSE OF HIGH WAGES AND THEIR
EFFECT ON METHODS AND COST OF PRODUCTION

BY

J. SCHOENHOF

LATE U. S. CONSUL; COMMISSIONED BY DEPT. OF STATE TO INQUIRE INTO
THE ECONOMY OF PRODUCTION AND THE STATE OF TECHNICAL
EDUCATION IN EUROPE; AUTHOR OF "THE DESTRUCTIVE
INFLUENCE OF THE TARIFF"; "THE INDUSTRIAL
SITUATION;" "WAGES AND TRADE"; "IN-
DUSTRIAL EDUCATION IN FRANCE,"
ETC., ETC.

WITH AN INTRODUCTION
BY
THOMAS F. BAYARD
LATE SECRETARY OF STATE, U. S. A.

G. P. PUTNAM'S SONS
NEW YORK   LONDON
27 WEST TWENTY-THIRD STREET   24 BEDFORD STREET, STRAND

The Knickerbocker Press

1892

COPYRIGHT, 1892,
BY J. SCHOENHOF.

INTRODUCTORY LETTER

FROM HON. T. F. BAYARD,
Late Secretary of State, U. S. A.

WILMINGTON, DEL., *June* 10, 1892.

JACOB SCHOENHOF, ESQ., NEW YORK.

My Dear Sir: I am gratified to learn that you are now prepared to lay before the country, in a compendious form, the results of the personal examination and intelligent study which, under instructions of the Department of State in 1887, you prosecuted in those industrial centres of Europe where technical education had been most highly developed and had proved itself to be productive of the highest economy and best results.

Impressed by a necessity of a practical and thorough comprehension by our countrymen of the actual condition of their foreign competitors in the arts and manufactures, to the end that their energies and intelligence could be successfully applied to keep them abreast of the world's column of artificers in the progress of science and invention, I considered it fortunate for the public that I was enabled to command your especial faculties in the execution of the task.

My only regret has been caused by the arrestation of your work, pending its satisfactory completion, by your removal from your position in the Consular service and the consequent subtraction of that support and furtherance which your official association afforded.

I had indulged the hope that the non-partisan nature of your employment, and the signal ability you had displayed in the execution of your Consular duties, would have constituted a protection to the public interests, and have shielded you from the desiccating blasts of "the spoils system."

Nevertheless, I congratulate you upon the result of your labors as now presented to the country, and which I cannot doubt will prove of great value in the campaign of education in political economy now happily in progress in the United States.

The scope and purpose of your investigations were not limited to reporting mere processes of manufacture and the bare statistics of the hours of labor, rates of wages, cost of machinery, of raw materials, utilization of wastes, etc., etc.

Such information, however interesting and valuable, was not wholly wanting, nor was it difficult to obtain. Your purpose was even more important, and its results were to contain a higher significance, which was to indicate and establish the power of education of the human hand and brain, and the application of sense and feeling in the expansion and improvement of the products of human industry; to show how "the sweat of the brow is lessened by the conception of the brain," and increased wages accompany increased efficiency.

The proofs contained in the reports of your investigations, go far to refute the shallow and repulsive theory that a human being is a mere machine—and to prove that, on the contrary, true economy and philosophy join in declaring that the cheapest labor is the labor that is most productive, and that the more the forces of cultivated intelligence, conscientiousness, and hopefulness shall infuse themselves into human industry, the more abundant and valuable the results, the greater the sum of human happiness, and the more stable the political institutions of a country.

No sophistry is more demonstrable than that contained in the phrase "the labor market," a phrase which grates upon the ear and offends the moral sense—for it seems to classify men with machinery, and fails to take into account human impulses and feeling, the heart and brain in their effect upon the energy and excellence of human industry.

When Turner, the artist, was asked with what he mixed

his colors, he growled out, "Brains"—and there is not a department of human labor, however mechanical, in which the enlistment of the brain, and with it the heart of the laborer, is not in a degree and way of its own of practical importance.

Amid the elements of the cost of production, labor is ever present and essential, and consequently in the fierce and strenuous competition of the industrial world the *true economy in labor, its quality as well as quantity*, is the question of controlling importance.

Before the item of profit can arise, the cost of the various elements combined in any product must be first deducted.

Wages, taxes, rent, insurance, interest, capital, material, waste are among these items, and labor is the ever-present and essential integer which imparts vitality to the whole.

An increase of any of these items trenches upon labor, and true wisdom instructs that labor is entitled to the chief consideration and outranks all the others in its importance.

The facts you have adduced and your deductions irresistibly establish the proposition that low wages do not mean cheap production, and that the best instructed and best paid labor proves itself to be the most productive—so that the rate of wages and the cost of production are not alternative nor equivalent expressions, although so frequently and ignorantly confused.

As the efficiency of labor is increased, prices will be lessened, and this creates new demands, so that successful and progressive industry implies a necessity for wider markets, and a minimum of artificial restriction upon exchanges in the commercial world.

Mechanical excellence is one of the fruits of technical education, and the command of every market follows the workman who can produce what is best and at the lowest cost.

Skill is the outgrowth of educated senses, and the superiority of labor consists in the degree in which mind aids muscle in its tasks—hence the discrimination in the rewards between "skilled" and "unskilled" labor.

The information afforded by your studies as now reported, cannot fail to prove a valuable contribution to the just and rational solution of the great labor problem of the present day, and will assist alike employers and employed.

I hail with satisfaction everything that tends to emancipate labor from the control, or as it is delusively styled, the "protection" of the State, and demonstrates the essential truth that excellence in skill and labor comes from each member individually, and not from an aggregate of members in which individual excellence is not recognized nor respected.

Nothing surely can be more unreasonable, unjust, and

delusive than the view or scheme of regulating the rewards of labor which excludes the value of individual intelligence, industry, skill, and the attendant moral force which are combined by the law of their creation with the labor of mankind.

There is gratifying evidence of growing recognition of the needs and just claims of labor in such institutions as the Metropolitan Museum in New York, which is a great public adjutant as a school of design; a well-spring of education of the earning capacities of manual labor, serving as a model for imitation as well as technical and practical instruction.

Akin to it in usefulness and beneficent purpose is the Drexel Institute of Art, Science, and Industry in Philadelphia—another splendid illustration of well-considered individual generosity and wise public spirit.

And thus in the education of the faculties for special results, general results must also be achieved in the expansion of their faculties and elevation of mankind.

Technical education, by means of which taste is cultivated and skill acquired, will greatly promote that healthy and self-reliant independence so desirable for a nation.

It is by such means that the true elevation of the industrial classes will be attained, and that relations of mutual confidence and good understanding between employers and employed, will be established. It will, in fact, be a resort to "the golden rule," productive only of benignity, and which will be found the most reliable means of exorcising from modern civilization its worst spectre—the antagonism of capital and labor.

I hope your work may hasten on the day when the honest individual may be permitted to enjoy the calm content of constant industry and the advantages of his own labor, free alike from the tyranny of numbers in his own class or of that other class "of prosperous plunderers who live in abundance surrounded by the victims of their injustice and rapacity."

You have certainly erected a modest porch to the great edifice of sound sociology, and performed a service to the people of the United States.

I am,
Very truly yours,
T. F. BAYARD.

TABLE OF CONTENTS.

PAGE

Introductory Letter from Hon. T. F. Bayard, late Secretary of State, U. S. A.................................... iii

PART I.

THE CAUSE OF HIGH WAGES.

CHAPTER I.

The Economy of Production and the Tariff interwoven 1
The Relative Positions of Producers............................ 4
The Tariff Reform Issue.. 5
In what Foreign Tariffs are Distinct from American Tariffs........ 8
Wage Differences in Protected and Unprotected Industries..... ... 10
The McKinley Act a Monument of Legislative Ignorance.......... 11
The Raw Material in Production 13

CHAPTER II.

The Labor Question in the Tariff 18
The Fallacy of the Old Theory of Wages........................ 19
Relative Productiveness of Labor................................ 20
Differences in Coal Mining...................................... 22
Increase of Earnings and Reduced Cost going Hand in Hand 24
The Same Labor Differences in Higher Products.................. 25
Maintaining Power of Labor.... 28
What Causes High Wages 31

CHAPTER III.

Low Wages, Stagnating Causes.—Improvement in Machinery more Profitable in High-Wage Countries 35
A High Standard a Prerequisite to Improvement.................. 38
Low Wages Indicate Low Productivity........................... 39
Irish Industries as Object Lessons.............................. 41
Working for a Home Market..................................... 44

CHAPTER IV.

	PAGE
Advantages of Old Methods in Certain Industries	50
How These Low Wage-Earners Live	51
How they Work in Lyons	53
Economic Advantages of the Old System.—Capital left Free	55
The Evolution of Industries	58
The Producer and Consumer are One.—Increasing Productiveness is Increasing Consumptiveness	61
The Economic Value of High Wages generally not Understood	63

CHAPTER V.

The Efficiency and Productiveness of Labor increased by Education.	67
Cheap Labor and Ignorant Labor Synonymous	67
The Ideal Part in the Economy of Production	69
Teaching Industrial Art	72
The Industrial Art Museum	74
Antique and Modern Art Industry	76

CHAPTER VI.

Science and Art Powerful Factors in the Economy of Production	81
Superiority of English Work	82
Helps in Technical Training	84
American Chemists Lagging behind	88
Scientific Improvements quickly adopted	89

CHAPTER VII.

Improvements and Inventions	91
Powerful Influence in Metallurgy	92
Steel Rails	93
Price Reductions in Other Forms of Iron	95
Other Illustrations of Superior American Methods	97
The Steamship an Illustration of Modern Development.—Science applied to Industry	103

CHAPTER VIII.

Proof of Principles laid down taken from Agriculture.—Results of Scientific Methods	108
Ignorance the Cause of Poverty	109

CONTENTS. xiii

PAGE

Difference in Results Traceable to Institutions 111
Modern Russian Agriculture on a Thirteenth Century Level of England... 115
High Results of Ownership by the Tiller under Free Laws. 119
General Farming Results in Europe Confirmatory of the Principle.. 122
Causes of Lombardy's Superior Agriculture....... 125
The Contrasts and their Causes..................... 130

CHAPTER IX.

Security from Famine guaranteed by Civilization.—Auxiliary Advantages by Improved Means of Communication 134
Truck Farming, a Creation of the Railroad and the Steamboat..... 136
The Richer Lands give the Poorer Crops........................ .. 138
Poor Results and High Results due only to Poor or Good Farming.. 138
A Practical Illustration of Results of Best Methods............... 144
Extent of Land required under Different Methods of Cultivation.... 150

CHAPTER X.

The Condition of the Workingman under the Old and the New Dispensation................................. 153
The Standard of Living under the Best of Old Conditions 154
The Measure of Progress expressed by the Budget of Consumables .. 160
Comparison of Budgets 163
The German Workingman's Basis of Living now, on that of the English a Hundred Years Ago................................... 167

PART II.

THE EFFECT OF HIGH WAGES.

Comparative Methods and Cost of Production in America and European Countries.

CHAPTER I.

Unreliability of Statements of Protected Interests.—The Potter's Industry in Evidence 175
The Industry in America and England.......................... 176

CONTENTS.

	PAGE
Assertions of the Trenton Potters	179
Inefficiency attracted by a High Tariff	184
Labor-saving Appliances in Pottery	186
Sanitary Ware	188
Brown Stoneware	190

CHAPTER II.

The Trust and Monopolies alone benefited by Tariff Legislation.—
   The Glass Industry in Evidence 194
Flint Glass, Table Ware, Hollow Ware, etc. 195
Mode of Pay and Comparative Rates in England and America 196
English Rates 198
Cut Glass, Decorated and Fancy Ware 202
Window Glass 204
Plate Glass 205

CHAPTER III.

The Insincerity of the Claim for Protection of Labor.—Demonstrated by a Comparison of the Cost of Coal and Iron Mining, here and abroad 208
America's and England's Position 212
Iron Ore 213
Coke and Pig-Iron 215
Steel Rail Making 218

CHAPTER IV.

The Injury of Protection to Industry.—The Advantages America reaps from Superior Methods and Low Labor Cost frustrated by Protection 222
Manufacturers' Tools and Machinery 224
Cutlery 228
Arms, Ammunition, Machinery 229
Europe's Methods Different 231

CHAPTER V.

The Textile Industries.—Labor's Higher Reward in America Due entirely to Greater Exertion.—Greater Output and Lower Labor Cost in Cotton Manufacture.—The Tariff Increases Profit Rates but Reduces Wages.—Print Cloth in Evidence 234

CONTENTS. xv

PAGE
Relative Positions of England and America...................... 236
Print Cloth.—The Comparative Cost and Rate of Wages.......... 237
Republican Contradiction....................................... 242

CHAPTER VI.

Ability to Satisfy the Taste of Buyers Determines the Course of Trade.—Cotton Goods, Printing, Finishing.—Our Importations Caused by Inability of Home Producer to Answer the Wants of the People.—New Departure in Tariff Legislation............. 246
Cotton Velvets 250
Cotton Hosiery.. 255

CHAPTER VII.

Futility of attempting Industrial Creations by Protective Tariffs.—Flax Cultivation and Linen Manufacturing.—Cotton Embroideries and Laces classed under Linen for Tariff Increase.—Reasons why they cannot be produced here 258
Linen Manufacturers... 262
Cotton Embroidery, Cotton Lace................................ 264
Embroidered and Hemstitched Handkerchiefs..................... 267

CHAPTER VIII.

Science and Skill in Manufacturing Industries.—Silk Manufacturing.—Lyons and Paterson compared.—Superiority of Lyons Goods.—Lower Cost Due to Other Causes than Differences in Labor 269
Loading of Silks... 273
Comparative Cost of Spinning................................... 275
The Dyeing of Silk.. 277
Weaving... 278
General Conditions of Silk Manufacturing in America............ 281

CHAPTER IX.

Silk Plushes.—Increased Duties to Foster Non-existing Industries.—Marked Decline in Silk Manufacturing in General.—Tariffs cannot Supply the Absence of Skill and Knowledge............... 283

CHAPTER X.

Wool and Woolens.—Protection frustrated by its own Excesses.—Wool artificially Dear Limits Consumption.—Decrease of Sheep.—Increase in England.—Decline in Wool Manufacturing Traceable to the Tariff.—Great Increase in the Use of Wool Substitutes 294
The Wool... 295
American Wool 298
Other Disastrous Effects of a Wool Tariff........................ 301
Decline in Wool—Increase in Shoddy 307

CHAPTER XI.

Woolens and Worsteds.—Methods pursued in Comparative Inquiry.. 310
Worsteds and Combed-Yarn Goods 313
The Labor... 314
The Yarn.. 318
Italian Cloths.. 323
Mohair and Other Combed-Wool Dress Goods.................. 325

CHAPTER XII.

Carded-Wool Goods.—Labor not Higher than in England......... 328
Dress Goods.. 329
Answering by "If"... 333
The Proof is in the Selling Price................................... 337
All-Wool Kersey Cloth... 338
6-4 Cheviots.. 340

CHAPTER XIII.

Plushes, Pile Fabrics, Knit Goods classed with Clothing for Duty Increase.. 342
Knit Fabrics.. 345
Carpets.. 348
Summary of Comparative Cost in Woolens and Worsteds.—What is the Cost Difference under Free Wool...................... 351

CHAPTER XIV.

The Making-up Industries.—Industries protected, but not by Tariffs. 356
The Manufacturing System of Berlin.............................. 361
The Sweating System.. 363

CHAPTER XV.

Improved Methods and Division of Labor.—Labor in Ready-made Goods here and abroad.—Great Export Articles.—Foreign Commerce restricted by the Tariff............................ 370
Boots and Shoes.. 373
The Foreign Trade Aspect.. 375
Reciprocity Treaties 379

CHAPTER XVI.

The Tariff in its Relations to the Industrial Problem.—Comparative Labor Cost in Principal Industries in America and England.—High Wages and Reduced Hours resulting from Improvement in Economy of Production................................... 383
The Cost of Production... 385
Economic and Sociological Deductions 390
The Cotton Industry, an Illustration 395
The Cause of Progress and Prosperity 401
Addenda... 406
Index.. 409

PART I.

THE CAUSE OF HIGH WAGES.

Eine einzige Thatsache vermag die Systeme ganzer Jahrhunderte über den Haufen zu werfen und ganze Bibliotheken in Makulatur zu verwandeln. Gegen die Thatsachen hilft kein Sträuben und Protestiren.— *Frauenstädt.*

A single fact is able to upset the systems of centuries and to turn whole libraries into waste paper. Neither resisting nor protesting avails against facts.

CHAPTER I.

The Economy of Production and the Tariff interwoven.—Impossibility to treat the One without a Thorough Understanding of the Elements of Production.—The Difference of Tariffs here and abroad.—The Raw Material, the Natural Starting-point in Production.—The Inherent Differences to be considered.

THE protective theory starts from the assumption that an act of legislation can equalize the differences which economically considered exist between one country and another in the ability of producing whatever is not absolutely withheld by nature. As within this wide limit there is very little which cannot be called into being in the range of products consumed by the people, provided the differences in cost can be balanced by enabling the home producer to charge the difference on the consumer, there can be very little difficulty to understand the genesis of protection. The taxing power of nations has not been loath to avail itself of the advantages which this dogma offered. By persuading the workingman that he could find more remunerative employment he was made an easy proselyte, wherever he had anything to say in the selection of his rulers, to the policy of excluding foreign products by tariff taxation, which might interfere with the sale of the products of his own industry. The manufacturer, of course, would be the stanchest advocate of the policy, as he could collect all the profits from the consumer which lie between his enhanced cost of production and the price he could realize from the sale of his goods. It was his interest, therefore, at all times to have this margin as big as possible. He did this very effectively, as is known to all generations of tariff-afflicted peoples, by getting the legislators to keep raising the duties to heights as demanded by every interest. Many things, however, have escaped notice, which, had they received due weight, would have tipped the balance in the opposite direction.

Taxation of foreign imports for revenue, selects only such articles as dutiable which will not interfere with home production. Articles of luxury or of immediate consumption—not requiring a process of remanufacture—are fit objects of such taxation. Taxation for protection, necessarily must gradually extend over all articles which go into every species of remanufacture. Every one concerned in the production of consumables will consider himself injured unless he gets his share allotted in the enterprise of creating universal prosperity by universal taxation. Taxation for protection, therefore, covers the raw material of the fabric as well as of the worker, the sustenance on which he must feed to keep up his tissue. It covers every advance in the scale of progression. Every new feature in the metamorphosis of production is made a subject of additional caretaking by taxation. Finally, by this inflating process constantly going on, the cost of production is increased so that protectionism would become extinct more by the curses of its beneficiaries than by the kicks of its enemies, were the former as enlightened as one might expect the producers to be on the economies of their own crafts and trades. Another cause of distress to the protected, growing out of protection, is in the attraction of capital and enterprise to these artificially fostered industries by which the very reverse of the early benefits frequently follow to those who embark with hardly any other qualification than the possession of capital.

The pressure which the unusually keen competition following therefrom exercises on prices cannot be alleviated by relief which foreign markets would give. The inflated cost of materials, though labor and capital become alike depressed in the struggle for survival by a merciless competition, would prevent this, if all other things were equal. The difficulties interposed by protection to the normal growth and expansion of industries are increased when further abnormities have been introduced which make it doubtful by what name to call a system of fiscal taxation such as encumbers the statute books of the United States. It has been doubtful at all times, from 1870 on, whether to call it a system of protection, obstruction, or destruction. It may be said to be one thing or the other as the parties concerned are affected by such a system of hybrid legislation. When the so-called Morrill tariff—the war tariff—was enacted, the terms were moderate compared to what they have become since by successive layers. The later increases, required by the exigencies of the war, in 1865 and 1867 were found necessary, in part at least, as offsets against the newly introduced system of internal revenue taxation, which taxed home products specifically, besides taxing the manufacturer on his sales, the banker and the merchant on their turnover, and then the net incomes of all concerned over again. All these internal rates have long ago become extinct, and nothing remains of the whole system, except those on intoxicating liquors, beer, and cigars, which are properly called excise duties and do not bear on the subject of discussion except in a very remote way.

The tariff on foreign imports, however, has not been

reduced. We cannot call the tariff act of 1883 a reduction. In all its essential features it was as burdensome as that of 1867; in one sense greatly more so, inasmuch as the decline in prices of almost all commodities since 1867 had thrown out of proportion the relations of the specific duties to the prices of the articles on which they were imposed.* Hence the tariff of 1883 weighed more heavily upon the people as consumers and producers than that of 1867, which was strictly a war measure.

The Relative Positions of Producers.

It is evident, confining ourselves more strictly to the concrete question as it presents itself in the United States, that the industrial interests would long have rebelled against this war tariff and its further excrescences had they not been held in check by fears and threats. The latter were more powerful than they would have been had they been met by a more thorough understanding of the principles which govern the economy of production than is the case among so intelligent a people as the producing classes of the United States, including the manufacturers. The latter soon found out that the taxing of raw material for protection's sake practically confiscated the advantages given by

---

* In illustration I will refer to the price of raw wool. In 1867 the price of greasy Australian was 12¼d. (25 cents gold) London price. The duty was 11 cents a pound and 10 per cent. ad valorem, equal to 54 per cent. The same wool is now quoted at 8d. or 16 cents a pound, and was a few months previous to this writing as low as 7¼d. or 14½ cents. Specific duty of 11 cents makes the ad valorem percentage to come to 70 to 75 per cent.— so that, even without the 10 per cent. ad valorem of the old tariff taken off (changed in 1883 to a net rate of 10 cents per pound), the new tariff taxes wool one-third more than the extremest war tariff rates have been. The specific rate of 11 cents in 1867 equalled 44 per cent.; in 1892 it equals 70 to 75 per cent.

protection to their respective industries. A large class of them, chiefly among those whose products had exceeded the limited markets to which they were confined thereby, made protestations. As early as 1882 they organized, and later took more decided action asking for radical reform of the tariff on the basis of free raw materials. In 1884 they sent the writer a representative to Chicago to urge the adoption by the Democratic National Convention of their views, contained in the following resolutions:

"*First*—The abolition of all duties on raw materials, such as wool, iron, and other ores, coal, jute, hemp, flax, dye stuffs, etc., in order that we may compete in home and foreign markets with other manufacturing nations, not one of which taxes raw materials.

"*Second*—The adjustment of the tariff, so that manufactures approaching nearest to the crude state will pay a lower rate, and manufactures that are further advanced, requiring more skill and labor, will pay a higher rate of duties."

The convention adopted these views, and they form now the credo of that party.

At first sight it may seem unjust to free the products of the farm or the mine and to protect the products of the mill. I admit the stricture to be correct. I consider all protective taxes injurious to that extent that they increase the cost of production. I consider them superfluous, as the economy of production in the United States clearly shows. It is the object of these pages to show that production is conducted on so essentially different a basis in the United States than in other countries that all the arguments hitherto employed for the maintenance of the protective principle become more than hypothetical. But no matter what the demonstrations, though they be based on the most reliable facts obtainable by personal investigations, the practical conditions are that the fiscal laws of the country cannot be changed at will.

Accustomed methods of raising revenue must be followed. Whatever the opinion of the most radical reformer, he must take existing conditions, the bias of the public mind, into very serious consideration. A tariff on imported commodities will maintain itself for some time to come, and it remains here only to say that a tariff on finished articles is the only possible way of meeting the difficulty. To raise a revenue and give relief from burdensome taxation to the producer and the consumer can only be done by cutting away somewhere. Leaving the raw material taxed and taking off the duties from manufactures would be too absurd even for mention. A child could see that it would shut up every workshop and mill. The producer of the raw material would not need to concern himself further about the advantages of his special protection. He would have killed the goose which lays the golden eggs. There would be no market whatever for his protected raw material. But, on the contrary, the best protection for the producer of the raw material lies in the healthy expansion of manufacturing industries—an axiom which, stated by the author, has always given extreme satisfaction to protectionists. The only difference is in the methods found necessary. The writer considers non-interference, his opponents constant interference, the best means to the great end.

The natural advantages and resources are so great, the impulses to exploit them for individual benefit are so powerful, in the United States, that no matter what other nations may deem necessary in consequence of a different historical development, considerations which may guide them do not apply here. In agriculture these differences of an economico-political character have at all times had the most decisive influence. It can be demonstrated from the most substantial facts, that the freest institutions give the greatest excess of products. The rude system of agriculture in America cannot be classed with the systems of the advanced countries of Europe. The settlers of new lands are not given to intensive cultivation. What gives the quickest returns to the labor of the husbandman is an extensive cultivation of comparatively large tracts of land requiring little manuring and preparing. A comparison of yield per acre is therefore inadmissible. But the great total result is that America, feeding her own people in abundance, sends perhaps twenty-five per cent. in value of agricultural products to make up the deficiencies of Europe.

A tariff for protection of agricultural products in America stands therefore much in the position of blinding the farmer while his pockets are rifled by highwaymen. The effect of a tariff stimulation on such products of the soil which for inherent differences have been previously imported in more or less important quantities, has always been an extended acreage allotted to the crop, in the anxiety of the farmer for something "that will pay." The consequence of fostering by "protection" has therefore always been an oversupply of undesirable and often unmarketable products within a year or so of the enactment, and a greater distress of the farmer than he had felt before he received the treacherous gift.

It is plain from this brief statement of an undisputable fact, that the American farmer cannot be protected by protective legislation. All threats of certain interested people would, from this cause alone, have been met with contempt had not the living generation of industrials been so filled with the protective mania that their understanding of conditions under which production is conducted had become obtuse. No wonder that this condition of the mind of the two classes of producers, the agricultural and the manufacturing, has been considered an excellent field for the designing politician to cultivate in his interest. By playing one interest against another the Republican party has been able to strike fear among all and thus make anxious victims believers in benefits largely the children of the imagination. From the agriculturist's point of view the only remedy for complaints, he has had ample reasons for advancing of late years, lies in the removal of import duties of a protective character affecting the price of his consumables, and not in the imposition of duties on what he produces. The surplus determining the price of his entire product, the price for him is made on European exchanges, buying that surplus. Absolute free trade being out of consideration—for reasons stated—the practical question remains to find a nearest approach, which would relieve the consumer without preventing the collecting of revenue by means conformable to ingrained notions of the people.

There remains then no other way to bring all these exigencies and seemingly conflicting interests into harmony than by such a policy as is demanded in the resolutions referred to as the only practical basis of tariff reform.

In what Foreign Tariffs are Distinct from American Tariffs.

From the American manufacturer's point of view—the protected interests chiefly—the only rational basis of a tariff is one based on free raw materials. The fact that no other industrial nation, with whom American manufacturers aim to compete in neutral markets, taxes raw materials, should be an object lesson strong enough for them. When we hear of Germany or France taxing raw materials it always means taxing food supplies. Foolish as this must appear, raising the cost of living, reducing the standard of life and in consequence reducing the productive capacity of the working classes, yet it is something quite mild in comparison with raising the price of the manufacturer's raw material—his " matière première "(first materials)—fifty to a hundred per cent. above the cost at which his foreign competitors use the same.

In a sense the foreign agriculturist stands towards his tariff in the position in which our industrial classes stand towards our tariff. There the landed classes, chiefly the landed proprietors, draw all the benefits from the tariff, while the small peasant, agricultural laborer, and all the rest of the people are heavily taxed on their food supplies. To benefit a few the whole nation is taxed and the nation's productive power curtailed. Here in America agriculturists cannot be protected, as has been shown. They are merely taxed, to support an artificial system in which make-believes go a great way to make burdens seem a blessing.

Of course, the same relates to all the occupations which are engaged in the professions, personal services, and the distributing trades. The same relates to all the industrial occupations which cannot possibly be benefited by a protective tariff: the building trades, railroad building, slaughtering, and other trades connected with food supplies, and all occupations operating on non-transportable objects. All told, there are barely 5 per cent. of bread-earners to whom any direct benefit can be said to accrue from the protective tariff, while all of them (even the 5 per cent.) suffer to the full extent of the whole measure of double taxation, viz., for revenue to the government, and for protection to a favored few. But even this very small class reduces itself to a smaller and smaller number, the closer one examines into the industrial fabric which is said to be benefited. It is in evidence that the greater the amount of protection dealt out,

10   THE ECONOMY OF HIGH WAGES.

the lower the rate of wages; while the freer the industry from all such influences, the higher the rate of wages.* In the cotton industry the daily wages are not materially different from English wages. If we take the greater number of looms and spindles worked, and the greater number of weekly

---

* I will give here the wages paid in the building trades and in cotton manufacturing, as evidence. The wages for Germany are taken from the wage lists prepared for regular periodical publication by the Sociological Society Concordia, in Mayence. For the building trades I take the wages for the Hansa towns, where the highest rates are paid. For England I take the wage rates for Manchester, Liverpool, and London from the lists prepared by the Trade Unions' Committee for the Royal Commission on Trade Depression. For America I take the rates ruling in New York City.

The wages, reduced to the hour, compare as follows:

	GERMANY.	ENGLAND.	AMERICA.
	Cents.	Cents.	Cents.
Bricklayers (34.7 pfg.)	8¼	16	45
Stonemasons	8¼	16 to 18	45
Carpenters (30 pfg.)	7¼	16	30 to 35

The percentage of wages of England over Germany is a round 100 per cent.; of America over England, 180 per cent., and over Germany, 430 per cent. and 330 per cent., respectively.

In the cotton goods industry I take the wages of spinners and reduce them also to the hour, so as to bring them to a common basis.

These wages are taken from mills which I visited, and they were given me by the parties paying, and corroborated by those receiving them.

	RHENISH GERMANY AND SWITZERLAND.	MANCHESTER.	LOWELL.
	Cents.	Cents.	Cents.
Mule spinners (men)	5.2 to 6	14 to 17	15 to 16
Ring spinners (women)	4.3 to 5.2	6	8.4

The English and American mule spinners stand about on a par, while they earn from 165 to 200 per cent. more than Swiss or German spinners. The American spinner-girl earns 70 per cent. more than the Swiss or German, and 40 per cent. more than the English girl. But this is balanced by handling eight sides with 960 spindles, against four sides with 576 spindles in England. The American spinner gets less pay per work than the English, Swiss, or German.

working hours into consideration, they are decidedly below the English rates. In woolens, taking all the differences into consideration, 25 per cent. would cover the higher rate of pay which our working people can call their own, and even this is frequently balanced by a higher output. In the building trades, which are certainly independent from all benefits a tariff can give, as houses cannot well be imported, the differences are from 200 to 400 per cent. in favor of the American artisan. Entirely different considerations than tariffs bring about the higher rate of wages which prevails in this country. What these causes are, will be the subject of the succeeding chapters. Here it can only briefly be mentioned that the wage earner does not draw any benefit from protective duties, and that so long as the tariff on raw materials prevails, he, along with the employer, is directly injured by the system. The facts in support of this will be brought out in the course of this treatise. Blind prejudice may strenuously oppose their application, but the force of facts is too strong to be long delayed before sweeping away artificially bolstered-up theories.

The McKinley Act, a Monument of Legislative Ignorance.

The legislators responsible for the act did what they were expected to do. They simply delivered the goods for value received in 1888, with a tentative hint to future campaign contributions. Still they might have shown an appreciation of the consumers' interests. They could have learned that they are entirely compatible with the true interests of the manufacturers. An inquiry into the productive methods of European countries would have shown them that these are based on vitally different principles. They would then have seen that our importations are due to only a limited extent to cheaper labor cost in Europe. They, as well as the recipients of legislative favors, should know that technical and artistic skill are elements of very great importance in manufacture. If we are deficient in the one or the other, it is only natural that we import what we cannot find equally satisfactory at home.

Our labor, being machine labor, is generally cheaper than European labor, which is to a large extent hand labor or inferior machine labor or unproductive underfed labor, as compared with higher productive American labor. What our labor suffers from, is the high cost of taxed materials. Free raw materials and a higher technical and artistic development would result in lasting benefits to our manufacturing industries, which periodic additions to already extreme tariff rates can never do. They increase the cost of production in spite of our cheap labor, and continue the congested condition so frequently complained of by manufacturers.

It was my good fortune to be charged by Mr. Bayard, the late Secretary of State, with the important mission of inquiry into the economy of production and the state of technical education in Europe. The information gained from my investigations fully bears out these views. I had not been able to make a final report, and it shall be my endeavor now to give to the public a review of the industrial situation from personal observation in the foremost industrial countries of Europe and the United States. From the insight into the competitive side of the productive process gained thereby, it will be not difficult to understand that the McKinley tariff is opposed to the best interests of our producing classes, the manufacturers included; that it failed entirely to accomplish what it set out to do, and that it could not end in anything but failure, because starting on entirely erroneous premises, even when it honestly strives to benefit American industries.

The Raw Material in the Product.

Before speaking, however, of production and the processes by which it is conducted in the different countries, of labor, its reward and its productiveness, of the true causes which lead on to progress, the basis of prosperity of the working classes, it is essential to say a word or two of the raw material, especially as the most important part—the inherent part, which gives character to the fabric—is given but little consideration by the tinkers in legislation.

Since nations have risen from barbarism and isolation they have become accustomed to exchanging their products. This exchange of commodities served to create more wants and develop taste. What is not produced, for reasons too varied to specify, by one country is obtained through commerce from another.

Now, among all things impossible to produce by all countries, gifted with the same intelligence and advancement in science and the arts, is that which is the product of nature, and this we call raw material. Everything else in the finishing into an article of use may be reached even by nations not having the same natural adaptation and artistic feeling, by proper teaching and training. To the raw material cannot be given the essence by cultivation which it derives from the soil and the climate. Great are the variations in minerals even. Take clay and stone. One of the reasons adduced for crazing in pottery is in the different properties which the clay of this country possesses compared with the clay and kaoline of Cornwall and Devonshire. In iron ore, not one ore has the same qualities as another. We cannot use our ores for Bessemer iron, except from the remotest sections of the country on Lake Superior.

In all these materials the chemical qualities and affinities of the parts determine the character of the product so entirely that only the grossest ignorance would endeavor to build up industries and put restraint upon the free choice of nature's gifts.

But even to textiles this applies with fullest force. For fine yarn spinning no cotton equals Egyptian. Our own Sea Island is something quite different from and superior to the upland cottons.

It is only of late years that our cotton manufacturers begin to see the advantages which they would reap from a greater use of Egyptian cotton. Though in small quantities yet, as compared with the use made of it by the English, Swiss, and German fine yarn spinners, the rapid increase during the last few years shows that even protected manufacturers cannot forever continue oblivious to the pressure of trade facts. Rays of outside facts creep into the fool's paradise of protection, and disturb the harmony of interests so dexterously fostered, no matter how carefully the blinds are pulled. Of the 500,000 bales of Egyptian cotton raised, we imported in 1885 a total of 4,553 bales and in 1890 some 9,000 bales. The bale is of 750 pounds.

Egyptian cotton has properties which even Sea Island cotton does not possess. Aside from the fact that it has a long fibre and is therefore excellently suited for combing purposes, making a very even thread, it has the very great advantage of a higher lustre, so that the fabrics made of it are softer and take more the character of silk goods. In the dyeing, the goods made of Egyptian cotton have more brilliancy of color, and for cotton and silk mixed goods it is of especial importance that the respective fibres blend well.

THE ECONOMY OF HIGH WAGES. 15

Besides all this the goods made from this cotton take a much finer finish. All this is well known to foreign manufacturers and is the chief cause why we import most of our fine yarn goods. In all American fabrics made to substitute these foreign importations, a lack of knowledge of this first principle in production, to have the proper raw material for the goods, is painfully apparent.

In no branch, however, are the differences so great as in wool. Our own wools show conclusively that almost every State of the Union produces a different grade. For instance: the wools raised in the far West in the new Territories and States are considered very inferior to those raised in the States east of the Mississippi. The pasturage consists of wild grasses, which during the dry season become parched, leaving the sandy soil underneath as a fine dust or sand, which permeates the fleece, adding much to its shrinkage and changing not only its appearance but the strength of staple, more especially where the soil is alkaline. Such wools lack in lustre and spring, and goods made from them show a dead, cottony appearance. They could not possibly be used as an offset in the manufacture of fabrics which we import, amounting in 1890 to $50,000,000, and which, adding duties, $35,000,000, represent $85,000,000 American value laid down at the ports, exclusive of freight and other charges.

For the replacing of this vast amount the American supply would be entirely insufficient. We raise the corresponding wools in very limited quantities (and, what is more to the point, in receding quantities) in the older States only. Texas and California wools have good felting properties. For combing purposes they are unserviceable. Of combing wools only a limited amount is raised in the States lying east of the Mississippi. But most of the goods used for outer wear have for years been made of combed and not of carded wool.

The same differences we find in English wools. The Southdown is different from the north country wool; the Scotch from the English; the Welsh wool different from the English and Scotch again. The best reputed kinds of Scotch tweeds can only be made from a particular class of Scotch wools. Irish wool is different again. Welsh, Irish, and Scotch wools shrink but very little when manufactured into flannels, knit goods, etc., in the washing; German and American wools, very much more so. Australian, Cape, and Plate wools differ again. But these differences can be made very valuable by adapting the varying qualities to the respective fabrics to which they give their special character.

The same can be said of silk. China silk, Japan silk, Italian, French, East India silks, they all differ. Breeding and cultivation can improve the product, but cannot give it the properties which it derives from the soil upon and the sun under which it grows.

In articles of direct consumption, this is so well understood that a reference to it will make the meaning plain to everybody. Nobody accustomed to the taste of Rhine wine will take American wines instead, nor would anybody who had a preference for French wines take the Italian growth in their place. No amount of cultivation will produce Havana tobacco in any part of the United States. Nor would tobacco grown in one part of the United States from seed transplanted from another part of the country produce the same tobacco.

A tax upon raw materials will always and necessarily injure home industries, because the people who for one reason or another prefer an article of foreign to one of domestic manufacture on account of the inherent qualities of its material, be they what they may, will buy the foreign article if by virtue of the duty the raw material is excluded from our workshops and factories, and thereby withdraw support to that extent from home industries.

Protectionists who always are so full of concern in behalf of the working classes and their employment at full wages omit to give this side their consideration.

CHAPTER II.

The Labor Question in the Tariff.—The Old Labor Doctrine opposed to Experience.—The Cheapness of Well-paid Labor.—Iron and Coal Mining-Machine Operating.—Foreign Labor not capable of Exertion like American.—Mostly Crude Labor from Abroad.—Slowness in Adopting Labor-saving Improvements in Low-wage Countries.

NOTHING in the whole catalogue of argument for protection by its advocates has been used with so much effect as the fact that the daily wage rate of American working people is higher than that paid by manufacturing nations of Europe. From this fact, that wages are higher in America, a fact not disputed by any one, the conclusion has readily been jumped to that the differences between the rate paid in Europe by competing nations and in America in the same lines of industry should be equalized by tariff duties laid upon the article of foreign manufacture.

The question here arises, What connection is there between the daily wages of the workingman and the cost of his work?

Until very recently the theory had been accepted without argument and criticism that a day's labor in any one line in one country would produce the same results as a day's labor in another country; indeed, it has been handed down as an axiom, and upon this the so-called iron law of wages has been built, which to a large extent is the cause of our present socialistic agitation. The so-called law arises from another so-called law, promulgated by the English school of economists, that, if wages rise in one part of a country above the general rate ruling, very soon an influx will follow of labor from the lower stratum, which will soon begin to press on and reduce the rate of wages to the old standard. This, then, necessarily would lead to a state in which it would be hopeless for the working classes to expect anything more than the mere means for their subsistence and for the perpetuation of their race. How ever such a view could have got abroad and taken possession of the thought of generations is one of these incomprehensible features which we meet in the history of thought. Views are accepted without being questioned if put forth with sufficient authoritativeness, even if the experience of every day shows their futility.

The Fallacy of the Old Theory of Wages.

The theory of wages which we combat in these pages is principally based on Ricardo. He formulates this so-called iron law, as a kind of dogmatic prison-cell out of which there is no escape for the working classes, and we cannot do better than to quote him in his own words:

"If the shoes and clothing of the labourer could, by improvements in machinery, be produced by one-fourth of the labour now necessary to their production, they would probably fall 75 per cent.; but so far is it from being true that the labourer would thereby be enabled permanently to consume four coats or four pair of shoes, instead of one, that it is probable his wages in no long time would be adjusted by the effects of competition and the stimulus to population to the new value of the necessaries on which they were expended. If these improvements extended to all the objects of the labourer's consumption, we should find him probably, at the end of a very few years, in the possession of only a small, if any, addition to his enjoyments."—(The Works of David Ricardo : London, John Murray, 1886, p. 12.)

Instead of being not true that the laborer would by these

improvements be enabled permanently to consume four coats instead of one, etc. (which is equivalent to reaping the full benefit of the improvements in the economy of production), history shows that the effect of these improvements has always been to increase the well-being of the laborer. The improvements referred to must by the natural force and the momentum given thereby, lead by necessity to the improvement of conditions wherein the laborer always gets the largest proportion of the gain. The facts lead to exactly contrary conclusions from those of Ricardo and the schools accepting them. Any one who has experience in manufacturing knows by his own observations that the laborer's wages increase in the proportion that his productive capacity increases, whatever the causes which bring this about. Not his money wages alone but his real wages, expressed in their purchasing power.

Relative Productiveness of Labor.

Every employer of labor knows and will readily admit that the laborer's value stands in exact proportion to the quantity of work turned out.

The productive capacity of the labor is a varying quantity, even aside from the aid given by machinery and invention. We find not alone that nation and nation differ in the same occupations, but the different sections of a country vary in results when output and output is compared.

Thomas Brassey, in his interesting book, "Work and Wages," gives an abundance of facts to show the superiority of English over continental labor in road-building and railroad-building—navvy work principally. For the best and most difficult work, that of making curves, etc., he could employ no other labor but English. English labor was paid at a much higher rate than continental labor, working alongside of it. But still, measured by the work done, in many instances the cost was higher at the lower wage rate per diem than the work done at the higher wage rate per diem. The better feeding and better muscular development of the Englishman is accepted now as explanation of this fact. But in reference to the differences in the effectiveness of crude labor employed in the same occupation, we can take an example from the United States to show clearly and distinctly that a day's work in the same occupation is something quite different in different parts of the same country.

Pig-iron-making is, perhaps, one of the crudest industries, so far as labor employment goes. The principal part of the labor expense at a furnace is wheelbarrowing and yard-work. In the Northern States, especially in the Pittsburgh region, where most of the ore used is from Lake Superior, a great part of the expense is due to the necessity of storing the ore on account of climatic influences, interruption of navigation in winter, and so on, thereby necessitating two handlings instead of one. In England, with its open winters, no such necessity exists. The ore is run from the mine on tracks to the furnace to be filled into barrows, put upon the lift, hoisted, and dumped into the furnace. If imported ores are used, the furnaces being situated along the coast, the steamers are run close by and the ore is taken direct from the ship to the furnace.

In the Southern States the ore beds are situated so near the furnaces that much the same condition prevails. Crude labor per day there is certainly not more than about two-thirds of what it is in Pittsburgh; still, with the seeming advantages of cheap day labor and the advantages of situation mentioned, I found in a recent investigation on the labor cost in iron-making in certain furnaces in Alabama, that the labor cost per ton is nearly the same as in Pittsburgh and a little higher than at furnaces in eastern Pennsylvania, which I visited in 1888—a time when labor, consequent upon high iron prices, had obtained twice an increase in pay of ten per cent.

This, my own observation, is fully corroborated in a recent statement published by the Labor Bureau at Washington. Taking about twenty-five furnaces from the Northern States, and about the same number from the Southern States, the average for both is nearly the same; leaving out of the average for the Southern States three furnaces which are given as making iron at the labor cost per ton of $0.595, $0.784, and $1.008 (which is an impossibility on the face of it, judging from the known conditions), the average for the other twenty-one Southern furnaces is about $1.70 per ton. This is a higher average price of labor than in Northern furnaces. Southern ores, however, are mostly cheaper ores of a lower percentage of iron, consequently, require more wheelbarrowing and hoisting. Therefore, on the same basis of work done, the cost would be about the same—if anything, somewhat higher—showing clearly that though cheap labor gets less remuneration per diem, its cheapness is no saving to the employers. More hands are required to do the same amount of work that better paid labor does at the same cost. More efficient labor in the North accomplishes greatly more in a given time, and thus renders its work, if anything, at a lower cost than the cheaper labor elsewhere.

Differences in Coal Mining.

Coal mining in the rich bituminous fields of America gives a further illustration. Taking the data from the census of 1890 for the mining industries of Alabama, Kentucky, Tennessee, West Virginia, Pennsylvania, Ohio, Illinois, and Indiana, we find the products, value, and wages as follows (tons at 2,000 lbs.):

	Annual Product.	Wages per Ton.	Value at Mine.
Alabama......................	3,378,000	$0.94	$1.10
Tennessee.....................	1,925,000	82	1.21
Kentucky......................	2,399,000	70	99
West Virginia.................	6,231,000	60	82
Pennsylvania	36,174,000	58	77
Ohio...........................	9,976,000	69	94
Illinois........................	12,104,000	69	97

The lower cost per ton goes hand in hand with the higher day rates. An approximate idea can be given from this table of the differences in the labor cost and relative working capacity in the same line of production in the different sections. The annual earnings of the laborer would not permit to base comparisons on, on account of the difference in number of days worked in the year. The nature of the coal and the depth and incline of the seams are also differences of importance in coal mining. But where a survey of production is taken on so large a scale a fair average of conditions may be assumed to exist. Allowing for all possible objections and eschewing all other generalizations we can certainly accept this as irrefutable evidence that coal is mined cheaper in the Northern than in the Southern States.

As to the earnings, we cannot take the yearly earnings as a criterion of daily wages. The days of employment in the year, varying so much in the different States, are at hand only for five of these States. But taking these and putting Kentucky and Tennessee for the Southern and the remaining States for the North we find the average day rate for

THE ECONOMY OF HIGH WAGES.

	Miners.	Laborers.	Wages paid per Ton.
	$	$	Cents.
Tennessee	1.98	1.26	82
Kentucky	1.75	1.56	70
West Virginia	1.86	1.47	60
Ohio	2.01	1.77	69
Illinois	1.96	1.68	69

Increase of Earnings and Reduced Cost going Hand in Hand.

The labor cost per ton, it will be seen, is lowest where the average of day wages is highest. But if this demonstrates satisfactorily our point, we can with equal certainty refute the statement cited above that labor does not permanently gain by the improvements which lead to a reduction in price.

We can show this by putting the average annual earnings of all employed in these coal-mining States, the labor cost per ton, and the value per ton, side by side with the same items from the census of 1880:

	Yearly Earnings.		Wages per Ton.		Value per Ton.	
	1880.	1890.	1880.	1890.	1880.	1890.
	$	$	Cents.	Cents.	$	$
Tennessee	332	392	68	82	1.27	1.21
Kentucky	261	334	73	70	1.20	0.99
West Virginia	295	391	72	60	1.10	0.82
Ohio	320	352	86	69	1.29	0.94
Illinois	382	357	99	69	1.44	0.97

A rise in the total of earnings is very marked, and goes hand in hand with a very decided fall in the price of the product.

The decline in the cost of production is due to nothing else but to improvements governing the economy of production in the mining industry.

The same practical results show themselves in other industries all along the line so far covered by the last census.

In woolens the earnings of all employed have risen from an average of $294 to one of $347. The price of wool having declined, as shown in the opening chapter, as much as twenty-five per cent. between 1879–80 and 1890, shows, in combination with a greater use of shoddy, cotton, and other wool substitutes in the industry, that a far greater bulk had to be manufactured than is expressed in the difference of values of raw material, which rose from $164,000,000 to $203,000,000. Divided over the product, the cost of production must necessarily be less. The bulk being, to say the least, by one-third greater in each dollar's worth of material consumed in 1890 over 1880, and the ratio in the rise of wages equal to the ratio of values in material, leaves no room for any other conclusion.

The Same Labor Differences Manifest in Higher Products.

In the making of finished iron, I was told by the President of the Amalgamated Association of Iron and Steel Workers that the piece rates at Southern puddling furnaces were the same as in Pittsburgh; that the labor there, however, is very wasteful, and that experience has shown that three white men do the work of five colored men. This proves conclusively that even work done by mere muscular labor, shows great gradations in efficiency of the workers; that no great competition and pressing down by help not used to the work, or of a lesser efficiency, can ensue, or offer serious dangers to those employed and possessing greater efficiency, is obvious from these examples covering crude labor processes.

It is held generally that labor-operating machinery of the same nature and construction would turn out in a given time the same amount of work. It has been my own experience that labor turned on the same kind of work, and using the same machinery, showed the most varying results. Sewing-machine operators in my employ turned out, in so simple a labor object as plain hemming, all the way from 2,000 to 6,000 and 7,000 yards a week, which, paid at the rate of twenty cents a hundred yards, gave wages varying from $4 to $12, and sometimes $14, a week.

The lowest grade of earnings may be due to lesser experience and skill, as that of beginners; but even among operators of experience differences exist, if we take $12 as the maximum, varying all the way from $6 to $12 under an equally ready supply of work, and in the same number of working hours. This is a very simple article, requiring only deftness of hand, and no special change and shifting.

Equal variations I found in more difficult parts—trimming and adjusting. There is, however, one very important point which will also be conceded by every one familiar with manufacturing: that the work done by those who earn the highest wages and do the work most rapidly is the work which, based upon its selling value, would command the highest prices, being done better, more regularly, and cleaner than that of those who earn the lower wages. This is a very important distinction, upon which too much emphasis cannot be laid for the understanding of the labor question as well as the understanding of the economy of production in general. In all my inquiries, abroad and at home, I always found this fact a predominating feature.

If such variations in the skill and productive power of the individual workers under the same roof and under the same direction, supervision, and training, impress themselves upon our view, how much more must we expect to find variations in the output when the production of the same lines of goods is carried on in different countries.

In almost every employment of an industrial nature a very great amount of training is requisite to make it effective or make it serviceable at all. Only in times of very great demand and scarcity of labor would any one employ crude labor in factories where skill is required. The first question at all times for an employer to put would be, What can you do? How skilful are you? What are your earnings? Never would he ask, How cheaply can you work? He would surely take the one offering his or her services first who had been in the habit of earning the highest wages, doing the greater amount of work, etc. In times of depression or lesser demand, he would surely dismiss those of his hands who earn the lowest rate of wages, and keep those who are best paid per diem, etc. How, then, can it be that wages cannot rise beyond the point of mere subsistence of the worker, when the skill of the worker is so powerful a factor in determining the rate of wages?

Nor can the rate of wages be seriously affected by an influx of new labor, because new labor is seldom labor accustomed to the occupation. There is never in any one industry a perceptible amount of desirable labor floating which could be used to effectively compete with the trained help holding the field. No sensible employer would engage new hands in place of the ones used and trained to his work, even were it offering itself for employment.*

---

* The most recent appearance of the bogeyman, that has come within my notice, is in Prof. R. T. Ely's "The Labour Movement in America." He says :

"The cost of production is the limit below which the price of other commodities cannot permanently fall, for the production is diminished as

But a main point for consideration is this, that labor cannot at the bidding of a sudden demand arising somewhere else be removed from old homes and associations. If transplanted to new spheres, even in the same occupations, it is seldom able, except after long application, to cope with the trained labor of the place, especially when the labor is of a

---

the price falls, and at times ceases almost altogether. But the individual labourer cannot diminish his supply of labour so long as he lives, and misery and death are the factors which must bring about a decrease in the supply of his commodity and raise its price to the cost of production, in other words, to what it costs the labourer and his family to live and to maintain the customary standard of life among the members of his class.

"Closely connected with the foregoing is the fact that the price of labour does not at once rise when the demand increases, as is usually the case with other commodities, for the first effect is that the unemployed receive work; and after the 'reserve army' finds employment competition among purchasers of labour raises its price.

"Finally, the only way to diminish the supply of the commodity labour in the market in the future is, by prudence in marriage, to diminish the birth-rate. But to accomplish this, will and intelligence are necessary, and some probability that the labourer would reap the fruits of his self-denial. No such guarantee exists, because the folly of his fellows will render his prudence of no avail. In addition to this, the labourer in America can hope to influence the supply of labour offered in the market of the future only when he gains some control over immigration."

The professor moves the army of the unemployed about like a condottiere, throwing it into this or into that camp which may be willing to bid for its services. The fact is not considered at all that, however large the army at any one time, those belonging to any one handicraft or employment are usually few and rather scattered. Given a "reserve army" of 1,000 of unemployed in a time of depression among a population of 50,000 (certainly a very large percentage), there would be, let us say, 25 potters among them. These would be the only ones that could possibly exercise a pressure on the existing rates of potters' wages. The other 975 would not be of the least consequence to the potting industry and could in no conceivable way endanger the equilibrium. The tailors, the shoemakers, the tinsmiths, the machinists, the seamstresses, the longshoremen could not possibly find employment in any trade except their own specialty. As working-

THE ECONOMY OF HIGH WAGES. 29

higher developed kind, as expressed in its higher earnings. Most of the labor brought from foreign shores is of the cruder kind, if industrial, or it is entirely agricultural and attracted by the facility of obtaining land.

The labor brought from foreign countries to America to work in American mills, even if used to the same machin-

---

men out of employment are usually the least expert ones, they cannot exert a depressing influence, even while they are engaged in the nefarious practice which haunts the vision of the professor. But the "reserve army" broken up into corporal's guards of occupations becomes more reduced yet in power of doing mischief. All manufacturing industries are minutely subdivided to-day. The sewing-machine operator on a Willcox & Gibbs, would be out of place where Singer, or Wheeler & Wilson machines are in use. The white goods sewer would not be able to get along in a factory working woolen goods. The straight sewer could not compete with the trimmer. In pottery, as we have chosen that example, the turner, the handler, the flat goods presser, the dish maker, the sanitary ware maker, the mold maker, the dipper, the decorator, etc., etc., would all be classed among our 25 unemployed potters. But each one ever so expert, let us assume, in his own branch would find it hard to make a day's wages in any one of the other branches of his trade. In a factory of boots and shoes employing 500 hands it is doubtful that as many as twenty are engaged in one and the same occupation, each one forming in itself a specialty, which to become expert in requires a good long apprenticeship. But wages are paid by the piece in all manufacturing industries, and it can well be understood what cleverness and skill it requires to make high earnings, and the advantages of the trained over the untrained are therefore entirely unassailable.

I can assure the professor that in a business experience of twenty-five years I never was able to find desirable accessions among the "reserve army," whenever business required me to increase my stock of help. I know that the experience of other manufacturers is of exactly the same nature.

Of course, the remedy of diminishing the supply of labor by voluntary or involuntary death increase is unfolded. The Malthusian skeleton is taken out of the cupboard and shaken whenever we find ourselves hemmed in by perplexing economic phenomena. But the performance is too anachronistic even for appeal to the gallery gods.

ery, is found at first to be entirely unable to compete with American labor. It is only after considerable time that it can take its place and earnings in common with American labor. Here these new-comers work side by side with the old practiced hands at considerably lower rates. But their lower wages are expressive of lower working capacity. American higher earnings are only, in other words, an expression of a higher working capacity. In England I frequently heard it said that laborers brought from Ireland usually break down after the first week's trial; had then, living with friends, to first get used to the English standard of life, and feed up in order to be able to do work at the English rate. Gradually, in keeping with their better feeding and living, they become as good and strong workmen as the English. Now, in American mills the very same holds good. The labor which we bring from Europe is seldom employed directly in manufacturing, except in special lines where the work people are brought over for industries newly created for which we have no American labor ready, wanting the training and experience requisite for their operation.

The foreign labor entering mill life usually takes up the crude labor processes, and with growing efficiency makes claim to and quickly obtains the standard rate of wages ruling in the respective occupations. Skilled labor does not emigrate so freely as is generally taken for granted by those who make definitions for text books, and take facts and conditions supposed to exist but really as far removed from the living experience of the day as the study of the writer is removed from the workshop of the worker.

In 1885 the emigration from the United Kingdom to the United States, of adult males, having been employed in mechanical employments, showed a total of 9,541 only. Of these 2,257 were miners and about 1,750 were employed in the building trades—bricklayers, masons, carpenters, etc.—the rest, of something over 5,000, were distributed over different manufacturing industries. In England I found, far more so than in America, that the artisan classes and mechanics can only with difficulty be brought to leave their occupations and homes. Their earnings are remunerative, their expenses low, on account of low cost of commodities due to free trade, their love of home and surroundings is intense; and I found during my consulship that very few left the potteries to emigrate, but that a goodly number were at all times returning from America, preferring, as they said, the old associations and steady employment with a sure income to the high earnings in America, frequent stoppages of work, and wages spent as freely as received. This applies even to Germany and certainly in the strongest measure to France. As to the former country very few skilled workmen are found among the myriads who leave the shores of fatherland, comparatively speaking. Of the French, not an emigrating people under any circumstances, the number of skilled workmen coming over by no means cover the demand which is always at hand from special industries for their higher skill.

What Causes High Wages.

It is a fortunate sign of the times that we are at last beginning to recognize the all-important and redeeming fact, that cheap labor by no means means cheap production; that, on the contrary, low cost of production and a high wage rate go hand in hand. This may seem paradoxical, but on closer examination it will be found to be entirely logical and in keeping with the facts and philosophy of the economy of production.

The leading principle can be stated in a few words.

The United States, with its vast resources, free laws, and extended territory, gives a field for employment of labor which no other country possesses, excepting perhaps the Australian colonies. The great stretch of unoccupied soil gives an opportunity for the satisfaction of what is one of the chief desires of man, to be the possessor of a homestead upon his own land. From the widely distributed ownership of land radiate all other employments. A high wage rate and a higher standard of living are thereby insured. So long as the land is able to absorb, in times of business depression and collapse in manufacturing industries, the surplus labor of the towns, a lower wage rate once reached cannot permanently maintain. Labor under all circumstances, instead of being always ready to submit to a pressing-down process by the exercise of the undue power of capital, as maintained by the old economists, under free laws and freedom of association maintains, and with slight variations, always regains, if temporarily lost, its old position and wage rate.

A perceptible rise in the rate of wages ruling in the United States and in England, and even Germany and France, has taken place within the last twenty-five years; while at the same time a decline in the price of commodities and provisions has gone hand in hand with this rise in wages. The facts are so indubitable and have so incontestably been demonstrated that we can dispense with introducing data in support of this.*

This in itself is sufficient to controvert the theory of wages alluded to above. It shows plainly that Ricardo's four pairs of shoes or four coats are absorbed by the workers and not

---

* See Schoenhof, The Industrial Situation. G. P. Putnam's Sons, 1885.

by the capitalists. A rise in wages and a decline in the price of commodities is the best evidence of this.

Even where the laborer's wages could become easiest depressed by the large influx of foreign labor as in the coal-mining industry, we find, as shown, not alone that the wage rate maintains itself upon the standard of the workers of ten years ago but shows a steady increase. This is quite natural and in obedience to the powerful impulse given by freedom to all labor to work up to the highest level of pay obtainable or ruling in a country. It is admitted on all sides that imported labor, like the month of February, comes in as a lamb and goes out as a roaring lion. At first ready to accept any conditions for obtaining work, no sooner does it feel itself securely lodged and able by the acquisition of the necessary skill to maintain the position, than it demands full rate of pay. Hence this being the case with the only possible menace to the ruling standard of wages, we cannot see that any danger can be discovered to the continuance of the ruling high standard of wages. The tendency of economic forces is a rising one in wages, as will be further demonstrated, and so long as freedom is the basis of action, the high rate once gained must be considered a permanent one, which cannot be interfered with or repressed. The influence of a protective tariff as a force to bring about conditions which create this happy state is, however, not more powerful than that of a fly on a revolving wheel, with due deference to the opinion of the fly.

Happy as the augury is for the working classes, the employer of labor is not only not injured, but fully as much benefited by the inevitable results of a high rate of wages. Indeed the law of gravitation is not more absolute than this, that where, as in America, the rate of wages of labor per diem is a high one, the first object of the employer is to economize its employment. The result is that in no country is the organization of labor in mills and factories so complete as in the United States. In no country is the application of machinery carried to the extent to which it is carried in the United States. Here invention and improvement are always most readily welcome in the labor processes involved. Manufacturers introducing a change in manufactures have a machine built to accomplish what in other countries would be left to hand labor to bring about. Machinery, used to the limit of its life in Europe, is cast aside in America if only partially worn, or while satisfactory in this respect, if an improvement has come out that can do the work quicker and consequently cheaper. The improvement introduced by one manufacturer in any line is quickly adopted by his competitors. Labor-saving is the result, and a cheapening of production ensues, which is the due outcome of the high cost of day labor in the United States.

CHAPTER III.

Low Wages, Stagnating Causes.—Improvement in Machinery more Profitable in High-wage Countries.—Peasant and House Industries.—A Picture of a Home-market Country.

IF a high wage rate is an impelling cause in this country to the introduction of improvements and the adoption of labor-saving processes, the low wage rate per diem ruling elsewhere is an equally strong inducement for the continuance of rusty and antiquated methods. The old labor methods, going parallel with low wages, become quite ingrained with the countries where they prevail, and offer sufficient grounds for their perpetuation. To the employer of labor, advantages are offered which are in themselves sufficient not to make him anxious for changing the old for the new methods. Conservatism becomes increasingly pronounced in proportion as the rate of wages descends to a lower and lower scale.

But the effect of this tendency in low wage countries to adhere to old labor processes and continue the employment of obsolete machinery and method, becomes obvious to all when their products compete with goods in the same lines produced by high wage countries. What in other instances would be a commendable quality, here often becomes a grave defect. Durability is considered an advantage. In the economy of production it has become a disadvantage when an improvement, or the introduction of new machinery, can effect savings equal almost to the whole labor cost, or reduce the labor cost to the extent that a profit can be realized where none existed before.

A few examples will illustrate the effect on the cost of production, of these rapid changes and improvements in machinery. In 1886 (a rather dull year) I found in cotton spinning in Oldham that, in ninety mills, thirty-four paid neither dividends on stock nor interest on loan capital; an equal proportion paid no dividends, but paid interest on borrowed capital, and only twenty-two were able to pay interest and a moderate dividend on shares. All these mills are conducted on the co-operative plan. The managers, superintendents, etc., get very little more than workmen's wages, and everything is managed on the most economical basis. Even their basis of capitalization is one which would give the greatest advantage to the profitable employment of capital. These Oldham mills are all established on a capital of which only half is raised on shares, while the other half is loan capital. As loans on a safe security and for permanent investment can be raised in England at the low rate of interest of three per cent., of course, the profits going to the shares must be correspondingly higher as soon as the earnings of capital go above the rate of interest paid on the loan, than if the whole capital invested were share capital.

But with all these advantages in the way of a substantial dividend on the shares, the results were as stated.

The latest reports from the Oldham spinneries (for 1891) covering the same number of mills, give even less satisfactory results to the invested capital than those of 1886.

While those Oldham mills, built mostly in the sixties, were showing such poor results, the workings of newer erections were of a very satisfactory character.

A spinning mill at Rochdale, run on the same basis as these Oldham mills, and whose work account I had the privilege to examine, and a statement of which can be found in No. 70, Consular Reports, paid a dividend of 5 per cent., besides carrying an amount equal to 2½ per cent. as surplus, to profit and loss. The mill was recently built, had the latest improved machinery, and not alone was enabled thereby to produce at a lower rate of cost in labor and expense, but had a lower rate of waste than I found the case elsewhere.

This shows, if nothing else, an advantage of machinery not being too durable. The adoption of an improvement, principally in the lower numbers, of cotton spinning, sometimes saves more than the whole of the spinning cost. An improvement in roving lately introduced promises a saving of 5 per cent. in cotton by diminishing the rate of waste to that extent. The mechanism is an American invention, was taken over to England, and there, on trial, was found to do all that it was represented to have done in America. An insurmountable difficulty, as it seemed, arose. Manufacturers who had shown themselves quite ready to adopt the invention after having given it trial, reported that it was of no use. It was soon found that the opposition came not from the manufacturers themselves, but from their foremen and mill managers, whose reluctance to adopt new devices is proverbial. It is an open secret, as has been brought out in many lawsuits, that an opposition of this kind is not an insurmountable obstacle; that it can be overcome with money.

If England is much slower in adopting improvements and exchanging less advantageous machinery for more perfected, the Continent of Europe shows this in a still more aggravated form. In Switzerland I found looms and spinning machinery that would be considered inadequate in England and America. The manufacturers prided themselves on the durability of their machinery, costing two and three times as much as the English, but lasting five times as long. This would in part explain that work done under such conditions, though the wage rate per diem be much lower in Swiss than in English cotton mills, is dearer than in England, barring the fact of lesser proficiency of labor, due to poorer nutrition. But the lower wage rate per diem accounts here also for the persistence in using machinery to the full extent of its natural life. The incentive is wanting for replacing, with large capital outlay, old and obsolete for new and improved machinery. Quite on the contrary, the cheapness of human labor where it prevails is the greatest incentive for the perpetuation of obsolete methods.

A High Standard a Prerequisite to Improvement.

A certain high rate of wages is essential for the profitable employment of machinery. It is said that in railroad building and canal work in India, it is found that the low day rate at which laborers can be hired for carrying the dirt away from the banks, makes the employment of machinery unprofitable and unnecessary.

"Many mickle make a muckle." A much higher rate of wages and a considerably higher standard of living of the working classes would have to be preëxisting before rapid and radical changes from one kind of machinery to other and more improved machinery would be practical or become an economic necessity.

In silk throwing I found the labor cost in English mills to be higher than in American mills. The wages, however, were in America double what they were in England.* I

---

*This was on a comparison of wages paid in Macclesfield, England, with wages paid in a silk mill in Massachusetts. For further information on this subject I refer to a succeeding chapter on the silk industry.

stated then, in my report, that one mill in America had lately exchanged old machinery for new, by which change the speed had been increased from 5,000 to 7,500 revolutions a minute. When my report was published in England, a silk throwster who read it told me that if they ran their machinery at such speed in their mills all their girls would run away, as they had not the nerve power to stand such a high rate of speed.

Later on I found mills in America that ran their machinery at 10,000 revolutions a minute, and one which ran at 12,000 and even 13,000 revolutions. Of course, to keep in line, all others have to follow the same rate of improvement.

The survival of the fittest is, therefore, so to speak, the result of a high wage rate; and a high standard of living in industrial countries, becomes the prerequisite to a low cost of production. The lower the rate of living, the lower I always found the industrial development of the country. I visited Ireland with a view of ascertaining whether low wages, even with the aid of improved methods of manufacture which I found in some mills, were an aid in production. Outside of Belfast and the linen industry, I found labor very inefficient. In woolens, on improved power looms, the results were far below those of English mills, while American mills exceed both.

Low Wages Indicate Low Productivity.

The peasant and house industries of Europe are sprung from the soil, in the process of evolution, the progenitors of the more improved systems of to-day. Small though the income is to the peasant homes from industrial work, their agricultural holdings are so small that without this addition the lot of these poor people would be still worse. Indeed, the power mill has nowhere created so much distress as among the peasantry who were accustomed to look to industry for part of their income. The change from hand embroidery to machine embroidery by the invention and introduction of the so-called Swiss machine has at once taken out of the hands of the peasant women of Ireland a source of employment and of earnings which cannot be replaced by other occupations. By generations of adaptation they have acquired remarkable skill and excellent taste. Living in the most frugal and primitive manner, they can subsist on the very lowest rate of pay, and hence make it questionable in many industrial fields whether the economic advantages are all on the side of the factory system.

How these people live and work can be seen from an examination of life in Ireland. The examination is an interesting object lesson. Two sister countries, only divided by the Irish Channel, a three hours' run by steamer. The one, England, holds the most advanced commercial and industrial position in Europe; the other, Ireland, the most backward. In England wages for men average, say four shillings a day; in Ireland, all along the west and south coast, where these peasant industries have given the population a most remarkable aptitude and versatility, men would be happy if they could be assured of regular earnings as high as a shilling a day. England, though not raising more than half her food supply, feeds her people with abundance; Ireland, exporting large stores of food produce, has a majority of her people underfed and frequently on the brink of starvation. All these conditions could not be coexistent if the old labor theory were correct. The cheap labor ought to have attracted capital sufficient to make it economically of value, or by being drawn over to England have repressed wages there. It is not possible here to draw all the deductions admissible from this parallel, but this one in proof of our thesis, that labor to become economically valuable, must have risen to a higher standard of living than these mountain dwellers occupy. In other words, this would be, that their standard of wages would rise with their greater efficiency. The advantages and disadvantages would soon outbalance each other, and practically this I found always the case. Wherever I met power-mills in Ireland, I could make a test of practical application. The low rate of wages and of living to which the Irish have become reduced through ages of oppression, has produced the result that at about one-half the rate of wages ruling in England, not one industry can hold its own against the latter country in the same lines of activity.

Irish Industries as Object Lessons.

The Irish industries are of peculiar interest and a fruitful source of study, as showing the conditions from which industrial life in general has taken its rise.

In the remoter parts of the country—Donegal, for instance—one finds the most primitive conditions of life; a sturdy, honest, and industrious population, anxious and willing to work. I was there after the evictions of the poor peasants from their homes on the Olphert estate. The men were erecting turf cabins, dug-outs, with walls and roofs of turf, as shelter for their families. After completing these primitive habitations the men tramped in gangs of twenty or thirty to Derry or the nearest harbor, to take ship to England and Scotland for harvest work, to bring home £4 or £5 for the winter. I met men who had been two or three times in America two or three years at a time, working for the support of their families at home. One was preparing to go a third time in his married life of seven years. After accumulating a few hundred dollars, they returned home, living with their families till their savings were used up. The children are sent to Derry and other Ulster towns, where regular labor markets exist. Here they are hired by the larger farmers and for work suitable to their tender age during the summer. At the end of the season they tramp home again with £2 to £4 in hand. In winter they attend school. Neither mountains, rivers, nor oceans are obstacles in the search after work and wages. Neither young nor old hesitate to seek abroad what is denied them at home.

This is in answer to those who ascribe the poverty of these sections to the want of thrift and to lazy habits of the people. Here we find labor at its lowest pay, and perhaps its lowest efficiency, and the tools equally primitive. Conditioned as it is, it finds no markets for its products, and English capital, always eager to enter into the most hazardous undertakings in distant countries, has not found the low rate of wages under which labor can be hired there a sufficient inducement for employing it, except on such work, principally hand work of women, for which they have a peculiar adaptation—sprigging handkerchiefs, knitting, etc.

The deftness of hand of these peasant women, spending their time largely in house and field work, is very remarkable. We find the same, however, in the mountain districts of the continent of Europe. A great deal of the fine needlework and embroidery, hand sewing, kid glove making, real lace making, and work in numberless notions known under the name of articles de Paris, etc., is done by the peasant women in France and Germany. The price paid for such work would not suffice to pay the expenses of the most penurious living here.

The linen industries of Germany, Belgium, Holland, and Ireland have taken their rise from peasant industries. The spinning wheel used to be found in every household. In Germany, until recently, home-made linen of yarn spun by the peasants was a regular article of trade. It is only of late that hand-spun linens are gradually being replaced by machine-made linen in the finer numbers, while the cheapened production of cotton cloth is gradually driving the coarser peasant-made linens out of the market. However, in my recent visits, I found a good deal of hand-made linen in use still in the northern part of France and Germany. Peasant women still bring their rolls of linen to market towns, and at Leipsic during the fair I found a good deal exhibited by peasants and traders.

The earnings per diem in all these occupations are very small. Still, taken collectively, they help to round out the family's income. Field work occupies the peasant, especially the female part of the family, only a part of the year. In the winter months these industries give very welcome occupation and a means for bridging over periods of scarcity. Many a highly developed industry of to-day, upon which the wealth and prosperity of nations are founded, took its rise from peasant and home industries.

It takes long periods of evolution till primitive peoples alienate themselves from producing everything that is needed in the home and on the farm, and till special trades arise to supply their needs. In the records of Strasburg, up to the thirteenth century we find no reference in cloth-making to weavers. We find, however, dyers, fullers, and finishers. It is evident from this that the weaving was done exclusively by the women of the peasantry and of the burghers as late as that. Before that period the dyeing of cloths was done in the same way. On the west coast of Ireland conditions of this primitive nature prevail to this day, which can be considered fitting backgrounds for the industrial development in progressive countries.

Working for a Home Market.

There almost everything is raised and produced on the land by the people. The soil is poor and does not yield much under the present system of agriculture. It is bog land, badly drained, or not drained at all. Where there is no bog the land is arid and stony. The soil has to be made by the peasant—actually created—before he can think of getting any but the poorest crops. From a little patch of land, not more than a few acres, under cultivation, I have seen heaps of stones collected that would build a goodly-sized stone fence. The bog has to undergo a far more serious treatment. It has to be ditched and drained. Then a subsoil has to be made. Sand and seaweed are carried from a distance, the top of the turf is burnt, and a manure thus procured which then, with the sand and seaweed, is mixed with the soil to loosen and fertilize it. I have seen the men and women carry seaweed in hampers upon their backs from the shore up steep hills for miles into the country.

It is evident that land which has to be worked in this way can only produce for the poorest living. Under conditions existing it can only be worked by the spade. A peasant and his whole family working such land could not raise much surplus for sale or exchange. Land of this sort has to be worked constantly or else it falls back into a state of aridity worse than before. The land where the tenants had been evicted a year or two previous to my visit began to assume the character of the surrounding bog and wild land.

A people living under such conditions would consider any addition to their earnings, no matter how small, a blessing indeed. The invention and adoption of machinery, replacing hand labor, has dealt the severest blow to the poor peasantry of European countries.

Formerly, all embroideries were hand made. White edgings and insertions in numberless quantities were made principally by the peasant women of Ireland and constituted a vast industry. All this employment has been taken from them and transferred to Switzerland and Saxony, the embroidery machine being now found in the Swiss and Saxon mountain homes, doing largely for an entirely new set of workers what, before the advent of the machine, the needle had done for the peasants of Ireland.

In such conditions the population, cut off from the sea for want of harbors with landing facilities for ships and by the absence of railroads from land communication, is obliged to perpetuate the old state of living in making everything that is required at home. The farmer is a farmer and a builder too. All the houses are built by the farmers. The houses built in the last few years show a great advance. They are better built and more commodious than those of older times. While the old houses were mere mud hovels, with the cow and the pig under one roof with the family, without partitions even, the new houses have separate buildings for the animals, and the dwellings are divided into three rooms, usually, the kitchen in the middle and a good-sized room on each side; windows and doors are well put in and the roofs are slated. This is due, not to a new acquisition of skill in the peasants, but to a change in the laws which prevents the landlord from exacting increased rents from the peasant upon every sign of improvement on the farm. Indeed, the old laws and conditions spread like a pall over the whole land and largely explain the anomalies mentioned above.

This I found not alone in poor, stricken Donegal, but in the famed Protestant part as far north as Portrush. The reputed Ulster tenant rights were by no means a guarantee against rack-renting on any visible sign of farmer prosperity, such as decent dwellings, slated roofs, and increased productiveness of the soil. Since the establishing of the land courts and other measures of protection against the rapacity of landlords, improvements have sprung up which are the natural outcome of greater security of tenure and a guarantee of the unhindered enjoyment of the fruit of one's labor.

This only in parenthesis, and to return to our peasant industries.

The clothing of the people is made by the women. They shear the wool, scour it, card it, spin it, and, if they have looms, weave it, or give it to a weaver, also a peasant. The dyeing is done with especial skill. They have many lichens and other plants which they gather and use in making dyes. Their friezes and tweeds look especially well when made up. They make very handsome cardinal and blue friezes for women's wear, frequently adorned with a colored border. I have been shown by a peasant woman some blankets and quilts of wool of a rich cardinal, very evenly dyed.

Such are the natural industrial powers, now going to waste for want of employment, of perhaps the poorest peasantry of Western Europe. They are a world by themselves. They show us more than anything else how easy it is to establish manufacturing industries where the population is naturally gifted with all the elements of knowledge pertaining to manufacturing. These peasants are confined to a home market. They work for a home market. They eke out a precarious living only by going outside of their own districts and home surroundings for earnings which they cannot possibly make at home, under the conditions that have been forced upon them by the ruthless conquerors who, in successive waves, have taken possession of the more productive soil, and whose spirit was well characterized in their ultimatum to the poor Irish, "to hell or to Connaught." But the picture given here shows us approximately what must have been the beginning of the industries of the modern world, the foundation from which Europe started in its industrial development.

On the continent of Europe other and far more complicated industries have taken their rise in the peasants' homes and are still successfully carried on there, some requiring great skill of hand and showing a depth of artistic feeling to an astonishing extent. I refer to the wood-carvers of the Bavarian and Tyrolese mountains.

These poor peasants, without any art-school training, with a hand made heavy by field-work, display a fineness of execution and a depth of feeling in some of their work which I have not seen approached by any of the numberless productions of pupils and graduates of the many industrial art schools of Europe. In Ireland, charming objects of wood-carving done by peasants are thrust under your eyes on every roadside by peasant women. They are cut from bog oak, an extremely hard wood. Though the designs are limited to Irish emblematic figures of a rather conventional character, they still show much natural taste. The carvers are entirely self-taught. The few art schools in the larger towns are certainly not reached by them, and have so far not exercised any influence upon this art.

Another industry, also largely a peasant industry, is the

making of real lace. It used to be a source of income to the poor peasantry of Ireland, but fashion, more than anything, has made this in all countries where the industry exists a precarious source of income. Irish lace designs are stiff and conventional, and while the lace industry of Belgium and the Saxon and Bohemian mountain districts has received a new impetus of late years, Irish lace-making can hardly be considered an industry now.

The proper teaching in design by art schools, brought into proper contact with the lace workers of Belgium, Austria, and Saxony, is freely acknowledged by the people as a constant and beneficent stimulus.

I can only passingly refer to the varied industries of Thuringia in glass, porcelain, toys, and other varieties of fancy goods too numerous to specialize. They reach into every household in the plains and the mountains. A far more complicated industry, however, than any of these—that of watch and clock making—may also be classed among the peasant industries. In the Black Forest of Southern Germany and in Switzerland this industry arose in the early part of the century. The work is distributed to every hamlet and home in the mountains. The earnings, small as they are, have helped to keep away starvation, which was formerly a frequent visitor. Lately, machinery has been introduced to make competition with American clocks and watches possible.

America, with its high-cost labor, is always the dreaded competitor of these poorest paid working people of the industrial countries of Europe. The employment of labor-saving automatic machinery of American origin in these trades is intended to bring about the basis upon which they hope to be able to maintain themselves. The use which I have seen made of American machinery in a watch and clock factory in Trieberg, in the Black Forest, has given me the impression however, that the results obtained there will fall quite short of the results obtained here, and that the machinery used in a country whose industries are entirely built upon the employment of machinery, largely automatic machinery, is something quite different when employed by a people whose industries have been built upon hand processes, and where the cheapness of labor is a bar to the introduction and economic employment of the American system of work.

4

CHAPTER IV.

Advantages of Old Methods in Certain Industries.—House Industries economically considered.—The Silk Industry of Europe.—The Mode of Living.—The Rate and Method of Paying.—The Master and the Weaver dividing the Piece Rate paid by the Manufacturer.—Auxiliary Help, how paid.—Neither Risk nor Expense to Manufacturer.

ONE of the leading industries, the silk manufacture of Europe, spreads far into the country districts from the respective centres. It is as well a country as a town industry. The work is still distributed into the individual homes, although power mills are run for some of the staple goods, ribbons, etc. The silk and velvet industry of Germany, Switzerland, France, and Italy is conducted on about the same basis.

In 1885, in Crefeld and surroundings, the power loom stood in its relation to the hand loom as one to twenty. The weavers receive from the manufacturer the silk and warp yarn dyed and ready to be put on the looms. The system has its advantages, certainly, in articles like silk and satin, over the new system of manufacturing in power mills. The advantages are so great, although the price paid by the piece to the weaver in power mills is below what the very poorly paid hand-loom weavers receive for their work, that it is not likely that the factory system, economically considered, will be found preferable, except in a country like America, which, for very weighty reasons, cannot possibly conduct its industries upon the basis of manufacturing just mentioned.

To illustrate the working system on this plan I will give a few examples. We obtain thereby the output, the price paid, and the standard of living of the working classes under the old system. For instance, a hand-loom weaver had a piece of satin on his loom, of which the following is an account: it was of two widths on the loom—47 centimeters wide each (17 to 18 inches) and 40 meters long. The price paid him per double meter was 58 pfennige, or about 15 cents. The quality was of 1,362 reeds of 4 threads each. (Power-loom weaving in America would not be paid at a higher rate, but a fairly good weaver would turn out three times as much. This class of goods, however, is made very little in this country.) Of this quality the Crefeld weaver could make three and a half meters a day, working twelve hours in summer, and in winter, by the aid of lamp light, longer hours yet, frequently as late as ten at night. The children did the spooling, and out of 24 marks for the piece he had to pay about 3 marks per piece to the loom fixer. It takes the loom fixer about a day for a double-width piece of satin of this description. The loom fixer goes from house to house to the weavers to make ready their warps.

All the weaver can earn, therefore, net for two weeks' work is 20 marks, or 10 marks ($2.40) a week. The question as to saving, where such scanty wages prevail, is naturally met with a laugh.

How These Low-wage Earners Live.

The mode of living of these poor people is of the poorest, and their pallid color and emaciated condition tell the whole sad story, but also that better-fed people and less run-down labor would undoubtedly produce more than what these were doing.* They do not work very steadily either. A good deal of time is spent in pauses. Every gossip brings a welcome interruption. I found in the whole district, wherever I went, pretty nearly the same state of things. Men's earnings on work of this and similar character were from 10 to 12 marks a week, and women's from 7 to 8.

---

* I came to one of these weavers at dinner time. They were husband and wife and two children and a baby on the breast. Their dinner consisted of soup, sourcrout, sausage, and bread. Under a plentiful supply this might be considered a fair meal. But the soup was water with milk. I could not detect a trace of fat even on the soup, though an evidence of it would have shown on the soup in the plates. The children, however, seemed to relish it. Remarking on the character of their soup and on my question what else their dinner consisted in, the wife lifted the cover off the pot on the stove, in which I saw sourcrout enough to fill a soup plate not overfull, and one little sausage of the size of a Frankfurt. Low as this fare is, and little strength as it can impart to the people who are raised, live, work, and die under it, it is by no means the lowest which supports life of the working classes of this and other districts of Germany. In the eastern provinces, Silesia for instance, the sausage even is not an everyday occurrence.

These people made silk velvet, 50 centimeters, or 19½ inches wide, for which they received 2.70 marks (64 cents) per meter. They work 13½ hours, commencing at 5.30 in the morning, and do about 80 centimeters (about 32 inches) a day. The wife at intervals relieves the husband, or she works on a separate loom (at the time worked by another workingman). They gave as their earnings for the past year 630 marks ($151), and estimated the husband's part of this as 450 marks, and the wife's part as 180 marks. This, however, I will add, was the lowest rate of earnings I met with. Leaving out the wife as an independent worker, as she cannot be counted as doing more than relieving the husband, we can say that their combined earnings would have represented at that time the higher wage rate of adult male hand-weavers, to wit: 12 to 13 marks, and the husband's earnings the lower wage rate, dependent either on the better paying work or on the greater capacity for work of the weaver.

Quite a number of them, however, have little patches of land, which supply them vegetables and potatoes, and thus render them considerable assistance. A few from better times own their own houses, but where they depend entirely upon the result of this industry they are frequently placed in a very pitiable condition, as so much in silk depends on fashion.

In the very article just mentioned, what was then being paid under a limited demand at the rate stated, of 58 pfennige a meter, used to be paid a few years previous on a brisker inquiry at 92 pfennige (22 cents) a meter. In this industry, therefore, more than in any other, the weaver's condition alternates between times of prosperity and fair living and times of depression and semi-starvation. Power-loom weavers at the same time and in the same district, were earning in sixty-eight hours' working time per week, from 18 ($4.32) to 22 marks ($5.28).

How They Work in Lyons.

In Lyons, hand-loom weavers make the finest goods, for which Lyons is renowned and unapproachable.

The master weaver takes his tram and organzine from the manufacturer and brings back the finished goods. He usually employs a number of workmen and women, with whom he and his wife work along, each on a separate loom. The master pays the rent of the workshop and furnishes the looms to his help. One master whom I visited had four looms on very fine silk and beaded stuff then in fashion (1887), for which he received 6f. ($1.15) a meter. To show the alternations of high prices and high earnings, and low prices and low earnings, as influenced by fashion and demand, I will state that for that very material the year previous the weaver master received 12f. ($2.30) a meter, and of course paid the workmen accordingly. Under the reduced demand and price of 6f. per meter, the workmen, doing two meters a day, received 3f. per meter. Their workday is from 7 A. M. to 8 P. M., with two hours for meals. Out of these 6f. the workman pays a girl helper 1.25f. (24 cents), and the master pays her an equal amount. This reduces the net part going to the master to 2.37f. (45 cents) per meter. The rent for the premises in which to place four looms, inclusive of house room for the master and his family, was 350f. ($68) a year. This master made 4.75f. (93 cents) a day on each of the two looms then worked by workmen, besides the full amount of what was made by himself and his wife on the loom worked by themselves. Of course full earnings could not be made by either on their looms, the master being occupied part of his time in going backward and forward to the manufacturer and doing the outside work. Part of the wife's time is taken up in household duties.

Another master, helped in a similar way, was engaged on furniture velvet of a very fine quality. He received 20f. a meter for a piece of fifty meters long. It takes an expert weaver about four months to finish a piece. It takes two weeks to mount the loom. The weaver gets 10f. a meter and makes about four to four and a half meters a week. He pays the boy helping, often a son or other relative of the weaver, 3f. (58 cents) a week, and the master pays him the same amount. This leaves to the workman 37f. to 42f. ($7 to $8) a week, or from 6f. to 7f. ($1.16 to $1.33) a day. The master makes an equal amount gross from the loom worked by his workmen, less the mounting of the loom and the preparing of the warp, which he has to pay alone out of his share.

This sort of work was also then not in very brisk demand, being somewhat out of fashion, and showed the influence of depression in trade on the earnings of the workpeople. On the whole, these three examples show how different the earnings of workpeople are, engaged in the same industry and in the same manner of home industries, supplied with the material from the manufacturer, and doing the complete work in their own homes or in shops under the eyes of masters.

The most depressed condition in the trade I found in Germany, where the average of wages was not over two-thirds of what it was in Lyons, and earnings in silk weaving varying between fifty as the mark of depression and a hundred as that of active demand.

Lyons is especially renowned for the beauty of its work in all silk goods of a rich character. It is the leader in fashion in silks all over Europe and America. Its taste in design and color is equalled nowhere. When silk fabrics are in fashion, its workpeople are the first to feel the effects, and it is difficult often to execute the orders pouring in upon them. Not alone does the wage rate per yard rise, but work supply is abundant, and high earnings result from both causes. Of course, the opposite effect results from decline of demand.

Economic Advantages of the Old System to the Manufacturer. Capital Left Free.

It seems to be settled in the minds of thoughtful observers that the system of work prevailing in the silk industry of Europe, as described, cannot easily be superseded. It offers to the manufacturer advantages which fully counterbalance the advantages accruing to him from the smaller rate paid per yard in power mills. First, the all-important fact that the manufacturer can employ all his capital as free and floating capital. He requires no fixed capital. He has not hundreds of thousands invested in brick and mortar and machinery. The looms belong to the weavers without any risk of ownership to the manufacturer. Mostly all manufacturers, owners of power mills, and especially so in America, are bound by the necessity of keeping their workpeople together. They feel impelled by this to supply work to them, even in times of slack demand. In America the workpeople are apt to leave the neighborhood for other employments wherever they offer. The manufacturers, having perhaps spent years in training their help to their work, know the difficulty of getting a supply when needed. For these reasons they quickly overstock themselves with goods made for stock instead of goods made on orders, soon become involved, have to raise money to keep themselves afloat, and have to sacrifice stocks in order to raise money and keep going. In times of prosperity and active demand earnings and profits are high. But few in America are circumspect enough to lay by their surplus profits to tide them over a rainy day, sure to come with the high-pressure industries in America.

The European manufacturer is not so eager to extend his works, adding machinery and buildings, but is satisfied to lay up his surplus profits as reserve capital. The American system gives great results in times of active demand and unrestricted outlet, but shows frequently disastrous results when depression sets in. The manufacturer in Europe in this and similarly conducted industries has no responsibility and no engagements. He works on orders; he does not start his looms till he has received the orders which come from all the markets of the world. Except in articles for which he is certain that he has a ready demand in the near future, he seldom does give work except after it has been ordered. A change of fashion can be easily met by him, and although dulness may be a loss of profits and trade, yet it is no risk to his investments, because he has no capital invested in a factory, and is not compelled to work on stock to keep his help.

The system of working on the domestic industry plan saves, besides all general manufacturing expenses, the interest on fixed capital employed and most of the auxiliary help necessary in the running of a mill. His items of cost are always given, fixed quantities. The savings in the general expense part of the manufacturing cost, interest, and fixed charges are so great that they would compensate for any saving in the power-mill rate of wages per piece.

There are, however, other advantages in hand-loom weaving in silks. First, cheaper silks can be used to advantage, while in power-mill weaving, and especially in America, with less skilled workpeople, a much stronger and better quality is required.*

Another point is this, that goods made on hand looms are quite different from those made on power looms. The hand-loom product shows greater softness, suppleness, and character than power-loom work. Of course, in a general sense what can be made on a power loom can be made on a hand loom, but to the eye the two are quite different things. People are guided by their tastes, and are determined to have that which pleases their senses most, their eye and their touch, and it is plain that they will continue to be guided by preferences in this direction. The hardness of American, the softness of Lyons fabrics are features well known to all wearers of silks.

---

* See chapter on silk.

The Evolution of Industries.

It is very important to keep these distinctions in view as starting points for an understanding of the industrial problem under examination. The industrial development of all Europe has sprung from conditions like those of Ireland, described. The conditions as we find them in outlying countries of Europe, mountain districts of the continent, the islands and highlands of Scotland, and the west of Ireland, are those which prevailed in more advanced industrial countries at more or less remote periods.

We can follow the process of industrial development of centuries under our own eyes if we go from the stagnant to the more advanced countries. We observe in the economy of production a process of evolution that has been going on from the remotest to the present time. We need not go back into the historical records preserved to us in libraries, or in anthropological museums, to get back to the beginning. The past from which our civilization has sprung is still living with us. All we need to do is to go among primitive people and study their methods of work, their tools and employments, and mode of living, and we can surely find the prototype of our own ancestors in the different stages of their development. As the tools have changed, so have the systems of work changed. The simple workshop is a step beyond the original house industry; the workshop of larger dimensions, with divisions of labor added, is an extension of the primitive workshop; the factory is an extension of the workshop, and the power mill an advance on the factory. The people employed are the people born and bred on the soil for generations, used to all the employments by heredity, as having been for generations, perhaps, the occupation and source of maintenance for all the members of the family. The introduction of machinery collected larger numbers under one roof, but they were always the same people, and always working the same materials. Nor has the power mill changed very much in that most important part of manufacture—the nature of the workpeople. They have all the peculiar fitness resulting from heredity and long contact with the industry in which they are employed. The workers in the Staffordshire potteries are all Staffordshire people. They all talk the same dialect and have the same interests. One does not find many that are not born in the same county. The cotton mills of Lancashire are all peopled by Lancashire people, the Yorkshire mills by Yorkshire men and women, and so on in all the countries of Europe.

Here, in America, industrial life starts from entirely opposite grounds. We have no house industries to start from. The population is a migratory one. Americans seldom keep to one industry all their lifetime. The children of Americans hardly ever now enter factory life. The factory is started on an artificial basis; that is to say, a collection of capital, building of a mill, stocking with machinery, and a collecting of workpeople from wherever they can be brought together.

While the American system has its great advantages, it has certainly its disadvantages equally pronounced. The highest stage of development in the productive process, however, has been reached in America. Of all others, the working classes are benefited by this industrial development. The conditions of the working classes necessarily are improved by every progress made in the economy of production. Actual wages measured by their purchasing power rise with a rise in the productiveness of labor. Where the labor processes are most advanced and aided by science and the application of its findings and discoveries to production, there, naturally, labor is most productive, and the share going to labor for its remuneration is the highest.

The labor cost by the piece is reduced, but the earnings of the laborer are increased, by the application of a new invention. ,The quantity produced in excess of the quantity produced by the former process must be large enough to outbalance by far the deficiency caused by the reduction in the piece price. The introduction of machinery or any improved method in place of an old one, without this compensating result, would not alone find serious opposition on the part of the worker, and therefore be adopted with reluctance by the manufacturer, but the manufacturer himself would otherwise not consider the inducement sufficient for the capital sacrifice it would entail on him.

The working classes, however, are not only producers, but consumers; and as consumers the purchasing power of their wages is of equal importance to them as their rate in the sense of earnings. Now, every improvement in the method of production which increases productiveness of labor not only leads to higher earnings, but also to a cheapening of commodities. The cheapening of products means nothing less than making the product accessible to classes of the population who had not been able before to make use of the article at all, or in a more limited way than they would and could under new and cheaper processes of production.

If we were to return to-day in our processes of manufacture and production to the economy of production ruling a hundred years ago in the most advanced industrial countries, we could not produce one-fourth of the goods which now, on account of their abundance, have become necessaries of life of our people. Their price would be so high that none but the wealthy could afford to buy them. The widening of markets, the necessary aim and object of manufacturers, can only be reached therefore by a cheapening, which follows improvement in the economy of production. The poorer classes, meaning the bulk of the nation, being those where an increasing ratio of absorption is almost unlimited, are therefore necessarily those benefited by every progress made. The inventor and employer of improvements is by necessity compelled, in other words, to carry into the humblest home, comforts to which it had not been used before. This is, so to speak, an automatic process, constantly going on, by which gradually but surely the progress in the economy of production brings comfort and well-being into wider and wider circles.

The Producer and Consumer are One. Increasing Productiveness is Increasing Consumptiveness.

In this self-acting principle of an ever-ready market opened by increasing productiveness, the statement quoted from Ricardo, and on which the general theory on labor and wages criticised above is based, and from which our dreary labor views obtain their principal support, finds its easy refutation. The four coats produced with the same amount of work which was formerly required to produce one coat, have to be consumed. If they could not find consumers, the employer of the machine or of the improvement by whose aid the plus-product in a given time can be turned out, would not go to the expense and inconvenience of the change. The economic inducement would be wanting—the change would not be made. But, leaving out the wealthy classes, the absorbing power of the people is in an increasing ratio with either a lowering of prices of commodities at steady wages, or with rising wages and steady prices, and, certainly, as the practical case stands now, with rising wages and declining prices. Either one or the other, and, as we have seen in our own time, the latter case results from improvements in the economy of production. The standard of living of a country makes the general rate of wages. From reasons given above (Chapter II.), the standard in America being, through general causes, a very high one, the rate of wages is a high one. The absorbing capacity of the people is the only limitation of market to which the plus-product is subjected. So long as 90 per cent. of our population have to support families on incomes below $500 a year,* it is self-evident that we have an open market at our immediate doors to absorb products which are now only accessible to that class of the population which lives at a somewhat higher rate of expenditure, *i.e.*, can expend a larger amount on products of labor. But $500 expresses a maximum average of earnings. A very large half of our population has to subsist, with a family group of three,† on less than $400, and from there downwardly, say $300, another large class have to subsist. If all these bread-winners could be made to live on $500 per family group, by a sudden change in their incomes, there would be a market for commodities created which would set our mills and workshops to a very severe test of ability to supply the demand. The endeavor to obtain the highest rate of wages ruling in the country and the industry, and the other endeavor of the working classes to maintain the rate of wages once reached, are not stronger ruling economic forces than the passion of man to obtain as high a rate of comfort

---

* For detailed statement of incomes of working classes see Schoenhof, "Industrial Situation," Chap. XII.

† This is based on the table of "occupations," in the census, where one wage earner represents three heads of the population.

and well-being as his income, under due provisions for the future, will allow him to indulge in.

To maintain themselves in their standard of life has given impulse to the most heroic struggles of the working classes. They have sacrificed immediate well-being, and even the wherewithals to maintain themselves and their children, rather than submit to wage reductions which, in their views, threatened a reduction in the standard of life.

But while sacrifice of immediate well-being for an ulterior end deserves our admiration, from the point of view gained so far by our inquiry into the " Economy of High Wages," it will be seen that, economically, these acts speak of a high degree of wisdom. On the other hand the attempts of the employing classes to depress the rate of wages show frequently an entire misapprehension of the principles under which production is conducted. Most of the strife would disappear if it were more fully recognized that a high rate of wages has all the time been the powerful lever to reaching the low cost of production which practically rules to-day in the industries of the United States.

The Economic Value of High Wages generally not Understood.

A high rate of wages expresses a high rate of productiveness, and its converse a high consuming power. A relatively high consuming power, high standard of living, is required to make the laborer efficient, strong in body and in mind. Without this, labor remains economically more or less sterile, for which an adequate proof will be given in the further progress of this work, treating the industries of the country *seriatim*. Employers can therefore under no possibility lose where a permanently high rate of wages rules. They cannot possibly lose under a rising rate of wages even, as a rise in actual wages is only possible with a rise of the productive power of labor. A higher rate of wages than the one of a previous period simply registers the change which has gone on in the direction of improvement in the economy of production. But, instead of being injured, the employer gains positively by the rise in the standard of wages through the increasing demand thereby created for the increasing product. The demand for this plus-product can come from the laboring classes only, the wage earners, and the people of small incomes. The well-to-do are numerically not a large class. Considerably less than one-tenth of our population would cover them. Of them, however, it can be said that they would not increase their rate of consumption of the necessaries of life either from a cheapening of prices or an increase in income. It is therefore of the working-classes alone, that a market for the plus-product can be expected. Of course, I include here the farmer who tills his farm without the aid of hired help, except at harvesting. With all of these a rise in income means an increased consumption of commodities.

Everything in the wide field of economic phenomena tending to show the benefits arising to the employing classes of a high rate of wages, it is not a little astonishing that such constant repressing force should be employed to oppose a rise in wages. In the lower wage countries this tendency exerts itself the strongest. In Germany, we find in mills a certain maximum day rate fixed. This is fixing the piece rate on the time wage basis. The workers to earn this rate have to turn out a fixed quantity. If they do less, proportionate deductions are made. Under more encouraging aspects they could produce greatly more. But not receiving the benefit out of the plus-product which is clearly due them, but on the contrary knowing that a greater quantity of work done would lead to a reduction of rates or increase of the ratio of output for the day rate fixed, they certainly in return make an economic use of their only salable commodity: their working power, vital power, which the employer considers himself not concerned to replenish.

Many manufacturers in Germany expressed themselves to me in deploring terms of this state of affairs. They were wise enough to see that this short-sighted policy is the chief cause of Germany's low productiveness of labor. Those following an opposite policy had most satisfactory results. " They don't eat and don't work," said a shoe manufacturer of Vienna, when we compared notes on the productiveness of Austrian and German labor and of American labor. "Bread and beer-swilling and an occasional bit of sausage cannot give strength sufficient to compete with you."

It is then clearly evident that there is no greater fallacy than the doctrine that a low rate of wages is necessary to insure a low cost of production. In fact, the opposite is shown to be the true principle upon which the productive processes of nations rest. Yet, how far are we still from recognizing this redeeming fact? The whole armature of possession, governments, and the schools of learning, were put into active service to defeat the attempts of the working-classes at bettering their position; to wit: increasing the rate of wages to enable the buying of sufficient food to replace the wear and tear of tissue. In England this was the condition in the first half of the century. It is the condition of the continent at the end of the century. The improvements in the condition of labor are due to this, that the working classes were in a position that they could wrench from the privileged classes the necessary concessions which alone could enable them to reach the position which they occupy to-day. This fortunate position is the only vantage ground which England possesses and which secures to her the safe and indisputable rulership of the commerce of the world. Reluctantly, sullenly even, the employing classes there, acquiesce in the new development. By education and association they are made to still cherish the belief, despite the world-facts surrounding them, that a low rate of wages is necessary to a low cost of production. The growing tide of democracy in England can afford to laugh at an occasional outbreak of rhetoric repression. It is not dangerous there, this sort of atavism.

But not so on the continent. There the governments are still the willing instruments. Recent years have brought so many examples, that we need not fear contradiction when we say that the repression of the working-classes is still considered to be one of the functions of governments. The more or less active interference of the military forces depends simply on the more or less extensive or intensive mode of protest of the working-classes against the old, incarnate labor theories, so destructive to the countries where they prevail and guide the economy of production.

CHAPTER V.

The Efficiency and Productiveness of Labor increased by Education.—The Ideal Part in Production.—Change of Sentiment in Europe.—Aid given by Art Instruction to Industries.—The Effect on English Industries.—The French System of Education directed to Industrial Ends.—The Industrial Help of Art Museums.

Cheap Labor and Ignorant Labor Synonymous.

PERNICIOUS as the labor views just treated were, and little calculated to reach the end at which they aimed, the ideas prevailing in regard to the intellectual outfit of the laborer were still worse. They were a necessary sequence of the low wage theory. Given the one, the other must follow. A plentiful supply of cheap labor can only be secured by depriving the laborer of all means of cultivating his mind. If he becomes intellectually improved and instructed he will become restive, dissatisfied, and ask higher and higher wages. This can be avoided only by reserving the educational facilities of the age to the privileged few.

In England, especially, the battle fought against education of the working classes was a long and bitter one. Manufacturers held, and I have met not a few who still hold, to the creed that labor would be the more satisfactory the less it knew, outside of the work in which it was employed. Starting on this doctrine, as a matter of course, the introduction of common schools was opposed by the employing classes with a vehemence reminding us of the Dark Ages. The science and art schools are frequently spoken of as instruments for spoiling good material, not alone in England. Though these voices are isolated, yet they are echoes from a not distant past, when they expressed the opinions of the employing classes generally.

These crude opinions are making room for more enlightened views since experience has taught a different lesson. Countries more backward in industrial competition were soon to make rapid strides toward gaining trade which English manufacturers were in the habit of considering their own heirloom. If anything, a loss of trade is an eye-opener in England. This successful competition was recognized by England as well as by France to be due to a more thorough teaching in science and art schools, especially in Germany, and the wider dissemination of knowledge among the German working classes. Now, of course, a different spirit is beginning to manifest itself in England and in France, the two countries where the introduction of more enlightened systems was opposed most bitterly by class interests.

As I have shown in my report on industrial education in France* the system of education introduced into and now extending over the whole country is based on the most enlightened and comprehensive theories of education. The end in view is to give to the people, the poorest included, all the advantages of mental, manual, and technical training that can be given in the school years up to the age of fourteen, and as much supplementary education as may be needed and desired by the youth of both sexes for special pursuits. As a practical educational system, with the object of making efficient workers, I do not believe that there is elsewhere a system of education equal to that of France. Eng-

---

* Technical Education in Europe. Department of State, Washington, D. C. (1888.) Part I. Industrial Education in France.

land, in its Technical Education Act passed two years ago, has laid the seeds for a most thorough reform in school education on as wide a basis as that of France.

In theory, at least, it is now everywhere conceded that the efficiency of the workpeople grows in proportion to their intellectual advancement. All the ages behind us have historically demonstrated this as a fact. But it is well known that facts were not always by deductive political economy considered a necessary ground for theories to stand on. If the facts contradict the theory, "so much the worse for the facts."

The brightness and quickness of youths who had gone through the schools, in the manufacturing districts of England, contrasted very favorably with the dulness of many of the adults who had none of the advantages of the younger generation. With the advantages which the industrial nations of Europe possess in the hereditary skill of their working classes in a variety of special industries, over America, and with a dissemination of knowledge and education among them, they occupy a very strong vantage ground. Europe is now full of the eagerness of nations not to be outdone by competitors in the establishment of such educational advantages as give the greatest facilities for the development and strengthening of industries.

The Ideal Part in the Economy of Production.

The ideal part relates not alone to the intellectual outfit of the laborer, but also to all the intellectual forces set to work in the creating of the huge productive machinery of the age.

For the full understanding of our problem we must separate industries into two classes: Those relating to finished products, articles of use and fashion, and the cruder manufactures. In the former, art is the great teacher; in the latter, science.

First, art teaching. Here England has been the first to recognize the importance of a national system of industrial art education. Experience of a disappointing nature has given the impulse to the creation of a system which has undoubtedly borne excellent fruit.

The Universal Exhibition of 1851 showed to the English how poor and tasteless in design and color many of their industrial productions were, as compared with those of France. Far-seeing and leading statesmen recognized the necessity of action in order to insure the full maintenance of the position of Great Britain in the world of trade and manufacture. To this the science and art department of South Kensington owes its origin. Art schools are now distributed all over the industrial centres of the United Kingdom. They produce good draughtsmen, designers, modelers, etc. To my mind, however, the system needs remodeling, and requires more independence of teaching in the different centres. All the work of the different schools bears one and the same imprint, that of South Kensington. It is too much after the same pattern, not enough scope being given to individuality and to the personal intuition of the art master as well as of the pupil. The paying by results is held by many to make the masters too anxious for drilling and getting prizes.

In spite of all this, the schools undoubtedly benefit the decorative industries. The pottery, metal, and glass industries, in their continued ascendency over their Continental competitors, would alone speak favorably for the schools. The mere fact that Continental competitors copy so much from English pottery and reproduce the richer work of English origin in cheaper production, not by any means through their cheaper labor, but mostly by following the same design, leaving out a great deal of the richer work, however, gives a silent but eloquent acknowledgment of the superiority of English work and taste in this branch of industry. The English take talent from wherever they can get it when they find it superior to the national product. Native talent, however, is coming more and more to the fore. A few of the leading art potteries and other art industries employ French directors. Foreign talent is undoubtedly attracted by the high pay which the English are always ready to give to superior skill and talent, but it plays no important part. Native talent in pottery, painting, modeling, cameo-cutting, in glass, and in metal chasing produces work in design and execution inferior to none of France.

The Royal Worcester factory's work ranks with the highest. If imitation is the highest kind of flattery the homage paid to this remarkable firm is certainly the greatest acknowledgment of its superiority. Yet, as I have been assured by the director and principal owner of the factory, they educate all their artists themselves. The director showed me, however, very costly pieces in their museum, which they buy regardless of price if they contain elements which, either by their originality or beauty of composition, color effect, etc., they can make useful in their own work. They do not shrink from spending hundreds of pounds for objects small in size, but full of leading ideas. A very small Japanese vase was shown me, picked up in 1876 in Philadelphia, for which an extraordinary price had been paid, by which, it appeared to me, many of the Royal Worcester ideas must have been suggested.

The Philadelphia Exhibition of 1876 showed us the

greatness of Japan as an industrial art country. In America articles of commerce of Japanese art are only cheaper specimens, selected with a consciousness of the high-tariff duties to which they are subjected when they enter this country. The Paris Exhibition of 1889 was full of pieces which the trade of England even, free of any tariff charges, would be afraid of handling. They gave an idea of the capacity of that wonderful people for art work. There is object teaching ready for every one able to understand and profit by it.

Teaching Industrial Art.

I take it for granted that everybody will understand that when I lay such importance upon industrial art teaching I do not mean that it is only the regular school which can give it. The school is only one of the many methods open for teaching. If art taught in schools connected with factories like that at Sèvres, the Royal Worcester, etc., makes the future workman more proficient in his special branch than in the special school, this mode of teaching is only substituting one for another. A proper teaching in well-organized schools, however, gives undoubtedly a broader foundation.

Industrial art schools abound especially in Germany. The World's Exhibition of 1876 in Philadelphia did much in opening the eyes of governments and industrial institutions in Germany by impressing them with the poverty of their productions compared with those of other nations. Great support has been given since to industrial art schools and technical schools, with a view to giving much-needed help to industries. The graphic arts especially have found great development through the influence of industrial art schools. In ornamentation, design, color, and general outside appearance, they have made great progress. This shows in the pressure which they have been exercising on foreign competitors in neutral countries, especially on the English. The intrinsic value and quality of their products, however, have not improved equally. It is undoubtedly due to this inferiority in quality that they not infrequently lose position in foreign markets. What progress Germany does make, however, is, more than progress anywhere else, traceable to the influence of the art and technical school, especially in color and chemical industries.

Some of the schools, like that at Crefeld, show remarkable completeness of organization, teaching all the elements of production in that most complex of all industries, the manufacture of silk. Schools of this character would be of the highest value to America, where industries are a matter of creation, and not of gradual growth and development, as in Germany and the industrial countries of Europe, and therefore only the more needful.

In France, art teaching as an organized course in public instruction is of recent times. The inherent artistic feeling of the French was considered a sufficient fund to draw from. The teachers and directors of art schools in Germany are to the present day fully conscious of this superiority in the French, and readily acknowledge it. The natural sense of taste shows so prominently in all articles of French origin, that little need be said on the subject. Still, with all this natural advantage, thorough art teaching in all branches of the industrial arts, wherever it can give additional impetus, has been considered necessary by those shaping the destinies of France. A course of art teaching has been established which could not be broader, covering the whole system of public instruction, nor higher in its reach, as it ultimately connects with the École des Beaux-Arts, the crowning edifice. At the Paris Exhibition of 1889 the exhibits clearly showed to any one following the industrial development of nations the great help which the schools have given the industries of France.

The exhibits at the Exposition of the different art schools, which I visited in 1887, were especially gratifying from the industrial point of view, giving a clear indication of what class of workers would soon be spread over the industries affected thereby. On the whole I found industrial art teaching in France more satisfactory than anywhere else, inasmuch as there is not the gulf between what is generally called real art and industrial art.

No nation understands so well as France, that art in its highest productions is but speaking the language of the people. The greater the art, the more direct and eloquent the appeal to the common understanding. The greater the art, the truer to nature. Hence, a saturation of industrial production with the true spirit of art cannot have any but the most salutary practical results. The more this quality becomes part of industrial productions accessible to the masses of the people, the more extended the markets, of course. And so it follows, that though the cost of production need not be enhanced, the benefits and profits to industries must grow with an extension of art teaching and artistic feeling to all classes engaged in production appealing to taste.

The Industrial Art Museum.

The superior advantages given to the industrial countries of Europe and the workers engaged in these industries, which we may class, for want of a better name, under the general name of taste industries, are by no means limited to hereditary skill, natural taste, and art teaching. The cultivation of taste by the sight of beautiful objects, the special productions of different countries, is certainly a great help in raising the art standard of a nation. There can be no doubt that the high perfection in industrial art works of the German master craftsmen of the fifteenth and sixteenth centuries was due to the custom of making it a condition for admission into the craft that every craftsman applying for his diploma of mastership should have spent some years away from home and in foreign travel. The workingman travelled from place to place, and frequently visited far distant countries. This custom prevailed up to recent times, being still in vogue within my own recollection. I remember the familiar figure, knapsack on back, stick in hand, tramping the highroad from town to town.

The workingman's tramping it certainly did not detract from his ability to take in the varying aspects and impressions of different countries. The trades then were, however, conducted on different principles from the modern idea and the factory system. The master workman had to be master of all the parts belonging to his craft. The builder was not only a bricklayer or mason, but also skilled in the art of drawing his plans and doing practically what a modern architect does to-day; the same with the cabinetmaker, the weaver, the worker in textiles and metals, etc.

By the modern system of division of labor, much of the task is taken out of the hands of the individual worker and given to special hands; still there is no doubt that even work so subdivided will be benefited if the worker doing only a part in the whole possesses trained skill and developed taste. The printer in calico print works does not make the design, but if he has no eye for the harmony of color he is very apt to spoil a good pattern.

Now craftsmen can no more take their lessons from travel in foreign countries. The importance of having the great storehouses of the past and present open has, however, been recognized, and art industrial museums have been created which offer an always-ready opportunity to everybody who wants to cultivate his taste and enlarge his ideas.

Here, again, England has been a leader, followed now by almost every nation of an industrial character except America. The South Kensington Museum contains treasures in every conceivable branch of industry, collected from all parts of the world, and leading us back to remotest times. Every industrial centre in England has an art museum of its own, to which South Kensington periodically sends exhibits from its vast stores, which loans are replaced from time to time. The South Kensington Museum, with its numerous branches and its whole organization, is a result of the Exhibition of 1851. Being first in the field as a collector from old treasures stored up in palaces, monasteries, and in the hands of private collectors, its task was an easier one than that of its imitators.

It does not belong to my present task to describe in detail these vast collections. Still, it may be well to call attention to specimens of what we are pleased to call industrial art, to show what treatment was given it by the ancients, to the collection of Tanagra figures in South Kensington and the British Museum. A figure of a reclining lady, four inches by eight and six inches high, was paid for at the price of £270 10s. The inimitable ease of pose, the grace and beauty of the figure, brought out even more by the charming arrangement of the drapery, which the Greeks employ to cover the nude form, not to conceal it, make the impression that such treasures are well acquired at any cost, though they be terra-cottas and produced in quantities as articles of trade and manufacture by the potters of Tanagra. Indeed, we see in the British Museum the moulds in which they were cast and a partly-finished model, part of the nude not yet covered by drapery.

Another specimen of ancient art may be mentioned here. It is the most expressive lesson extant of the highest perfection in what we should call to-day industrial'art objects. I speak of the famous Portland Vase. It is the greatest masterpiece of its kind, and is fitly placed in the gem room of the British Museum. It is made of two layers of glass. The lower layer, forming the body of the urn, is of black; the top layer, of white glass. By cutting away the upper part, enough is made to remain to make the design, as in all cameo cutting. The difficulties of the task are very great. The Webbs, of Stourbridge, who have made a specialty of cameo plaques, and produce beautiful pieces on this principle at a value of a hundred guineas and upwards, showed me a piece which cracked in the hands of the artist when only a few hours more work was required for completion. The bringing out of the design depends on the darker or lighter tones. These are produced by the cutting away of more or less of the white substance. Now, mistakes cannot be remedied as when the matter is only laid on as in paste-on-paste decorations in pottery. If the technique offers great difficulties in a plaque, a flat surface of the size of a dinner-plate, how much more in a round body like a vase! Yet the figures of gods and mortals actually live and speak. Posture and bodily perfection would do high honor to the greatest sculptors of modern times. The limbs show that they are meant to do service on earth; that even if some of the people represented are used to living in ambrosial heights part of their time, their feet and ankles are in proportion and fit for use among mortals.

In the work of Sèvres and of Mintons' in Stoke we see still too much of a pandering to a taste which runs more after an imaginary than the real type of the beautiful. In ancient plastique art we see the best living models reproduced; in the modern we see them " improved " and " idealized." *

---

*How the "improver" and "idealizer" is equipped for his ambitious task is apparent from the many examples of his skill, which he has seen fit to place along with the specimens of ancient art which have received his attentions in the restorations. They fill all the museums of Europe. The forms of gods, heroes, and mortals are made grotesque by the additions of arms, hands, and feet evidently stolen from some clumsy clown of awkward manners and appearance. They had even attempted to restore the holy lady of Milo, the goddess of incomparable hauteur and loveliness, of unsurpassable lines and forms. The artists who attempted the work were unable to come within an approach to the task. The age seems at least to have reached a first step to progress, a consciousness of its incapacity, and so the restorations were removed and the foam-born Aphrodite stands to this day, in her solitary retreat in the Louvre, without arms and without her left forefoot, and without toes to her right foot. More fortunate than her brother of Belvedere, though mutilated, she will never be an object of derision should the gods ever return from their exile among the barbarians, who have gone so far as even to scrape the classic forms and thereby destroy their beauty forever.

But the most astonishing example we find in two statues in the Louvre—two statues called "Venus Accroupies." The one was found at Vienne, and the other at Tyre. Though sepulchered at distant places, they were evidently twin sisters, exact likenesses of one another in size, pose, and character. The one was found in a perfect state of preservation, the other only the upper part of the body including the hips. The missing lower body had to be restored by the artist, equipped with all the art cunning of his craft. The restoration stands an eloquent admission of "non possumus." At about thirty feet distance from the complete classic work stands this half-classic, half-modern work of art, a sort of hermaphrodite, because the upper part is that of lovely womanhood, the lower seems to belong to one of the more massive, coarser sex. Aside from the absence of the fine accentuations in lines, which make classic statuary so wonderfully alive, this restoration, with the original actually completed before the restorer's eye, is in dimensions of a body twice the weight of its upper part. The statue restored is a standing

Therefore, a return to classic art means a return to nature and its never-closed storehouse of information.

These few types show us how the ancients regarded "industrial art."

We cannot go astray if we follow closely in the track cut out for us.

From my observations I carried away one general impression, the expression of which will not be out of place here: that, at least in the æsthetic side of industrial art, the present, no matter where, with all its unbounded auxiliaries, has no standing before its ancient teachers. The skilled weaver who makes his own design and dyes his own colors is not reached by all the complexity of modern textile industry. The illuminations in the old missals of the fourteenth and fifteenth centuries show a delicacy and richness of tints which after five and six centuries have more wealth of color than if products of yesterday. While the wall paintings of Pompeii and Egypt, not to speak of those of the Renaissance, live to the present day, the frescos of the Maximilianaeum in Munich, hardly forty years old, have already crumbled away.

The most remarkable work of graphic art is the Book of Kells in the National Library at Dublin. This is a work of about the seventh or eighth century of our era, a time when all Western Europe was still steeped in barbarism. The delicacy of colors, the treatment of concentric lines, the general harmony, give the illuminations an ornamental effect unexcelled in any period or any country.

Nowhere, however, have I found a museum as an aid to

---

accusation that our age has lost, or, perhaps, not recovered the correct vision which antiquity possessed and which enabled it to produce masterpieces in the workshop, perhaps, where the atelier and the studio stand aside in dull mediocrity.

the development of a special industry so complete as the industrial museum at Lyons, of which I have given a full description in my "Report on Industrial Education in France." Here, also, the remoter period shows the greater wealth and warmth in color and design. There we see all the greatness of the Venetians of the thirteenth century mirrored in their silks and velvets, as we see it in South Kensington and elsewhere in their ancient glassware. We understand why they prohibited their craftsmen from going abroad, why they made hostages of the relatives of these craftsmen, even to the penalty of death, if they did not return within a given time.

In the æsthetic part of art industries we have a great deal to learn; we find, when examining the treasures of these museums, very little to be proud of in our own achievements. In Germany and Austria almost every town has its museum, many of them organized with a view to helping existing industries. They are, however, on a smaller basis than the South Kensington Museum, but are all excellent in their way. Yet being new, supplied only with limited funds and largely dependent on aid given by private individuals, they cannot, of course, be put in the same category with their English prototype.

In addition to the objects exhibited in these museums, the art libraries attached to them are of great usefulness. These libraries are open to everybody, and contain almost every known work relating to industrial art. Their portfolios are full of designs and reproductions of artistic work. In this manner a constantly flowing source is open, from which those interested can take refreshing draughts.

CHAPTER VI.

Science and Art powerful Factors in the Economy of Production.—Cheapening of Price.—Influence of Science Schools.—Technical Training.—Art and Technical Schools greatly needed in the United States.—Scientific Methods are quickly adopted.—American Inventors easily lead the World in improving Mechanical Appliances and are ably assisted by the Workmen who handle the Machines, but the Chemists of this Country are far behind those of Europe.—Cheapening the Cost of Production.

I HAVE endeavored to outline the elements which combine in giving character and value to manufactures, aside from the material part of the work that may be in them. I have found it necessary to show the superiority of Europe over America in possessing a stock of working people, born and trained to the trades in which they are engaged. They bring to their work a certain indefinable skill of eye and touch which shows itself in the fabric, and which cannot be put into it by any substitution from without. How this manifests itself practically in all our importations from Europe, I shall show later on in dealing with the special schedules of our tariff act. The word taste alone will hardly express the full meaning I wish to convey. But I find no better word by which to express all that makes an article attractive and induces people to pay a higher price than for the American counterpart. Our large importation in finished goods is due to the fact that they show attractive points in their general appearance, color, design, and finish, which for lack of skill or adaptation are wanting in those produced here. Others we cannot manufacture, because other conditions may be wanting. In what we do manufacture successfully against foreign competition, the labor cost is very seldom a consideration. Wherever quantity of production comes into play, our superior machinery, working methods, and the energy of our workpeople are fully able to cope with that part of the question. In many lines training given in art and technical schools would be of much greater service to our industrial classes than all the tariff increases repeatedly enacted for the fostering of home industries. To this proposition our manufacturers generally answer that they can buy talent cultivated abroad much better trained than they could expect to get here, even if they had these schools. This may be true so far as leading artists and designers are concerned. It certainly cannot apply to the many who would be benefited by this training and distributed into very important though minor subdivisions of manufacture. Besides, experience speaks against it. The same views were formerly held in European countries, but they are abandoned in the light of the manifest advantages of the introduction of art and technical training in the different excellent schools that have sprung up all over Europe.

Superiority of English Work.

There is no manufacturer or workman so proud of his rule-of-thumb efficiency as the English, and speaking from practical results no one else has a right to be so proud of it. Strange to say that in many lines of manufacture where technical skill and science play the greatest part, Germany, with all the help it receives from its school training, has not been able to approach the superiority of British work. The color and finish of cotton velvets, for instance, and of seal plushes in silk, to name only a specimen or two, are of such acknowledged superiority that the English more than hold the market against the rivalry of Germany. Still England recognizes the importance of technical training, and has gone to work with open hand to supply its coming generations with the means of increasing efficiency. This is due to the fact that while Germany has not been able to supersede England in neutral markets, the English see clearly that their rivals are approaching them perceptibly, and by means of nothing else than their technical and art schools. If any nation by reason of its development from an agricultural into a manufacturing nation (whose working classes are mainly recruited from European unskilled labor) has the need of such institutions as we have been describing—art schools and technical schools—it certainly is the great republic of the United States. Strange to say that, few as have been the attempts to establish industrial art schools, most of them seem to die of inanition due to the neglect of government and industrials. General McClellan, while governor of New Jersey, interested himself earnestly in establishing an art school in Trenton. He succeeded so far as to get it started with the support of the manufacturers. But even this useful enterprise in a centre whose chief industry is an art industry, viz., pottery, went to pieces again after his retirement from the governorship. The waste in American mills and much of the bad work done are due to the absence of special skill in labor as well as in the laboratory and the management in different branches of the works. Loose and even corrupt practices on the one side and incompetency on the other have frequently led to destruction of wealth where all other elements of prosperity were present. Since the establishing of the Institute of Technology in Boston it is acknowledged in that centre that much has been done toward the eradication of these evils.

Helps in Technical Training.

The great corporations in our leading textile industries would be especially benefited by schools furnishing trained American help in science and in art. Our people are still engaged in the task of subduing a continent. The extent of the territory progressively covered by an enterprising population still absorbs, so to speak, the intelligence of the nation. Quantity and immediate results are the main objects of all enterprises. The railroad engineer in uniting continents, the inventor turning out a new machine, the scientist discovering a new process, all have the same purpose—to make production serviceable to the masses and all classes of people. Necessity is the mother of invention. We are inventors by compulsion. Some of the greatest inventions and improvements for cheapening production were either made here in America or adapted and improved from foreign types. All industrial countries must be quick in accepting scientific discoveries of a far-reaching nature, but that the United States outrun the world in the contest for mechanical and scientific improvement is proved by the fact that in iron-making, steel-making, cotton-spinning, silk-throwing, and in the coarser wool fabrics (after reducing the cost of raw wool to the foreign free wool basis), though paying higher wages per diem, America fully holds her own, frequently at a lower cost of labor by the piece. The higher wage rate per diem ruling in the United States enables the operatives to enjoy a better mode of living and better nutrition of body and mind. They eat more and better food than any of the operatives of Europe, and their general mode of living is upon a higher standard. They operate more spindles, more looms in the textiles. In steel-making, coal-mining, coking, etc., an equal number of hands turn out more tons in a given time than any of their competitors in Europe, England not excluded. They work more steadily in every hour of their working day. The steadiness of the worker, the application of his whole time and energy to his work, is most intense, and is only possible where good nutrition prevails. Every moment is made use of to turn out the greatest number of pieces that can be ground out of his machine or run out of his hand while at work. This alone explains the high rate of earnings in some occupations, coupled with the low piece-price paid, which, when I stated it to manufacturers in the same industries in European countries, caused astonishment. Many of our foreign rivals are aware of this and dread a reformed tariff (in the Democratic sense), a low tariff on a basis of free raw materials.

Much of this is due, aside from the superior quality of American labor, to the scientific development of the age. Many a new industry has been called into being of which the last generation was entirely ignorant. Quickest of all are the United States to avail themselves of these. Thus, what may be called the new science of our generation—electricity—has found new developments and applications in America. I will not speak of the telegraph and the telephone, which play so important a part in the world's commercial life, and, in saving time and employment of capital, have become very important factors in cheapening prices, but of the application of electricity to productive processes. Here we have an entirely new vista of possibilities still in store for us. The feats accomplished within the short time since the application of electricity to industries are so wonderful that we may well indulge in prophecies which a decade or two ago would have been considered flights of imagination of the most fanciful kind. In metal industry especially, is electricity destined to play a most important part, and I will allude to only a few of the results attained within the last few years. The welding of different metals had resisted all attempts. Electricity has solved the problem very effectively, and a process has been invented by which iron and copper, or any other metals are welded now at a nominal cost. Welding by electricity cheapens many a form of iron that had formerly to be welded by subjecting the different parts to a separate heating process. Another direction in which electricity has shown its wonderful capacity for cheapening cost is in the recent development of the manufacture of what may be called a new metal, aluminium. Aluminium possesses qualities which make it of the highest value industrially. It unites with great tensile strength great specific lightness. It does not oxidize in moist air, nor is it affected by water. Its softness makes it easily workable. It can be hammered and drawn into wire. For these reasons it would be an excellent material for almost every article of use now made of iron, steel, copper, or brass. Its specific weight is 2.56 against 7.84 of iron. Wherever lightness combined with strength is desirable, and this is the case in almost everything made wholly or largely of metal, its capacity for employment is unlimited. For military equipments it would, for this reason alone, prove of the greatest value, either pure or as an alloy with other metals. The supply is unlimited, as it is contained in all clay to the extent of about 35 per cent. The use of this valuable metal was, however, up to recent years almost impossible on account of its high cost. Aluminium was produced for practical purposes and in a compact form by Ernst Wöhler in 1845, and by Deville in 1854. The French Government, seeing the great advantages to be derived from this metal, assisted with large sums and enabled the erection of works at Javelle, and the manufacture in quantities. The process, however—the Natron process—was too expensive to give the metal much scope for employment. The price at first was as high as fr. 1000 per kilogram (about $90 a pound) and was gradually reduced by various inventions and discoveries to about $10 a pound, at which price it was sold but a few years ago, when the world was informed of the invention in America of a process of reducing aluminium by electricity. Factories were started in America and in England and put in successful operation. The price was quickly reduced to $2 a pound, and something over a year ago to $1. It was then said that this reduced price would not leave a profit to those operating by the new electro-chemical process, that the price was reduced to discourage the employment of new inventions rapidly coming into the field, by which the cost of production is again reduced considerably. The patentee of a later process which has come under my notice claimed then that the metal can easily be produced as low as 30 or even 25 cents per pound.

But before any new process had been put into operation, the employers of the electric process who had claimed that aluminium could not be profitably produced at $1 a pound, have since seen fit to reduce the price to 50 cents a pound.

It is useless in a discussion of the kind that we are engaged in, to task the reader with technical explanations as to the difference between one invention and another. I only wish to point out the effect of scientific discoveries on the cost of production. The difference in wages, whatever their day rates may be, sinks into insignificance when compared to this destroying factor in price making. Last summer it was stated in England before the British Association that the cost of aluminium bronze (with 10 per centum of aluminium) was but a few years ago $1.20 per pound, and at the time of the reading of the paper 33 cents. At the present price of aluminium, the aluminium bronze can be produced at considerably less cost. The governments of different countries are preparing for the extensive use of aluminium as an alloy with steel in their ordnance and small arms, ship-building, armor-plating, etc. Here, then, science has again called into existence new industries, a new metal of great serviceability, probably to be produced in the near future at what, compared with the past, will be merely a nominal cost.

American Chemists Lagging Behind.

In chemistry equal results can be noted. But here America lags behind European countries, and science schools and technical colleges with extensive laboratories would be of the highest value. In this branch Germany especially has had remarkable success. Many of its most flourishing industries are pre-eminently chemical industries, and their establishment and very profitable operation are traceable to the excellence of its polytechnic schools and the high science training in its universities. Some of our colleges have very good chemical schools and laboratories. But they seldom reach high enough. In most instances they lack the means for sufficient extension. American colleges and universities are generally endowed schools, based on bequests and legacies; hence they are in most cases hampered by provisions which direct the application of the funds and interfere with the free exercise of judgment as to the teaching. The direction of the teaching is taken from the faculty and left to the trustees. But teaching must be as free as science in order to show the best results.

Returning now to applied chemistry, I will cite an

example to show the cheapening effected by the introduction of science into manufacturing industries. Paper making has especially gratifying results to show, and this within a very brief space of time. I take here the English prices, because England has for a long time had the advantage of cheaper prices for its materials, and has been the seat of the industries which furnish the chemicals for most paper makers, and largely so for our American manufacturers. A fine quality of glazed packing paper, known to almost every user of English goods, sold in 1879 at £39 per ton. In 1890 it had come down to £18 10s., or less than one-half the old price.

This reduction is partially due to improvements in machinery and the manufacturing methods. The largest part, however, is owing to the improvements—mostly chemical—in the reducing of the manufacturing materials used. It costs less to make the pulp because, as we discover improved processes, chemicals used in reducing the fibrous matter are cheaper. Bleaching powder, which had been £14 the ton in 1879, is now £5 to £6 a ton. Soda ash, etc., have come down in proportion. Soda pulp when first introduced sold at £22, and sells now at £9 unbleached and £11 bleached, a ton; while the mechanical pulp, mostly from Germany and Sweden, sold last winter at Hull at 34 shillings or $8 a ton. Sulphite pulp is a long fibre pulp which owes its creation as an industry to the chemistry development of Germany. It largely replaces rags in paper making. In England it is now sold at rates between £11 10s. and £12 10s.

These improvements in pulp making have, of course, largely reduced the value of rags. Jute end cuttings and rope ends, formerly largely used, have come down from £14 to £6 in sympathy with the decline of price in the other materials. America has kept in line in the progress made in the industry. A number of improvements are of American origin. Although it has to import its soda ash, bleaching powder, and other chemicals, and pay duty, it produces soda pulp as cheaply as England, and by means of its consolidation of works and a quicker eye to improvements is even able to export pulp.

The labor cost here is also infinitesimal, independent of the remuneration per diem. A product of 5,000 pounds a day of one converter would not require more than four or five men at $1.50 a day. The wage rate per pound would not be more than one-tenth to one-seventh of a cent. Reduction of wages would not accomplish very much toward reduction of price, alongside of the cheapening influences recorded above.

Great saving of expense and cost has been effected by improved methods in the recovery of soda ash and other chemicals used in the manufacturing process. In this the Americans have made great strides of late, and in soda pulp making are fully able to compete on a free trade basis with the whole world, and carry off the honors besides.

Equal progress has been made in America in paper making. In spite of the onerous burdens on materials, we are able to export to England with higher prices for our chemicals, and even pay the freight for the paper, and undersell English makers in their home markets.

This is due to the fact that in America, wherever industries can be so conducted, a special article or special line is made by one mill, year in and year out. Infinite machinery keeps grinding away and produces infinite quantities. The general cost is reduced pro rata with the increased quantities run out by the mill.

In England, as I have repeatedly been told, paper makers

make all kinds of paper that are wanted. This principle applies as well to other industries to which I shall have reference hereafter. One of the leading men controlling and selling the output of a number of mills, told me that one house prides itself on manufacturing not fewer than 160 different sorts of paper. By its different methods America is enabled to pay high wages and undersell Europe.

CHAPTER VII.

Improvements and Inventions.—Labor Cost enormously reduced.—Iron in Finished Forms.—Metallurgy.—Automatic Machinery.—Its Effect on Cost.—Labor Cost an Insignificant Item.—Cheapest Cost and Highest Wages with Highest Scientific Development.—The Steel Rail and the Ocean Steamer, Creations of Science.

Powerful Influence in Metallurgy.

THE greatest savings in the cost of production have, however, been realized in metallurgy, and in the production of pig iron and steel the most astonishing and gratifying results have arisen. It is not more than sixty years ago, as I was told by an old ironmaster of North Staffordshire, that it took six tons of coal for the production of a ton of pig iron, where one and three-quarters are used now. The introduction of the hot blast and the better construction of furnaces have brought this about. Not only is less coal used, but the ores yield now almost all the iron they contain, while formerly there used to be considerable waste. Of course the labor of carting the materials was then proportionately greater too. The value of the fuel saved alone is sufficient to more than cover the present price of pig iron. The difference is equal to the labor cost in ten tons of pig iron at the furnace average labor cost in England. While we may say that labor employed about furnaces receives from one-third to one-half more pay, the cost of pig iron has been reduced to less than one-third the price it commanded then.

In the manufacturing of steel, both on the Bessemer and

the basic process, improvements have led to economies by which the price of steel has been reduced far below the price of puddled iron, which is gradually making room in almost all employments for steel. English steel rails, which had been in 1869, $55, and in 1873, $80, are now about $20, and were as low as $18 in 1888. American steel rails had to follow, of course, in this price decline. In 1869 they were $132 currency a ton, or $88 gold. They are now $30 a ton, and were sold as low as $25, about three years ago.

American rail mills, it is not saying too much, are the best equipped in labor-saving methods and appliances, and an American rail can be produced now from the pig iron at less cost on the average in labor, although the daily rates are considerably higher, than in Europe. These are truly achievements of science applied to industry. The far-reaching effect is brought home now to every understanding. Railroad building could otherwise never have attained the extension which it has. Hundreds of thousands of homes and farms would not have been established. The food supplies of Europe, principally of England, would be still subject to scarcity, and want and misery still be the lot of the working classes of England, not to speak of Germany and France, if iron and steel were still produced at the cost and by the methods of the time when railroads were first started.

Some of the most important inventions for reducing the cost of rolling the rails are American. But whatever their origin, they are applied to better advantage here than abroad. The effect is a much smaller number of men employed for the same output, even where we compare American with English rail mills. The resulting higher wage rate per day and lower labor cost per ton will not surprise, therefore.

The invention and introduction of the three-high blooming-

and rail-mill instead of the two-high mill did a great deal in cheapening the cost of production. Automatic tables and travelling cranes do now the chief work in American rail mills. "Before the introduction of automatic appliances, from fifteen to seventeen men were required to operate a three-high rail mill. The automatic tables reduced this number to five, including the roller in charge of the train," says one of our great engineers, Mr. Hunt, the inventor of the tables, in a paper in the *Engineering and Mining Journal*. They were first introduced in 1884–85, and we can well see from this that the labor cost of steel rails from the ingot to the rail is a necessarily decreasing quantity in the train of these inventions and improvements.

To give the reader an idea of the workings of an American rail mill of to-day, I will quote from the paper referred to above:

"After the ingot is reduced in the blooming mill it is carried by power rollers toward the first rail train, and through a shear by which the end, which was the top of the ingot, is cut off, and the long bloom sheared in two, each half making two or three rails, according to the weight of the intended section. The first half at once passes through the rail roughing rolls, the second one being held for a few seconds, or until the first has made three passes, when it is also sent forward.

"If from any reason the bloom when sheared should have become too cold to be safely and successfully finished, an overhead traveller is provided to carry it at a right angle into a ring at the side of the mill, in which heating furnaces are located with a Wellman charging and drawing crane in front of them. When sufficiently heated the same carrier conveys the steel back to the table rollers.

"By this arrangement cold cobbles, or other rail blooms, can be heated and delivered to the rolls. In the roughing rolls the bloom receives five passes in three-high rolls. It is then passed to the second roughing tables and is given three passes in three-high rolls. The partially formed section is elevated to the back tables of two-high rolls, and making one pass through them reaches a dummy table in front, from which it slides down to driven rollers, and is by them carried back to the

THE ECONOMY OF HIGH WAGES. 95

three-high set of rolls which are in line with the first roughing rolls, and driven by the same engine. In these it receives four passes, making, in all, thirteen rail-mill passes. It is now a finished section, long enough to cut into three 30-foot rails. This is done at one operation by four saws. After passing through the cambering machine, the rails are carried by power down the hot beds. When sufficiently cool they are loaded by power on a spider car, which is handled by a special locomotive. The rails are conveyed to the several cold beds, located conveniently to the cold straightening presses, and are unloaded on these beds by an automatic arrangement of arms or levers, receiving their power from steam taken from the locomotive boiler."

Here it is all self-acting machinery which does the work. The few men seen about in an American rail mill direct and guide. In Germany, near Aix-la-Chapelle, and in England (Middlesborough, and Darlington) I saw at what was reputed as the best equipped works no arrangements even approaching this complete system of scientific apparatus. In rolling and handling the rails men were employed to do what is done here by automatic appliances. We turn a ton of rails out of the pig iron at a labor cost of $2.50 at the present time, which in England costs $3.04. At the same time our labor per diem receives two-thirds more pay than the comparatively well paid English labor.

Price Reductions in Other Forms of Iron.

If we look into the prices of iron at remoter periods, with their crude methods, we can well understand the backwardness of European countries. Indeed, the progress of the ages can almost be measured by the progress made in the production of iron. In the early Middle Ages especially, iron had become so scarce an article, that almost every remnant of it brought down from the Roman period was made use of in one form or another. Thus, for instance, it is recorded that the iron clasps which had been used in the huge masonry of the

Porta Nigra at Trêves were removed and forged into weapons and utensils. For the fifty years previous to 1830, when railroad building took its rise, the price of English pig iron, according to Tooke's "History of Prices," averaged about £7 per ton. From old accounts we learn that the price of bar iron not further back than the seventeenth century was 25s. 8d. a hundredweight, which is equal to £25 13s., or about $125, the gross ton, which the value of money at that time would make considerably higher yet, compared to our present prices. About the middle of last century the price was yet £20 a ton. At the present time English bar iron varies between £5 and £6.

The reduction in price of finished articles of iron, caused by the application of improvements and mechanical inventions, is greater yet, and here again America shows most astonishing results. Our principle laid down above, that high wages lead to cheapened production by a necessity like a natural law, finds excellent proof in the iron industry, principally in finished forms. Here automatic machinery replaces hand labor in almost all except the finishing processes. By this means we are able to indulge in the luxury of what, compared with the prices paid in free trade countries, must be called high-priced iron and steel (to help the infant industries of Pennsylvania and their millionaire owners), and still undersell European free-trade countries with the finished products.

The drop-hammer has been lately introduced in American plow works, and contracts are taken at $4.50 a plow. I heard of one order for 20,000 plows to Argentina at that price. This was in 1890. In that same year I visited one of the principal English works of world-wide reputation. There the hammer and the anvil alone were in use, and the blacksmith wielded his craft unassisted by any mechanical auxiliaries. The cheapest plow which they produced was 30s. or $7.29. But as in other trades so in agricultural implements, their trade, being principally an exporting one, has adapted itself to the local variations of the demand. We know how tastes and habits determine the character of tools and implements no less than of commodities. England, trying to give the people of foreign lands the articles which they claim to be suitable to their purposes, accommodates her manufacturing system to the conditions most suitable to the purpose. The many variations do not permit of a system, except under very great modifications, which can afford to build and use machinery for one specialty or pattern even. This factory not alone produced a variety of plows for the different countries, but mowers, reapers, and other agricultural implements. Our system of work may somewhat interfere with a rapid extension of exports by not being elastic enough to adapt itself to special local demands. Much can be done, however, to assimilate the American working system to a readier compliance with foreign tastes. But be this as it may, we hold the inner circle. We certainly cannot be dislodged from the hold on the home market by any possible emergencies arising out of foreign labor and manufacturing conditions as here outlined.

Other Illustrations of Superior American Methods.

One of the most interesting labor processes by which the difference between the old methods and the American methods can be illustrated is that involved in the making of an article largely used in building—a piece of iron for uniting beams, turned into its proper shape after it has been heated. The uniting of beams by means of this beam hanger is preferable to mortising, as mortising weakens the beam to the extent that the timber is cut away. The beam hanger leaves the beam intact, and unites the two beams equally firmly. In Germany and other foreign countries it is forged by the blacksmith on his anvil. In America, where its use is far more extensive on account of the more general employment of wood as a building material, it was formerly made in the same way. Lately a machine has been invented by which, after the iron is heated, it is rolled by one operation into the proper shape.

In Germany, as I found out by personal inquiry, a blacksmith and his helper would not make more than twenty of these irons in a day, and wages at three marks (or 72 cents) a day would be considered high pay. The selling price of these irons is about 9 cents a pound in England and Germany. In America, though iron is higher than in England and Germany, the roller at the machine earns from $3 to $3.50 a day; the helper, $1 to $1.50; and the iron is sold at $3\frac{3}{4}$ cents a pound, with a good profit to the manufacturer. A day's work on one machine turns out 600 to 700 finished beam hangers. The cheapened product and the rapidity with which orders can be filled now, creates markets which formerly were wanting through lack of ability to supply them. Here again cheapness is not at all due to any individual labor exertion (except that close and exhaustive application which is possible only to well-paid labor), but almost entirely to the inventive spirit so characteristically American.

These labor processes are always paid at piece-work rates. The time occupied in rolling is the same, whether the irons be of larger or smaller size. It takes ten seconds to run a

THE ECONOMY OF HIGH WAGES. 99

bar through the rollers. The heating of the larger pieces, however, takes more time than that of the smaller, and on this account the larger irons occupy more time in making.

A machine can roll three tons of iron a day at less than a cent per pound for the labor, as against perhaps five cents under the old hand process. Other forms of iron are treated in the same way, but this will suffice as an example to illustrate the influence of invention upon prices. In pin making, screw making, chain making, and kindred industries, automatic machinery does all the work, while human labor is confined to feeding the machine which turns out the work. It sounds almost ludicrous to hear the question of wages or labor cost mentioned in connection with operations of this kind.

What difference would it make in the cost of the product in pin making whether the day rate of the workman tending the machine be \$2 or \$3 under working methods like these? In a factory in Connecticut I found 70 pin-making machines in operation. They were tended by three men and one machinist and a boy helper for the repairing. The combined output of these self-acting machines is 7,500,000 of pins a day or 25,000 papers.* The pins are even put on the paper by the machine. The difference in the cost, whether the combined wages of the five men be \$7.50 or \$10.00 per day, is infinitesimal. Allowing for stoppages, and taking the output at 20,000 papers, the difference would not be more than one-eighth of a cent.

---

* It was considered a great triumph of progress of his time by Adam Smith that ten persons under proper division of labor could make among them upwards of 48,000 pins a day.

Forty-eight thousand pins the product of ten men a hundred years ago, against 7,500,000 pins the product of five men to-day. A four-thousand times greater product by the aid of modern machinery than possible by the aid of the best system then known.

The most surprising results are attained, however, in composite products, articles of immediate use and wear, when different parts of so complicated an article as a watch, a clock, or a pair of shoes can be made by an application of the American system.

As shown in the Introductory Letter to the Secretary of State to my report on Technical Education (Industrial Education in France) a Waterbury watch is made at the trifling labor expense of fifty cents. The material in no instance is further advanced, when it enters the mill, than sheet steel. All the springs, wheels, screws, pins, pinions, etc., are made by self-acting machinery. Yet the factory had at the time of my visit 420 employees on its pay-roll, fully one-half of whom were women, at an average of wages of $10.71. . We see here a remarkable illustration of a low cost of labor consequent upon a high rate of wages. But here every improvement or device tending to cheapen cost is quickly introduced. A machine was lately put in by which 1,200 to 1,500 springs are turned out a day with two machines and two men, to take the place of other machinery which exacted the employment of twelve men for an output of 1,000 springs. In Germany, in the Black Forest, I visited the works of a "stock company" turning out clocks by the help of machinery and power. Screw-making was done by a man putting pieces of copper cut from the rod into the required sizes into the receptacle of the machine. Of course the machine had to stop for each operation of turning out a finished screw. The whole looked somewhat funny to one accustomed to the operation of automatic machinery, grinding out incessantly without any human labor, except that of a boy, putting in a new rod when the old is worked up and the last screw has fallen into the bag. Under such differences and distinctions, it becomes apparent that labor in watch and clock making at $10.71 is cheaper in Massachusetts than labor at ten or twelve marks ($2.40 to $2.88) in the Black Forest.

We find the best illustration of the superiority of American workpeople in quantitative production over their English and foreign competitors when using and handling the same kind of machinery.

The application of these methods and employment of self-acting machinery, plays nowhere a more important part than in machine building itself. Not alone that a machine made by machinery can be made more cheaply than by hand labor: the parts also are usually more exact in the fittings, and offer the very great advantage that they can at all times be easily replaced simply by specifying the number of the part, and therefore of great practical value for shipment into countries where skilled labor for repairs is scarce. Here, also, every part is usually accompanied with the building of a new machine for the purpose.

The effect of these tool machines may be measured from one little example that I noticed in a factory making dynamos. The cutting of threads in the racks in the electrical mechanism was formerly done by hand, and the racks (about eighteen inches long) cost about fifteen cents apiece in labor. This is now done by a machine specially constructed for the purpose, with unvarying exactness, at a quarter of a cent. With such help, utilizing machinery wherever possible, one of the dynamo works which I visited lately turns out one dynamo per day, of sixty arc lamps, with all the lamps, hanging boards, cut-out boxes, ampères, switchboards, and all the innumerable little supplies, too numerous to mention, for equipping so complicated and highly-developed a mechanism. For 160 persons, with a large proportion of helpers (boys and young men), the weekly payroll is $2,200, including superintendents, office and shop rent, as well as office help. The help employed in the factory averages about $12 a week. Considering the large proportion of minor help, the rate of pay for the more skilled occupations, of course, is very much higher.

But whatever the amount of weekly earnings might be, would here again not be of great importance if held against the commercial value of the article produced.

The total labor employed in the production of an apparatus as described would be $400 (on the basis of calculation given above)—while the gross selling price is, or was at least at that time (1890), $4500. The high selling price, quite disproportionate to the cost of production, is due to an extent to the guaranteeing of the dynamos. They require constant attention and repairing on account of the binding of the journal in the bearing, arising from the heating, through the high-speeded machine. Many inventions are being put into requisition which are calculated to obviate this difficulty and to bring down the price.

So far as the labor cost stands to the value of the product it can be easily seen that the question of wages is but an unimportant item. The manufacture of products so thoroughly protected by patents as these are, becomes an absolute monopoly, and the profit rates are large as bespoken by the high dividends on watered stocks and other evidences of rapid capital accumulations out of the earnings.

The question of the relations of labor to the cost of production resolves itself entirely to one of equipment. Whether labor be equipped with all the improvements and inventions or not, whether labor be well conditioned and fed or underpaid and overworked, decides the contest, not the relative difference in day wages. It is the output after all which makes the price of a commodity.

It has been my unvarying experience that, even with the employment of machinery, the number of people employed for a certain output is proportionately much larger where the rate of pay is lower. In other words, that a higher rate of pay more than compensates in the output by the results.

The Steamship an Illustration of Modern Development. Science applied to Industry.

A collective picture of what science has done for the progress of the race in the field of industry is given by the steamboat. The greatest results of the combination of science and work are seen in the iron monsters which traverse the oceans and balance the deficiency of one zone by the abundance of another. All the sciences hold congress here. The latest achievements are quickly introduced, lest some rival line would offer cargo space at a fraction less. But comfort and health of the passengers, steerage or cabin, have to be studied no less than the ability of carrying the greatest bulk at the minimum of cost. The economy of space and of power becomes the chief end here. Chemistry supplies cold storage room and removes from sea-water the salty substance. Electricity gives lights and signals and power to the many inner arrangements of these swimming hotels or rather towns, considering the number of temporary inhabitants. There is hardly a trade which is not set to work at the building and equipping of a steamer. But none of the advances in the other sciences would have availed had it not been for the great improvements in machine building. It would hardly be possible to carry bulky freight long distances on board steamers, were their machinery still constructed on the patterns in use some thirty or forty years ago. Nearly all the storage room now consigned to freight tonnage would be given to fuel. The compound engine, first introduced by Randolph, Elder & Co. in 1854, was soon followed by the triple and quadruple expansion engine. I will not do more here than allude to these facts and let the reader judge of the economic importance of these marine inventions by the results. The first steamship which crossed the Atlantic (1819) was the *Savannah,* an American vessel. But as she was a sailer fitted up for steam, partly sailing, we cannot bring her in except as a matter of record and to do homage to the flag. In 1833 the *Royal William* crossed from Quebec, but all her hold had to be filled with fuel. It was said by a competent authority in 1835, that "As to the project which was announced in the newspapers of making the voyage directly from New York to Liverpool it was altogether chimerical, and they might as well talk of making a voyage from New York or Liverpool to the moon." If prophesying was a hazardous undertaking even in an age of faith, it is still more so in the age of science. The *Great Western* sailed from Bristol first in 1838 and consumed between 12 days 7½ hours, her shortest, and 22 days her longest passage. Carlyle said in connection with this, that "The success of the *Great Western* left our still moist paper demonstration to dry itself at leisure." These earliest steamers used 10 pounds of coal per hour to the indicated horse-power. From this, by the rapid introduction of improvements, the consumption of coal has gradually come down to less than 1¼ pounds per horse-power per hour. With less than one-eighth of storage room required for fuel,* the impetus given to steam navigation and

---

* I give the concise history of the improvements from a paper of Mr. Henry Dyer in the *Scottish Review:*

"The chief stages in the development of the marine engine are clearly marked by the pressure of the steam used, and the amount of coal con-the carrying trade can be readily imagined. The reader is too familiar with all the great gifts, civilizing, liberalizing, enfranchising from the thraldom of poverty and want even, to need much demonstration from the author, whose object it is only to point out the road upon which the human family is progressing from misery and dependence to freedom and prosperity.

But what is of equal interest in the consideration of the steamboat, in our review of the industrial aid given by science, is the parallel illustration of the method applied to the building of the iron monster of the sea, and the result

---

sumed per-indicated horse-power per hour, and these may be briefly recapitulated. Until about 1830 the pressure seldom exceeded three pounds on the square inch above that of the atmosphere. From that date a gradual increase took place, and in 1845 the average was about ten pounds on the square inch. By 1850 it had reached fifteen pounds. In 1856, Randolph, Elder & Co. employed pressures of thirty pounds in their compound engines, but it was not till almost ten years later that such pressures became general in the merchant service. On the compound engine becoming common, pressures rose suddenly to sixty and in some cases to eighty and one hundred pounds on the square inch, and now for triple expansion engines the average is over one hundred and fifty pounds, while for quadruple expansion engines it is two hundred pounds on the square inch. With regard to coal consumption, the earliest marine engines must have used nearly ten pounds per indicated horse-power per hour. In the well-known side-lever engines it was about seven pounds, while for engines in use before the general introduction of the compound type four to four and one-half pounds was the average. Randolph, Elder & Co., as we have seen, had an average of from two and one-half to three pounds. In 1872, when two-cylinder compound engines had been in use for some years, the average was found to be about 2·11 pounds, being a saving of nearly fifty per cent. over the ordinary engines, while in 1881 there was a reduction to 1·828 pounds, or a further saving of 13·37 per cent. With triple and quadruple expansion engines there has been a still further reduction of about twenty-five per cent., the consumption of fuel in some of these engines being as low as one and one-half or one and one-quarter pounds per indicated horse-power per hour."

expressed in wages. The outfit of a yard is a marvellous collection of labor-saving appliances. Operations are now conducted by machinery of the highest efficiency, which formerly were all done by hand and hand tools. It is impossible here to do more than to notice in a general way an all-important fact with which we can fitly conclude the general discussion of the cause and effect of a high wage rate in the mechanical arts. A general statement will, however, cover the whole case. The effect of all the improvements and inventions in the immense mechanism required has been a constant reduction in the cost of building per ton. The wages paid in the yards of Scotland and England are the highest paid in any calling. At times of activity the earnings in the trades connected with the building rise to £4 and £5 a week, two and three times the rates paid in outside occupations. Still England is the iron-boat builder of the world, and is only equalled by America in regard to high wages paid to the worker and low cost of construction by the ton. In 1888 I visited the yards of the chief steamboat builders in Philadelphia. They were building then one of the fast cruisers. Their equipment with labor-saving apparatus for riveting and other processes was as perfect as one is accustomed to find in American shops. The firm's protective proclivities are known. Yet they had to confirm my conviction that protection did injury to their trade by preventing them from building steamers as cheaply as the English, by the following statement:

In the contract for the cruiser, estimates were invited from English builders. Their estimate on the same specifications was $1,200,000. The American firm obtained the contract for the sum of $1,850,000. But the American inside fittings are far superior and more expensive than those submitted by the English firm. A member of the firm told

THE ECONOMY OF HIGH WAGES. 107

me that on the basis of the English specifications and with the materials at the English level of cost, they could have produced the cruiser at the same price. The force of the argument that the labor differences would not stand in the way of Americans in the building of iron steamers, were the duties on their materials abolished, is increased by the statement of a fact illustrative of the development in shipbuilding. The firm referred to above employs a riveting machine for riveting boiler shells, the shell turning on a rotary platform. Before the introduction of the machinery the riveting engaged the work of a gang, composed of two riveters, one holder, and two boys, for two full weeks. The same work is now performed by the same number of hands in one and a half days' time.

A saving of seven days out of eight enables the payment of a higher rate without interfering with the competitive capacity of the builders.

With this we will conclude this general consideration of the economy of high wages in industrial employments, and turn our attention to the question of the supply of the wherewithals which uphold the force and strength of the labor, the supply of the staff of life which determines the actual value of the rate of wages.

CHAPTER VIII

Proof of Principles laid down, taken from Agriculture.—Application of Scientific Methods.—Great Results.—Extending the Margin of Starvation.—Every Addition to the Productiveness of the Acre an Addition to the Soil.

THE questions treated in the preceding chapters find nowhere better illustration and support than in agriculture. In no other branch of industrial activity are the gratifying results so easily traceable to what we must consider the primary cause of all progress and prosperity, freedom from restraint and security of possession, as in agriculture. In no field of employment can it be shown so clearly that even the difficulties which nature may impose are as nothing against the indomitable will of man employing his best faculties for the acquisition of possessions guaranteed to him by free and just laws. The question of a high rate of wages is practically the question of food, etc., the raw materials of which are the produce of agriculture. It is evident that we cannot well consider the questions here introduced, as satisfactorily treated, without examining the development of agriculture along with the other branches of human activity. It will serve, therefore, a double purpose: first, in allaying apprehensions that growing populations are necessarily causes of poverty; and second, to show intellectual force to be equally effective in this as in all other employments, and able to overcome difficulties of the most formidable character.

Ignorance the Cause of Poverty.

The end of the eighteenth century gave birth to theories which made everlasting poverty the preordained condition of the working classes, death only alleviating the miseries which would be the inevitable consequence of growing populations.

It is reserved for the end of the nineteenth century to dissipate the fears which have ever since haunted the imagination.

Poverty—abject poverty—was the general characteristic of that time. Negro slavery, with all its disgracing features to the civilization which bred it, had this silver streak in the cloud—that it fed its victims. Hunger and want did not infest the cabins of the slaves, any more than the stable of the horse or other four-legged cattle. But who can read the history of those days, and not be moved at the condition of nine-tenths of the people of England and Continental Europe? There bread was scarce indeed, and hunger, the gaunt spectre that haunted the poor man's home. The populations were sparse compared to to-day. In England the population has trebled, while it is not too much to say, the consumption per head has doubled. True, the population could not subsist on to-day's cultivated area, under the present system. But that a much greater population could subsist if the land were more distributed among cultivating owners, admits of no doubt. As it is, every year more and more land goes out of cultivation and is put under grass. In the last twenty years not less than three million acres have gone out of tillage. What this means can be seen from the fact that three million acres would grow nearly all the wheat which is imported now from abroad. By improved cultivation the average yield per acre has risen to thirty bushels. We can easily appreciate the significance of this fact, when we consider that the average yield in wheat, for France is from 16 to 17 bushels, for Germany 21 bushels, and for America 12 bushels. English soil and climate are by no means as propitious to agriculture as those of the other countries.* England's superior yield in all branches of agriculture, root crops and hay as well as cereals, is due

---

* On this point it is well to hear the testimony of the highest authority on comparative agriculture, since the days of Arthur Young, Mr. Léonce de Lavergne, "Essai sur l'économie rurale de l'Angleterre, de l'Écosse et de l'Irlande (1854)": "Le sol et le climat de l'Angleterre seront-ils donc naturellement supérieurs aux nôtres? Bien loin de là. Un million d'hectares sur 13 sont restés tout à fait inproductifs et ont resistés jusqu'ici à tous les efforts de l'homme ; sur les 12 millions restants, deux tiers au moins sont des terres ingrates et rebelles que l'industrie humaine a eu besoin de conquérir."

(Are, then, the soil and climate of England superior by nature to our own? Far from it. Out of 13 million hectares one million have remained entirely unproductive and have resisted so far all human efforts. Of the remaining 12 millions two-thirds at least are irresponsive and rebellious soils. which the industry of man had to conquer.)

He then proceeds to analyze the country by sections and to speak of the unpropitious climate, its proverbial fogs and rains, and of the excessive humidity, "est peu favorable au froment qui est le but principal de toute culture" (little favorable to wheat, which is the chief end of agriculture), and winds up in the comparison: "Combien le sol et le climat de la France sont supérieurs! En comparant à l'Angleterre, non plus seulement le quart, mais la moitié nord-ouest de notre territoire, c'est-à-dire les trente-six départements qui se groupent autour de Paris, à l'exclusion de la Bretagne, nous trouvons plus de 22 millions d'hectares qui dépassent, en qualité comme en quantité, les 13 millions d'hectares anglais."

(How much superior the soil and climate of France ! Comparing to England, not one-fourth but the northwest half of our territory, to wit: the thirty-six departments grouping around Paris, with the exclusion of Brittany, we find more than 22 million hectares which surpass in quality as in quantity the 13 million hectares of England.)

And with all this natural inferiority, there results : nearly two bushels of England to one of France.

alone to the more thorough husbandry and introduction of improvements dating from the early part of last century and continuing through modern days through conditions peculiarly favorable to agriculture.

Capital, enterprise, and free labor (though handicapped and depressed) were turned to the soil at a time when all Europe was looking with contempt on agriculture, and, excepting the countries where a free peasantry had survived, agricultural labor was chafing under oppression worse than that of slaves.

A reaction has begun to set in which makes capital withdraw from land. This may be a forerunner of a new era in the tenure of land, by which even a greater productiveness of the soil may be brought about than is the case there now. A survey of the field shows distinctly that where holdings are cultivated by the owner, supplied with sufficient stock and capital, in gross and net yield he surpasses by far the great landowner or the tenant farmer, even of England. This is to show how rash it must appear to set a limit to the food-producing capacity of an acre of ground of which an immense area is yet awaiting the advent of the tiller. It is equally shortsighted to base deductions and predictions on existing facts. It is safer to accept the present as a halting station from a remote past, and if we have to do predicting, let at least experience guide us.

Difference in Results traceable to Institutions.

Four to six bushels an acre was the average net yield, after allowing two bushels for seed corn, in the thirteenth and fourteenth centuries in England. It was clearly an extensive cultivation of a large area of soil by economically dear and individually cheap labor. Under conditions then existing this was the best system, if for no other reason than because it was the only system available. The modern system gives a net yield of twenty-eight bushels. Subdrainage, proper manuring,* rotation of crops, etc., after six centuries

---

* The efficacy of manuring was not unknown to the early periods of husbandry in England, but the practice was of a very rudimentary kind. The sheep were driven into the corn-fields after harvesting, as the droppings gave the manure before another crop was sown. The owners of flocks were paid a rent in money, or in kind, for the lending of their flocks for the purpose by cultivators who had no sheep. "Sheep were occasionally hired to lie on the ground. This must evidently have been in inclosures. A hundred and fifty sheep were folded on an acre at from 1s. 4d. to 2s. the acre, or two hundred sheep were kept on a field at 8d. a week for eight weeks. It would seem, then, that such a flock was kept on land from three to eight weeks in order to fertilize it, the owner, of course, feeding them."—(J. E. Thorold Rogers, "Six Centuries of Work and Wages.")

The results were satisfactory enough where even this sort of manuring could be applied. But it must be seen, from what we know of the state and condition of live stock in the middle ages, that even this fertilizing method could not cover a very large proportion of the land then under cultivation, proportionately greater as the yield per acre was so much smaller than to-day. Fodder was scarce, root crops unknown, and what live stock could not be carried over the winter was slaughtered and salted at Martinmas.

The advantages from this natural manuring explain why so much land is allowed to go out of cultivation and become grazing land in England.

The best general results of farming, on the one hand, and a relapse of the same agricultural land into grazing, on the other : An anomaly, a paradox. Yes and no. If the cultivator and the owner were one and the same person, he would probably continue to cultivate the soil and besides raise and keep a large amount of live stock, as in Holland and Belgium, etc., on the farm. As it is, the two interests clash. Each wants to draw as much out of the joint business, and put as little into it, as possible. The landlord wants to get his rent. The tenant is restricted by his lease in ways hardly known to outsiders. For instance, he must not sell any straw or hay, as it is expressed in some leases of which I know. The object of this is to force him to feed it all to live stock on the farm, so as

of cultivation, not alone yield five bushels where one grew before, but the net results, after all deductions are made for labor and capital employed, are far greater and are in distinct opposition to maxims handed down, of diminishing returns, etc. This can be shown to have followed in the

---

to keep the property in good condition, though it be ever so hard to get the landlord to do anything in the way of improvements or even repairs, his part in the transaction. A friend of mine, a pottery manufacturer in North Staffordshire, bought a stack of hay at quite a reduction for immediate delivery and for cash, because the landlord's agent was soon expected to be on the farm. The farmer feared that, if the landlord knew that at the time so near haying he had hay to the value of £75, he would raise his rent, while, on the other hand, the farmer wanted a reduction. The reader can understand that the results, ever so satisfactory from a statistical point of view, are by no means equally pleasing to the farmer. That he could make his position greatly superior to what it is to-day (even paying his rent of 25s. to 30s. per acre of good wheat-land) I can prove by facts gathered in my investigations. But to do this would require more space than I can give the subject here. I am not writing a treatise on general economics, but simply on the facts which have contributed so powerfully to make the position of the working classes superior to any which they have ever occupied in the history of man.

Here I will only say that a good deal of land is allowed to go out of cultivation because, under present conditions, stock-raising pays better. A landowner of my acquaintance had about a thousand acres of land. Part of it he let to a tenant, another part he farmed himself. The tenant's holding came back to him because of his inability to pay the rent, 25s. to 28s. The owner turned the land into grass, and put lean cattle on to fatten. It has become quite an extensive practice to buy lean Irish cattle in the spring. After grazing five months the cattle are sleek and rounded. After allowing for the help required, a man and a boy for about 300 head, the year's operation yielded to my friend about £3.10 a head. This, deducting for the value of the land a rent of 25s., still leaves a net income of £2.5, and points a very strong moral in the direction indicated. But the point which I want to emphasize, the natural manuring, comes here into view. The land on which the cattle had been grazing, and over which I went with the proprietor, was decidedly the richer for it, as was shown by the density of the growth compared with adjoining grass-land on which the cattle had not been. A

successive stages marking the period of evolution from the rudimentary to the high cultivation of the soil. But the distinctions which mark the two ends of our chronological line exist to-day, though the line is now a geographical one. Let us take Russia and its mode of cultivation. The gross average yield per acre for all Russia is not more than that of England was then. It follows that the yield of the more backward provinces is smaller yet than this average. The system of cultivation (if it can be called a system) is of such nature that it would be surprising if better results were reached. The terrible famine now devastating a territory where twenty millions of human beings drag out a miserable existence even in good years, is eloquent testimony. Plowing is done in the most superficial manner, with wide spaces left between the furrows. A German traveller, pointing out to a nobleman farming his own estate, the wastefulness of this system, was answered, "Oh, we grow corn enough for our own purposes. If we grew more we should not know what to do with it." And this, in part, explains, as it illustrates, existing conditions. As it is, the commissioner sent by Germany on a mission of inquiry as to the prospect and aspect of the wheat cultivation of the world, told me that he found that the peasants and cultivators cut only what corn they require for their own use or what they can find a market for, and let the rest stand for the hogs to feed on. Improvements in methods follow in the wake of an extension

---

double advantage, which, of course, explains a great deal in the changing agricultural conditions of England.

Of course, the best quantitative returns are not produced thereby, as by the combination of the two systems in Holland, Belgium, the Rhinelands, Lombardy, Switzerland, and the best farmed parts of France and the Scandinavian countries. But here I desire only to explain certain rather contradictory phenomena in contemporaneous agricultural history and the efficacy of natural manuring under certain conditions.

of markets, or rather, of roads and railroads. But even such advantages as would elsewhere arise from this, are largely neutralized by the prevailing system of political and economic oppression standing in the name of government.

Where roads are absent, plenty may rule in one province and famine in the adjoining one. Still, no relief can be given to the suffering neighbor, while the plenty may be of no economic value to the possessor of it. This is the normal condition of countries like Russia, plenty alternating with scarcity and starvation. The present famine is only an intense aggravation of evils which show themselves almost every year. They show themselves where agriculture has no other resources than the rudimentary labor processes of olden times, and has to trust to the elements for the rest.

Modern Russian Agriculture on a Level with English Agriculture of the Thirteenth Century.

How the peasantry of Russia are equipped mentally and materially for their struggle with mother earth can be seen from an extract of an article in the *Fortnightly Review* for February, 1891, by Lanin, a writer most fully informed on the economic conditions of what Carl Emil Franzos very properly calls "Halb-Asien" (Semi-Asia):

" Plows are so scarce among petty farmers that the Moscow Zemstvo lends a number of them gratis every year in the hope of inducing the peasants to buy them ; and as for scythes—a primitive instrument enough in these days of mowing machines—the peasants of large districts of some of the finest meadowlands in all Russia have not yet begun to see their utility. In the rich meadows of the Dvina Valley, the peasants mow the grass with an implement called a 'hump'—a large reaping hook, two feet in diameter, which, though too heavy for one hand, has but one handle for both. In order to mow with this the laborer must double himself up, holding the short handle in both hands, and turn the 'hump' round after each stroke from right to left and from left to right, so that its edge may be turned towards the grass to be cut down by the next stroke. It is a species of torture to mow thus: 'It is hard to breathe, the blood rises to your head, and on a hot day you have not the faintest shade around,"

says the *Moscow Gazette* to emphasize the torturous proceeding.

Agriculture is not conducted on a higher level in Poland either. Cause and effect are everywhere the same. Stupefying the tiller by oppression, and robbing him of the fruit of his labor, cannot produce other results.

Instances related in "Die Grenzboten," the experience of one who studied the conditions by living for years among them, explain in an unmistakable manner the low state of agriculture resulting from the oppression under which the Polish peasants have languished.

"I lived for nearly a year on the estate of a Pole, as a guest. I had consented to introduce some German improvements into his economy. My first act was to have the stones and boulders removed from some of the nearest fields. The peasants helped with pleasure. But now there was to be an attack on their beloved fruit-trees. When I gave the overseer the order to remove these wild trees the next morning they looked at each other with long faces. I had hardly gone to sleep when by a hundred voices the cry was raised: 'Oh, dear sir, we beseech you.' They asked for a hearing. I was more gracious than is the custom here, sprang from my bag of hay—a bag of hay under the sleeper, a silk quilt over him, and a horsehair pillow under his head, is the bed of the Pole—and opened the door, which led immediately into the open, as is very frequently the case in Poland.

"Some thirty men and women, the tears running down their faces and screaming wildly, rushed into the room. Their only words were: 'Oh, we beg of you, forgive the fruit-trees!' meaning, preserve the trees. I assured them that it was on account of the injury to the growing crops that I wanted to remove them. But this did not quiet them. Finally I promised every head of a family a dozen cultivated fruit-trees as a present by next spring. 'Oh, no, no, sir,' they answered; 'these we cannot have.' 'And why not?' 'No, the count would not allow it.' 'And why not?' 'Such fruit is reserved for the nobility.' 'And have you asked the count about it?' 'No, but we know it.' 'Yes, kind German sir' (gütiger Herr Deutscher), a venerable peasant returned, 'we know it for certain. I once planted behind my cottage two plum-trees, which a seed-dealer had given me in payment for some carting I had done for him. Hardly had our gracious lord (der gnädige Herr) noticed them than he broke them up with the remark, "Such fruit does not become the peasants to eat." And I got some cuts from his whip into the bargain.'

"Of course," continues our author, "under such conditions it would have been barbarous to execute the order. I revoked it, and the abominable trees are no doubt on the field to this day. It is easy to see, from this, how closely connected the low state of Polish agriculture is with the conditions of the people and how difficult it is to reform it."

"Every face bespeaks the relation of serfdom; laziness, hopelessness, dread and fear show at once in look and gesture. If possible, the peasant evades the noble and the well dressed—as every such he considers a nobleman. But if not possible, he uncovers his head at a distance of forty to fifty paces, and passes with his head bowed nearly to the ground and his cap stretched towards the recipient of the homage."

Everything in the life of the peasants depended on the good will of the owner of the soil. Any sign of prosperity would result in greater exactions. His direct efforts were, therefore, to make the part open to observation look as miserable as possible, the land bear the poorest crops, and the hovel in which he lived as forlorn as a human habitation can be. All his cunning was directed to concealment from the rapacious eyes of the landlord.

"If the peasant cultivates his farm with care, and realizes good crops, the owner would not hesitate long to take away a piece of land. If the peasant has luck in raising stock, if he raises a few bullocks, or increases the number of his sheep, immediately the landlord will appear and take away his surplus stock with the remark that he has no right to own more than what had been turned over to him, and that he is entitled to raise a head only, if he has killed or lost one from the inventory. Consequently, if the peasant would utilize stock raising, he has to act like a thief, conceal the additions in every conceivable manner (to which proceeding the pasture in the dense, dark forest offers the best opportunity) and to bring them as slyly as possible for sale to the nearest town. He has to anticipate the robber proclivities of the landlord by the cuteness of the thief."

Such conditions explain everything in the political, economic and social situation of these countries.* We need not

* Serfdom was abolished in Poland in 1807, but the peasantry, though nominally free, had, in return for land, stock, etc., to give the landlord their services, and were held in a state of dependence and oppression fully as bad as it had been under serfdom. That the state described above pretty fairly illustrates the general condition and is not overdrawn, is proven by the fact that in the Polish revolution of 1861-63 the peasantry sided with the Russians. All the endeavors of the Insurrectionary Committee to draw them to the national cause by ever so many fine promises would not prevail with them. But on the contrary they sided with the Russians and were the only effective instrument to break up the revolutionary bands. In return for these services the Russian government materially advanced the position of the peasants by making them free owners of the land which they held, wherever it was found that the landlord had sided with the revolutionists. But though the conditions have changed outwardly, the improvements in agriculture and in general prosperity are not yet very marked. For this an entirely different system of government is required than Russia can give. The facts here stated are a lesson of great significance. The Nemesis of history has wreaked her revenge on the Polish nation. By separating the peasantry from the life and interests of the nation by cruelty and oppression, the privileged classes gave the chief instrument of destruction into the hands of the Russian executioner.

If we took our lights from the history and conditions of the common people, we should easily understand the political aspect and prospects of nations, which the descriptions of the doings of kings, of wars and diplomatic scheming, can never make clear. Searching the archives helps us little if we neglect to look into the open book of a people's daily life. If we find a nation so separated, as by impassable barriers, that nine-tenths are in a state akin to slavery and a very small class of the privileged exercise power, it can be easily understood why the, apparently, most powerful nations are so easily overthrown whenever they come to a testing of their strength. Little are we inclined to look into the economic status of the Russian peasant when we try to explain the almost proverbial discomfiture of Russia on measuring her strength even with Turkey.

Little do we look into the socio-economic fabric of Poland when we write about her overthrow and the futile attempts of her people to regain their liberty. The "people" were always a few. The masses were serfs, and took little interest in the heroic struggles of their superiors. The peasantry

search for other causes in explanation of the low yield of their agriculture.

Compare this with the best systems of cultivation, such as pointed out above, for England, as regards large tenant farming, not nearly so productive as where proprietorship of holdings under fifty acres prevails, and land worked under the best methods with sufficient stock etc., as in Holland, Flanders, Lombardy, the Scandinavian countries, and many parts of Germany and France, and draw a balance. We can then compare what an acre can be made to yield by the grace of nature and the work of barbarians held in ignorance by a despotic govenment, and what by the work of intelligent beings helped by all the appliances which modern science has put at their disposal.

High Results of Ownership by the Tiller under Free Laws.

Holland is the best field from which to draw the proof that some of the worst natural conditions can be changed so that they produce the very best results. The alluvial regions made by the deposits of the three rivers—the Rhine, the Scheldt, and the Meuse—are extremely fertile. The flat lands require constant, careful labor to protect them from being swept away by the ocean. Up to the early part of this century great inundations were matters of regular occurrence. They destroyed the fields, swept away the improvements, cattle, and men. It is stated that from 525 to about 1825—a period of 1,300 years—some 200 great floods have gone over the land, which would make an aver-

could not possibly fare worse in changing masters. The Russian was looked upon with favor even, if for no other reason than because of the enmity of the Polish nobility to him.

age of one in seven years. To lay dry the Harlem Meer and to build the works of defence of the 17,000 hectares (about 40,000 acres) gained therefrom, took an outlay of 9,000,000 florins. To keep the lands in cultivable condition implies constant pumping operations. Wind-mills are erected all over to operate pumps emptying the water into the network of canals traversing the country. The annual expense to the government for its water-works is about 6,000,000 of florins. This is independent of the burdens of the communes incurred for the purposes indicated. The good soil is considerably less than one-half of the total acreage of the kingdom. It comprises but 1,500,000 hectares (3,700,000 acres). The other part, about 1,800,000 hectares (4,400,000 acres), is mostly indifferent, and a very large proportion very poor land. One-fourth of the acreage, or some 800,000 hectares (2,000,000 acres), about twenty-five years ago were waste lands. But even these heath and turf lands are gradually brought into subjection. The most refractory soils are brought under the yoke of cultivation. Of course, the labor expended is so incessant, so meagre of first results, that no inducement could make people undergo the hardships involved unless directed by the most dire necessity. No incentive could hold people on such land except ownership of land so directly the result of the laborer's exertions. This is not the place to give an account in detail of the labor involved to make the sands of the dunes, the unproductive soil of the heath, and the bog become gradually but permanently productive. They become productive with increasing yield to the free peasant owner. Capitalistic exploitation would be entirely inadequate. But possession of the fruits of one's labor is here, as in other fields of employment, the incentive for the fullest exercise of the individual's exertions. As it is, with the land owned

THE ECONOMY OF HIGH WAGES. 121

by the farmer all over Holland, and under the most intelligent methods applicable to the varying conditions of the soil, the 6,500,000 acres now under cultivation produce enough to feed abundantly the 4,500,000 of the population of the kingdom. The imports and exports of food products about balance each other in value. No farming population of the most favored countries of the world can be compared with the Dutch in wealth, comfort, culture and general well-being. The treasures of gold, silver, rare china and furniture heaped up for generations and found in plain peasant farmers' houses, would in themselves be a most forcible demonstration of the difference, were not other and more direct testimony at hand. But what escaped the covetousness of the powerful in the critical centuries when land grasping made serfs of the peasantry of most European countries has now become the corner-stone of Holland's prosperity when all other resources have given way before the rivalry of more powerful nations. Even in the thirteenth century the Hollanders and Frisian peasants sent home with bloody heads the barons who had ready for them the yokes of feudalism and serfdom, then slipped so deftly over the shoulders of the peasantry of less fortunate countries. William of Holland had no more satisfactory results from his mission of armed persuasion than the Leopolds of Austria in Switzerland.* Switzerland and Hol-

---

* The lessons here written in the impressive language of the bloody field are as interesting, and, in their consequences, far more important to the Anglo-Saxon student than those of the battles of Marathon and Platæa. (I by no means undervalue the importance of these.) But how many out of a thousand who know of the Athenians beating in open battle the hosts of the Persian, have ever heard of the day when the peasants of Drenthe, Groeningen, Friesland, and Oldenburg, defeated William, his valorous knights, and an army of 30,000 men? Poor William! A Dutchman himself, he ought to have known something of the nature of the mind of his

land, the guardians of the sources and of the mouth of the Rhine, were left in the fortunate possession of the only incentive powerful enough to overcome all other obstacles —the possession of liberty. They were left in the possession because they had the manliness to defend it against all who were rash enough to try to wrest it from them.

General Farming Results in Europe Confirmatory of the Principle.

Figures, if correctly read, convey more intelligence than argument. To be convincing they must not contain in their make-up unrelated parts, and their application must not be misdirected. Comparisons of agricultural returns of all the

---

countrymen. A Dutchman, the most unimaginative of men, to value correctly the romance and glory of the Middle Ages, monkery, chivalry, and lordly manors, chatelains and chatelaines, and the benevolence of mighty lords to humble serfs, in exchange for such unpoetic realities as time-old liberty and freehold, allodial instead of feudal tenure and serfdom ! Well, William paid dearly for the mistake. In trying to make proselytes of his countrymen to the new idea, he lost his crown and his life. His German kingship, no more than his fine armor, protected him against the irresistible argument of the Saxon battle-axe. The Dutch blows fell with equal impartiality on the heads of the highest and of the lowest on that day almost forgotten by history. The victory was as important and far-reaching in its consequences as any event in the days when the battle was fought against Spanish oppression on the same fields. Without the former the latter would not have taken place.

Nor were the bishops and knights more successful when they tried their efforts on parts to the southwest. The peasants of Utrecht, Harlem, and other parts of Holland were equally unwilling to bear a yoke which their neighbors to the northeast had so rudely rejected. It was some fifteen years later that they, too, made short work of the missionary hosts in armor sent against them. Ever after, the soil to the south of the German Ocean was very unpropitious to the growth of a landed, privileged class, a rich and powerful nobility, and a poor, enslaved peasantry. Neither of them ever took root.

different nations leave us free from any imputation of indirectness. The annual returns of farming in Europe prove so fully the correctness of the views expressed, that it seems strange that, published as they are from year to year by the respective governments, they have not made more of an impression on the public mind and dispelled the fears still haunting the imagination. Not to weary with too many figures I have reduced the total product and average of each crop of the cereal products to number of bushels per acre, leaving out decimals for easier tabulation. I have usually averaged the crops of three years, so as not to fall into spurious comparisons, such as comparing an extraordinary harvest of one country with poor harvests of other countries, falling into any one year.

YIELD IN BUSHELS PER ACRE OF THE DIFFERENT COUNTRIES OF EUROPE IN THE DIFFERENT CORN CROPS AND POTATOES.*

	Russia.	Italy.	Austro-Hungary.	France.	Germany.	Denmark.	U. Kingdom.	Sweden.	Norway.	Belgium.	Holland.	Great Britain.	Ireland.
Wheat...........	7	10	16	17	22	22	29	25	24	23	29	30	28
Spelt............										42			
Barley..........	9	12	19	21	20	28	33 }	30	30	40	40	33	36
Oats............	16	14	22	27	19	29	37 }		37	44	40	39	40
Rye.............	10	13	17	17	18	28		25	27	23	22		
Maize...........		16	19	28									
Buckwheat......	12		12	18	10	15				23	20		
Potatoes........	80	67	138	121	140	115	180	150	220	112	200	234	140

It will be admitted by everybody that the trinity of causes, directing the current of civilization, according to

---

* Agricultural Returns of Great Britain.

Buckle: soil, climate, and the general aspect of nature, is in favor of the first-named four States and against the sequence of States following. Italy certainly ought to give the richest results; Sweden, Norway, and Denmark, the poorest. The mere mention of the name of the southern country is connected in our imagination with fecundity and abundance. The north opens up visions of sterility and scarcity under bleak winds and forbidding skies. And, indeed, the early inhabitants of the thinly settled countries were driven from the inhospitable shores by scarcity, and attracted to the southern countries by the abundance which they promised. The southern climes certainly held abundance compared to the poor returns of the home farm under this rude system of agriculture. The younger sons had to go abroad under the lead of a chieftain, the dreaded royers of the sea. The land could only support a very limited number. But how are things changed! Italy has to import large quantities of cereals under a system of cultivation which, with all the advantages of nature's smiles thrown in, does not produce more than one-half to one-third of the returns of the northern countries. Holland, Denmark, Sweden, Norway, it is true, import corn; but their exports of animal products largely exceed in value the imports of bread-stuffs. With a yield as high per acre as in the northern countries, Italy would be a large exporter of bread-stuffs, as nearly half her area under cultivation is planted in wheat. The average represents the advanced farming of Lombardy as well as the backward condition of the rest of Italy. Allowing for this the *pro rata* for the rest of the kingdom would find a diminution of 20 per cent. in the respective figures of the above tables.

While the average of the provinces outside of Lombardy and Piedmont would not be above 8 bushels in wheat and

14 in maize, Lombardy gives over 22 in wheat and over 40 in maize. The 12,000,000 acres under wheat would at the latter rate give 260,000,000 bushels, and the 4,500,000 acres under maize, 180,000,000 bushels; instead of the actual yield of 120,000,000 of the former and 75,000,000 bushels of the latter cereal (the chief food of the common people).

Causes of Lombardy's Superior Agriculture.

Lombardy's agriculture not alone feeds her populous towns but adds largely to the export values of the country; principally raw silk, rice, cheese, and even wheat are articles of export from Lombardy.

> "By means of her silk, Lombardy pays for her purchases from abroad, and turns the balance of trade in her favor. It is estimated that the product of silk amounts annually to a hundred millions of francs." *

This was written some thirty years ago. The silk product amounts to much more now. The exports of raw silk, alone, amount to some two hundred millions of francs, the greater part of which is raised in Lombardy.

The wealth of Lombardy is based on agriculture chiefly, widely distributed among a large number of peasant proprietors. The foundation of its wealth could not be sapped even by the rule of the Hapsburgs. The energy, as well as the love of liberty, of its early citizens planted the roots of the tree from which, after centuries, the descendants reap golden harvests. Nature, like the fierce Brunhild, has to be conquered by the strong will of man before she yields

---

* "C'est au moyen de la soie, dont une grande partie est exportée, que la Lombardie paie ses achats à l'étranger, et qu'elle fait pencher la balance des échanges en sa faveur. On estime que la soie produite annuellement vaut plus de 100 millions de lire."—E. de Laveleye, "Études d' Éc. Rur.: La Lombardie."

her rich treasures of love. Émile de Laveleye states the case of this most interesting piece of wooing, which has gone on on this classic soil since the days of the Etruscans, in such graphic language that I cannot do better than to quote him:

"But this happy country is under no sort of obligations to the favors of nature, as it holds to a large part its fertility from the hands of man. It required the labor of a hundred generations to raise these terraces which hold the soil on the mountain sides, to lay dry these swamps, to dig these canals, and dispose with an admirable art these water conduits, which, descending from high valleys, circumventing hills, crossing each other and passing the one over the other at different levels, carry to distant fields a marvellous fecundity. Without the embankments which enclose the rivers a part of the plains would be a vast swamp; without the irrigation works another part would be burned by the consuming sun of summer. The Lombard is not even allowed to enjoy the work of his ancestors in peace; he has, without relaxation, to defend himself against the inundations of the Po and its tributaries with as much solicitude as the Dutch employ to protect themselves against the attacks of the ocean. . . . The Ligurians built the first cities . . . ; the Etruscans, an industrial and painstaking race, built the first canals and undertook the first irrigation works; the Gauls established the basis of commercial organization; Rome gave the language and the laws; the Germans founded the feudal system, of which the last remnants are passing away in our days. Even Spain has left a trace of her short-lived dominion, a sad trace, it is true, the example of idleness." *

---

* "Cependant cette heureuse contrée est loin de tout devoir aux faveurs de la nature: c'est des mains de l'homme qu'elle tient en grande partie sa fertilité. Il a fallu le travail de cent générations pour élever ces terrasses qui soutiennent la terre aux flancs des montagnes, pour dessécher ces marais, pour creuser ces canaux, pour disposer avec un art admirable ces conduites d'eau qui, descendant des hautes vallées, contournant les collines, s'entrecroisant et passant les unes au dessus des autres à différents niveaux, vont porter au loin dans les campagnes une fécondité merveilleuse. Sans les endiguements qui contiennent les rivières, une partie de la plaine serait un vaste marécage; sans les irrigations une autre partie serait brûlée par le soleil dévorant de l'été. Il n'est pas même permis au Lombard de jouir en paix des travaux de ses ancêtres; il doit sans

Leaving out the last-mentioned element, the mixture of races left a population such that fifteen years after Barbarossa had razed Milan to the ground and passed the plow over its ruins, the freedom-loving burghers rebuilt their city and completed the great canal, il Naviglio Grande, as far as Milan, an entirely agricultural end. Two hundred years before this, Milan had hardly begun its rise among Italian cities. The land was still in great part cultivated by slaves. The country was largely covered by forests, and large tracts were stagnant waters. It was brought under cultivation by the men who, fifteen years after their terrible visitation, could break forever the power of the feudal hosts which Frederic brought a second time against them.*

The excellent system of cultivation is in keeping with the great works mentioned. Arthur Young gives an equally glowing account, visiting Italy three-quarters of a century

---

relâche se défendre contre les inondations du Pô et de ses affluents avec autant de sollicitude que le Hollandais en met à se préserver des atteintes de l'Océan. Tous les peuples qui tour à tour ont occupé le pays y ont laissé des traces toujours subsistantes de leur passage ou de leur domination.—Les Ligures ont bâti les premières villes et l'étymologie retrouve encore dans certains noms modernes les racines de l'idiome primitif. Les Etrusques, race industrieuse et laborieuse, ont creusé les premières irrigations; les Gaulois ont jeté les bases de l'organisation commerciale ; Rome a donné la langue et les lois, entr' autres celle du colonat ou métayage ; les Germains ont fondé la féodalité dont les derniers restes s'écroulent de nos jours. L'Espagne même a laissé une trace de sa domination passagère, trace funeste il est vrai, l'exemple de l'oisiveté."—Émile de Laveleye, " Études d'Économie Rurale : La Lombardie."

* At the peace of Constance (1183) the free republics of Lombardy were given equal recognition with the bishops and princes of the empire. A new element was thereby introduced in the body representative, the burgher. To the Lombards belong the everlasting glory of having made the breach in the constitution of the empire by which society and the body politic became transformed. Legnano (1176) is the birthplace of modern society.

before M. de Laveleye. Contrast these pictures with another account of the state of agriculture concerning the greater part of the rest of Italy, and we can well understand the low average of yield in our table as contrasted with the high yield of countries where the same causes are at work which made Lombardy's prosperity.

"In the matter of implements the Italian agriculturist is far behind. The old Roman plow, as it is described by Virgil and Columella, may be still seen in use in various parts of the country. In Sardinia, the plow which figures on the ancient monuments of the island, might have been copied from that at work in the fields. Great improvement, however, has taken place in the more progressive regions; iron has taken the place of wood, and the coulter and share have increased in massiveness. But even in the Veneto the heavy plough drawn by as many as six pair of oxen, cuts the furrow not deeper than nine inches. As we proceed southward the fashion becomes more simple and antique. Manuring, even of a very ordinary kind, is but little attended to in a great part of the country."

Though Italy is so distinctively an agricultural country and has been subject so long to regular processes of cultivation, a large proportion of its arable land is still in a state of utter neglect. Large tracts formerly cultivated have become wastes. Unhealthy marshes distribute fever miasms where the husbandman would create a paradise were he supported by the spirit which animated the creators of the Lombardian republics. Their wisdom saw clearly the source of wealth was to turn to the soil the enterprise and energies of the people. The works created by them are lasting monuments of a liberty-loving race. The builders have long passed away, yet, through all the vicissitudes of war and turbulence, all succeeding generations have annually reaped wealthy harvests from these wise investments.

Jacini, the Italian economist, says, in "La proprietà

fondaria e la populazione agricola in Lombardia" (Milan, 1854), on this subject:

"It is the general belief that the expense of introducing the system of irrigation could not be less than a milliard of francs; and, in fact, it would be above that sum. This assertion will not appear exaggerated if one reflects on the number of canals necessary to carry the waters to the land under cultivation, and on the work which made it ready to receive them. To this end one had to change entirely the surface of the plain, to construct, if I may express myself that way, the soil on which we live in the same way in which the Venetians have constructed their wonderful city. Venice displays its magnificent edifices and its sublime masterpieces where formerly the desolation of the lagune ruled. With us, one admires the richest vegetation of Europe in a plain which nature seems to have abandoned to the marsh, and to the sands and the pebble. This is what has been done in the ancient times, what conserves itself and grows each day in this dead land in the country of sweet idleness." *

---

* What lends this picture a peculiar charm and background is that the irrigation works which challenge the admiration of Europe, were begun by the barbarians who overthrew Rome and the antique world. The great Theodoric employed an engineer whom he had come from Africa to teach the Italians the art of controlling the waters for irrigation. It is recorded that the African was publicly rewarded for his services by the king. Pavia, the residence of Theodoric as well as of the Longobardian kings, who were equally earnest in this meritorious work, seems to have the honor of having built the first canals. At least, the first part of the great canal from the Tessin to Abbiategrasso was completed long before the Milanese took up the work to unite the Tessin with the Adda and their city.

"If one takes an impartial account of the time, of the circumstances, of the beauty of the work, the canal of Milan, which unites the Tessin and the Adda, can pass as the masterpiece of what we possess of the kind. From what Sigonio says, it appears that the first part, between the Tessin and Abbiategrasso, exists since the oldest times, commenced and finished by the Pavesans for irrigating their land. It was in 1177 that the Milanese carried it along from Abbiate to Corsico and Milan."

"Con tutto questo pero, si imparzialmente si vorrà avere riguardo al tempo, alle circostanze, alla maestria del lavoro, il naviglio di Milano che forma la communicazione del Tesino e dell' Adda, potrà passare, per il capo d'opera che abbiamo in questo genere. Per quanto dice il Sigonio

A population of four millions subsists and has to spare for export. But what is the extent of this·land, reclaimed, so to speak, from the desert and the marshes? The territory of Lombardy, according to Jacini, had of its 2,141,700 hectares (about 5 million acres) only 1,132,795 under regular cultivation. The rest, or nearly one-half, is uncultivable mountain, mountain pastures, forests, watercourses and lakes, houses, and some large stretches of bog which have so far withstood cultivation, "but which are being put into contribution by planting them with pines." An arable soil of less than 3 millions of acres is made to support more than 4 millions. Three-quarters of an acre of refractory soil suffices to support a human being and to create the material upon which the wealth of the country is built.

The Contrasts and Their Causes.

The resources of the new kingdom are consumed in the attempt to be a great military power. This policy taxes the country beyond its ability, drives the tiller from the soil and sterilizes the land. Were the hundreds of millions spent on armaments, employed in works of irrigation, of drainage, and improvements, as in Lombardy, Italy would as intended by nature, be the richest instead of being the poorest of all the modern countries of Europe.

The people are the makers of their own destiny. The institutions make the prosperity of the citizens. Agriculture languishes, and the returns show it, wherever oppression, whatever the agency, rules the nations.

---

nel libbro XIV. del regno d'Italia all' anno 1179, pare che il primo tronco dello stesso naviglio dal Tesino ad Abbiategrasso fosse già dai tempi più antichi, incominciato e finito dai Pavesi per irrigare le vicine loro campagne. Fù nell' anno 1177 che i Milanesi condussero lo stesso cavo da Abbiate a Corsico e a Milano." (Verri, Nuova raccolta.)

Arthur Young, one of the keenest observers and most enlightened critics, in speaking of France and Flanders gives the correct explanation of this phenomenon a hundred years ago, which is applicable to the parallel as if it were written to-day.

He notes that the soil from Orleans on is of the same nature as that of Flanders. Yet the returns are so far inferior in the old French provinces to those of French Flanders that he looks for an explanation of this remarkable fact. He says ("Travels in France"):

"It has to be noted as a curious subject for reflection for all who occupy themselves with the nature of governments that Bouchain (the border of French Flanders) is situated a few miles from the Austrian side of the old border of the kingdom. The line of division drawn between the good and bad cultivation corresponds then pretty nearly with the old boundary of the provinces of France and of the low countries. The French conquests, as everybody knows, have carried their dominion far beyond these old divisions, but without effacing them. It is remarkable to see the agricultural merit form a frontier corresponding not with the actual political borders, but with the ancient, and dividing the despotism of France so hostile to agriculture, from the free government of the Burgundian provinces which encouraged it. This fact cannot be attributed to the nature of the soil, because there is hardly a finer one than the greatest part of this vast and fertile plain extending almost uninterruptedly from Flanders to the neighborhood of Orleans."

On the one side of the ancient line, excellent cultivation of the same soil gives a remarkably rich product, while the other side shows the most meagre results. French Flanders, though for a hundred years under the discouraging regime which had sapped the energies of what, under more favorable conditions, is the most thrifty and toilsome population of Europe, preserved all the advantages resulting from the enjoyment of the laws. The land gave rich harvests every year under the lessons derived from the fathers, while the people living on the other side of the old line still clung to the primitive system of three-field cultivation: fallow and two crops. The comparatively small yield of the France of to-day is traceable to these historic causes. For good and for evil the past has its hand on the future:

> " Laws and rights become transmitted
> Like an eternal malady ;
> From place to place are dragged, and fitted
> From fathers down, by slow degree."*

To understand the present we must study the past. The economic development of to-day cannot possibly be understood or explained without a glance at the institutions which created the conditions upon which it stands. The agricultural development is expressed in the yield of the acre. No other branch of human industry can be used to such good purpose in proving the principles laid down as those upon which the prosperity of nations is built: liberty the mother of all progress; because here the results can be so directly traced to cause. What brings about the remarkable phenomenon represented in the tables of the comparative yield in agricultural product may involve collateral causes calling for further elucidation. But after all is said, the chief factor remains, that no exertion is equal to that of the individual who hews out his own road, under the guarantee of free laws, to possession, the fruit of his unhindered toil, and that countries with the freeest institutions show the highest results. In all states where this is the case, property in land is nearly always in the hands of the cultivator, and though by no means endowed with all the knowledge at the disposal of

---

* Es erben sich Gesetz und Rechte
   Wie eine ew'ge Krankheit fort ;
   Sie schleppen von Geschlecht sich zum Geschlechte,
   Und rücken sacht von Ort zu Ort.
                      —Goethe, " Faust," Part I.

his industry, nor faultless in his method of cultivation, yet he has arrived at a stage as favorable as presented above and not reached by any other system of tenure. Property becomes cut up into small holdings wherever free institutions prevail, because no one finds land so valuable as he who tills it and knows that the results of his thrift and toil belong to him and his children after him, that neither the landlord nor the state can despoil him. The highest wages obtainable are those resulting from the cultivation of the soil by the owner himself. They are limited only by the degree of intelligence he employs to extract fecundity from the soil. What these variations are has been shown in a general way in an illustration of farming as conducted by different nations, where every indication points to the irresistible conclusions pointed out.

In another chapter I will bring proof that in no appreciably near future time the question of pressure of population on the means of subsistence need cloud the apprehension of the social reformer, and that the rate of wages will not suffer a diminution from that source. I will do this from an examination nearer home. It will be seen that the present evil is not a scarcity of land but a wasting of energy consequent on an over-supply of land.

CHAPTER IX.

Security from Famine guaranteed by Civilization.—Auxiliary Advantages by Improved Means of Communication.—Truck Farming.—Creations of Railroad and Steamboat.—Results of High Farming in America.—Farming Results contrasted and applied to Territorial Dimensions in America.—Conclusions concerning Food Supply.

The Famine Danger, always threatening under Barbarism and Oppression, becomes Extinct under the Rule of Freedom.

THE rude, unintelligent farming of Russia is an illustration of the condition of the forward countries of Europe in remote times. The Slav of to-day occupies the position, intellectually and materially, of the Teutonic nations of six hundred years ago. In the wake of barbarism we have plenty and starvation in frequent alternation among scanty populations. Civilization secures to the densest populations an equable supply of food. General failure of crops is not known in countries whose early establishment of free institutions turned enterprise and intelligence to good account, as for instance Lombardy and Holland. The illustrations stand for all other countries similarly conditioned. Their intelligent cultivation knows, under the most adverse circumstances of unpropitious seasons, how to exact an equal tribute from the inimical forces of nature. While short corn crops were general in Europe through equally unfavorable and unseasonable weather, the failure was complete at the eastern terminus of the line, marking the lowest stage of civilization. In a western direction, with increasingly civilized methods of agriculture, the decline of yield becomes gradually less and less, and almost disappears in England, etc.*

What we have said so far has not at all taken into account the great machinery which civilized countries possess to-day for supplying deficiencies or distributing surplus. The railroad and the steamboat have made one country of the globe. Every hamlet within reach of the lines of communication has the abundance of the remotest part at its feet.

Except so far as hampered by stupid protection laws, which are interposed to prevent the blessings of civilization from reaching the working classes in the form of cheap food and life's necessaries, no country in the world supplied with roads and railroads has to suffer from the absence of a full supply at uniformly cheap prices. Distribution and its huge machinery is but a part of production. Whatever improvements are realized in the former by the inventive spirit of the age are the same in their results as if an improvement had brought about a price reduction in the more direct elements of production. Civilization draws from the remotest corner, and has nature under its dominion. Barbarism is confined to the immediate soil, and is the abject

---

* England had the most inclement weather all through the summer of 1888. Up to the end of August there was barely any sunshine to break the monotony of cold and rain. Of course, the prophecies of calamity were universal. The journals were full of predictions which, had they been verified by events, would have produced universal bankruptcy among the farmers. The outlook fully justified the lugubrious forebodings, the wheat beaten down by incessant rains and everything wearing the most forlorn air. But after all, when the disastrous season was fairly booked, the general average was 28.05 bushels of wheat against 29.36, the average of the three preceding years, barely five per cent. difference. In all the other crops smaller differences still appeared, except in potatoes, where 1888 gave 5.18 tons against 6.27 tons the average of 1885–87.

The starvation limit is extended, food is supplied in abundance to the generation that knows how to bridle even the most destructive forces of nature and make them obedient conductors of man's will.

slave of nature and her caprices. Not only that an acre can be made to yield an illimitable product, up to $2,200, as is the case with kitchen gardens near Paris (maraichers), but that it is immaterial now what the distance between the producer and the consumer. What the railroad and the steamship can do in this connection is familiar to everybody, in so far as it relates to bringing wheat and other coarse agricultural produce to Liverpool. Transportation over 10,000 miles of sea or 2,000 miles of land is as nothing, seeing that with competition so distanced, English wheat does not command a higher price than 4s. to 4s. 6d. (Mark Lane prices) in a year of general failure over the chief agricultural states of Europe. The tremendous crops of America of 1891-92, and a generally rich yield in India and Argentina, have equalized things, so that in England, where the law does not interfere to help the producer exact a tax from the consumer, the difference in corn prices is but between 32s. 9d. in January, 1891, and 36s. in January, 1892. In March the old price of 32s. was reached again. Truly, progress has done something for the working classes.

Truck Farming, a Creation of the Railroad and the Steamboat.

But the railroad not alone guarantees cheap food to countless millions, it creates new agricultural pursuits, otherwise impracticable. No other branch shows so well what agriculture under the best available methods can produce, as does truck farming as conducted in the United States.

Truck farming is a comparatively new industry. Fifteen years ago it could hardly be said to exist. It is the creation of our modern means of transportation. Like kitchen gardening, it caters to certain localities, centres of large populations. But while the former is conducted in the immediate neighborhood of populous cities and towns, the latter is carried on in remote parts of the country, hundreds and even thousands of miles away from the consumer. The truck farmer has a free choice of territory among all the States of the Union. He has only to keep one point in view in choosing his ground, that the railroad or water connection with his market is good and works with reliable accuracy. Truck farming has grown to such dimensions within a little more than a decade, that the shipment of this perishable freight has become a very important factor in the earnings and calculations of railroad and steamship lines. It is to be taken as a matter of course, therefore, that transportation lines will study the convenience of their patrons and not interfere with their prosperity. The kitchen gardener is usually his own distributor; the truck farmer, on the contrary, ceases to be connected with his product as soon as he has handed it over to the common carrier who delivers it to the commission agent at perhaps 2,000 and 3,000 miles distance. Whole fleets of steamers carry cargoes of truck from Norfolk, Charleston, Savannah, and Jacksonville to Northern ports, just as the trans-continental roads carry their loads from California to the Eastern termini.

It is not my province here to describe at any length any system or part of a system, but simply to give an idea of what height of yield an acre can be brought to if conditions exist which make the further advanced system the more profitable to the farmer. And here we have by the mere advent of the great transportation systems and their more useful employment in America than anywhere else, an industry which yields annually a product of $100,000,000 from 534,000 acres of land.*

---

* The Census year gave $95,000,000 gross. After deducting transportation expenses and charges of commission merchants, the farmers netted

Of course, the yield varies according to the greater or lesser degree of energy and intelligence applied to the individual farm. "New and better methods of culture are gradually introduced with the growth of wealth of the poorer producers." As it is, we have even here differences, according to the census, which make the net income per acre in New York and Philadelphia as the higher rate, and the Peninsula of Virginia as the lower rate for

Asparagus	$183.60	and	$84.00
Beets	150.00	"	80.00
Celery	214.00	"	66.00
Cabbages	133.00	"	95.00
Watermelons	81.00	"	43.00
Other Melons	158.00	"	51.00
Peas	67.00	"	26.00
Irish Potatoes	90.00	"	77.00
Spinach	80.00	"	32.00
Sweet Potatoes	75.00	"	48.00
Tomatoes	165.00	"	43.00

Whatever the causes of the differences, the poorest returns are so far ahead of the proceeds of ordinary farming, that we can very well observe what gradations exist in the food yield from an acre of ground and to what heights it can be carried, starting from the lowest returns of cultivation.

The Richer Lands give the Poorer Crops. Poor Results and High Results due only to Poor or Good Farming.

The difference in net yield between the Northern and Southern districts is by no means due to the greater distance

---

$76,500,000. The labor cost consumed of this sum $9,919,000, seed $1,420,000, fertilizers $9,919,000, and other charges $3,794,000. There was left a net profit of $48,106,000, $90.00 for each acre of ground so employed (Census for 1890).

THE ECONOMY OF HIGH WAGES. 139

from the consuming centres. It does not cost more to ship a barrel of potatoes or other produce to New York, Boston, or Philadelphia by steamship from Savannah or any other of the South Atlantic ports than from any of the truck farms located within a dozen miles from any of the places of destination mentioned. The Southern farmer competes with the home farmer on fairly even terms so far as transportation charges go. And he has a great advantage: he has the monopoly of sunshine, while the Northern farm lies buried in snow or is subjected to summery winters followed by wintry springs. Being a month or two ahead of the home supply, the Southern truck farmer realizes much better prices than his competitor, and the freight rates become but nominal charges.

The charge for carrying a barrel of potatoes or other vegetables from Savannah to New York, Philadelphia, or Boston is thirty cents (in shipments of 100 bbls. to one consignee, twenty-five cents). Early potatoes bring to the shipper from $4 to $5 per bbl. according to the state of supply in the receiving markets. At the time of this writing (May, 1892), I find in one of the Savannah papers the statement that truck farmers send their potatoes to Cincinnati, because there potatoes command $5.50, while a sudden accumulation has reduced the price at New York to $3.25 per barrel. Watching the markets is not the least of the truck farmer's tasks. Indeed, few industries offer a more varied field for the employment of a high degree of intelligence and handsomer rewards in compensation. Now it will be seen that all the natural advantages are on the side of the Southern truck farmer, and his yield ought to be the reverse of the actual, both as to gross and net results.

I will show here what the gross and net yield per acre is in the principal articles, taking the New England and the

New York and Pennsylvania divisions for the one extreme and the Norfolk and South Atlantic divisions for the other.

INCOME PER ACRE (AFTER DEDUCTING FREIGHT CHARGES).

	Asparagus.	Beets.	Celery.	Cabbages.	Peas.	Cucumbers.	Watermelons.	Potatoes.	Spinach.	Tomatoes.
	$	$	$	$	$	$	$	$	$	$
New England................	216	200	266	183	130	*2,000	100	100	175	300
New York and Pennsylvania..	183	150	214	133	67		81	90	80	165
Norfolk....................	98	88	68	101	27	25	46	80	33	45
South Atlantic..............	93	95		113	57	175	32	101	70	94

The soil of New England is not known to be possessed of any extraordinary degree of natural fertility. The wail of distress which we hear from the mother of the country down to New York and Pennsylvania, supported by the constant demonstration of the increasing ratio of abandoned farms, accuses nature of having done poorly by her first born, the Eastern tillers of the soil. Neither has the South Atlantic farmer any reason to be proud of his soil. Though the sun smirks and smiles on him, yet he often suffers by drought to such a degree that the climatic advantages would seem fairly counterbalanced. Still, with all these admissions, it is fair to say that the long stretch of territory from Baltimore to Mobile (including some very rich soils), covered by our census report, showing all over the same differences as against the North in the yield, enjoys sufficient advantages to jus-

---

* The high yield of cucumbers is explained by the fact that in New England they are grown under glass, which adds largely to the labor expense. But how trifling in comparison to the enormous net profit realized by the farmer.

tify us in saying that nature's favors go with the sunny South.

That man, by means of higher intelligence of work, here again is the instrument of wresting the high prize from nature's forbidding attitude, is seen from the following statement of labor expense, and of the amount of fertilizers expended on the respective crops:

LABOR EXPENSE PER ACRE OF THE FOLLOWING CROPS:

	Asparagus.	Beets.	Celery.	Cabbages.	Peas.	Cucumbers.	Watermelons.	Potatoes.	Spinach.	Tomatoes.
New England...............	$34	$75	$58	$36	$29	*$137	$24	$16	$37	$75
New York and Pennsylvania..	36	18	44	26	26	16	14	16	14	30
Norfolk..................	18	22	17	20	10	15	13	12	15	27
South Atlantic............	21	12	17	16	10	7	7	16	13	22

COST OF FERTILIZERS IN DOLLARS PER ACRE OF THE FOLLOWING CROPS IN EACH OF THE NAMED GEOGRAPHICAL DIVISIONS:

	Asparagus.	Beets.	Celery.	Cabbages.	Peas.	Cucumbers.	Watermelons.	Potatoes.	Spinach.	Tomatoes.
New England	$52	$40	$93	$68	$40	$30	$21	$50	$65	$60
New York and Pennsylvania.....	31	40	42	31	27	28	24	24	32	45
Norfolk..................	21	26	47	36	10	28	13	32	25	21
South Atlantic............	25	16	...	22	11	10	7	27	15	21

Deducting the cost of labor and fertilizers from the income per acre (freight being already deducted), the truck farmer receives as

NET INCOME IN DOLLARS PER ACRE OF THE FOLLOWING CROPS IN EACH OF THE NAMED GEOGRAPHICAL DIVISIONS:

	Asparagus.	Beets.	Celery.	Cabbages.	Peas.	Cucumbers.	Watermelons.	Potatoes.	Spinach.	Tomatoes.
New England................	$130	$85	$140	$79	$61	$1,833*		$55	$34	$73 $165
New York and Pennsylvania..	116	92	128	76	14	.....		43	50	34 90
Norfolk	44	40	4	45	7	†		20	36	‡ §
South Atlantic..............	47	67	...	75	36		168	28	59 ‖	42 49

The labor is more intelligent in the Northern sections than in the Southern. Its higher rate of wages controverts the time-worn theories that low wages are a requisite to high profits.

The day wages on truck farms are: for men, in New England, $1.25; in New York and Pennsylvania, $1.19; in Norfolk, 75 cents, and in the South Atlantic division, 85 cents. For boys and girls they are 65 cents in New England, 50 in Pennsylvania and New York, and from 35 cents

---

* See note, p. 140.
† Minus income of $18 per acre, but unexplained.
‡ Minus income of $7 per acre, but unexplained.
§ Minus income of $3 per acre, but unexplained.
‖ High prizes realized in comparison, on account of early growth.

down to 25 cents in the South. Here again a demonstration is given of the difference between piece-rate wages and time wages, wherever piece rates find employment, as in gathering the crops. The higher day rates simply express the higher working capacity and greater productivity of the worker. While the day rates are higher in the North, the piece-work rate is less than in the South, showing in the few instances stated that in a given time the cheap labor of the South turns out considerably less work than the better paid labor of the North. Picking string beans, for instance, is paid per bushel at the rate of 10 to 12 cents in the North and of 12 to 15 cents in the South; peas at 15 cents North and 20 cents South. Not alone are higher day wages expressive of higher intelligence and working capacity of the laborer, but they always carry with them a higher working of the farm. The Northern farm employs more hands and more farm animals to the acre, more manure, and, all told, the highest degree of tillage under scientific methods.

The differences in intensity of cultivation are made clear by the subjoined exhibit of the varying ratios of hands and farm animals to the acreage of truck farms. (I count two women equal to one man.)

	No. of Acres.	No. Hands employed.	No. of Farm Animals.	No. of Hands per Acre.	No. of Farm Horses and Mules per Acre.
New England	6.838	7.810	3.468	1.14	.50
New York and Pennsylvania..	108.135	69.654	26.232	.64	.24
Norfolk	45.375	20.152	5.790	.44	.125
South Atlantic...........	111.441	34.983	6.686	.31	.06

As truck farming does not employ labor equally throughout the year, the above figures could not very well be taken as illustrative of anything more than that the different sections employ labor, in greater or smaller degree to the acre, in the ratio given. Nearly the same proportion of farm animals being employed, and these not being supplied according to demand, but being a fixture of the farm the year around, it is evident that the general test of intensity of cultivation by the labor employed is as correct as the other test of the fertilizers employed.

A Practical Illustration of Results of Best Methods.

The best proofs of the high results of farming on the most approved scientific methods, employing labor as extensively as in the New England section, and fertilizing as freely, I collected on a recent visit to the South. From Savannah to Jacksonville, Florida, and from there to Suwanee Springs, about a hundred miles west, and thence north and east again to Savannah, I found nothing but sand in endless abundance. The forest stretches in every direction. But the soil is so poor that the pine, though getting all the fecundity which is in the soil, disputed only by a sickly looking growth of very thin grass, seldom grows to be a respectable tree. The land around Savannah does not look more inviting. The live oak, rooting strong and deep, seems to be the only growth courageous enough to spread out. We have seen the average yield of the South Atlantic division. The division includes a large stretch of country from above Charleston down to and inclusive of Florida. If the Savannah district alone were investigated, it would perhaps show a smaller yield than given in the

THE ECONOMY OF HIGH WAGES. 145

above abstract. My visit to the truck farms around Savannah was in May, and at a time when for six weeks not a drop of rain had fallen. Field after field of early vegetables lay parched and withering, and with many of the farmers the results, not always satisfactory at the best of times, were quite discouraging. Everything seemed changed when I came to the fields of one of the most successful farmers in the district. Here not a yellow leaf was visible, and I found the farmer directing his help who were busily engaged in gathering crops and packing for shipment. Deep plowing and a thorough preparation of the soil allow his roots to go deep enough to get all the moisture and thus to escape the drought affecting surrounding fields so injuriously. He keeps the soil and the plants in good condition by successive plowings. He uses on every acre of his farm fully thirty dollars' worth of artificial guano and twenty dollars' worth of farm-yard manure, part of which he gets from his own stock, and part from the town, brought out by scavengers. He employs from 35 to 40 hands permanently, and from 200 to 300 at gathering time. He works now 120 acres. When he obtained the farm, only 60 acres were in fairly good condition. The rest has since been broken, drained, and cleared. All is now in fine condition, the land well built up by rotating crops and rich fertilizing. He has three crops from the land, if he can gather his first crop so that he can plant corn in May. June planting is injured by worms. He raises on one acre from 150 to 200 crates of cabbages, as a second crop 40 bushels of corn, and after harvesting the corn from two to two and a half tons of hay. In Irish potatoes he gets 200 bushels to the acre, after which follows a crop of hay. He could raise larger crops of potatoes, but that early potatoes are frequently frost killed. This happened to him a year ago; then he plowed them over, planted cabbages, and came out with a good profit on the cabbages and two crops of hay on top. Crowfoot and crap grass spring up immediately after a good rain where the land is well manured, though without manuring nothing would grow. The money yield of these crops depends so much on the conditions of the market that the prices fluctuate very greatly. The quantities of produce raised give therefore a better impression of the most improved methods of farming when we hold them against the results of farming as generally practiced in Georgia, where, be it remembered, the average in corn is not more than twelve bushels, and, for South-eastern Georgia, ten bushels per acre.

The salable value of one species of farming is $6. of the other $200. After providing feed for stock—35 head on the farm, among them 18 mules, and 5 pleasure horses, which my informant keeps in Savannah for the use of himself and family—he sells annually from 200 to 250 tons of hay, netting from $2,500 to $3,000. His permanent help is paid at the rate of 50 and 60 cents for males, and 40 to 50 cents for females. He houses them in cottages on the farm (for which they pay no rent) and allows them what vegetables they require for their own use. Yet he has realized as much as $25,000 from his sales in a single year under favorable conditions of the market. The net results are not less satisfactory and may well be classified among the best in the country.*

---

* Equally important data can be introduced from an examination of other agricultural departments. The average per acre planted with cotton is about 160 pounds for Georgia. This represents the well and the poorly farmed acre, the fertilized and the non-fertilized. The land with constant cropping takes five to six acres to produce one bale. The same land supplied with 2 hundredweights of fertilizers produces a bale to two acres. Land has lately been given 10 hundredweights of fertilizers by a class of farmers who have but begun to bring intelligence to the cotton

Greater concentration of effort, a higher cultivation, more intelligent working of a smaller acreage seem to be the only fields, with the yield of a bale and a half from one acre. The highest net profit resulted from the highest degree of cultivation.

Even under the present low price of cotton, giving but 6 cents to the farmer, high cultivation leaves a fine profit. The cost of raising cotton under the two last-mentioned degrees of fertilizing distributes itself as follows:

COST PER ACRE AND NET PROFIT RESULTING FROM RAISING COTTON, FERTILIZING WITH—

A : 2 hundredweights.		B : 10 hundredweights.	
Yield : 250 lbs. lint cotton, @ 6 cts.	$15.00	750 lbs. cotton @ 6 cts.	$45.00
Cost of fertilizers	$3.00	Cost of fertilizers	$16.00
2 to 3 hoeings	2.50	1 hoeing *	1.00
Ginning	1.00— 6.50	Ginning	3.00— 20.00
	$8.50		$25.00

This assumes the farmer to do his own work, as is now very generally the case.

The picking expense is about covered by the price received for the cotton-seed.

But even when hired labor is employed, the results are highly satisfactory under the improved method. Four dollars for plowing is taken to cover the cost of man and horse per acre.

The two statements of cost under hired labor to cultivate twenty acres in cotton would be as follows:

A.		B.	
Cotton : 10 bales @ $30	$300	30 bales @ $30	$900
Seed, 300 bushels @ 15 cts. to 18 cts.	50	900 pounds seed	150
	$350		$1,050
5 months' labor, man, @ $10	$50	Labor	$50
5 months' support @ $5	25	Support	25
Picking @ 50 cts. per 100 pounds seed cotton	75	Picking, 450 cwts. @ 50 cts.	225
Ginning per bale, $2	20	Ginning	60
Fertilizing per acre, $3	60— 230	Fertilizing	320— 680
	$120		$370

Whatever deductions may have to be made yet from these net results, commission and freight ($2 to $2.50 per bale covers these two items) must be balanced by the consideration that the labor of the owner is here replaced by hired labor.

* One hoeing, I am told, is enough with richer fertilizing, where 2 to 3 are required on the poorer farmed land.

opening the Southern farmer has left for improving his by no means satisfactory condition. The planter is becoming more and more a part of history. The pressure of prices, the consequence of improvements and discoveries, is becoming too intense to allow wastage and high expenses. Farming as described, scientific farming alone remains profitable. The large truck farm worked under the eye and management of the farmer by hired help, may be only a transition to the ten-acre farm worked by the farmer and his family with the same satisfactory results of a surplus at the end of the year after providing a comfortable living for the family—conditions which the forty or fifty acres of a one-horse farm of the white farmer, and the twenty-five acre farm of the colored man, cannot begin to secure. Everything, by the force of competition, is in a moving condition, and, as Goethe says:

"Und wer nicht schiebt, der wird geschoben."
(Who does not push, he will be pushed.)

We have here only given the product in the different countries, per acre, under cultivation by the plow. The possibilities under spade culture have not been considered at all. The Lombard saying is: "If the plow has a share of iron, the spade has an edge of gold." *

Two pieces of land of equal fertility and equal manuring have given on a test a result of 66 by the spade and 28 by the plow.†

A laborer employed by the landlord of the Glengariff hotel (in the southwest of Ireland), had a piece of land of a quarter of an acre free of charge from his employer, which he worked with the spade in his spare time, and on which he raised, as he told me, 25 bags, or 75 bushels, of potatoes. The land itself was no better than the average in that

* "Si l'aratro ha il vomero di ferro, la vanga ha la punta d'oro."
† É. de Laveleye, Économie Rurale : La Lombardie.

section, mostly bog and reclaimed mountain land. Either requires much preparatory work till it is brought to a point where the spade can be set in.

Those living in large cities can easily inform themselves on the results of the highest degree of cultivation practiced by the market gardener. An example of it has lately been reported in the *Contemporary Review*, in describing the maraichers in the suburbs of Paris. The yield of an acre, it will be seen from the example, can be carried, indeed, to an extent to which it would be as rash to set a limit as it would be to set a limit to the inventive faculty of the mind. I will quote the illustration in evidence. Speaking of the gardener, it says :

"His garden is only 2¼ acres in extent ; ¼ acre is given up to asparagus. From Sept. 1 to April 30 he sends every day to Paris from 200 to 1,000 bunches, getting for them on an average through the eight months 6*d*. a bunch. They grow in frames 50 feet long, 5 feet wide, floored with slates ; under these, hot-air pipes, above them a shallow layer of earth. The roots are crammed in as thickly as possible, covered with two inches of good soil, and the glasses are drawn over ; in eight days they are ready to cut, the stocks lasting for two months. He has also 1,000 bell-glasses, costing 1f. each, for salads. Every year the whole surface of the garden to the depth of six inches is taken out, sold to the neighboring bourgeois for their flower gardens, and replaced by manure from Paris, which we saw standing in large ricks ready to be spread. He employs fifteen men and pays £35 per acre rent on a fifteen years' lease, with right of pre-emption. We sat down with him to calculate his profits. Here is the balance sheet we made out :

Wages	£1,000	Sale of asparagus	£2,550
Rent and taxes	100	Sales from rest of garden	178
Manure	100		
Firing and repairs	200		
Interest on capital	150		
Horses and carts	100		
Sundries	50		
Balance (profit)	1,028		
Total	£2,728	Total	£2,728

Net profit of £1,028 on a little over two acres of ground."

Here fifteen men find employment on 2¼ acres. They receive wages of $320 a year, as high a rate as is paid in many of the trades of Paris, requiring considerable skill. A rent of $168 is paid an acre, and still this victim of diminishing returns and of the rent gatherer pockets £454, or $2,200, net profit from each acre of soil, impoverished by successive generations of cultivators since the days of Julius Cæsar.

Without wishing to avail myself in the argument of these examples of highest cultivation, and returning to general agriculture, we get the most striking proof of the inadmissibility of the ruling theories, here criticised, when we apply the varying results to territorial comparisons of the United States. The crops of the United States in 1887 covered an area of 200 million acres. Of this the corn crops covered 42 million; potatoes, 2.4 million; cotton, 18.6 million; hay and grass, 37.7 million acres. Considering the exports, this acreage would have been sufficient to feed and clothe seventy millions of people. Allowing ten millions of acres for small crops, not here enumerated, tobacco, etc., kitchen-gardening and truck farming, this ratio would take three acres of soil for every head of population. To raise all this enormous product under the rough methods still prevailing, and under a therefore comparatively small yield per acre, a territory of the size of the states of Texas and Louisiana would be sufficient, and leave all the rest of the states and territories open for increasing population to settle upon.

Advancing to more intensive systems of cultivation, as in the chief agricultural states of Europe, but only selecting the self-supporting ones, we arrive at the following interesting comparisons, as we progress from the lowest to the highest yield:

Austria-Hungary, on the same method of computation, averages 1¾ acres per head of population, allowing for excess of exports. On this basis of yield the territory required for the United States would be 125,000,000 acres, and be covered by the State of Texas, with one-fourth of the territory to spare. The same ratio represents France. *Germany's* cultivated lands cover 65,000,000 acres, and with a population of 50,000,000 requires 1¼ acres per head: equal to 88,000,000 acres on the American basis of population, covered by a territory half the size of Texas. Of the cultivated area of Belgium and Holland, one acre suffices, and for the United States this ratio of cultivation would only require 70,000,000 acres, equal in size to the State of Colorado.* On the basis of Lombardy, not more than 53,000,000 acres would be necessary, or a territory of the size of Minnesota. On the ratio of yield per acre, as instanced by the truck farmer at Savannah, whose farming account I examined, half an acre would suffice where three acres are employed now. On this basis, 35,000,000 acres, or a territory of the size of the State of Wisconsin, would be required.

* I give here the acreage under different crops supplying food for man and beast in the European countries here named. Fallows are not included.

	CORN CROPS.	POTATOES.	ROOTS, GRASS, MEADOWS, ETC. VINEYARDS.	TOTAL.	POPULATION.
	Acres (Millions).	Acres (Millions).	Acres (Millions).	Acres (Millions).	(Millions.)
Austria-Hungary...	38	3.7	30	70	40
France............	37	3.6	22	62	38
Germany..........	34	7.2	17	60	50
Belgium...........	2.4	.5	1.8	5	6
Holland...........	1.5	.4	3.1	5	5

The same measure of comparison applied to European countries would be equally impressive. From the application of the highest degree of cultivation to the countries subject to the lower degree, an extension of the supply of products is realizable there, which, figuratively speaking, would be equal to adding new continents to the cultivable area of the world.

With these data in hand, we can safely relegate the question of food supply to remote generations. Even these may not feel more grateful to us for our worry on their behalf than we have occasion to feel obliged to our ancestors at the beginning of the century for the fears they entertained on our account. The question of pressure of population on subsistence is taken out of the possibilities of ages to come. The growth of intelligence, the application of science to production under the protection of liberty, has given us the surest guarantee that the positions gained are safe possessions of the race. The source of poverty is not to be sought any more in increasing populations, but in the yet imperfect organization of the machinery of distribution of the products of toil and science. More and more we begin to learn to master the new development. As the masses progress in intelligence they will become able to absorb and to enjoy the great prosperity which all classes of workers, by the hand and the brain, have been instrumental in creating. The chief obstacle in the way to this end, however, is in the mistaken policy of governments, that they can contribute to the well-being of the masses by interference and by taxation.

CHAPTER X.

The Condition of the Workingman under the Old and the New Dispensation.—Progress measured by the Budget of Consumables.—The German Workingman on the Basis of the English of a Hundred Years ago.—The Great Purchasing Power of England the Result of the Plus Earnings of her Working Classes.

THE condition of the working classes a hundred years ago and down to the time when the new development began to break down the old barriers, compared with their condition to-day, furnishes the strongest evidence in support of the positions here taken. So plainly do the facts point in this direction, that it appears strange that so little use has been made of them for refuting the contrary theories from which so much misdirected agitation has sprung.

The comparison will show that the comfort and well-being of the working classes of to-day are due entirely to the economic progress outlined in the preceding chapters, and that the contrary conditions still prevailing are entirely due to the neglect of the causes which have led to that progress.

The effect of high wages in cheapening production has been correctly estimated by old writers. Not to mention earlier apostles of this sound theory, Arthur Young ("Travels in France") declares most directly in favor of it, and was the more worthy of practical consideration, because his declaration is the result of actual comparisons after long years of observation by travel in France, Italy, Spain, England, and Ireland.

"The great superiority of English manufactures in general over those of France, in connection with the higher cost of labor, is a subject of great interest and of the highest political importance. It shows that manufacturing industries are not benefited by a nominally low price of labor, as they flourish most where, on the contrary, labor is nominally at the highest price. They flourish perhaps on account of this—that labor nominally the highest is in reality that which costs the least. The quality of the work, the skill with which it is performed, go for a good deal in the balance; these depend to a great extent on the ease in which the workman lives. If he is well fed, well dressed, if his constitution preserves all its vigor and activity, then he will surely do his work far better than a man to whom poverty leaves but a meagre pittance.' (Arthur Young on "Manufactures in France.")

The Standard of Living under the Best of Old Conditions.

But this superiority of English wages over French by no means entitles them to be called satisfactory in the light of the position gained by the English-speaking nations of to-day. The French average of wages is stated by Young as 13d. for men, 7½d. for women, and 4½d. for spinner-girls. For England he gives the average as 20d. for men, 9d. for women, and 6¼d. for spinner-girls.

In Germany the rate of wages was much lower still than in France. The degree of comfort and working power which the English working classes could buy for their higher wages was balanced to an extent by the high price of wheat then beginning to make itself felt, the effect of the corn laws which made the succeeding fifty years the darkest in their history.

Nothing perhaps has been so productive of good to the working classes of England and contributed so much to the greatness of the nation as the remarkable period of fifty years of low corn prices from 1715 to 1765. It was during this time that the working classes were enabled to get that superior strength and working power on which Arthur

Young dwells and which laid the groundwork for the industrial revolution which has since overturned the world.

The average price of wheat for that period was about 35s. a quarter of eight bushels, varying from 23s. in 1732, as the lowest price, to 53s. in 1754, as the highest price, for the fifty years of the period. This must have been indeed the golden time of the working classes, compared to the later period in which the price of bread was doubled, to say the least; while, as Frederic Eden says, in "The Condition of the Poor" (1797):

> "To counterbalance this the rise in price of labor was very little, if anything, more than 2d. in the shilling, except what money is earned in piece-work, which ten or twelve years ago was not nearly so plentiful as at present."

He gives the wages for 1737 and 1787:

	1737.	1787.
For out-door labor per day	10d.	12d.
" thrashers	9d.	12d.
" laborers near great towns	16d.	16d.
" scribblers	14d.	15d.
" shearmen	15d.	18d.
" weavers, 2d. higher.		
" women spinners	6d.	7d.

For the period of 1765 to 1796 the average price of wheat stood at about 50s., with 42s. in 1776 and 1786 as the lowest, and 81s. in 1795 as the highest, price of the period. The 25 years from 1796 to 1820 were terrible years indeed for the working classes. The average price of wheat was near a hundred shillings. The lowest price was 60s. in 1803, the highest 128s. in 1801 ($4.00 a bushel).

That matters did not improve up to the time of the repeal of the Corn Laws is presumed to be a fact so well established that we need not dwell upon this part of the subject. The time when the worst aggravation had not yet been reached, when war, gold premiums, and all the evils of taxation for the maintenance of government and of the privileged classes had not yet brought things to their climax, may, therefore, be selected as a fair basis for comparison. The time is, furthermore, well suited for the purpose, as it represents the "good old time" when the factory system had hardly begun to invade and press upon the house industries. The whole idyl of the good patriarchal period was still in full bloom, with the manor-house at one end and the "home"* at the other end of the social structure. Work was still distributed and done entirely as it is still done in many parts of Germany † and other Euro-

---

* The name given to the poor-house by the people in England.

† According to the Industrial Census of Germany in 1882, more than one-half of all engaged in manufactures, where small groups of workers can at all be employed, were employed in groups of less than 5 to each establishment. In

	A Total of	Worked in groups of less than 5 persons.	Worked in groups of more than 5 persons.
In metals............................	459,713	298,125	161,588
In machinery, instruments, etc.	356,069	127,565	228,524
In chemicals	71,777	16,867	54,910
In textiles..	910,089	440,573	469,516
In paper and leather industries........	221,698	107,293	114,395
In wood industries...................	469,695	367,688	102,007
In nutriments, food and drink.........	743,881	468,652	275,229
Total	3,232,932	1,826,763	1,406,169

Organizations large enough for profitable employment of power machinery would have to be aggregates of many more than 5 persons. The number of people employed in domestic industries, those working in their own homes, for account of business-houses, merchants, exporters or manufacturers, is very large. A total of 754,550 persons are so engaged. The kingdom of Saxony alone employs 138,000 persons, and Rhenish Prus-

pean countries, England herself not excepted. Steam power certainly had not yet begun " to run down human labor" and "made human flesh so cheap," as we are so often told in speech and song. Manufacturing was entirely based on home industry. Even spinning was done in the rural homes. Weaving was a house industry well into the first half of the nineteenth century. As late as 1830 the cotton industry of Lancashire employed 250,000 hand looms against 50,000 to 80,000 power looms, according to Porter (" Progress of the Nation "), and Ellison (" The Cotton Trade "), who is authority for the latter number.

The work of Sir Frederic Eden gives us a full insight into these halcyon days, which, in contrast to the succeeding period and the bread-riot times, were certainly to be remembered with longing. Nearly the combined earnings of a family were consumed in bread alone. Two examples, one of a smaller and one of a larger family, may serve for many, reported by Eden, to give the earnings and explain how they were expended.

---

sia and Westphalia 102,000 in domestic industries ; 230,000 are engaged in textiles, mostly in weaving. Hosiery still occupies over 40,000 people in house industry. The principal lines in textiles occupy in home industries the following position ; I set side by side the total of all engaged in the representative branches :

Percentage of all Employed.		Engaged in House Industries.	Total in Industry.
	Per cent.		
Silk weaving and velvet (Rhenish Prussia 49,022)..	70	53,286	76,264
Woolen weaving..	22	23,799	106,007
Linen "	40	41,045	103,808
Cotton "	42	52,295	125,591
Mixed goods weaving	30	22,212	73,750
Knit goods, hosiery (kingdom of Saxony alone, 30,513)	55	40,528	73,828
Total..	42	233,165	561,248

The first family consisted of husband, wife and three children, one of them able to earn a little money.

	s.	d.
The husband's earnings per week were	8	0
The wife and oldest child earned	4	6
Parish aid	1	6
	14	0 ($3.40)

This was laid out for:

	s.	d.
Bread, 12 loaves (4 lbs.), @ 11 d. or	11	0
Butter, 3 lbs. (bought of the master at a reduction), @ 6 d.	1	6
Clothing and other expenses	1	6
	14	0

The house was built on waste land, and, "the landlord not having asked rent for many years, may now be considered freehold."

Had they had to pay rent, the contribution from the parish would have had to be larger or the bread cut smaller. One shilling and sixpence a week, or $20 a year, for clothing and other expenses of a family is not a reducible sum. The wardrobe could not be more fully supplied than that of many of our German house weavers of to-day.

As the second case, I will cite that of a weaver in Kendall, wife and seven children. They earned:

	s.	d.
Man	9	0
2 daughters	4	6
3 daughters	2	6
Oldest boy	2	6
One girl knitting	0	6
Parish allowance	1	0
	20	0

THE ECONOMY OF HIGH WAGES. 159

This was spent as follows:

	s.	d.
Provisions	14	0
Other expenses, soap, fuel, rent, clothing	5	6

Of the first part:

	s.	d.
Bread and flour absorbed	6	0
Meat, 6 lbs. @ 4½ d.	2	3
Milk, 7 qts. @ 1½ d.	0	10
Butter, 2 lbs. @ 9 d.	1	6
Tea and sugar: tea, 2 ozs.; sugar, 1¼ lbs	1	6
Potatoes, 2 pecks	1	2
Ale	0	6
	14	0

Bread was 11 to 12d. a quartern loaf; flour, 2s. 8d. to 3s. 2d. a stone of 16 lbs.; potatoes, 1s. 9d. a bushel; beef, 4d.; pork, 3½ to 5d.; mutton, 5d. If the wife baked the bread, instead of buying it, a family of nine good bread eaters would not have had more than 5 pounds of flour for bread, and perhaps 2 pounds of oatmeal a day, out of the shilling spent under that heading.

Meat at 4½d. would give 6 pounds a week. Milk at 1½d. a quart allows one quart per day. Tea and sugar, at the high prices which these articles then commanded, gave precious small quantities for the 2½d. a day left for them. Potatoes would allow something over two pecks a week at 1s. 9d. the bushel. So we find the daily consumption of nine eaters to have been:

In bread and flour	7 pounds.
" meat	⅔ pound.
" milk	1 quart.
" potatoes	5 to 6 pounds.

This was all the obtainable supply of food of the great majority of the working classes in the good old times.

The Measure of Progress expressed in the Budget of Consumables.

Let us now see how a workingman's family lays out its earnings to-day, and what is the food supply it consumes.

I shall give the earnings and budget of an English potter from his own statement to me. From other personal inquiry I know that it is a fair average of earnings as well as of living expenses. Many individual earnings are less than given in this case; others are considerably higher. But in manufacturing districts the wife is usually a far greater wage-earner than in this case; in the potteries especially so.*

---

* That this represents very fairly an average of earnings is proven by copies which I made from the wage lists of a pottery manufacturer at Hanley in 1889:

A jollyer, £5 2s. 8d. He pays out of this two lads at 8s. and 6s. 6d., and three women at 10s., 16s., and 10s. = £1 16s., and has left, therefore, £2 12s. 2d., or $12.81.

A second one earns gross £5 16s. 10d., and with the same deductions for his help has £3 6s. 4d., or $16.11.

A third earns £5 14s. gross, and net £3 3s. 6d., or $15.38

Women jollyers : First case, £2 13s., out of which go £1 4s. for three helpers at 8s, which leaves her net £1 9s., or $7.04.

A second one, £2 5s. gross, less 9s. and 7s. each to two helpers, leaves net £1 9s., or $7.04.

A man plate maker earns £3 16s., less 12s. for helper, net £3 4s., or $15.54.

Still another earns net £3 3s. 6d., or $15.42. He has between £200 and £300 in the savings bank.

Another (a young man of 24), £2 18s., with 16s. 6d. off, nets £2 1s. 6d., or $10.08.

A turner, £2 14s., less 9s., net £2 5s., or $10.93.

A mould maker, £2 5s., less 6s., net £1 19s., or $9.48.

Another mould maker, £2 7s., less 6s., net £2 1s., or $9.96.

A kiln man, £3, less 14s., net £2 6s., or $11.16.

A woman in fancy work potting made 30s., or $7 30.

To take these earnings and say they represent the Staffordshire potters'

THE ECONOMY OF HIGH WAGES. 161

The family under consideration consists of husband, wife, and three children.

The husband earns	30 shillings.
The wife	6 "
Total	36 "

We can here safely set a man's wages of 30 shillings against a rate of 12 shillings in corresponding occupations a hundred years ago, and, as in the case of male weavers, of 24 shillings against 9 shillings in the good old times. But let us see what we get for a shilling to-day in food supplies as against the period we have dealt with above. Bread is about $4\frac{1}{2}d.$ a loaf to-day. This is 11 lbs. for a shilling, while at $11d.$, the price then, the workingman could only buy $4\frac{4}{11}$ lbs. Of flour, a shilling bought from 5 to 6 lbs. Now (1s. 8d. the stone) it buys $9\frac{3}{5}$ lbs. Meat is the only article which has become dearer. But it has become so, because the workingman has become a great consumer of flesh food, which he was not then—glad enough, then, if there was always enough bread and potatoes.

Of beef a shilling bought about $2\frac{1}{2}$ pounds on an average. To-day imported frozen beef is sold at 4d. to 6d. a pound,

---

wages would be as unfair as the practice usually adopted by American manufacturers for an effect, and which practice has been criticised in these pages. That 30s. ($7.30) is below rather than above the average, and 36s. ($8.74) more expressive of the individual worker's earnings in the potteries, is proven from a statement of the average wages of fifteen pottery works, taken from their books at the time of a general strike in 1882-83. They are as follows : (1) Flat pressers, $7.75 ; (2) dish makers, $9.67 ; (3) cup makers, $9.97 ; (4) saucer makers, $7.97 ; (5) hand-basin makers, $9.71 ; (6) hollow ware pressers, $8.18 ; (7) hollow ware jiggerers, $11.69 ; (8) printers, $6.59 ; (9) oven men, $6.59 ; (10) sagger makers, $8.50 ; (11) mould makers, $10.29 ; (12) turners, $8.05 ; (13) handlers, $8.43.

and English beef 8d. to 12d. for the choice pieces. A shilling buys 2 to 3 pounds of the former and 1½ to 1 pound of the latter.

The same is true of mutton. New Zealand mutton of very fine quality is sold at 4d. to 5d. a pound. Were the English workingman not so fastidious, he could have his meat as cheap as his ancestors, what meagre portions they could buy. But he insists on his home-grown beef and mutton. He even wants the best cuts, and disdainfully leaves the poorer pieces to be taken by the "classes." A story is current in the potteries, that in the flush days of the early eighties a lady asking the price of a fine cut of beef was answered, "Oh, you won't buy this nohow! None but the collier ladies buy these pieces." -

Butter averages 1s. 4d. a pound now. Hence a shilling buys ¾ pound against 1½ pounds a hundred years ago.

Tea was 4s. 7d. to 8s. 6d. at the company's warehouses; at retail 6s. to 10s. Taking the lowest price, a shilling bought 2⅔ ounces. To-day, at 2s. 6d. or 60 cents a pound, a shilling buys 6⅖ ounces.

Refined sugar was 7½d.; now it is 2⅖d. a pound. A shilling's worth was then 1¾ pounds, and. is now 5 pounds.

Potatoes are now 8d. a peck. In 1797 they were 6d. to 8d. a peck (1s. 9d. to 2s. a bushel). Hence a shilling buys 1½ pecks now, against 1⅔ to 2 pecks then.

We see from this, that a workingman in England can not alone buy to-day more food products all around for 1s. than his forefathers could a hundred years ago, but that he has a far greater number of shillings at his disposal.

As this is a very instructive object lesson, we will tabulate here:

THE ECONOMY OF HIGH WAGES. 163

WHAT A SHILLING BOUGHT IN 1790, AND WHAT A SHILLING BUYS TO-DAY, IN THE CHIEF FOOD PRODUCTS CONSUMED BY WORKINGMEN IN ENGLAND.

	1790.	1890.
Wheaten bread, pounds	4¼	11
Wheat flour, pounds	5 to 6	9¾
Beef, pounds	2½ to 3	1½ to 3
Mutton, pounds	2½ to 3	1½ to 2½
Butter, pounds	1⅓	¾
Tea, ounces	2⅓	6⅔
Sugar, pounds	1¾	5
Potatoes, pecks	1¾ to 2	1½

When three-fourths of the earnings of a family have to be devoted to food, and most of this goes to the purchase of bread and flour, we can well understand the significance of these figures.

Taking now the budget of the working potter mentioned above, comprising a family of 2 adults and 3 children, we find him laying out his 36s. as follows:

	s. d.	$
1. Food supplies	15 7	= 3.74
2. Other expenses, rent, taxes, fuel, sundries, clothing	14 2	= 3.40
3. Balance	6 3	= 1.46

Food takes only 43 in a hundred of earnings, leaving 39 per cent. for other commodities and expenses, while 18 per cent. go to savings. The savings bank has taken the place of the poor-house. But what is more to the point yet in illustration of our case, we have here a family of 2 adults and 3 children consuming as much and, taking other products than bread, more than a family of nine mostly grown up persons in the old days.

We have here the following items as the weekly food bill of the potter:

		s.	d.
1.	Bread, 6 loaves, @ 4½d.	2	3
2.	Flour, 4 pounds	0	5
3.	Meat, 7 pounds	3	11
4.	Milk, 4 quarts	1	0
5.	Butter, 1½ lbs.	2	0
6.	Lard, ½ lb., @ 6d.	0	3
7.	Tea, 10½ ounces	1	3
8.	Sugar, 5 pounds, @ 2½d.	1	½
9.	Potatoes, 1 peck	0	8
10.	Ale and tobacco	1	2

Besides these articles, which also appear in the food budget of the workingmen of 1797, we have:

11.	For spices, other vegetables, etc.	1	8
	Making up our food bill of	15	7½

I inquired into the finances of another family which consisted of father, mother, and six grown-up children, all earning money, except the youngest boy of the age of fifteen.

This family baked its own bread, and consumed a sack of flour of 224 pounds in five weeks. Hence per week:

		s.	d.
1.	Flour, 45 lbs.	4	5
2.	Meat, 16 lbs., @ 9d.	12	0
3.	Milk, 10 qts.	2	6
4.	Butter, 4½ lbs.	6	0
5.	Tea, 1 lb.	2	6
6.	Sugar, 5 lbs.	1	0½
7.	Potatoes (about), ¾ pks.	0	7
	Does not smoke or drink.		
8.	Other food products	0	9

Placing side by side the two groups, we behold the relative positions of the working classes of the two periods. One is representative of the old, the other of the new civilization and development. We cannot better show the advantages resulting from the progress made than by setting in parallel columns the quantities of food consumed by

Family A, 2 adults and 3 children. (1790.)	Family AA, 2 adults and 3 children. (1890.)	Difference in Consumables.
Bread.....12 loaves......	6 loaves..........	− 6 loaves
Flour..................	4 lbs.............	+ 4 lbs.
Meat..................	7 lbs......... ...	+ 7 lbs.
Milk ......3 qts.........	3 qts.............	—
Butter.....3 lbs.........	1½ lbs............	− 1½ lbs.
Tea....................	10½ ozs...........	+ 10½ ozs.
Sugar..................	5 lbs.............	+ 5 lbs.
Potatoes...............	1 peck...........	—
Extras.................	2*s.* 8*d.*..........	+ 2*s.* 8*d.*

But here we may be told that the outlay of the family's earnings of a hundred years ago in bread alone was not judicious, as bread was so high and meat relatively cheap. Very well, let us reconstruct the table of outgoings on a basis of six loaves of bread and assimilate the bill of fare to the more diversified plan of our modern example. According to the prices of commodities stated above:

Family A.	*s.*	*d.*	Family AA.	*s.*	*d.*	Plus or Minus of AA.
Bread, 6 loaves, @ 11*d.*....	5	6	6 @ 4½*d.*....	2	3	equal.
Flour, 3 lbs., @ 2¼*d*.......	0	7	4 @ 1¼*d.*....	0	5	+ 1¾ lbs.
Meat, 4 lbs., @ 4½*d.*.......	1	6	7 @ 7*d.*.....	4	1	+ 3 lbs.
Milk, 3 qts., @ 1½*d*........	0	4½	3 @ 4*d.*.....	1	0	equal.
Butter, 1½ lbs., @ 9*d.*......	1	1½	1½ @ 1*s.* 4*d.*.	2	0	equal.
Tea, 2¾ ozs.	1	0	10½..........	1	8	+ 7¾ ozs.
Sugar, 2 lbs., @ 7½*d.*......	1	3	5 @ 2½*d.*....	1	0	+ 3 lbs.
Potatoes, 1 peck..........	0	6	1..........	0	8	equal.
Sundries.................		10	0	2	10	+ 2*s.*0*d*.
Omitting sundries....	11	10	and	13	1	

represent the money value of the respective budgets.

But on only 1*s.* 3*d.* more outlay the workman of to-day can live so much better than a workman of one hundred years ago, as the plus figures above indicate, not to speak of the large surplus left over for other purposes.

On the basis of consumption of 1790, to-day's budget would stand as follows:

Family A.	*s.*	*d.*	Family AA.	*s.*	*d.*
Bread, 6 loaves, @ 11*d*.	5	6	6 @ 4½*d*.	2	3
Flour, 3 lbs., @ 2¼*d*.	0	7	3 @ 1¼*d*.	0	3¾
Meat, 4 lbs., @ 4½*d*.	1	6	4 @ 7*d*	2	4
Milk, 3 qts., @ 1½*d*	0	4½	3 @ 4*d*	1	0
Butter, 1½ lbs., @ 9*d*.	1	1½	1½ @ 1*s*. 4*d*.	2	0
Tea, 2¾ ozs.	1	0	2¾ @ 2*d*	0	5½
Sugar, 2 lbs., @ 7½*d*.	1	3	2 @ 2½*d*.	0	5
Potatoes, 1 peck.	0	6	1.	0	8
	11	10		9	5¼

A minus expense of 2*s*. 4¾*d*.

At the same rate of living, the workingman of to-day can buy for 9*s*. 5¼*d*. what it took a hundred years ago 11*s*. 10*d*. to obtain. If he were to live on bread and butter, as in the first illustration taken from Eden's amount, 8*s*. 6*d*. would buy what required an outlay of 12*s*. 6*d*. then.

The parallel is more complete when we take the actual budget preserved by the Kendall weaver's account and of the potter's family of eight members for comparison, the letters B representing the former period, and BB the latter:

Family B. Bread baked at home.	*s.*	*d.*	Family BB.	*s.*	*d.*	Plus or minus of BB.
Flour, 2¼ stones	6	3	3 stones	4	5	+ ¾ stones.
Meat, 6 lbs., @ 4½*d*	2	3	16 lbs., @ 9*d*.	12	0	+10 lbs.
Milk, 7 qts., @ 1½*d*	0	10	10 qts., @ 3*d*.	2	6	+3 qts.
Butter, 2 lbs., @ 9*d*.	1	6	4½ lbs	6	0	+2½ lbs.
Tea, 2 oz., @ 4½*d*.	0	9	1 lb.	2	6	+14 oz.
Sugar, 1¼ lbs., @ 7½*d*.	0	9	5 lbs.	1	½	+3¾ lbs.
Potatoes, 2 pks., @ 7*d*.	1	2	¾ pks	0	7	−1¼ pks.
Ale.	0	6	None.			
			Other food products	0	9	+ 9*d*.
	14	0		29	9½	

THE ECONOMY OF HIGH WAGES. 167

This fairly characterizes the change in the conditions of the working classes, the progress from the old to the new. The transition from a bread and potato diet to a meat diet is unmistakable. The surplus of earnings applicable to the purchase of commodities other than food, the savings put into banks and loan and building societies, are the direct result of this higher and better living. The beef eater overcomes the bread eater as the latter overcomes the potato eater. The economic position of nations is one of food and of standard of living. Only the ratio is the reverse of the general assumption. The lower the rate of living, or the rate of wages, the higher the cost of production. Of course, the economic position of the nations corresponds to this.

The German Workingman's Basis of Living now, on that of the English a Hundred Years Ago.

The rate of living of the working classes explains everything, the standing of nations in industrial competition as well as all other phenomena in the economic world. Germany's present status is not farther advanced than England's before the free-trade era. The living of the working classes is not so high to-day as that represented by case B of a hundred years ago. From the many investigations undertaken by governments, economic societies and individuals, I will introduce two examples, representative of the better situated. The fact that a large proportion live beneath this rate, stated in these pages, in speaking of the condition of the poor weaver (Part I., Chapter IV.) adds weight and force.

I take the budget of a German workingman from Professor v. Schulze-Gaevernitz's admirable book ("Der Grossbetrieb, ein wirthschaftlicher und sozialer Fortschritt, Leipzig," 1892) and one from my own examination. If we place these exhibits beside the showing of B and BB, the demonstration will be complete.

The family consists of husband, wife, and four children. The father earns 15 marks a week, and the two oldest children, employed in a textile factory, contribute 7 marks. These combined earnings of 22 marks are spent mainly for food—17.85 marks. Rent takes 3.20, and barely one mark remains to pay old age insurance and school rate. For clothing, no provision is made at all. But the composition of the budget for food speaks volumes:

WEEKLY FOOD BILL FOR A GERMAN WORKINGMAN AND HIS FAMILY, IN ALL SIX PERSONS.

		Marks.	$
Rye bread, II. quality*	42 lbs.	5.60	1.35
Rolls	2 "	2.00	.48
Wheat flour, II. quality	2 "	.40	.10
Meat (Sundays only)	¾ "	.45	.11
Lard	¼ "		
Vegetables, peas, beans, rice, etc.	...	3.40	.80
Potatoes	30 qts.	1.80	.44
Corn coffee	...	.20	.05
Butter	2¼ lbs.	3.40	.80
"Half" milk (skimmed milk)	6 qts.	.60	.15
		17.85	4.28

The price of bread and flour is stated here somewhat higher than I had it quoted to me by workingmen in 1886, at the time of my visit among the Crefeld silk weavers. But it must be remembered that the duty on corn was raised since that time. The budget of supplies, taken down by myself, however, does not vary materially from that given by Dr. von Schulze-Gaevernitz. The family was composed of father, mother, grown-up son, and widowed daughter with three

---

* Rye bread is here quoted at the rate of 3¼ cents a pound against wheaten bread in England at (9 cents the 4 lb. loaf) 2¼ cents ; wheat flour at 5 cents against 2¼ cents in England.

children. They owned the house and about a quarter of an acre of land. In the previous year (1885) father and mother had earned 624 marks together, or 12 marks per week. At the time they did not work, as trade was dull. The daughter earned 10 marks and the son from 12 to 18 marks, according to the work. It will be readily understood from the fact of the house being owned by the father, and through the aggregation of earnings of the family, that this is one of the most favorable cases, from my own observation as well as reported on by others.

BUDGET OF A FAMILY OF FOUR ADULTS AND THREE CHILDREN. (FROM MY OWN INVESTIGATIONS.)

1. FOOD.

	Marks.	Marks.
Rye bread, 20 lbs., @ 10 pfg		2.
White bread		2.
Rolls		.50
Home-baked white bread:		
Flour, 10 lbs., @ 13 pfg	1.30	
Yeast	.30	
Milk, 1¼ liter, @ 15 pfg	.22½	
Baker's wage	.50	
		2.32½
Flour, 4 lbs., @ 13 pfg		.52
Butter, 2 lbs., @ 1 mark		2.
Milk, 6 liters @ 15 pfg		.90
Beef (Sundays), 1½ lbs., @ 60 pfg		.90
Salt pork, 2 lbs., @ 65 pfg		.97½
Sausage, 1 lb., @		.80
Potatoes, 1,000 lbs.	24.	
" about an equal amount raised on own land.	24.	
Cabbage for sourkrout, 400 lbs., @ 1 mark per 100 lbs	4.	
Cabbage, cutting	10.	
Coffee, 40 lbs., @ 1.25 marks	50.	
For 52 weeks	112.	2.15
Carried forward		15.07

	Marks.	Marks.
Brought forward		15.07
Sugar, ¼ lb., @ 40 pfg	.20	
Olive oil and spices	.44	
Soap, 1 lb	.20	
Beer	1.20	
	17.11	

2. CLOTHING.

Father	40.	
Son	40.	
Three children	54.	
(Children's shoes are 3.50 and boy's shoes 5 marks a pair.)		
Mother and daughter	78.	
	212.	4.08

3. FUEL AND LIGHT.

Coal, 4 tons, @ 7.50 marks	30.	
Coal oil	12.	
	42.	.80

4. RENT.

Owns the house, mortgaged for....2,400.		
Interest	120.	
Repairs	20.	
	140.	2.70

Total expense		24.69 *

No allowance is made here for taxes and school money, or for any other unavoidable expense. Nor must it be forgotten that no full allowance for rent is made, which would be considerably higher were the house not their own. The two statements, together with the other illustrations, clearly explain the position of labor and of the laborer in Germany.

We see that a German workingman of to-day cannot live as well as an English workingman lived a hundred years

---

* The mark at 24 cents round, and 100 pfennige the mark, will help computing German into American money.

ago, poorly as the latter was situated as compared to conditions of to-day.

Meat disappears almost entirely. So do tea and sugar. Everything is reduced to a point below which it is hardly possible to produce the strength necessary for earning even the scant wages that keep the family alive. A surplus is unimaginable. The purchasing power for other commodities is destroyed,* as every possible increase in earnings

---

* A few cases taken from the better situated classes of workingmen will evidence this fully. Other proof exists in abundance. "A family of a type-setter at Leipsic—consequently belonging to the highest class of workingmen—with only two children has only 174.40 marks ($37) to spare for shoes and clothing." "To save shoes the children have to go barefoot in the warmer season." "The house-furnishing of a German workingman's family is hardly ever bought new, but, as in numerous cases, the clothing also from second-hand dealers, or obtained through charity." ("The factory system, an economic and social progress." Dr. Gerhardt von Schulze-Gävernitz, Leipsic, 1892.)

"Eine Leipziger Buchdruckerfamilie—also der höchststehenden Klasse der Arbeiter angehörig—mit nur zwei Kindern hat für Bekleidung und Schuhwerk jährlich nur 174.40 M. übrig. "Um Schuhwerk zu sparen, laufen die Kinder in der wärmeren Jahreszeit barfuss." Der Hausrat der deutschen Arbeiterfamilien wird fast nie neu gekauft, sondern, wie in zahlreichen Fällen auch die Kleidung, vom Trödler, oder durch Wohlthätigkeit erworben."

"A workingman's family with four children and an income of 1145.19 marks ($283) spent for clothing, linen, furniture, and repairs only 100.78 marks ($24). The head of the family buys once in a while a pair of working trousers, or some other indispensable article, but has not for fifteen years bought a new suit of clothes. As a rule with workingmen, the furniture is bought second-hand when the family starts housekeeping. A sofa or lounge is absent in most cases. A separate sitting-room is found nowhere, the same room being used to sleep and to live in. Frequently the same room serves the whole family as living and sleeping-room, and in many cases is shared with boarders."

"Schriften des freien deutschen Hochstifts, Frankfurt-a.-M., 1890. Eine Arbeiterfamilie mit vier Kindern und 1145.19 M. Einkommen gab für Kleidung, Wäsche, Haushaltungsgegenstände und deren Reparatur nur

would be consumed in meat food, so necessary for the nerve of the worker.

The contrary position in England, allowing for so large a surplus over food expenses, explains the great absorbing character of the English market, the dumping ground of the surplus products of the whole world.

The high importance, the economic and sociological value of a high rate of wages, the preponderating power it gives to nations blessed with it, has been so fully demonstrated by the facts here adduced, that further argument seems superfluous.

Nor need I dwell here upon the conditions in America, where the forces that have been so powerful in creating the advanced position of England have had fuller sweep yet. The results have been fully dwelt upon. Their effect will be made clear in the second part of this volume, when the different industries will be separately reviewed, and when it will be shown that the hindrance to reaching the highest development is the interposition of laws, mistakenly called protective, but in reality preventive.

100.78 M. aus. Vom Familienvorstand heisst es : "Er kauft wohl einmal eine Arbeitshose oder ein derart unentbehrliches Kleidungsstück, hat aber seit 15 Jahren keinen neuen vollständigen Anzug mehr sich angeschafft." Die Möbel der Arbeiter sind meist schon bei Begründung des Haushaltes gebraucht gewesen. Selbst das Sofa fehlt in den meisten Fällen. Einen besondern zum Wohnzimmer benutzten Raum giebt es nirgends, vielmehr wird in demselben Raume geschlafen und gewohnt. Häufig dient ein Zimmer der gesamten Familie zum Wohn- und Schlafraum, in vielen Fällen wird derselbe mit Aftermietern geteilt."

PART II.

THE EFFECT OF HIGH WAGES.

COMPARATIVE METHODS AND COST OF PRODUCTION IN AMERICA AND EUROPEAN COUNTRIES.

IN the first part of this treatise it has been shown that a high rate of wages is the primary, the moving cause to all industrial progress, and that a low cost of production must necessarily follow where favorable conditions have created this basis. It has been shown that these conditions are created by freedom, and that restrictions, like tariffs, even be they called protective, cannot possibly be otherwise than obstructive.

In the second part the chief industries of the world, competing in trade, will be discussed and reviewed in the light gained from the general inquiry into the causes of high wages, contained in the first part. It will be shown by an analysis of competing industries, methods, and cost of production, that all the available facts prove the correctness of the principles treated in the previous pages.

The analytical review will fully corroborate the main contention, that the industries of America want the reverse of what the McKinley Act has given them—room for freer and higher development. The latter can only be given by what has been suggested, a higher training, technical, scientific, and artistic. These are the requisites which would make America industrially independent. A few millions annually spent on these necessary elements in the productive machinery would conduce more to this end than ever so many efforts in the direction which Mr. McKinley has induced the Republican party to follow.

That the act he has identified with his name would prove a disastrous failure ought to have been self-evident at the outset, from a consideration of the true principles of the economy of production. Blindness and mere party greed alone could have prevented a correct estimation of the logical results which are now open to everybody's view.

CHAPTER I.

Unreliability of Statements of Protected Industries.—Exaggerated to obtain High Rates of Protection.— The Pottery Industry in Evidence.—English and American Positions contrasted.—Sanitary and other Ware.—Making High Rates of Profit though selling Goods considerably under English Prices.—Brown Stoneware.

PROTECTION has its strongest ally in the general ignorance of the relation between the method and cost of manufacture in countries competing for our market and our own. Not able to cover the field of inquiry for themselves, the lawmakers had no other sources of information than the manufacturers themselves. Where the latter did not wilfully mislead, it is certain that they showed only such facts as would most surely prove the need of continuing or imposing excessive duties. Facts from abroad were entirely wanting. The consular reports had no information on the subject worth considering. The consuls gave all they could give—the daily rate of wages, the mode of living, the hours of labor, the commercial statistics of industry, etc. But upon such data no intelligent comparison can be based. No points on industrial competition can be determined therefrom. With the object of obtaining the information required for establishing a basis for comparative manufacturing statistics, I commenced my investigations with the pottery industry, it being the chief industry of the district to which I was appointed. The pottery industry has always attracted general interest. It is, strictly speaking, an art industry, and as such offers many useful hints and points for comparison. The technical processes are very important subjects of study. In many directions, industrial improvement would follow a more careful consideration of them than they seem to have found among American manufacturers in the scramble for high protective duties. Under the cheapening of prices following the adoption of improved methods of manufacture, and under a rising standard of life among the masses, white ware in pottery finds a very much wider market than in former times. White and decorated pottery can now be brought into every cottage, giving an inviting appearance to every dinner table, by replacing the pewter and common earthenware of former days. Increasing commercial importance is thereby secured to this article of manufacture, in addition to the importance attaching to it from the educational point of view.

The Industry in America and England.

An industry like this naturally invites the attention of everybody who is interested in the general question of the æsthetic and industrial development of a country. What lends to pottery in England especial interest is that it has there, unaided by government support, developed into one of the leading industries, and holds a position which enables it to send now to the United States twice as much as Germany, France, Austria, and all other exporting countries combined.

To get to the cost of production, it becomes necessary to examine into the cost of materials, the cost of labor, and piece-work prices. In a report on the pottery industry of North Staffordshire I made a comparison of the English and American potteries, the weekly earnings in both, as well as the piece-work rates, transportation charges, methods of working, improvements adopted in the methods; and I added a description of the system of art education in England, the cost and mode of living, and finally the methods employed between master and man for the settlement and adjustment of disputes by boards of arbitration. It will be taken as a matter of course that in an industry like the finer pottery, white earthenware and china, America cannot produce on equal terms with England or other European countries. America lacks everything that European countries possess in abundance—skilled workmen who have imbibed all the elements of their art from childhood, foremen, managers and masters, knowing by intuition and rule of thumb the requirements of their trade, the treatment and combination of materials, the body and the glazing, the degree of firing requisite, etc.

Many of the manufacturers who have had the greatest success started as workmen from the bench. Their sons, if raised in the same way, devoting close attention to the management, bring to greater prominence the works inherited from their fathers. Where this is not adhered to, capital and reputation do not save from bankruptcy.

If such be the case in England, where the industry, so to speak, is to the manner born, how much more so in America, where it is ingrafted upon a not very willing tree? Our manufacturers, periodically laying claim to an increase of protective duties, are in the habit of pointing to the higher rate of wages paid in this country. They want it understood that their inability to keep out importations is due only to the insufficiency of protection, insufficient on account of higher labor cost. They never point to other deficiencies which are far more important.

I had endeavored to inquire into these. I alluded to them in my report without, however, enlarging upon them.

It was important to show the methods of manufacture pursued in England and the aid given to this industry by the state as well as by individuals. As pointed out, all the aid consisted of the intellectual aid given, that of science and art education. I was not remiss in stating the difference of wages, both by the week and the piece rate between Trenton, N. J., and North Staffordshire.

My report was of February, 1886. The potters of Trenton, under the headlines, "Shall the pottery industries of the United States be destroyed?" in a pamphlet dated March 12, 1888, and presented to the Ways and Means Committee, took exception. Their contention will be quite interesting and instructive to the reader as illustrating a system of arithmetic, which may very properly be called protection arithmetic. According to this system, 3 plus 4 are made to figure 8 or 6, as the exigency of the case may require. Though I had cited in my list of comparative piece rates quite a number of items at over 100 per cent. above English rates, they considered the case unfairly stated. They objected that in comparing piece rates of wages and rates of cost, I did not accept the whole list and draw a general average. My reasons for not taking the whole of the list, and for confining myself to such items of comparison in piece rates as were made by the same processes in both countries will prove ample in the light of later information. Various improvements in the mode of manufacture in England had not been adopted in Trenton. They had not adopted them even in 1888, a year or two later, when I again visited Trenton. The reason given was the same as is always given, that the workmen would object to their introduction, and not be willing to accept a lower wage rate with the new device than with the old. In England the manufacturer had met with the same difficulties, but the

THE ECONOMY OF HIGH WAGES. 179

higher wages per diem possible under the improved methods, in spite of the reduced piece rate, had gradually overcome these objections.

High protective tariffs are preservers of obsolete methods until closely pressed by home competition. In this instance the cheapening in England was especially prominent in flat dishes and pressed ware, where improved methods led to great savings in the labor cost. I confined myself to hollow ware and larger dishes, where by the nature of the articles the process could not vary much in the two countries.

The drawing of an average can only be misleading. It is unscientific and must lead to error. A comparative list of prices may contain articles paid at equal rates, but employing most of the time of the workmen, while other articles may be paid at double the rate, but be of small importance in the output. Thus a much higher average would be established than that practically existing.*

Assertions of the Trenton Potters.

The claim, however, of the Trenton manufacturers will stand in very good stead here. No figures could be more

---

* This is only one of the methods resorted to, when claim is made for legislative favors. The Trenton manufacturers in their statement give full week earnings, while the English in my report only cover actual time employed. The time of 58 hours in Trenton against barely more than 45 hours in Staffordshire ought to be considered. The work-people are still devoted worshipers at the shrine of Saint Monday. But the Staffordshire aggregate earnings are further increased as the weeks of work are 48 to 50, while in the Trenton earnings only 34 to 42 weeks' work appears in the occupations and for the year in comparison. All this, of course, gives an entirely different construction to their wage lists, especially when we bear in mind that the Trenton manufacturers, like their brethren in other industries, select for required effect the highest paid individual earners, and set them against an average or against lower earnings in the same occupations for England.

profitably invited for the proving of the unreliability of averages, to use a mild term. By adding the articles which are made in England, either entirely by machinery in pressing moulds, or with improved tools, batting machines, steam jiggers, etc., they show differences of 158 per cent., and in some instances as high as 275 per cent., and finally draw an average and say "that where the whole list is taken, English and American, the difference is 112 per cent. instead of 57 per cent. [what they make my comparisons to average], and these figures in England are good 'from oven' prices, while the American prices are good 'from hand,' a difference variously estimated at from 10 per cent. to 20 per cent. additional, in round figures, therefore a difference of 125 per cent. in wages." Now let us see what a comparison of the actual conditions demonstrates.

It is important for an understanding of the general factors in price making in pottery, and especially that kind of pottery which is most extensively used in the United States —white earthen ware or white granite ware—to know that in the cost of production the labor cost stands in about one-half of the net selling price, the material (coal, clay, etc.) and the gross profits taking the other half. In Staffordshire the exact relations, as from the account books of manufacturers (copied by myself), stand: Labor, 47½; gross profits, 23½; material, 29—equal to 100 as price unit.

Clay and coal are higher in Trenton than in Staffordshire. Coal is nearly double. Ball clay, much of which is imported, pays $3 a ton duty, about 50 per cent. If, on top of all this, labor is 125 per cent. higher than in England, it would be difficult to see how it is possible that many a manufacturer in potteries, who twenty years ago was a poor man, has realized a fortune since. And this, up to 1883, under a duty of not more than 40 per cent. on white ware, since raised by various pushings and the application of the methods usual on such occasions, to at present about 55 per cent.

That the increase of duty obtained in 1883 was not demanded by the exigency of the case might be taken from the fact that even up to then the manufacturers had prospered when they understood their business. It was, however, only partially an increase, important in higher cost goods, but insignificant in the lower cost ware, where value was comparatively small in relation to the bulk. How these increases were brought about will be seen from the following computation :

The net cost of a crate of white granite ware was at that time £5 15s. 7d. ($28.14). The net charges upon this are £1 6s. 9d. ($6.86), bringing the cost up, when landed free of duty, to £7 2s. 4d. ($35). The duty before 1883 on these goods at 40 per cent. was levied on the whole amount of £7 2s. 4d. ($35). This made the duty borne by the goods equal to 49 per cent. on the invoice value. The tariff of 1883 raised the duty to 55 per cent., but abolished the duty on charges. The McKinley tariff bill makes no change in the rate of duty, but the McKinley administration bill restored the duty on packing charges. These amount to about 16s. 6d., or $4; hence, an additional protection of $2.20 has been realized, making the duty on the net cost of the goods ($28.14) $17.68, or 62¾.

Of course, in decorated goods and finer ware the charges and duties upon these latter become comparatively insignificant. The white ware, however, is the most important in this consideration of comparative values and costs. It is upon this, also, that the contention of the Trenton potters was based in answering my report.

Having shown what rates of duty are being levied, and how the increase in rates was brought about in a roundabout way, we can now build up a cost comparison on the statement of the men of Trenton.

	Staffordshire. Per cent.	Trenton. Per cent.	
Material.............	29½	29½ plus 50 =	44¼
Labor...............	47½	47½ plus 125 =	107
Profit and expense...	23½	23½ plus 97½ =	46*
Total.........100			198

But the American manufacturers, in the statements published by their association, themselves show a higher percentage of profits than the English manufacturers. These relations of labor, material, and profit also appear in the census figures of 1880.

These statements show material 26½, labor 46½, and gross profit 27 in 100 as the selling value.

Hence, according to this, they show a cost statement which compares with the English normal rate of 100, as follows:

	English.	Trenton.	
Material.............	29½	26½ plus 50 =	39¾
Labor...............	47½	46½ plus 125 =	105¾
Profit...............	23½	27 plus 100 =	54
Total.........100			199½

Accordingly the relations of profit to the rest of the manufacturing charges are 10 per cent. higher than those of the best showing of English pottery manufacturers.

The English gross profit, however, is above the normal average. The year 1882–83 was highly profitable for the potteries. The impending change in the American tariff threw a very large business into the hands of the Staffordshire potters. The American shippers, anxious to make use of the time given them for filling their warehouses with

---

* The plus percentage of 97½ is arrived at by taking the English material and labor of 77 and the American co-relative cost of 152 as a basis.

goods under the old rates, were foolishly wasting the duties saved, in the enhanced prices they paid to the Staffordshire manufacturers. The latter did not fail to improve the opportunity. The year 1884-85, for which I made my examinations, was therefore more normal. This only showed a profit rate of 12½ per cent.

It would be utterly impossible for the Trenton manufacturers to keep going and pay running expenses under a rate of gross profit which would pay a handsome income to a Staffordshire manufacturer. The waste in manufacturing, the allowances for claims from customers, etc., are in themselves sufficient reasons for necessarily greater gross profits. But waiving this for the present, and accepting the rate as above, the question remains to be answered, how manufacturers can exist with goods costing (according to their showing) a full 100 per cent. more to produce than English goods under a protection of 49 per cent. (up to 1883), and 55 per cent. up to the present tariff bill. But this is not all. American goods do not command the prices of English goods. They are, so far as quality goes, considered inferior. At equal prices everybody would buy the English goods in preference. As it is, a great many white goods are brought from England to be decorated here. The decorating works, putting considerable labor on the goods, prefer paying a higher price to the taking of risks that the goods on which they have expended much time and labor would craze after being put on sale.

The selling prices of English and Trenton goods show the corresponding positions very plainly. The goods are sold at equal prices in English shillings. But the shilling of Staffordshire goods (after deducting the discounts and adding duty, etc.) is sold at 18¾ cents by the importer, the Trenton manufacturer's shilling at 16 cents.

Thus a difference of some 15 per cent. is considered to exist. In the face of such facts, it becomes difficult to see how the extraordinary wage-rates can be paid by the Trenton manufacturers, and leave them sufficient margin to exist and to make very handsome accumulations besides.

We can see the absurdity of the statements upon which their claims are rested, when we observe that the English goods costing 100, paying duty 55, charges 5, and importers' profit, say 15 per cent., equal to 25, are sold accordingly at 182, and that against this the Trenton makers have to sell their goods at only 160, goods which at their own showing cost them a full 200 to put on the market. Arithmetic of this kind is not apt to impress business men seriously. It would invite contempt rather than the consideration of Congress, were it weighed there in the balances in use in the commercial world.

Inefficiency attracted by a High Tariff.

If the average cost of labor were 125 per cent. more than in England, it would be difficult to understand how so many of the manufacturers, twenty years ago poor men, could realize large fortunes under a tariff of 40 per cent., or adding duty on charges, 49 per cent. One of the manufacturers, a thorough-going old English potter, who at all times opposed the endeavors of the later generation of Trenton potters for higher duties, emphatically declares that he made most of his money under a tariff of 25, and later on 40 per cent. This is quite natural. The higher tariffs inflated cost and increased competition by incompetent hands. Of these, after depressing the industry, a number have failed. In view of the general prevalence of high profits, these failures must be attributed not to insufficient tariff duties, but to incapacity and mismanagement.*

Few things eat into the profits and the capital of a pottery so much as waste, due to breakage, to imperfections in the firing, and to crazing. Here is the touchstone of capacity, skill, and technical knowledge of master, manager, and workman.

At the time of the great coal strike in the anthracite region, Trenton potters suffered especially heavy losses from crazing of their ware. They had to substitute bituminous coal, and this change in the fuel led to some very disastrous results, not universal, however, thereby proving the effi-

---

* The high profits made by the Trenton manufacturers have recently been brought to light by the prospectus of the "Trenton Potteries Company," organized by the union of five of the leading firms. Of the $3,000,000 capital, the $1,250,000 of preferred stock represents nearly the whole property, undoubtedly at the highest possible valuation. (The value of real estate, machinery, patterns, merchandise, and cash in bank is given at $1,390,000). The $1,750,000 of common stock is, therefore, almost all water to absorb the surplus earnings over the 8 per cent. on the preferred stock. The prospectus shows that for the last three years the average earnings on the common stock were 11 per cent., and for 1891 they were 16 per cent. after providing for the expense of management. On the appraised value of the entire property, the average annual net profits for the three years 1889, 1890, and 1891 were equal to a dividend of 22½ per cent. The net earnings for 1891 were $401,000, equal to a dividend of 29 per cent. on the same basis.

This is in singular contrast to the statement of one member of this consolidation made before the McKinley Committee on Ways and Means in the spring of 1890. Said he: "It is for you, gentlemen, to say whether this struggling industry shall be destroyed for the benefit of foreign manufacturers."

Struggling infants, and deeply concerned for the wage-earner are they, when the tariff is discussed. But no sooner have they carried home permission to levy increased taxes, than they reduce the wages of their workmen.

ciency or inefficiency of the management as the cause of the difference. The trouble in crazing is that it often shows itself months after the ware has been burned, and so the manufacturers often get goods back long after they have been sold.

This condition of the industry largely explains the scramble for higher rates, though discountenanced by the older and wiser heads in the trade. To cover and perpetuate inefficiency ought not even be the object of paternal legislation. To this inferiority alone is due the continued and increasingly large importation of ware from the Staffordshire potteries despite high duties. It has been a common saying among leading North Staffordshire manufacturers that they do not wish the American tariff reduced on their own ware; that the American manufacturer now lives in a fool's paradise, and does not make improvements and savings, and a close study of his business, such as he would make if harder pressed by England.

Labor-saving Appliances.

How the introduction of labor-saving devices in pottery making has helped in reducing prices of the ware, and at the same time increasing the workingmen's earnings, will be seen from a few facts which I took from the books of a pottery in Hanley (North Staffordshire). Dinner plates (the unit of price is per score dozen, or 240 pieces) in 1880 were made by hand tool and jigger, at the rate of 4s. 6d., or $1.10; men could make one score dozen a day. In 1889, employing the steam jigger and steam tool, or monkey, they could make two score dozen a day, at the rate of 3s. a score, or 6s. day wages ($1.46.) Slop jars used to sell at 6s. 6d. ($1.58) in 1880, and sell now from 2s. 6d. to 3s. (61 to 73 cents). The quantity made by hand was not over a dozen, and is now six dozen a day. Jugs were paid for in 1850 at the rate of 15d. a dozen, when a workman made four dozen a day. In 1880 the rate had gone down to 10d. a dozen, and the workman could make six to eight dozen a day. Now they are made by machinery. In 1889 they were paid for at 4½d. (9 cents) a dozen. In 1880, with an output of forty dozen a week, at the rate of 10d. (20 cents) per dozen, the workman made 33s. 4d. ($8.08) a week. At the present time, with the help of machinery, at the rate of 4½d. a dozen, he makes from 250 to 300 dozen a week, earning from 94s. to 112s. 6d. ($22.87 to $27.35), leaving for himself, after paying his help, about £3 ($14.58).

Equally important with the improvements just noted in cheapening prices has been the improvement made in the building of kilns and the consequent saving of fuel. The cost of fuel in ordinary white ware is about one-third of the cost of all other materials used in English potteries. A manufacturer in the Staffordshire potteries told me that when he began he used for firing a bisque oven fourteen tons of coal, but that now, with the down draught, he could do the same with ten tons of slag and two of coal, and slag does not cost more than half the price of coal. In America the quantity is larger by one half.

The cost comparison in this instance would be, taking coal as it stood in 1885, at the time of my report, coal, $2.07 per ton and slag $1.09; and including cartage from the pit, $2.31 and $1.33, respectively. With the old firing method the firing of a kiln stood $32.34, against $17.92 with the present mode—a saving of $14.42 in one firing. In Trenton as much as 50 to 60 per cent. more fuel is consumed in the firing, as I am informed by the best authorities.

It is well to bear these facts in mind. They show how complex the questions are that we have to consider when estimating price-making in so variegated an industry as pottery; and that it is one thing to set up claims, and another thing to have them tested in the light of reality. At the same time it is necessary to keep in mind the fact, here so strongly marked, that high protective tariffs are an injury rather than a help to an industry. They attract people unfit for the work, lead to wastefulness, perpetuate obsolete methods; and while the well-qualified make fortunes in the end, the gift is for them, even, not an unmixed benefit.

Sanitary Ware.

Many manufacturers admit that competition among themselves, and especially the rushing in of incapable men into a branch of which they have little or no knowledge, are far greater dangers than English competition. This has shown itself to a marked degree in sanitary ware. A number of manufacturers have gone into this branch originally on account of higher profits and the large demand resulting from the almost universal employment of stationary washstands and sanitary appliances instead of the chamberware of old. Competition in consequence has become so keen among them, that, if price alone were considered, some of the articles could not be imported even if there were no duty at all. English goods are taken in preference by builders and architects, on account of their superior quality; yet the price differences are so greatly in favor of the Trenton goods, that this alone must insure them a considerable market. The manufacturers would wish to raise prices, but they are deterred by the fear that so much competition would be invited, that they soon would be worse off than before. I have obtained the price of some of the leading articles from an importer of English and jobber in Trenton sanitary ware. They are as follows:

	JOBBING PRICE.	
	Best English ware.	Best Trenton ware.
14-inch round plug basin	$1.12	$0.65
15 x 19-inch oval plug basin	2.50	1.90
Large Bedfordshire urinal, lipped	6.30	3.80
Washout	10.80	7.35 to 8.50

In England the manufacturers of sanitary ware maintain their prices far more easily and more firmly than the Trenton potters. The same is true of almost every industry in the two countries.

A most important economic principle derives its vital support from these trade facts, and a few words on the subject will not be out of place here. The manufacture of sanitary ware requires a much larger capital than ordinary white ware. In this latter branch, in England, many workmen and small beginners start almost every year on their own account. They rent small factories, they and their wives work on workingmen's wages; and by economy and close attention frequently succeed in building up a lasting business, if things keep running smoothly, industrially and commercially. Others not so fortunate, or wanting in the commercial requirements, are forced, after a life's savings are worked up, to return to the bench, which they had better never have left. These men are always pressed for money, and keep a close run with the older, wealthier houses. This has much to do with the closeness of prices and smallness of profits in English pottery, referred to above. It is by no means American competition and the American tariff which reduces prices and profits there, as we are taught by the economists of the American school.

In sanitary ware the situation is different. No small

man can engage in it. The manufacturers are all wealthy. The outfit in moulds alone absorbs a small fortune. The new era, the era of change, requires a constant additional outlay for new patterns. Another important fact is that the heavy body of clay of these large pieces takes much time to dry. It takes a month to turn out sanitary goods against a week in ordinary ware. This has enabled the sanitary ware manufacturers to maintain their prices and rates of profit.

In Trenton the very opposite has occurred. The money rapidly made in the highly protected pottery ware turned a very fierce competition into this, with results as noted. Yet, in spite of all these unfavorable influences, the profits of sanitary ware manufacturers are so high that they yield the dividends pointed out above. The five firms which have formed the combination mentioned above, besides manufacturing toilet and table ware, make "about 75 per cent. of the entire output of the famous sanitary plumbing ware made in this country," as the prospectus says. The public remember the strike of the Trenton sanitary ware makers of last winter, lasting several months, in resistance to the reductions which the masters wanted to impose on them. The facts here stated bring the wages question in the tariff into proper relief.

Brown Stoneware.

The owner of a pottery, manufacturing brown stoneware, requested me to obtain for him the prices paid in England for corresponding work. A strong tariff reformer, he had his suspicions that the claim of the protectionists that the high wage earnings of American potters implied high labor cost, requiring high duties as an offset, was not borne out by the facts. In his branch he was of opinion that the higher earnings were due only to the greater quantity turned out. I obtained the revised price list from the Secretary of the Associated Stoneware Throwers, England, for 1889, and my correspondent in Minnesota supplied me with the data from his wage books. I take articles which are well known, and which are called in both countries by the same names. I will quote the essential parts relating to this branch from the letters of my correspondent, Mr. O. M. Hall:

"The Red Wing Stoneware Company, of which I am secretary, and in which I am personally interested, claims to be the largest single stoneware pottery in the United States. It has been in existence fifteen years, and, after a struggle for life, is now in a highly prosperous condition. The demand for our ware so far exceeds our capacity that we make all we can; we do not limit the amount of work which the men are allowed to do. They, however, work by daylight only. In accord with the technicalities of the business, men are paid by the 'day,' that is, the 'potter's day,' which consists of a fixed number of gallons of a certain kind or size of ware. The average potter will do five 'potter's day's' work in one calendar day, and he can do six if an expert and not limited in quantity. The potter at his wheel, even though he only turns out the common jug and pot, is a skilled laborer. He commences on the smaller sizes of ware, and as he becomes more skilful he advances to the larger sizes. Consequently, the skill of the workman is indicated by the size of the pots he turns.

"The data I send is absolutely reliable, and is taken fresh from the company's books. You are at liberty to use it, and the name of our company and of its president, John H. Rich, and my own name, in any manner you wish."

This company ships ware to Winnipeg, where it competes with ware made in Ontario, although the Canadian tariff imposes a duty of 3 cents per gallon, equal to 60 per cent. *ad valorem*, the selling price on cars at Red Wing being 5 cents per gallon for butter tubs, and 6 cents per gallon for jugs.

192 THE ECONOMY OF HIGH WAGES.

Comparing, after this explanation, the English labor price with the American, the reader will find a flood of light thrown on the subject of high wages and low cost of production. As the English price is per 100, I reduce the American ratio of day work to the same unit of 100:

Gallon Butter Pots.	Wages, English, per 100.		Red Wing, per 100.	Number turned out per calendar day.
One-half.........	4s. 6d.	= $1.09	$0.71₁₇⁷	*420
One	6s. 6d.	= 1.58	1.00	*300
Two.............	12s.	= 2.93	1.62	*200
Three...........	18s. 6d.	= 4.50	2.44¾	†162
Four............	25s.	= 6.00	3.75	†120
Five	30s.	= 7.30	5.83⅓	†90
Six.............	50s.	= 12.00	6.66⅔	†72

The first two numbers are now mostly made by machinery and moulds at Red Wing, at a cost of 35 cents for the half-gallon size, and 50 cents for the gallon size per 100—about one-half of the turner's rate. The men pay 25 cents per day for steam, and 50 cents to the ball boy, in the smaller sizes, and $1 in the larger ones.

The weekly earnings, taken from the pay roll, of five good average turners, for fourteen consecutive weeks, show the following, the conditions being normal and wages at the standard rates above specified:

	Kind of work. Gallons.	14 weeks' pay.	Reduced to week.	Net weekly.
A	2	$218.59	$15.61	$11.31
B	3	269.35	19.24	14.74
C	4	310.25	22.16	16.16
D	5	335.00	24.00	18.00
E	6	463.65	33.12	25.62

I am informed by my friends in England that London potteries pay rates somewhat below those obtained from the

---

* Five potter's days.   † Six potter's days.

Secretary of the Associated Stoneware Throwers. The difference would not be material, and would in no way invalidate the proposition that high weekly wages, where the best energies of master and men are engaged in the work, by no means preclude a low cost of production. But such results are reached more by close attention to, and thorough understanding of, all the manufacturing details than by politics raising duties even after they have become inoperative as protective measures, as to an extent in ordinary white ware, and to a much larger extent in sanitary ware.

CHAPTER II.

The Trust and Monopolies alone benefited by Tariff Legislation.—The Glass Industry in Evidence.—The Piece Rate of Wages Lower than in England.—Dividends declared of 30 and 50 Per Cent.—Tariff Increase in Spite of these Facts.

IN the preceding chapter we have demonstrated the sophisms employed by manufacturers in vindication of their claims for high duties. The industry described is one of which we admitted at the outset that it could not exist, in white ware at least, and under present conditions, without a protective duty. The people are willing to pay protective duties for cultivating home industries, and if any industry deserves cultivation, certainly pottery as an art industry does. We only object to the methods at hoodwinking the public, and to the constant claim for increasing duties, when the lower rates had proven ample. None of the extenuating circumstances, however, can be applied to the glass industry. None of the difficulties exist which have to be contended with in the white earthen ware. The pots of glass matter are easily made if you have the right materials, and these are not difficult to obtain. Poor workmen are not so apt to spoil good material, though the low piece rates would give them but a poor chance for making a comfortable living. But in spite of all this, tariff increases were asked for and granted when no need for any protective duties was apparent. To ask for increased duties here, shows plainly the insatiable nature of protectionism.

In the whole line of tariff exactions imposed upon a long-enduring nation, nothing offers a more impressive showing of false pretense, of the debasing of the law into a handmaid of exacting monopolies and selfish interests, than the tariff status of this industry. Indeed, it is a regular *pons asinorum*, calculated to inspire the most timid politician, afraid of his constantly menacing bugbear, "the labor vote," with confidence in the importance and strength of the tariff reform issue as an ally to secure the support of every thinking workingman.

Flint Glass, Hollow Ware, Table Ware, etc.

From beginning to end the law is full of increase of duties. I will briefly state the old rates, and the new rates replacing them :

Green and Colored and Flint and Lime Glass Bottles, etc.—New duty, 1 cent per pound; old duty, 40 per cent. Increase in the heavy grades of some, 50 per cent.

Flint and Lime, Pressed, Plain Glassware.—New duty, 60 per cent.; old duty, 40 per cent. Increase, 50 per cent.

Flint and Lime, Cut, Engraved, Painted, Colored, etc.—New law, 60 per cent.; old law, 45 per cent. Increase, 33⅓ per cent.

Thin-blown Glass, including Glass Chimneys, etc.—New law, 60 per cent. ; old law, 40 and 45 per cent. Increase, 33⅓ to 50 per cent.

Heavy-blown Glass, Plain, blown with or without a Mould.—New law, 60 per cent.; old law, 40 per cent. Increase, 50 per cent.

Now, then, there must have been tremendous importations of European pauper-labor goods to justify an increase of 50 per cent. in duties. To discourage these importations and to give the American workingman a chance to maintain his preponderatingly high wages is undoubtedly the object and reason of this new addition. By no means! Of the goods which come into competition with the class of glassware now under consideration, and which form the bulk of our manufacture, we imported in the fiscal year of 1889 a total of $830,000. In this sum is included $530,000 worth of bottles and vials which came in filled, and are separately dutiable. So the whole extent of flooding the American markets with plain glassware is about $300,000. But if it were not for the high duties, we should have our industries at once destroyed on account of the high wages ruling in this country, and the reverse conditions prevailing in Europe. Well, we shall see in the sequel on what foundations of facts this pretense stands.

Some highly interesting facts bearing on this subject in England and America will throw light on the relative cost of labor.

Mode of Pay and Comparative Rates in England and America.

In America generally, flint-glass workers are paid by the move or shift. A move means half a day's work, and contains a varying number of pieces, according to their size, etc. The day is divided into four shifts. One shift commences at 7. At 1 P.M. another shift comes in. The first shift comes in again at 7 P.M., and at 1 in the morning the second set of men relieve the first again. The set of men working one pot are called a shop. A shop consists generally of one blower, a gatherer, a helper, and three or four boys. In the glass-bottle department the wages per move for the blower are $2, for the gatherer $1.10. The boys are paid by the day, and average less than a dollar a day.

Some of the works work by the day. Flint-glass works in Pittsburgh gave the output as about forty gross in half-ounce bottles and about fifteen gross in sixteen-ounce bottles as a day's work. Those works were operating from

7 in the morning till 5 P.M. The list prices per shop (three men and four boys) of a gross of two-ounce flint bottles is 58 cents, or less than five-twelfths of a cent apiece; of sixteen-ounce French bottles, $1.45 a gross, or about 1 cent apiece. These bottles of blown glass are used very extensively by druggists and in all putting-up industries. The quantity turned out is greater per move or turn than anything I have seen in Europe.

In another leading factory I found a day's work of large-size beer mugs with handles to be between 1,000 and 1,500. This work requires considerable labor. The glass is put in the mould and pressed with perpendicular pressure by the presser; he gets $2 per move of from 500 to 700 pieces, according to the size. The finisher gets $1.65 per move, and the gatherer $1.30, total, $4.95; which for two moves per day makes $9.90; adding the labor of about five boys at about 75 cents per day (the boys, mostly sons or other relatives of the workmen, are paid from $3 to $6 per week), makes a total for the day's wages of a shop of glass pressers $13.65, equal to $1.36 per gross for the largest beer mug with handle, and something less than a cent apiece for the pony beer glasses. For the further illustration of the lowness of the piece rates in this industry of pressed ware, I will give the quantities turned out in a move for the wages paid.

Pitchers, three-quart, cylinder mould, $1.90 per move; presser, $2.50; finisher, $2.25; gatherer, $1.60; handler (the one who puts on the handles), $2.50; total, $8.85. Seven boys at, say, the rate of 50 cents a move, average, $3.50; total, $12.35; bringing the cost of labor on a three-quart pitcher to 6¼ cents. One quart pitcher, number per move 305, wages same, or 4 cents apiece. In solid stem bowls, unfinished, the wages are for the presser, $2; for the gatherer, $1.20 ; for four boys, $2 ; total, $5.20. The output of 4½-inch bowls, is 650, and of 10-inch, 300. So the former cost about ⅘ cent, and the larger size about 1¾ cents apiece in labor. Comports finished run from 3-inch to 10-inch, at an average of $7.15 for labor of presser, finisher, and gatherer, and four boys. The output is 900 pieces for the smaller, and 300 for the larger size—from ¾ cent to 2¼ cents. Berry dishes, 4-inch to 10-inch, finished, average labor of three men and three boys, $6.60. Output, 825 for the smaller, and 300 for the larger size; cost, per piece, from ¼ cent to 2¼ cents apiece. Finger bowls, round finished—total labor, $7 ; output, 550, or about 1¼ cents apiece.

Fruit jars (one quart), presser, $1.92½ ; gatherer, $1.20 ; four boys, $2 ; total, $5.12½ ; number per move, 500 in block mould, and 600 in joint mould, or ⅞ cent and 1 cent, respectively.

I confine myself in this statement to a few articles well known to every housewife. By comparing the wage rates per piece paid for the making, with what the purchaser has to pay, how small the actual labor cost does appear !

Having shown the royal pay given to our labor in one of the most exacting industries, let us see now what the British workman gets, this living example of unbridled free trade.

English Rates.

The method of arranging pay and the regulation of output are nearly the same as ours. According to a rule of the Glass Blowers' Trade Union, the makers or blowers work three hours, which is called a "move," and they work two moves at a time, which is called a "shift" or a "turn." According to a very old custom, eleven moves constitute a "week's work." All over that is reckoned as overtime, and

THE ECONOMY OF HIGH WAGES. 199

paid for at about the same rate; eighteen moves, *i.e.*, from Tuesday morning to Saturday afternoon, is considered a full week's work. In some cases the men produce three of these moves in a turn of six hours, so that with eight turns, the usual number per week, they can make twenty-four moves.

In dishes, lamps, bottles, tumblers, goblets, etc., the eleven "moves" or "week's work" are paid:

```
Presser .................................. £1  6s., or $6.82
Melter ....................................  1  6s., or  6.32
Gatherer .................................    16s., or  3.82
Three boys, 6s ...........................    18s., or  4.38
                                              ─────────────
    Total ................................           $20.84
    Or per single move ...................             1.90
```

In blown work the pay of the blower is higher than the presser's, but, with two boys only, aggregates about the same:

```
Workmen ................................. £1 16s.
Servitor .................................  1  6s.
Footmaker ................................    17s.
Two boys .................................    12s.
                                           ─────────────
    Total ................................ £4 11s. = $22.11
    Or per move ..........................              2.01
```

We can now make a few comparisons:

FIRST—*Bottles*, Sixteen ounce.—American, ⅞ cent to 1 cent apiece; English, 220 in a move, at $2.01, equals $\frac{11}{12}$ cent; two ounce American, $\frac{1}{12}$ cent apiece; two ounce English, 350 in move, equal to $\frac{7}{12}$ cent apiece.

SECOND—*Decanters*, one quart.—American, 275 per move, total pay $10.10, equals per piece, 3¾ cents; English, 45 per move; total per move $2.01, equals per piece 4½ cents.

THIRD—*Pitchers*, one quart.—American, 4 cents apiece; English, 40 in move, at $1.90, or 4¾ cents

FOURTH—*Goblets*.—American, 650 per move; total pay per shop, $8.40, or per piece, 1$\frac{3}{10}$ cents; English, per move, 150, per piece, 1$\frac{3}{17}$ cents.

FIFTH—*Tumblers*.—American, 700 per move; total pay per shop,

$6.62½, or per piece, 1⅜ cent ; English, similar size, 240 per move, ot ⅞ cent.

SIXTH—*Finger Bowls.*—American, per piece, 1.25 cents ; English, 130 in a move, or 1.46 cents.

These few examples must suffice, taken at random from the respective trade lists. They have to be confined to items which are easily distinguishable and cover the same article. They dispose of the myth of the high pay which American workingmen receive. In most instances the piece rate is below the English ; and if American workingmen obtain a higher weekly rate, it is due solely to their greater exertion during each working hour of the week, and to their working a much greater number of hours in the week than their English brothers. To this alone (the cheapness of American labor) is due the fact that we export annually nearly a million dollars worth of this class of American glass ware.

But in this industry, the same as in the pottery industry, the higher weekly rates by no means express the earnings correctly. The time not worked makes so serious an inroad into the workingman's earnings, that, on a yearly computation, he is really not so much better off than his brother in England, with his evenly distributed work, as the weekly comparisons would lead to believe.

The average earnings of glass blowers in Pittsburgh by the week, rated on the statement of the president of the Flint Glass Workers' Association at about $30, do in reality not give more than an aggregate of $900, or $18 a week the year around. The English glass blower, with his well regulated control of the working machinery of his trade, earns under full employment 54s. for 18 moves at 3s., or $13.12.

If he has 24 moves coming to him, as happens under the regulations of the trade when work is plentiful, at 3s., he earns as high as 72s., or $17.28. The difference between actual and ideal earnings is quite a considerable one in glass as well as in pottery.

The materials which compose the body of flint glass are: Sand, 52 per cent.; potash, 14 per cent.; and lead, 33 per cent. Sand and potash are not different in price from foreign cost. But lead, dutiable at 2 cents a pound—about 70 per cent. *ad valorem*—adds two-thirds of a cent to every pound of glass made beyond the foreign cost, and helps the Lead Trust.

But besides the low cost of labor, we have advantages of another nature in glass making. First, the factories are usually situated where land is cheap. Indeed, the land becomes valuable only through the erection of the factory. Townships are eager, therefore, to obtain the location, and grant valuable privileges. This is no slight advantage in competition with old countries, where every acre of land has at least the tenfold value of similarly situated land in America.

Secondly, the fuel is cheaper, even where coal is used, as in Pennsylvania, Ohio, and West Virginia (where two-thirds of the capacity is situated) than in Europe, not excluding England, prominently in Belgium and France; but they have now the great advantage of natural gas. This is a twofold benefit—first, in that it saves the crucible, which lasts three times as long as under the use of coal; second, saving is effected in the labor, as in a six-furnace glass factory in Pittsburgh, as given me there, the saving in labor amounts annually to $5,000, formerly paid out for supplying coal to the furnaces. Another considerable saving, although gas charges are high and the waste is very great, is in fuel cost by the introduction of gas in the place of coal.

After what has been said, everybody can see that the tariff

argument is here used merely to throw dust into the eyes of the consumer and the workingman. The same wages could be paid with a fair profit to the manufacturers without any tariff. A fair protection in an article like glass ware to the manufacturer and the work-people arises from the low price comparative with the nature and bulk of the goods. In this line of goods—plain hollow ware of flint and lime glass —the packing charges and freight rates pro value are very high. Much loss is furthermore suffered by the importers by breakage in these goods carried from so great a distance, and subjected in the reloading to a great deal of handling. The McKinley Administrative bill, by doing away with the former rebates on breakages, and by imposing duties upon packing charges, adds considerably, by this change, to the former rates of duties. What, then, is to be said of the new tariff, which, besides this covert increase of tariff exactions, enormously increases duties in an industry entirely independent, so to speak, of European competition? The answer is always the same, dropping an anchor to windward, fostering trusts, and thus enable them to grab "what the traffic will bear" when opportunity is favorable.

Cut Glass, Decorated and Fancy Ware.

In decorated and fancy glass ware, America has attained an equal efficiency. At one of the leading glass works which I visited in Western Pennsylvania they turn out, among a variety of other articles, a large product in etched globes, and I have it from the superintendent himself that he can make them cheaper than any one in Europe, that he can sell them in England, and does send a good many to Norway and Sweden. The superintendent came from one of the leading glass works in England. The chief designer and head of the etching room was a German, as, in fact, nearly all the designers in America are, there being very little native talent to select from.

Our importations in cut glass amount to about $1,000,000. The goods are mostly of a lighter, fancy character. This is work dependent much on the taste of special industrial sections, work in which we have not attained efficiency. Our product is mostly heavy cut-glass ware. America has made great progress in this class of goods, in which it outruns Europe. The body of this heavy glass ware is largely imported from Europe, on account of the greater purity of the foreign casts, and is then cut in American works especially devoted to the purpose. The work being laborious stands to the cost of the body at least as ten to one. Still, with all the high wages paid per diem to our workmen, the work is done as cheaply as in Europe, or at least very much below duty-paid rate. Practically, all importation of this kind of work has ceased long ago.

A glass cutter at Stourbridge, England, gets about 32s. ($7.80) a week of fifty-eight hours' time. In Meriden and other American glass works glass cutters earn from $14 to $21 a week, according to efficiency. This shows plainly that the day rate does not, so largely as the output, determine the cost by the piece. The higher character and efficiency of American labor fully compensate in the larger number of industries, especially where physical endurance is of importance, for the difference in day wages. The pieces sent from America to the Paris Exposition in 1889 always drew a large circle of admirers. Although of high cost, they were bought very freely by people of wealth, who had, in annexed exhibits, the work of all other nations for comparison. This shows that where we boldly strike out on original lines, we can easily become masters of the situation, and hold our own against all odds. The imitator and copyist will always lag behind in the race. Still, with all this gratifying condition and virtual independence of our industries, and the special character of our importations, our lawmakers have seen fit to advance duties in this line also from a former 45 per cent. to 60 per cent. when, so to speak, protective duties had already become obsolete.

Window Glass.

The rates on window glass are specific. They were, before the new tariff came into force, over 100 per cent. Certainly so excessive a rate of duty as 100 per cent. on common window glass is not necessary for the protection of labor. The window-glass making combinations knew before this how to make use of the opportunity given by the Government for enriching themselves by taxing the people all they can get out of them. But still, in spite of that, some of the duties have been raised even in plain window glass. The increase of duty affects a class of window glass, the *ad valorem* equivalent of the specific duty on which amounted only to the bagatelle of 132.29 per cent.

A short review of the situation will show us how much in need of an increase of protective duties these manufacturers stand.

They have the same advantages related above—land, fuel, gas. The capacity has doubled in the last ten years in Pennsylvania, Ohio, New Jersey, and Indiana. They have a very strong organization—the American Window-Glass Manufacturers' Association—which regulates prices and the output. They allow importations to the extent of a million and a quarter dollars, and keep up the prices of their own goods to about duty-paid prices of foreign glass rather than have indiscriminate competition and the consequent forcing down of prices and profits. They are helped in this by the workingmen's association, which regulates and limits very strictly the employment of apprentices. In an industry which requires years to learn and get efficient in, and supported otherwise by the alien labor law, it is practically impossible to break down a monopoly, as unrestricted competition undoubtedly would.

In consequence of this closely managed organization, window glass in America, with slight variations in one kind or another, stands on an average at about the same prices it stood in 1860. On the other hand, foreign window glass within the last twenty years has fallen in price about 50 per cent. This is a fair example to show how the tariff reduces prices, and yet things are not always serene between workingmen and manufacturers. There are disputes and even strikes. The situation could not be better expressed than by quoting from a speech of Senator Plumb:

"They [the window-glass manufacturers] are in a quarrel about half the time out there, and it seems to me, from the investigations of the quarrels as they appeared in the newspapers, that the manufacturers make trouble with their employees in order to have a pretext for cutting down and shutting up, and they take only such portions of the market as they can make the best profit out of. It is certainly thoroughly well understood. I do not think that it can be successfully disputed that, notwithstanding their plants have been enormously increased in value, they have made very large profits. They have made such large profits that they have become the objective of the English syndicate, which has been seeking to buy them up, I understand ; at any rate, one of their representatives has so stated that the profits have been as high as 180 per cent., and they have never been lower than 30 per cent. or 40 per cent."

Plate Glass.

Such are the results of legislation in favor of trusts and combinations. They show more tellingly yet, however, in this line of goods, how easy it is, under the ægis of these pernicious laws, to roll up immense fortunes within a few years, and at the same time keep labor down to the grindstone. The increase in the consumption of plate glass of late years has been very heavy. The production in 1880 measuring 1,700,000 square feet, of which 1,042,000 square feet was polished and 377,287 feet sold rough, has risen to a capacity of 8,000,000 square feet. Three new works in process of erection in Pennsylvania will raise this soon to 10,000,000 square feet. With the advantages stated above, the profits present an equally dazzling spectacle. No plates are cast smaller than 24 by 60 inches. Smaller sizes are cut from plates that have been broken or are otherwise defective. On plate glass above 24 by 60 the duty is 50 cents per square foot, an *ad valorem* rate of 141.43 per cent.; and on 24 by 30 to 24 by 60 the duty is 25 cents, equal to 72.49 per cent. *ad valorem* on the importation lists of the custom house. But as the sizes above 24 by 60 chiefly concern our manufacturers, it is easy to see what an advantage they have in hand, and how deeply they must feel in the perpetuation of the paternal principle in government.

The dividends of the Pittsburgh Plate Glass Co., with works at Creighton, Tarentum, and Ford City, Pa., were 31 per cent. last year. The workmen fare not quite so well in the division of the spoils. In no other occupation requiring equal skill, and equally exhaustive, are wages so low. In the casting hall, wages are from $2 to $3 a day, the latter for the master teaser; in the grinding room, from $1.50 to $3; in the polishing room, from $1.80 to $2.75; and in the cutting room, from $1.50 to $2.50; in all averaging, perhaps, $2, as the lower rate always means the most numerous class of workmen. Indeed, the census of 1880 shows an outlay of $292,253 for wages in the plate-glass industry, divided among 822 men, 91 women, and 43 children. Counting women and "children" at half the rate of men, we get 889 men, which gives a grand yearly earning to each adult workingman of $328. " *Tant de bruit pour une omelette.*"

But the "workingman" will continue to send committees to Washington, and prove to a nicety to the lawmakers in the House and the Senate that a great industry would perish if anything were taken off the existing duty, or if the increase demanded by his employer were not granted. These poor people do not see that by their action they most effectively help to build up the immense capital power which in the end will crush them into slavish submission.

On polished cylinder glass, or German looking-glass plates, the duty has been raised 10 per cent. in spite of the fact that none is manufactured here, and against the earnest protest of furniture manufacturers, who for that reason wanted it put on the free list. The high duty on this article is a bar to the extension of our export trade in furniture where this kind of glass forms a very important item. But it so happens that glass knows how to make its power felt, and furniture had no influence in court. Furniture and the innumerable other industries similarly placed, as well as the consumer, ought to have remembered that nothing different could be expected from the Congress and the party which they elected and put into power in the memorable election of 1888.

CHAPTER III.

The Insincerity of the Claim for Protection of Labor.—Demonstrated by a Comparison of the Cost of Iron Mining here and abroad.—Pig-Iron and Steel Rails.—Large Profits secured to the Steel Rail Makers.—The Men on Strike to resist Wage Reductions.

THE insincerity of the claim, that protective duties are required for the sake of the laborer, cannot be better demonstrated than by a thorough discussion of the facts of our mining and iron-making industries. Nowhere has the general ignorance of the corresponding facts of foreign cost been exploited to such a degree as in these branches. Nowhere has the difference in the day rates of wages been used so tellingly to advance the selfish interests engaged, and nowhere more injuriously than against those who use the products of the mines, furnaces, or steel works as raw materials.

It is not a little astonishing that on a question of constant public discussion during the lifetime of this generation so little should have been done to gather the facts of cost of production and rate of output per man, employed in competing countries. The industries here concerned are the industries upon which the industrial life of the nation is founded. The whole structure of modern society rests upon them. Take coal and iron from the support, and the whole structure falls into ruins. The cheap and unhindered supply of coal and iron is the first essential of life of industrial States. To make a country, or sections of a country, tributary to the rapacity of other sections, in such vital materials,

THE ECONOMY OF HIGH WAGES. 209

out of political considerations, is nothing short of a crime. It could find extenuation and apology only in the general belief, that legal restrictions were required to protect American labor against the underpaid labor of European mining countries. This belief had nothing to rest upon, except what was known as the rate of wages paid by the day. How misleading this is will be seen from the sequel.

It was one of my first endeavors, after entering on my mission of inquiry, to examine into the comparatives mentioned above. The results were given in a report to the State Department (No. 64 Consular Reports) of June, 1886, of which the following statement represents the chief items:

COAL MINING.

Country.	Gross Tons Mined per Head........	Cost of Labor per Ton......	Annual Wages Earned per Head........
		Cents.	
United States, 1880, bituminous (census report)	377	86¼	$326.00
Pennsylvania, 1880 (representing one-half product of U. S.)	560	66	337.00
North Staffordshire, Great Britain, 1884...............	322	79	253.00
Prussia, Saarbruck Collieries, (Government)	256½	89	225.12
Dortmund Collieries (private)..	281	79	222.00

The tons are all reduced to the gross ton of 2,240 pounds. The census average cost per ton is higher than the labor cost at our great bituminous fields, chiefly in Pennsylvania, which here, for our consideration, stands as the chief factor. The coal of the Western States is mined at a higher cost. But this coal could not possibly be interfered with by foreign coal. As has been seen in one of the previous chapters,

14

even that coal is not mined at a much higher labor cost than the mining cost in Europe, as seen from the above.

The American average cost per ton is but little different from that of North Staffordshire, England, taken from actual working accounts of collieries by myself. It is lower than in Prussia in the Government's mines, and by a few cents above the labor cost of the principal Westphalian mines. The greater output per miner alone explains the high earnings of Great Britain over Prussia, and of America over both. The average for Pennsylvania, from where all the clamor for protection comes, is away below all other countries of the world. The total labor cost per ton of an output of no less than $32\frac{1}{2}$ million gross tons is 66 cents (60 cents the ton of 2,000 pounds). To protect, then, 66 cents' worth of labor, a tariff of 75 cents is imposed. The grim irony of facts. Every four years a fierce battle is waged, and half the nation, to say the least, made to tremble at the fearful consequences if, by their neglect to vote in the right way, this wholly imaginary safeguard of their prosperity should be removed. The travesty could not be more complete.

With all the details of the case added, it will be seen not only is the English mining cost higher to the mine owner, but the miner himself receives more pay by the ton, as indicated, than the miner in America. The English miner receives pay for the slag, which the Pennsylvania miner does not get, but the colliery owner takes as a profit. The total mining cost in the Staffordshire potteries, including materials and expenses, and exclusive of royalty (amounting from 18 to 24 cents), was between $1.09 and $1.42 in 1885 (a year of depression and low prices). The total cost in Pennsylvania for the product of 1890 (the census year) was $85\frac{1}{2}$ cents. With the royalties added, coal costs the mine operator nearly double what it costs to the mine operator in Pennsylvania. In the Clearfield region the mining cost, formerly 52 cents, has been reduced by one-fourth by the introduction of machinery since 1886.* At Connellsville coal is mined at considerably less cost than in both these regions. The mines are deeper (about 8 feet deep). The miners are paid on a sliding scale, according to the selling price of coke. At the time of my inquiry coke was selling at $1.35 (in 1883 it had been selling as low as 90 cents). The labor for mining 100 bushels was 90 cents to $1.10 then (1887), and twenty-seven bushels to the ton, equal to about 25 to 30 cents a ton, or the long ton 27 to 33 cents. In Durham, the coking coal district of England, the labor cost of mining and putting into trucks a ton of coal was 51 cents at the time of great depression in the iron and coal industry in England.

---

* While the cost has been reduced since 1880, the earnings have risen in obedience to the principle formulated in Part I. Chapter II. The cost per mined ton in 1880 was $1.02½ against 85½ cents in 1890. The output per head, 504 tons gross, in 1880, rose to 617 tons (685 short tons) in 1890. The earnings, $337 for the year 1880, were $391 in the latter year, a most forcible demonstration of the fact that reduced cost, increased output, and higher earnings go hand in hand. The earnings of miners would be much higher in Pennsylvania but for the existence of the pernicious truck system. To this is due the practice of drawing a great many more miners to the mining settlements than would be needed under full employment. The truck stores are owned directly, or indirectly through some relative, by the superintendent or the owner of the mine. He naturally finds it to his interest to have the men always dependent on his truck store, always under advances, and seldom with cash in hand, which can only be done by having a surplus of labor about and the earnings at a minimum. This accounts for the short time worked by the Pennsylvania miner, which is not more than three-quarter time in the bituminous and not quite two-third time in anthracite coal. In the latter branch the evil effects on wages show themselves far more gravely on that account.

The English miner with full employment and the truck system entirely stamped out is therefore better off than his American competitor.

America's and England's Position.

The advantages of cost difference in coal are clearly on the side of America. In regard to the nature of the coal, the Pittsburgh fields and the Staffordshire and Lancashire fields for ordinary soft coal, Connellsville in America and Durham in England for coking coal, would stand on a fair basis for comparison. What operates against the British coal owner the heaviest, are the royalties which he has to pay to the owner of the soil.

In America, where mining lands are owned by the mining companies mostly, royalties are charged only in cases where the mines are leased. In Prussia no royalties are paid, or are at most only nominal. It is necessary to call special attention to this fact. In England, as well as here, great stress is laid by protectionists on the higher wage rate. Though the causes be different, it can invariably be shown that if the cost of production is a higher one, it is due to other causes than the labor cost. The royalties in the materials contained in one ton of pig iron in England run from 91 cents to $1.58. The cost of labor in these materials, roundly speaking, two tons of coal and two tons of ore, amounts to $4.46. This gives the Prussian ironmaker a premium of nearly 25 per cent. against England, which, if there were anything in the plea of higher labor cost on account of higher earnings per diem, would surely enable the Prussian ironmaker to flood England with cheap iron, especially as freights are in his favor. English railroads are corporate concerns, which "charge what the traffic is worth." Each line is independent by agreement with the other roads, and controls its own field. Inland charges are higher than transit charges for foreign shipment or from foreign ports to inland places. In Germany, the state owning the roads, much care is taken to foster commerce by low charges. All the southern ports of England can be supplied with iron from Prussia at lower transportation rates than from North of England furnaces. Yet but little of that takes place, although England has no duties to protect any of its industries.

From what has been said above, it is clear that what price differences do exist are due to extra capital charges and privileges enjoyed by the landed classes and railroad corporations, and not the higher pay of labor. Privileged classes always attend to covering themselves from the searching eye of public inquiry, by making their victims believe that it is to their benefit that obsolete conditions continue. The names are different; the game is the same. In America, away from the mines, coal is high because the outlet from the coal-mining district is controlled by transportation companies. They either charge extravagant rates, making the development of the whole section impossible, or giving otherwise cheaply-mined coal an inflated price; or they own the coal fields themselves, as in the anthracite coal fields, and put a price of transportation on the coal to pay dividends on enormously watered stock. It is only competition between the lines which reduces the price of coal at terminal points.

Iron Ore.

The same argument applies to iron mining. The cost of mining, the labor cost, does not differ much in America, England, and Prussia. The cost of mining ore in the rich ore fields from Virginia down to Alabama and in Pennsylvania is as low as in Europe, if not lower. The same may be said of the Lake Superior region. The only differences that do exist are again in transportation charges. Iron, in an industrial sense, is a rather varying quantity. The ores of different sections possess different qualities, and for different purposes different iron is required. For this reason, with all our great production of iron, we cannot do without some special qualities of foreign iron. Steel is now largely taking the place of puddled iron. The Bessemer process of steel making is principally employed in America. For this process few of our ores, except from Lake Superior, have so far been available. Large quantities are imported annually from Spain, North Africa, and Cuba—last year 646,000 tons at an average value of $2.25. To this has to be added the cost of transportation from these countries. In times of great demand ocean freights are high, at periods of depression correspondingly low; 5s. expressing about the one, and 10s. the other extreme of protection to the poor mine owners on Lake Superior by ocean transportation. But an additional cost of 75 cents per ton from tide water to the works in Eastern Pennsylvania must be reckoned, when ore is turned into iron and steel, which compete in the east with iron made of Lake Superior ore. These high transportation expenses explain the difference in the cost of iron making of a higher grade.

In parts of the country where the iron is situated near the coal fields, we can produce iron as cheaply as any country. That class of iron, however, cannot be used for Bessemer steel, though it is an excellent iron to use for the basic open-hearth process. Now, in spite of the high cost of imported ore, the mine owners exact a duty of 75 cents on each ton brought into this country, for the protection of labor. A ton of Bessemer ore without a duty on cannot be landed at tide water, freight paid, at less than $3.50 and up to $5. If carried only 80 miles inland, it has an additional 75 cents to pay. Its being carried to Pittsburgh is an impossibility. The Lake Superior ore owners have, therefore, a clear field for the whole country west of 100 miles from tide water, and still, with a mining cost for wages of not more than $1.40 a ton, as the average for the Lake Superior ores of Michigan, census of 1880, and $1.19 in the census year of 1890 *—in Pennsylvania the softer ores of the Cornwall hills are mined as low as 20 cents a ton in labor expense—they have the audacity of claiming 75 cents duty on imported ores for protection of American labor, as they say. As it is, the 55 per cent. ore cost from $4.50 to $5.50 a ton in the eastern district for Bessemer steel making, changing according to freight rates, etc.

Coke and Pig-Iron.

Coal being cheaper in the United States, the cost of coke follows in the same wake. Coke in Connellsville varies, put on board cars, from 90 cents a ton to $1.75. The basis of price on which the sliding scale of wages rests is $1.35. The cost of production is $1.17 on the statement of the masters, and on the men's basis, 99 cents, according to Mr. Joseph Weeks. Accepting the former calculation, which includes all additionals, this is $1.30 the gross ton.

---

* Here, also, we observe the same tendencies as pointed out in coal mining, reduced cost per ton and increased product per head, and higher annual earnings. Michigan furnishes now nearly one-half of all the iron ores of the United States, to wit : 5,856,000 tons out of a total of 14,-518,000 tons; and what is said of Michigan here in this connection, applies to other mining districts so far as comparisons can be traced.

	1880.	1890.
Labor per ton	$1.40	$1.19
Mined per head, tons	295	450
Annual earnings	$413	$535

In Durham I found the net cost, barely covering expenses, to be 7s. 6d., and the price put on board cars 8s., or $1.95.

This was at a time of very severe trade depression. Since then the price has made the most remarkable gyrations up to 32s., or $7.78, and commands now in the neighborhood of 12s. a ton.

Laid down at Middlesborough, the iron-making district nearest Durham, an additional 2s. 6d. (60 cents) for carriage has to be added, which would more than equalize the freightage from Connellsville to Pittsburgh.

This, then, exhausts the subdivisions contributing to pig-iron making. All these positions are lower than in England. The labor at the furnace, however, aggregates more in Pennsylvania. Most of it is rough labor, wheelbarrowing, and yard work. The rate of day wages would not so much affect the cost per ton, though about 40 per cent. above English rates ($1.58 in Pittsburgh, $1.25 at Bethlehem, Pa., against 87 cents in Staffordshire), but that there is a great deal more labor connected with furnace work in the Northern States. In England the Bessemer furnaces, at least, are so situated that the ocean steamer carrying the ore can be run almost within a stone's throw of the furnace. It is loaded on trucks and run on rails close to the furnace. In Middlesborough the mines are situated equally fortunately. In America, where the mines are separated, and either ocean or lake navigation has to bring the ore and coal to the furnace, storing of the ore and consequently a great deal of extra hauling are required. But still, with all these drawbacks, I did not find the actual labor cost in a ton of Bessemer pig-iron in Eastern Pennsylvania to exceed the English costs by more than 50 cents.

The comparative cost of labor of making a ton of Bessemer pig-iron, including the ore, the coal, and the coke, stands as follows, from actual working accounts:

Middlesborough, England.		Pittsburgh, America.	
2 tons of 50% ore, @ $1.46	...$2.92	1⅔ tons Lake Superior 60% ore, @ $1.19	$1.99
1¾ tons of coal, @ 51 cents	89	1¼ tons Connellsville, @33 cts.	50
		1/10 ton Pittsburgh, @ 79 cents.	08
1 ton of coking, including incidentals	48	1 ton coking	45
⅝ ton of limestone, @ 50 cents	20	Limestone	25
Furnace labor	79	Furnace labor	1.58
	$5.28		$4.85

The total labor cost is therefore less by 43 cents in a ton of pig-iron in America than in much-decried England and the Continent with their "pauper labor."

The cost of production, inclusive of extra charges to cover the economic quantity of natural disadvantage of distance from the ore, as in Bessemer iron, compared in 1887 for Bethlehem, Pa., was about $7 above the English price of 1888, though the total of labor did not foot up very differently. The causes of this have been explained as partially legitimate extra transportation charges, and partly due to inflation, caused by the boom in iron and steel during 1887 in America, and great depression in prices in England. At present the difference in the cost of production has nearly disappeared. The cost of coal and ore has become diminished in America, and coal and coke have advanced in England. The selling price of Bessemer iron is now $14, while in England it is now 48s., or $11.65. Under free trade the difference would be wiped out by freight and other charges. The development of the iron industry within recent years has been of such a nature that the vastly increased means of production and the improvements introduced will make this lower cost of production permanent. The high duties, however, do the useful service of enabling the producer to make the large extra profit between the full duty charge and his low cost, whenever opportunity favors him.

Steel Rail Making.

Cheap iron makes cheap rails. The cost in the rail mill is a very small item now under conditious demonstrated in Part I. Chapter VIII.

At the time of my inquiry, trade and prices in rails being at their highest since 1881, as noted above, and English trade and prices at their lowest, I found the labor cost in England and America to be about the same. But wages have been raised twice in that year, 10 per cent. each time, in America, while in England they were at their lowest. At the present time the labor is lower in America by nearly 20 per cent. ; that is to say, a rail which costs at Darlington, in one of the best English mills, 3.07 cents in labor, is turned out at about $2.50 from one of our well-equipped rail mills.

The difference in 1888 stood as per my report to the State Department as follows:

COST OF PRODUCTION OF ONE TON OF BESSEMER RAILS.

England.		Eastern Pennsylvania.	
1$\frac{1}{10}$ tons pig-iron, @ $10.93.	$12.03	1 ton pig-iron.......	$18.00
1$\frac{1}{2}$ cwt. spiegeleisen, @ 97c..	1.44	3 cwt. spiegeleisen...	4.00
14 cwt. coal, @ $1.85......	1.26	Fuel..............	2.00
Labor.................	3.07	Labor............ .	3.04
	$17.80		$27.04

To-day, taking iron at the market price, though it must not be forgotten that the rail mills make their own iron (and, therefore, an additional profit), the cost comparison stands as follows:

THE ECONOMY OF HIGH WAGES. 219

COST COMPARISON ON PRESENT BASIS OF IRON.

England.
1 1/10 tons pig-iron, @ $11.65.$12.81
1 1/4 cwt. spiegeleisen........ 1.44
Fuel...................... 1.45
Labor.................... 3.07

$18.77

America.
1 ton.............. $14.00
3 cwt. spiegeleisen... 4.00
Fuel. 2.00
Labor.......$2.50 to 3.00

$23.00*

To sum up, I subjoin in parallel columns:

COST OF LABOR CONTAINED IN A TON OF BESSEMER STEEL RAILS AND THE MATERIALS ENTERING INTO IT.

In England.
Pig-iron per ton....$0.73 to $0.97
Bessemer rails....... 3.07
Coal mining, Staffordshire............ 0.79
Coal mining, Durham 0.51
Coking, Durham ... 0.24
Ore mining, Staffordshire, 50 per ct. ore. 1.46
Ore mining, Cleveland, 33 per ct. ore. 0.30

In America.
Eastern Pennsylvania.......$1.25
"   " $2.50 to 3.04
Average   " 0.66
Pittsburgh.................. 0.79
Clearfield.................. 0.50
Connellsville............... 0.33
" 0.32
Lake Superior, 55 to 65 per ct. 1.19

Cornwall ore, Pennsylvania.. 0.19

The difference in the cost of a ton of Bessemer rails is $4; the difference in the selling price, however, is $10; the price of rails in America being $30, and in England £4 2s., or $20. A profit of $7 and above is realized by the American steel-rail maker at a time when the English maker has to be satisfied with $1. Under the present prices in iron and steel the steel-rail combination secures a profit of three times

---

* On the basis employed in the English mills, 1 1/10 tons of iron and 1 1/4 cwt. of spiegeleisen and labor taken at full rate of $3 a ton, the cost stands : Iron, $15.40 ; spiegeleisen, $2 ; fuel, $2 ; labor, $2.50 ; total, $22.40. The additional weight of iron going into the furnace covers rail-ends and scraps. They have a value, however, and cover the additional expense, or whatever extra charge there may be.

the amount paid to all the labor employed. A steel mill employing 1,048 men and turning out 4,500 tons a week, and having a pay roll of $13,680 (as taken from the amounts kindly given to me by a rail mill in 1888), would in a year produce 225,000 tons and pay out $684,000 in wages, but make a profit, on present computation, of fully $1,680,000. But with all this enormous profit guaranteed by act of legislation, at the present rates the outlay for wages would now not be more than about $575,000 (about $2.50 a ton).

This, however, by no means exhausts the golden effects of protection to the protected enterprise. The usefulness of the tariff was seen again, after the golden shower of 1880, in its fullness in the time of brisk demand in 1887. The selling price of rails had fallen in 1886 to $28, but the demand springing up in 1887 raised the price to $40, and it averaged for the year $35. To a single concern turning out 500,000 tons a year, this extra profit guaranteed by the tariff is equal to a bonus of from $2,500,000 to $3,000,000 above the ordinary profits at the $30 price. Should the benevolent and patriotic mill owner not urge the maintenance of this blessing to the American workman—urge it with intense eloquence and energetic zeal?

The combination of rail mills has it in hand to raise the price at will to any height within the tariff limit. While in slack times the prices are, as now, below the foreign duty paid price, the full price is always sure to follow in the wake of an increasing demand. Combinations and trusts are the logical consequences of protective legislation.

The laborer's share in the value of the product, as has been shown by an abundance of proof, is less in the United States than in England and on the Continent.

If there are any advantages derived from protective tariffs, the laborers engaged in mining, coke-burning, iron and steel making certainly do not receive a particle out of the fund contributed by the nation, in the erroneous belief that it is required for the laborer's protection against the "pauperized" European labor.

The two million odd tons of rails annually manufactured give the combination of manufacturers a profit of $15,000,000, three times the wages paid to the ten thousand men engaged in turning them out. "Cultivated fruit is not for the peasant to eat," said the Polish nobleman in uprooting the trees.* The present strikes against wage reductions in the steel mills show very plainly the meaning of a protective tariff to the workingman.

---

* See page 117.

CHAPTER IV.

The Injury of Protection to Industry.—The Advantages America reaps from Superior Methods and Low Labor Cost frustrated by Protection.—Comparisons which are beyond Controversion.—Fighting over the Shell long after the Substance is gone.

In no other branch of industry is the effect of high wages in reducing cost of production shown so plainly as in all forms of finished iron and steel. The genius of the nation shows here to the best advantage. Labor saving by invention is enhanced by the best constituted help of all times and countries congregating under our factory and workshop roofs. The earnings are higher, the labor results cheaper than in other industrial pursuits, generally speaking.

But in no other industrial line has tariff protection become so plainly tariff oppression as in manufactures of metals in the finished form.

If, as a measure of protection to labor, the tariff has grown out of all proportion to the cost of production in all forms of crude iron and steel, which, barring the additional transportation charges on account of geographical disadvantages, can be produced cheaper than in Europe, its application to finished forms becomes decidedly a most harmful hindrance to full industrial development.

It is certainly one of the most forcible objections raised against the protective system, that it is unjust to the consumer to make him pay a high bounty to the American producer, so as to balance the favor nature dispensed to his foreign competitor and withheld from him. Yet, severely as it bears on the consumer, the system is not less burdensome to the American producer, to whom, in one form or another, these crude and unfinished forms of iron and steel serve as material for remanufacture.

If it is just to put a duty on iron ore and on pig-iron because of the differences in the cost at which Lake Superior ore can be placed at Pittsburgh, and the price at which foreign ore and foreign iron can be landed at Eastern ports, it is certainly a very unjust proceeding against the Eastern manufacturer. It, virtually, is a prohibition against manufacturing crude forms of iron in the Eastern States, and makes them tributary dependencies of the Pennsylvania iron lords. A tariff on these crude bulky materials—coal included—is tantamount to a confiscation of the natural advantages of situation. But this is practically the purpose of protecting the raw material, to balance nature's gifts by piling dead weight on those able to make freest use of them. Location on the seaboard is an advantage, so it must be guarded against by discriminating duties, lest the markets for Lake ore, Pennsylvania coal and pig-iron should become impaired.

The tariff is made a sectional measure, which adds not a little of the gall of injustice to the wormwood of vexatiousness. With the exception of puddled iron, where the labor cost is about $5 over the English cost (being all hand labor), the labor does not differ materially from foreign cost. Why, then, not give New England, New York, and Eastern Pennsylvania the same facilities? Free ore, coal, and iron would enable the Eastern States to make their own iron and steel and give them cheap materials for their hardware, machinery, and mill work. Free pig-iron would take from Pittsburgh only the Eastern trade, and leave to the present iron kings all the field from Harrisburg west. What a start this would give to the iron and kindred industries of the Eastern States can be estimated when we examine the positions these industries have made for themselves in the world's markets even handicapped as they are by the tariff.

Manufacturers' Tools and Machinery.

If one has made it an object to examine the tools and other automatic machinery and the working methods in the metal and machine industries of this country, and has made parallel observations in Europe, he can hardly help speaking in words of admiration of the genius of our people, who, impelled by causes already discussed, have worked from the most difficult beginnings into fields never trodden before, where a tariff could hinder, but never could help. I will take the reader to a few of these industries, where machinery works and men or boys only guide or feed; where machinery, as a porter taking me through a factory fitly said, "can do all but speak."

The old and the new cannot be more fitly contrasted. While here the fittest only survives in the struggle, in the old it is hard to shake off the tenacious hold of the unfittest upon the industries it controls.

When I speak of the "survival of the unfittest" in the methods of manufacture, I do not refer to the Hebrides, or Orkneys, Donegal in Ireland, or some mountain districts in Germany, but to England and to the very heart of this most progressive of all manufacturing nations of Europe. Some years ago, the present Superintendent of the Census, Robert P. Porter, went about to collect information for the New York *Tribune*. I remember the black picture he unrolled of the pitiable condition of the nail makers of South Staffordshire and Worcestershire, commonly called "the black country." He was wise enough not to mention the working methods or the output, so different from American conditions. A statement of such facts would have entirely frustrated the object of his mission, which was, to impress the American public with the danger of degenerating into similar conditions if they reduced their high tariff. His picture was not by any means overdrawn. But without the application of the other part alluded to—well—"A half truth is worse than a lie."

Work there is not limited by the factory act, as it is scattered all over a large district—entirely a house industry. Old and young, husbands, wives, and daughters, all work at nail making from four or five in the morning until late at night. Tea and bread constitute almost exclusively their diet. An expert nailer, working a whole week, would not earn more than 12s.; man and wife working together not above 16s. From this pittance about 2s. would have to be deducted for firing. Rivet makers earn better wages, about 20s. a week, because, on account of the heavy work, women have not encroached upon this branch. Exhausting as the working methods are, they cannot give very great results in an age in which machinery, more and more perfected, automatic machinery even, is encroaching constantly upon the domain of hand labor. The principal tool is the so-called "Oliver." It is a sort of spring-tilt hammer, operated by the foot of the worker, mostly of home construction. It is a clumsy and heavy instrument, trying the strength of the worker to the utmost extent. Besides this, the nailer uses a hand hammer in addition to the blowing of bellows. As considerable force is required in the use of the "Oliver," the effect upon the woman's health is very injurious. But in spite of the very pitiable wages, women have grown so accustomed to looking on this sort of work as their allotted task, that, even where the husbands work at other trades and earn fairly good wages, the wives go on as nailers or chain-makers. As a consequence, the women are mostly flat-chested, pale, and thin, and home life is at the lowest ebb. Nails are paid for by the bundle, which means 56 pounds of iron. Of ordinary nails, two bundles of the larger size constitute a good male nailer's day's work; of the smaller sizes, proportionately less. For horseshoe nails, now also made by machinery, the price paid is 2s. per 1,000, which here means 1,200. Six thousand is a good week's work. Rivets are paid for at the rate of 5s. 6d. a hundredweight, and a half hundredweight is considered a good day's work. Spikes 4½ inches by ⅓ inch, are 1s. 6d.; 5 by ⅜ inch, 1s. 3d. a bundle. That working by such antiquated methods cannot produce better results is not so much a matter of surprise as the fact, that it still gives employment to from 15,000 to 20,000 people—a clear proof that old trade habits are not so easily superseded as many imagine.* How this compares with American methods, output, earnings, and labor cost, will be seen from a few parallel facts. Nail making, as well as rivet making, spike making, and even chain making, also a considerable product of the "black country" in England, are in this country carried on by machinery. One nailer can attend three machines. The output of ten-penny nails is 18 kegs per machine a day, so that three machines turn out 54 kegs a day. The list price per keg is 16 cents, or one-half the English cost. The English nailer earns from 10s. to 12s. a week. If helped by a lad, the combined earnings do not exceed 16s., or $3.87. An American nailer, employed in a Pittsburgh

---

* See J. Schoenhof, "Destructive Influence of the Tariff," G. P. Putnam's Sons (1883), for parallel facts from the nail makers in the Taunus district in Germany.

nail mill, gave me $5 a day as a fair average of a nailer's earnings, and $1.50 for the feeder, or some $30 a week for the nailer alone. But we have here an output of over two tons and a half against barely two hundredweight in England. Twenty times the output against ten times the wages still leaves a comfortable margin of 100 per cent. in favor of the new method. Of late steel nails have been largely taking the place of wrought-iron nails. The price is somewhat lower even than that of the latter.

Spikes 5 inches and below by $\frac{3}{8}$ inch, per keg of 200 lbs., 40½ cents, against English, 1s. 6d. per bundle, or 6s., or $1.46 the two hundredweight; 5 by $\frac{5}{8}$ inch American, 22½ cents per keg, against 1s. 3d. per bundle, or 5s., or $1.21½ per two hundredweight in England.

A rivet-making machine which I saw in operation not long ago would turn out easily from one and a half to two tons of rivets a day, and required one machine tender and a heater. They got between them $5 a day, but at not one-fifth the English labor cost, though six times the wages. Still, in a recent speech, the author of the last tariff act pointed, "with pride" I presume, to the fact that the famous act to which he gave his name, reduced the duties on iron and steel nails and spikes from 1½ cents a pound to 1 cent, the heavier grades of the wire nails from 4 to 2 cents. Where has Mr. McKinley been while all these revolutions in the economy of production were wrought—revolutions which would give America the world's trade, were the low cost of its labor not neutralized by such measures as the McKinley act?

Screws, pins, etc., are made automatically. A wire rod, or a coil of wire, is put into the machine, which performs a number of operations, as the results of which the finished screws drop into a receiving bag, and the finished pins are fastened on the papers. An attempt at protection of labor of this kind, aided by the quickest and most inventive brains, is like helping the speed of a race-horse by tying cannon balls to its legs.

Cutlery.

Cutlery of American make is almost entirely of a heavy character, very serviceable for farm and country use, somewhat clumsy, but only the more appropriate for the purposes it is put to. Machinery is used for almost every part. Our plated table-knives do not cut, it is true, as they are neither ground nor polished, nor are they a thing of beauty when the plating has worn off; but, being of one piece of iron, give everybody a ready impression that very little hand labor, aside from the casting, has been expended on them. American cutlery has never been interfered with by foreign importations. It even finds a ready sale abroad. Foreign cutlery is of an entirely different character. It is essentially hand-made. In Germany, Westphalia is the chief seat of an industry which sends the different parts far out into the country districts from two or three centres. The smith-work, the grinding, the finishing, may be done miles away from the other. The smiths, grinders, finishers are all small masters, supplying their own shops, fuel, and tools.

The work of the so-called manufacturer is confined to paying the different labor items as the work is delivered in its various stages, and to packing up and shipping the finished articles, the same as the Lyons and Crefeld manufacturers in silks, most of the Chemnitz manufacturers in hosiery, etc. To Sheffield, England, excellence more than cheapness has given its world-wide reputation. Even there, though we find large factories, most of the work is distributed in small shops. But, small shop or factory, the working is pretty nearly the same kind of hand-work, skill and experience giving to the steel that excellent temper and finish which make a Sheffield blade, after many years of use, retain its keenness. As we have nothing to fear for our cutlery, and cannot easily supplant foreign cutlery for the reasons stated, one ought to have supposed 35 per cent. to be a sufficiently high tariff tax. But no; probably to satisfy a few greedy individuals who are looking out for the great possibilities in store, the old expedient is tried of remedying lack of skill and experience by an additional infusion of tariff taxes. Henceforth anybody who wants a serviceable pocket knife or razor has to pay an additional specific duty which will more than double the old rate. On table knives, forks, and all other knives, like plumbers', "painters' palette, and artists' knives" (to encourage art and the arts), the addition will be at least one-half the old rate of duty.

Arms, Ammunition, Machinery.

Whenever machinery can be set to work to turn many parts into a completed article ready for use, no competition need be feared. The world moves slowly on the other side of the Atlantic. In nothing is this better shown than in highly composite articles, where frequently hundreds of small parts form a very complicated mechanism.

Let us take, for instance, the manufacture of rifles. What a gigantic plant to bring out the best results! What a variety of machinery is here required! One of the principal and most successful firms, employing 1,400 work people (including a large proportion of girls and women employed in the cartridge department), with a weekly pay roll of from $12,000 to $14,000, has no less than 6,000 machines on its premises used in the manufacture of ammunition and firearms. Wages are a small consideration, when, as is the case of most automatic machinery, three or four machines are tended by one man. This firm finds it unprofitable to work for governments on account of the precariousness of work, the risks, and the expense connected with obtaining contracts. It finds it the same with the home government. The firm made application some time ago for a contract to the United States government, under great expense, had to make extra tools, etc., to suit the specifications, and had 300 stands ordered. Nothing further was ever heard from there. They have a general and widely-distributed trade, and have to cater to taste and changing fashions.

They find it profitable to lay out $20,000 at a time for tool machines for a special piece of work required by a change of pattern or style. The number of hands a rifle has to go through, and the pieces of machinery required, can be estimated from the fact that the lock alone goes through 131 different operations. A fine magazine rifle is sold at retail at $18, with a discount to the trade.* Under no other system of work and organization could such a result be reached. As these goods go all over the world, it is evident that high-priced labor does not stand in the way of the great achievement of underselling the labor of lower-wage countries in their own domains, but directly leads to it. Cartridges are made in a like manner; *i. e.*, with special machinery for each separate part of work. In this department mostly girls are employed. Even the wads are made, felt-covered, cut, and oiled by machinery. The same system of working and an equally high average of wages, as com-

---

* Trade discounts are always pretty high. The expense for advertising, etc., are all included, and the list prices are in no possible way a criterion to estimate the cost on, or even the price netted to the manufacturer.

pared with other industries employing an equally great percentage of female labor, is found in the clock and watch industry of New England.

But machine making itself is now carried on mostly by self-acting machinery, and several pieces require chiefly the eye and very little the hand of one attendant. One is surprised, in going through the vast workshops, to see so few people about, so much work turned out, and still so many hundreds on the pay roll. This impression is especially strong in going through the rifle company's works as well as through the works of a concern engaged in making tool-machines for machine makers, and instruments of precision for measuring gauges, screw-threads, etc. It can be well understood of what perfection and exactness this work has to be. Yet, though they employ some seven hundred men, five or six machines tended by one man was nothing unusual.

Europe's Methods Different.

This, the American system, stands still in remarkable contrast with Europe. I have pointed out in my report on "Industrial Education in France" how the Government as well as industrials exert themselves to keep the people to the old hand method. The technical and trade schools have all the same end in view, to give the new generation the same opportunity of perfecting itself in hand work. Excellent as it may be from their standpoint and traditional development, yet it must be seen that it is not likely that our metal and machine industries could be seriously pressed by competition trained under such diametrically opposed views.

But more than anywhere else, I found proof of this in

Germany, at the very heart of industrial push, Berlin. The Ludwig Loewe-Company have been made an object of special mention in the Reichstag, as they pay fully double the wages ruling in the trade. Ludwig Loewe, the founder, had lived in America and studied the system described above. On his return to Germany he established a small-arms and machine factory. The first machinery he employed for fitting up on the American plan he procured from the firm whose works are mentioned above, but now his company make all their own tools. This I heard independently from both parties. Messrs. Loewe told me it pays them well to adhere to this plan. They have none but picked men, and with the system borrowed from America the day wages are not such a consideration as the output and the reliability of their help. This fully proves how slowly the world follows in our footsteps. The reason is plain: it requires American conditions, not American example alone, to bring the world to the same high standard of production and productiveness.

But why demonstrate further? Handicapped as America is by high-priced iron and fuel, she exports in manufactures of iron, hardware, cutlery, mill work, machinery, and implements, agricultural machinery and cars, 65 per cent. more than Germany, and about 25 per cent. of England's exports in corresponding articles.

The positions are:

Exports of England, 1890.....................$150,000,000
Exports of America, 1890..................... 37,000,000
Exports of Germany, 1890..................... 22,000,000

What better proof can there be that labor and capital are discriminated against to favor a few noisy and domineering interests? The higher cost of raw materials on account of "protection" is an impediment to extension of trade.

The duty on tin plate raised from 1 cent to $2\frac{1}{5}$ cents shows more than any other the unpardonable ignorance of the lawmakers, and their indifference to the rights of the producer of finished articles, as well as of the consumer. Tin is an article that is not manufactured in America and cannot be manufactured in this country even under the new rate of duty, because the conditions are absent in America which are so abundant in Wales—hand labor, male and female, which for generations has brought down hereditary skill. After a year's operation of the new tariff it has been made clear by experience that, unless at rates far more exorbitant than the new duty, tin plates cannot be manufactured for commercial purposes in America against Wales, which, by long traditional development, has acquired a monopoly of the world's trade. The attempt of Germany is not considered successful in this line. It has still to depend on Wales for its supply. In view of these facts, which ought not to have been unknown to the makers of this law, the act of saddling the people with an additional eight millions of taxes on their tin plate appears as sheer madness.*

---

* The high rates of duty put on tin plate seem to have frightened the producers in Wales. The heavy falling off in their trade, after the new act had gone into operation, gave support to their fear that the business was going to be diverted from them. They were reported to be active in making Australia and Argentina rivals of the United States in the canning industry. If they succeed, the American farmer will have another illustration, added to the many he has already received, how he has his markets stolen away from him by the protective tariff. The necessity for such action, however, will become less urgent to the English merchant and the Welsh manufacturers when they see the real nature of the tin plate industry created by the McKinley act. The importations were very heavy in anticipation before, and became, of course, correspondingly light after the act took effect. But now, over a year that the act has come in force on tin plate, the shipments are as heavy as ever.

CHAPTER V.

The Textile Industries.—Labor's Higher Reward in America due entirely to Greater Exertion.—Greater Output and Lower Labor Cost in Cotton Manufacture.—The Tariff increases Profit Rates but reduces Wages.—Print Cloth in Evidence.—Senators' Pettifogging Methods to stifle Results of Investigations.

THE woven fabrics used by every country under the old dispensation of things had almost entirely been produced by the people themselves. Since steam has given such development to manufacturing, with the help of machinery, and to transportation, many inroads have been made and much displacement of labor used to the old methods has been going on. A *priori* reasoning would lead to the belief that nations of the highest potentiality in manufacturing development, especially in lines where machinery can be kept running constantly on the same goods, as in plain cotton goods, would produce the cheapest fabrics and command the trade of less advanced countries, did not general statistical knowledge of the facts of trade support these rational conclusions.

The political economists of protectionism in America, however, have persuaded a good percentage of otherwise acute reasoners, that a curved line is shorter than a straight one, and it is for this that so much work had to be undertaken to set the people right again. An inquiry into the cost of production of industrial articles here and abroad would certainly furnish the only reliable premises to build upon. I selected print cloth in this instance, and for the following reasons: It is made in America of the finer count of yarn than the bulk of our cotton fabrics (28 warp by 36 weft). If the spinning cost in these numbers does not exceed the foreign labor expense, the test will then certainly cover fully nine-tenths of American spinning, which in the low numbers is admittedly cheaper than in England, the cheapest spinning country of Europe.

Print cloth is easily described and found in different countries, as representing the same goods under the same formula—28 inches wide, 64 by 64 threads to the square inch, against 28 inches wide, 16 by 16 threads to the quarter inch, in England, which means the same thing.

In America it is made in mills which run entirely on this one article, and hence produced under the most favorable circumstances. This is true, more or less, of all our cotton manufacturing. It is different in England, where mills are engaged on a great variety of goods. The spinning is done separately, with very few exceptions. Generally the weaving alone is considered to be legitimately called cotton manufacturing. Going through a mill at Salford, near Manchester, which spins its own yarn and consumes weekly about 150,000 pounds of cotton, running 3,100 looms on twills and fancy cottons mostly, I found not twenty looms employed on the same article. The variety of their fabrics was something amazing to one accustomed to American methods. In print cloth this is different. I found Burnley, in Northeast Lancashire, to run exclusively on print cloth. As the weaving of print cloth gives so much greater output per hand through the greater number of looms worked in America than in England, the proof is certainly equally conclusive for the heavier yarn fabrics.

Relative Positions of England and America.

I found the relative positions to be as follows: American print cloth is made, as said before, of 28 warp by 36 to 38 weft yarn, while the English make it officially of 32 by 40 to 42 weft, but in reality the clothmakers take from three to four numbers finer. This gives them at the outset a very great advantage. A pound of yarn is thereby made to give a greater quantity of yards, and a saving of cotton plus the spinning cost is effected, which very largely outweighs the advantage we have in the cheaper labor cost of turning a pound of cotton yarn into seven yards of print cloth, the standard American weight. I had been told by an American manufacturer of print cloth that he knew that his spinning was cheaper than the English, and that if, as he said, our weaving was cheaper, he could not understand why he could not export to England. He had tried it by sending goods over to England, but had not found it a success. The English practice above described offers a sufficient explanation. But to make doubly sure, to have a demonstration of facts which could not be contradicted by any "ifs," I bought a piece of print cloth of the width and count mentioned above, and found it to measure exactly nine yards to the pound. A saving of two-ninths in the weight of the yarn is, therefore, at the start carried to the credit of the English, as competitors with American manufacturers. We certainly cannot become successful exporters of American cotton goods if we neglect the study of such simple lessons, the exact analysis of the goods of our successful competitors, the purveyors of the markets we hanker after. A little more alertness of our manufacturers and shippers would be of some use in the endeavor to extend our markets in cotton goods, which even Mr.

Blaine's reciprocity treaties cannot prevent from making progress in a backward direction.

Protectionism, chiefly concerned in defending a home market against intrusion, dulls the intellect of all who come under its baneful influence. The safe possession of neutral markets is thereby guaranteed to all those who have emancipated themselves, and are thereby able to strike out for themselves, unaided by laws and untrammeled by impertinent restrictions.

Print Cloth. The Comparative Cost and Rate of Wages.

In England the wage rates are by no means universal in the same line of industry, and it is by no means an easy matter to get to the bottom of things. One section pays differently and has different trade rulings from another, even in so plain a thing as cotton spinning. Still, the rates paid for the counts of yarn given below cannot vary much from those paid elsewhere in England. I obtained them from a mill at Rochdale for mule spinning, and will set them side by side with those paid in America, according to the price list of the Mule Spinners' Trade Union at Fall River:

WAGE RATES TO MULE SPINNERS.
(Per 100 Pounds.)

No. of Yarn.	Fall River.	Rochdale.
20	$0.45	$0.50
28	0.64	0.61
32	0.72	0.73¾
40	0.98	1.00
46	1.14	1.12
50	1.29	1.35

In the lower numbers the American rates are below the English; in the medium numbers they approximate, and only in the numbers above sixty the English begin to show a progressively increasing difference in their favor. Mule spinning is all male labor. Throstle spinning is done by girls; but while in England one girl attends four sides of 144 spindles, in America one girl supervises as many as eight sides of 120 spindles each, 576 spindles against 960 spindles.* Doubtless, in consideration of these facts, which must have found their way in some yet unexplained manner into the Ways and Means Committee room, the tariff on cotton yarns, "whether single, or advanced by grouping or twisting two or more single yarns together, except spool thread," was amended by reducing the rate of yarn in one instance from 23 to 20 cents a pound; but in order not to be found guilty of getting too near the free-trade heresy they increased the duty of yarns costing not less than 25 cents and not more than 40 cents a pound, and yarns costing not less than 50 cents and not more than 60 cents a pound, each three cents a pound. If this is not trifling with the industrial demand for lower taxes, then language must invent other terms.

English yarns, especially warp yarns, are superior to American yarns, being far more even and better twisted. They are preferred for manufacturing purposes on this

---

* The daily earnings in the leading branches taken from mills accounts I found to be:

	SWITZERLAND AND GERMANY.	ENGLAND. Rochdale and Salford.	AMERICA. Lowell and Fall River.
	Cents.	Cents.	Cents.
Mule spinners	57 to 60	125 to 168	150
Helpers	..	64 to 72	60 (boys.)
Spinners (women)	48	50	84
Carding (women)	38	48 to 71	..
Drawing	38	60 to 68	..
Weavers	44 to 55 [1]	65 to 83 [2]	90 to 120 [3]

Fine yarn spinners at Bolton earn 50 shillings a week, equal to $2 a day. The day wages stand in an inverse ratio to the cost of production.

---

[1] 2 to 3 looms.   [2] 3 and 4 looms respectively.   [3] 6 and 8 looms.

account. Even in the lower numbers, which cost no more to produce than English yarns, we import considerable quantities, and pay a duty of 50 per cent. In mixed goods of silk and cotton this is not a light burden, but where nobody objected, except the consumer, the framers of this odious law did not seem to consider it their duty to reduce rates even where a necessity for the continuance of duties had long ceased to exist.

While in the spinning of lower numbers of yarn we possess advantages, we possess them to a still greater degree in the weaving. In England four looms is the most a single weaver would tend. Some tend six looms, but then they invariably have the help of a boy. In Switzerland and Germany two is the rule, and exceptionally three, while in America four looms is the lower and eight looms the higher limit. I found in the Lowell mills six and three-quarters to be the average tended by one weaver.

The average earnings per loom in Burnley are 5s. 3d., or $1.25. This gives $3.75 to a three-loom weaver and $5 to a four-loom weaver. "A guinea a week is considered very good wages for good weavers." The rate of pay per 100 yards was 51 cents, and the output of a four-loom weaver was stated to me to be 980 yards. In Lowell the rate of speed is slower, but the average of six-loom weavers in one mill I found to be 1,270 yards, and in another mill 1,350 yards. But in Lowell the pay per cut of 50 yards is 20 cents, per 100 yards 40 cents. A six-loom weaver would average $5.08 in one mill and $5.40 in the other mill. Hence a six-loom weaver in America is not much better situated than a four-loom weaver in England. Eight-loom weavers, of course, earn correspondingly higher wages, from $6.40 to $7.30, according to the above ratio.

In both instances I took my data from mill accounts.

Making allowance for all of these differences, I found the

COST OF MANUFACTURING A POUND OF PRINT CLOTH:

SPINNING COST PER POUND OF YARN.

	Average No. 37¼. Lancashire.	Average No. 32¼. Lowell.
Total wages................................	1.708	1.992
Power and taxes........................	.418	.298
Supplies....................................	.240	.240
Repairs and depreciation.............	.6	.475
Interest on loan, etc...................	.36	
Carriage...................................	.18	
Expense, etc..............................		.150
Addition...................................		.000
	3.506	3.205

WEAVING COST PER SEVEN YARDS TO THE POUND.

Weavers' wages........................	3.57	2.8
Dressing or sizing.....................	.479	.469
Beaming, twisting, winding, etc....	.753	.428
Extra board.............................		.039
Labor.....................................	4.802	3.736
Supplies and expense................	1.38	1.335
	6.182	5.071

OR A TOTAL COST PER POUND OF FINISHED GOODS.

Labor cost of spinning...............	1.708	1.992
Labor cost of weaving................	4.802	3.736
Cost of supplies and other mill charges....	3.175	2.823
	9.685	8.551

We have here a credit of 1.134 mostly due to cheaper labor cost, against which stands a credit of two-ninths pound of yarn in the English cost of seven yards of print cloth. With cotton in England (inclusive of waste) at 11.8 cents, this makes a difference of 3.258 cents, and, deducting cheaper

American cost of 1.134 cents, still leaves a balance of 2.124 cents in each seven yards of American cloth; or, allowing for the difference in the cost of cotton on account of freight to Liverpool of, say, half a cent, about $1\frac{5}{8}$ to $1\frac{3}{4}$ cents.

The American cloth stood (cotton and waste, 10.695 cents) at 19.246 cents a pound, or 2.766 per yard, which yard the Englishman is enabled to sell at about a quarter of a cent less to our "natural customers" by giving them a finer cloth. Though with less cotton and more sizing, it seems to be taken by them willingly in spite of our convincing one another of its unwholesomeness and inferiority as to "intrinsic quality." It is not necessary to deal seriatim with Germany and Switzerland. The fact that the Mulhouse and Elberfeld printers use English print cloth for exportation, in which case they get the import duty refunded, does of itself prove conclusively that they cannot produce as cheaply as England, and far less America, without introducing direct and detailed evidence.

That this applies with equal force to heavier cotton fabrics, drills, sheeting, etc., is seen from another comparison touching a 4-4 sheeting. My sample represented goods counting 48 by 40 threads to the inch, and measuring 2.90 yards to the pound. For these our labor cost for weaving, inclusive of warping and beaming, etc., comes to 1.186 cents per pound, which is .405 cent a yard. English goods of the same count are paid at the rate of 1s. 5d. for weaving a piece of 80 yards, and 2s. 3d. for beaming and warping 720 yards of warp, or about 3d. for the 80-yard piece—total 1s. 8d., or 40 cents, the 80 yards, which is .5 cent against .405 cent in America. Still, although cotton is about $\frac{1}{2}$ cent higher on account of ocean freight, the English goods, with a finer yarn, but more dressing, were a shade lower in price than my American samples.

It must be admitted that, no matter how we may be affected as exporters by these important facts, the ability of the United States to exclude from its own shores foreign competition in cotton goods, even if there were no tariff protection whatever, cannot be denied. The higher duties are maintained, and are of great use in times of great demand. Then prices are put up. For instance, in print cloth, which when I made my investigation sold at 3 cents to $3\frac{1}{4}$ cents per yard, and later on, under a brisk demand, at 4 cents a yard, cotton being not more per pound. This gave a very wide margin of profit, and showed that a high tariff is not a thing to be despised, even if not required for the protection of labor, which, per work done, gets less than any other labor the world over. But these violent changes in prices, while competing nations keep their prices stable, are great inconvenience in our efforts to become extensive exporters of cotton goods. Many a time had I to hear English merchants make the remark that it was of little use to buy American goods: that no sooner was there an active trade in the United States than the prices were raised so high that the goods could not be used any more. This is an additional hint to those who cannot see that it requires something besides reciprocity treaties to extend foreign trade in cotton fabrics.

Republican Contradiction.

I do not know why such efforts should have been made to contradict my statements, in my official reports to the State Department, bearing on the cost of manufacturing here and in England, except that the proof of labor being paid less per piece or pound than in the Old World was damaging to the claim, that a high rate of duty was required to protect American labor. Facts need no defense. They stand on their own merits. But on the other hand, broad denials and "refutations" on the Senate floor by such authorities, for instance, as ex-Senator Chace, a cotton manufacturer himself, could not fail to make an impression, and might throw doubts upon the accuracy of the statements, which, if correct, must be of vital importance, not alone in the tariff issue, but in their applicability to the labor question and the whole range of social and economic dynamics.

But to show the nature of this "refutation" is also to show its futility, and is, perhaps, the strongest indorsement of the accuracy of these reports. On this account it will serve a public purpose to call attention to it. In answer to Senator Gray of Delaware, who referred to my reports to the State Department, Senator Aldrich said:

"If the Senate will turn to the speech made by my late colleague, Mr. Chace, in this body in the last Congress, he will find the statements of Mr. Schoenhof taken up seriatim, and shown by figures and facts within his knowledge to be inaccurate."

The speech referred to is contained in the *Congressional Record*, vol. 20, Part II., page 1,041. A brief statement will, therefore, suffice, as any one wishing to obtain the full facts can get them by reading over those pages. From the above sentence reported in the papers I had expected to learn terrible things about my "inaccuracy," and it turned out to be as follows: My report stated that No. 33 yarn was paid for in spinners' wages at the rate of 75 cents a pound, No. 37 at 84 cents, and No. 39 at 93 cents a pound, while, as Senator Chace correctly stated, the whole pound of yarn, No. 40, is sold at 18 cents. But he did not quote my statement immediately following, that the whole labor expense for turning a pound of cotton into yarn (average No. 33) is not more than 1.992 cents.

The whole difficulty arose from the omission of decimal points. The figures ought to have read, ".75, .84, and .93," etc. Senator Vance called the attention of Senator Chace to this fact, but quickly the senator from Rhode Island pointed to other figures equally damning. I will give the senator's words. "He [Schoenhof] says: 'They spin 1,792 pounds at $540, which is equal only to $\frac{3}{10}$ cent a pound.' I have figured it all sorts of ways, but I cannot figure it out," etc. Now, I had given the explanation myself in the very sentence quoted; namely, that 1,792 pounds at $\frac{3}{10}$ cent equals $5.40 (or, closely figured, $5.37½). The omission of a decimal point by the printers, here again as above, was all the senator could find to base his attack on. But it was evidently sufficient. It served the purpose, as Senator Aldrich's answer to Senator Gray plainly shows.

Another example of almost amusing pettifogging may be stated yet. Senator Chace quotes me as saying in one place that the charge per pound of cotton yarn in Lowell for water power and taxes was .298 cent, and in another place saying that it is .568 cent. The one referred to yarn, and the larger sum to the pound of finished cloth, including the yarn, as I had explicitly stated. Printer's proof was sent to me as I had requested, and when I saw these misprints I cabled from England to delay printing for corrections. But the matter had gone through the press already. This was fortunate for Messrs. Chace and Aldrich. What would they have done for a basis of attack had the decimal points been put in their proper places? Truly, if the defenders of a discredited system have to stoop to puerile tactics in order to find a foothold for attacking an opponent, then their case must be a weak one indeed.

It may be asked why these supreme efforts on the part of manufacturers and their representatives in the houses of Congress to uphold the high tariff even on cottons, when wages, measured by the piece, are below the English, and we export the products of the cotton mills.

The answer is easily given.

It has been shown that with cotton at 10.695, the finished cloth cost 19.246 cents. This was from mill accounts for October, 1886. Print cloth was selling then at $3\frac{1}{4}$ cents a yard, and even at 3 cents, at one time, as trade was depressed. This is 21 to $22\frac{3}{4}$ cents the pound, and no great margin was left for profits. But since then print cloth has sold as high as 4 cents a yard, with cotton no higher, and gave, therefore, not less than 8 to 9 cents, or about 50 per cent. over cost of production. For print cloth not the best quality of cotton is used, and the present price of cotton, best middling at $7\frac{3}{4}$ cents, would give an extra profit of 3 cents. The price of print cloth to-day is $3\frac{5}{8}$ cents, or $23\frac{5}{8}$ cents the pound. On the basis of present cotton prices we have 16.246 cents as cost, and 7.379 cents as profit, or 1.651 more than the cost of all the labor contained in a pound of print cloth.

I take only 3 cents as the difference in the cost of cotton between 1886 and to-day. The price having varied between $6\frac{1}{2}$ cents and $7\frac{1}{2}$ cents during this year, the average would be 7 cents, instead of $7\frac{3}{4}$ cents, and give an additional $\frac{3}{4}$ cent to the profit of the mills. The whole of the decline in cotton, so disastrous to the farmer in the South, is absorbed in extra profits.

If labor receives more pay by the piece to-day than in 1886, I have not become aware of it. At any rate it will be seen that there is sufficient inducement in the other quarter for the strongly urged injunction "not to disturb the tariff."

CHAPTER VI.

Ability to satisfy the Taste of Buyer determines the Course of Trade.—Cotton Goods, Printing, Finishing.—Important Points in Exporting.—Our Importations caused by Inability of Home Producer to answer the Wants of our People.—New Departure in Tariff Legislation.

BEFORE taking up the branches of cotton goods which we import, I shall have to say a few words of what the Germans call the "Veredlungsprozess," which I may translate into "æstheticizing." It comprises color, design, and finish in dry goods, everything that makes the article attractive to the eye. I shall confine my remarks more to printed fabrics, because the subject throws additional light upon our exporting trade, and likewise explains why we import fabrics regardless of price and the duties heaped upon them.

The printing of cotton prints is done by means of engraved rollers. For each color in the design a roller is supplied, which is fed from a separate color box. The separate colors closely fitting into the design together form the pattern. Three, four, as well as ten and twelve color patterns are thus printed in one running of the printing machine. In America, where quantity is the end and aim, 400 pieces of fifty yards each were given me in Lowell print works as an average of output for three to four patterns, and 250 pieces for eight to twelve color patterns. This is 20,000 yards of the former and 12,500 yards of the latter as one day's work. An owner of print works in another part of the country told me that in his works they run as high as 700 pieces a day. With a printer at $4.50 a day, and a helper at $1.50, the direct printing cost in labor (and accepting the first statement of output for the example) is not more than three one-hundredths of a cent per yard. The finishing is done by running the prints through a calendering machine, which would not add very materially to the cost.

English print works, as well as Mulhouse and Elberfeld printers in Germany, whom I visited, are unable to turn out work as cheaply as we do. A leading Manchester printer who took me through his works showed me an endless variety of patterns in his pattern book. Some of them are years old. But still he has to keep his rollers on hand, as orders may come at any time from the remotest corners of the world. Working for all countries and zones, each has to be supplied in its own peculiar tints and tastes. They buy the cloths as they require them for their orders. This printer had about 10,000 to 11,000 engraved copper rollers on hand, and some 800 living patterns. Rollers which are not to be used any more are ground off and re-engraved. Of course, they cannot keep grinding out the stuff for days without a change of rollers, as we do, and their cost is consequently considerably higher. The labor cost in Manchester for printing was given me from the books. It is 7¾d. for a piece of thirty yards, inclusive of finishing, engraving of rollers, and designing. Half a cent against less than one-twentieth of a cent in America. What applies to England, as against America, applies with greater force still to Germany, which gets the gleanings where England harvests the bulk.

I was told by the owners of extensive print works in Elberfeld that they had given up trying to compete with America in Mexico, for instance, or wherever the people have accommodated themselves to our style of goods. This does not seem to have cut as deeply into their trade, and certainly not into England's trade, as they imagine in Germany. And for very good reasons. Cheapness alone does not conquer foreign trade. Especially not where the tastes have to be considered. Southern countries, with their fine color sense, large consumers of printed fabrics, would certainly not be largely influenced to turn to our goods because of a difference of a third of a cent, even if this difference were not so effectually wiped out by savings in other directions, as shown in the preceding chapter. As it is, England exported in 1890 £11,450,482, or about $56,000,000 of cotton prints. Of this sum $15,000,000 went to the West Indies, South and Central America.* Of dyed and colored cotton fabrics an additional amount of £8,765,000 was shipped, and to the South Americas about $7,000,000 of this sum; to all countries some $98,000,000, and to Central † and South America and the West Indies about $22,000,000. Our export trade in colored cottons is $2,800,000, and half of this expresses our trade figures to the American divisions named.

What gives England this firm hold of the world's trade in cotton goods (in all kinds of cotton fabrics £75,000,000, or $375,000,000 in 1890 against our $12,000,000) is not cheap labor as against America, her only possible rival in cotton goods, as has been demonstrated. It is not alone the saving effected by giving a lighter cloth, but that the English really give a sightlier fabric. The finer yarn, though it be sized up, does something toward this; but that in color and finishing they are far ahead of us, and by being ready and able to give to the different markets what they require, is a fact of greatest force, and makes it certain that they cannot easily be supplanted unless we do likewise.

---

* Including Mexico.   † Ibid.

Our colorings show a certain crudeness against the English, which makes them somewhat harsh to the eye. Theirs have more of a softness and pleasing depth. Skill in color mixing there is more or less a matter of rule of thumb. Art schools and technical schools have not had much to do with the forming of the staff of English factories, but if the secure possession of the world's trade is a proof of the superior character of the goods, then no one can deny that skill is inherent there which we do not possess, and, moreover, neglect to acquire by proper training. The poverty of coloring effects may be due to ignorance as well as to other and worse causes. Corrupt practices in the buying of supplies, taking commissions, etc., especially in the dye department; the consequent using of inferior dyes and supplies, and wastefulness as a general result, have not infrequently been brought out before the public eye as the cause of disaster, or at least serious losses, of manufacturing corporations. At any rate, close watching of all details by a thoroughly-posted owner seems to be the only reliable safeguard against these dangers.

The material, out of which the leading officials of American textile corporations are usually taken, is not apt to be endowed with the necessary practical knowledge.

The question may here properly be raised whether the English system of subdivision of branches of industry, each under its own responsible management and ownership, is not more satisfactory in the results, though profits be saved in the subdivisions, and only one general profit be the charge in the other system. In machinery the English hold in this department a leading position, nor are they afraid of expense. A so-called Scotch finishing machine is attached to a printing machine, prints and finishes the cloth in running it over hot rollers and folding it at the same time. Other finishing machinery shows equal perfection. To give description of it here would be going too much into details which have only technical interest. We are here only concerned in results, and a passing notice of the means employed in reaching them suffices. The operations for the higher finish given to finer goods are mostly conducted by special firms. They are outside parties, who take the goods from the print houses and return them when finished. The charge is by the yard, at a comparatively low rate.

A plant for finishing 500 pieces a day would cost about £5,000. The finer the finish the smaller would be the output, so that a high satin finish, the silky lustre—not the one applied by a heavy varnish of glue, as given by our finishing concerns—would only turn out 300 pieces a day.

By pains-taking and a close attention to details a stage of perfection and results have been reached by the English, which our system, in cotton goods at least, has not yet attained. The wish to make everything in which the English excel is a very praiseworthy one, but it is not a sufficient qualification for the doing, as will be seen more pointedly in other cotton manufactures.

Cotton Velvets.

Up to the time of the conception of the new bill, protectionists were satisfied with the claim, " Give our industries protection until they are firmly rooted and can stand alone, when we shall gladly accept free trade, as it is the only rational end to strive for." They could well afford to be generous in promises. To-morrow is a strong bank to draw upon, as it will break only when the last to-morrow is reached. The people gave extensions willingly, though they knew the day of honoring would never come. But who had ever heard this claim: "We have never made these goods, in fact no one has ever attempted their manufacture; but if you put on a duty of 100 per cent., or double a 35 per cent. or a 40 per cent. duty, we will go to work and show the world what we are capable of"? It required only a few yards of velvet and other things of equal reality to be laid before the author of the act, and to him the demonstration was complete and satisfactory evidence that the goods could be produced in America without limit. Forthwith the decree was passed, and millions of taxes were added to the consumer's burdens.

Cotton velvet is not an article of luxury. It is a sightly and dressy fabric, serviceable both for dress and ornament. The working classes, especially, are large consumers. Some one in Rhode Island made the statement that he could very well make the velvet, which is now imported, and keep the money in the country, if the duty were so adjusted that the foreign goods could be kept out. The duty was raised, actually more than doubled. This was not done openly, but by the old trick of changing an *ad valorem* duty to a specific one. The duty was 40 per cent. *ad valorem*, and was then and there changed to 14 cents per square yard and 20 per cent. *ad valorem*. This applies to colored and dyed velvets, etc. The rates on gray are 10 cents, and on bleached 12 cents per square yard and 20 per cent. *ad valorem;* but none of these are imported. Now 14 cents per square yard and 20 per cent. *ad valorem* to those unacquainted with the run of prices does not look materially different from the old rate. In answer to Senator Carlisle's remark that this change implied an increase up to 100 per cent., Senator Aldrich stated that he had sent to all the retail stores in Washington, and had not been able to find any velvets cheaper than seventy-five cents, hence there could be no increase. A perfectly logical demonstration if the import price were anything like 75 or 60 or even 50 cents.

But the senator's premises were wrong. The Washington retail stores are not the best sources of information on the country's import trade. The great importing houses of New York volunteered information gratis, as the senator knows. I obtained from one of the principal importers a copy of an importation order, which may serve as illustrative of nearly all our importations. I will copy it here and give alongside the *ad valorem* equivalent of the present compound duty:

Colored Velvet.	Width, in.	Price.	Duty, Per Cent.
3,500 pieces.	18	5⅛*d.*	88
1,000 "	19	7½*d.*	70
315 "	22	9¼*d.*	69
4,815 pieces.			
Black Velvet.			
1,600 pieces,	18	4¼*d.*	102½
800 "	18	4⅜*d.*	92
400 "	18	5 *d.*	90
400 "	19½	5¾*d.*	92
500 "	19½	6½*d.*	82
400 "	21½	7¼*d.*	77
160 "	21½	8 *d.*	72
120 "	21½	9 *d.*	66½
40 "	21½	6½*d.*	63½
40 "	21½	10 *d.*	61½
4,520 pieces.			

In an importation order of 9,335 pieces, 7,260 pieces pay duties between 82 and 102 per cent. *ad valorem*, against a former 40 per cent.; 1,875 pieces between 69 and 77 per cent., and only 200 pieces between 61½ and 66 per cent. As packing charges are made dutiable under the new law, they add something like 2½ per cent. more to the duty.

The lower quality black velvet under the old law and under the new law would stand the wholesale buyer as follows:

	Old Tariff. Cents.		New Tariff. Cents.
Cost, 4¼d................	8.50		8.50
Boxes, commission and freight......	1.60		1.60
Duty, 40 per cent................	3.40	Duty, 105 per cent.,	9.00
Cash discount, 7 per cent..........	1.10		1.60
Importer's profit...................	1.60		2.30
Total........................	16.20		23.00
Add 25 per cent. to cover retailer's profit........................	4.05		5.75
And we have a total of.........	20.24 against		28.75

or a charge over the old duty of 8.50 cents on the lowest quality of velvet by the time the consumer gets hold of it in the most direct way—an extra charge, due to the tariff increase, equal to the price at which the goods are put on board ship in England. But velvets go mostly through more than one hand. They are distributed through jobbers to country dealers, or are converted into other articles of manufacture, and it would be a fair estimate to say that the bulk of these goods cost fully 10 cents a yard more to the masses than this eight-and-a-half-cent velvet would have cost them under the old 40 per cent. duty. Some people are silly enough to maintain, and some are sillier yet and believe, that the foreigner pays the duty. This example is introduced to demonstrate *ad oculos* who pays the duty, the increased duty, plus profits on duties and charges paid to the importers, dealers, manufacturers, and middlemen, who make themselves useful to the public as distributors of this fabric.

Now all this has been done because of the assurance given

by a few claimants that velvets could be produced as good as the English goods, if the duty were raised high enough. What "high enough" means has been shown. We have not heard anything of American velvets since the increase was engineered through, though the law is in force for nearly two years. For very good reasons we shall not hear of them again. The manufacture of velvets is one of the most difficult processes of all textile industry. In cotton velvets England is unapproached by Germany or any other country. The dye and finish of English goods alone are something to which all users of these fabrics will attest superiority. I know this by my own business experience. But this is only the final stage. Before we get to this the yarn, the weaving, and pile cutting have to be considered. In the two former we are deficient; in the last process, and the most important and difficult one, we are entirely ignorant. It is all done by hand. The goods are stretched on a frame some eight to twelve yards long, and the cutter walks up and down the frame cutting the pile with a knife. An unskilled handling of the knife would spoil the goods. The work is distributed all over the country, to towns as far as thirty miles from Manchester. Towns near the Staffordshire potteries, especially Congleton, are extensively engaged in velvet cutting.

The wages are extremely low. Special skill and very dexterous work are necessary to enable the workman to earn 12s. to 18s. Girls and women, also largely engaged in this work, earn less than that. The employment of machinery was talked about at the time of the new tariff enactment. If we had special machinery which could do the work, we should be far ahead of England. But England seems to know something about machinery in velvet cutting. It is a near relation to the Keely motor

—full of promise of a great future, but never successfully worked. Many inventions have been tried, but none has proved satisfactory. I have it stated from manufacturers that the chief difficulty has always been the pile being burnt wherever machines, by no means new inventions, have been tried.

These considerations should satisfy any one that cotton velvets cannot be an article of manufacture in this country, and no duty increase can make them so. We may take this as an illustration of the way the late tariff act was prepared, when any one who wanted an increase even for experimenting had only to step forward and ask for it. The greater the lump the surer the grant. The only thing refused with scorn was a demand for lightening tariff duties. The claimants made good use of the golden opportunity.

Cotton Hosiery.

Cotton hose rank with velvet as objects of criticism in the recent tariff legislation. In order to understand fully the wanton character of the proceeding, it is necessary to consider the character of the hose we manufacture and of that which we import. The two do not at all interfere with one another. In times past, happily for the wearer's sake, the goods were cut out of the piece and sewed together. They were clumsy, ill-fitting abominations. We make now an entirely different class of goods—mostly men's half hose, and a small quantity of ladies' hose. They are full knit on knitting machines, of heavy yarn, very serviceable, though they could be improved in make and character all around. Labor does not need protection in this class of goods, neither do the goods. I have taken the account of a knitting mill. These are the figures:

Ladies' Hose.

2¼ pounds of yarn, @ 20 cents per pound	$0.45
Knitting cost	.23
General labor	.10
General expense	.12
6 per cent. discount	.07
6 per cent. commission	.07
Total	$1.04
Selling price	1.20

Men's Half Hose.

26 ounces of yarn, @ 17 cents per pound	$0.27
Knitting	.17
General labor	.08
General expense	.10
6 per cent. discount	.05
6 per cent. commission	.05
Total	$0.72
Selling price	.80

This class of goods is our main product, and the tariff was not increased on their account. But we import some five million dollars' worth of cotton hose and half hose, which somebody seems to have convinced Mr. McKinley could be made here if the duty were doubled. These importations are full-fashioned goods, made on frames, and sewed together—so-called seamless hose, with flat, even seams without any ridges. Heels and toes are doubled, and in the half hose the elastic part being separately knit and afterward knitted on makes a close, even fit and appearance, instead of the somewhat raw and ruffled looks of the elastic end of the article mentioned above. The people who buy the imported article are not of the well-to-do classes exclusively. All classes buy them, the poor as well as the rich; all who desire fine, even-yarn goods, well shaped, and fitting the foot well, in color effects pleasing the eye, and answering a somewhat subtler taste. But they are to be prevented from doing so hereafter, by making the lower grades so high by tariffs, that by excluding the foreign they will be kept more strictly to the American article.

The prices at which goods having all these requisites are produced, principally in the Chemnitz district, are so low that even with a 40 per cent. duty they remained an article of large consumption. We have never made these goods, and, what is more, could not make them if the duty were trebled. But some manufacturers seem to feel that no foreign goods, be they ever so different, but interfering in price, at least, with their goods, ought to be brought to this country. Hence they claimed, and easily succeeded in obtaining, a specific duty additional to the *ad valorem* rate. Goods in the lower price-range pay as high as 80 per cent. now, while the average duty amounts to 65 per cent. against the old 40 per cent. The importations continue, however. They are as extensive as ever, if we take into account the increase in 1890 and 1891. Both years show abnormal figures, expected increase in duty having been anticipated in increased importations. The year 1889 is better fitted for comparison. The year shows in all kinds of cotton hosiery $6,300,000. The eleven months for the fiscal year of 1891-92, of which reports are just published, show $5,500,000, with the month of July added, on the basis of last year's figures (over $600,000), then certainly the normal importations continue, undisturbed by our fostered home industries. The additional duties will be borne by the consumer without even the solace which the consciousness of contributing to a patriotic duty would give him.

CHAPTER VII.

Futility of attempting Industrial Creations by Protective Tariffs when Natural Conditions are wanting —Flax Cultivation and Linen Manufacturing.—Cotton Embroideries and Laces classed under Linen for Tariff Increase.—Reasons why they cannot be produced here.

The cultivation of flax for the fibre and the manufacture of linen are by no means infant industries. The old mummies unearthed after 5,000 years are wrapped in linen. Babylonia carried on an extensive trade in linen fabrics centuries before Herodotus chronicled the fact. Tacitus tells us of the ancient Germans being clad in linen, and away into the Middle Ages linen tunics and sheepskins were the chief articles of clothing of the peasantry. The lake dwellers, too, were acquainted with the cultivation of flax and the use of the fibre for weaving into garments on their crude looms, as any one can see for himself if he visits the museum at Zurich. This takes us back to the first beginnings of civilization. The serviceability of the fibre as a suitable material for dress must have impressed itself upon primitive man. There are valid reasons for the assumption that flax was the first fibre used in the preparation of artificial dress when stone and wood were the only materials out of which his rude implements were wrought. Hence, the cultivation of the fibre and its manufacture cannot be reasonably called infant industries.

Nor can they be be called so in America. The North of Ireland Scotch Presbyterians are the principal cultivators of flax in Ireland. We know what a large percentage of our early settlers they were, and how well they returned in the War of Independence the injuries which England had inflicted upon them, and which had driven them over to this side of the Atlantic.

Before the spread of cotton manufacturing, pretty nearly all the "linen" was made of flax spun and woven in the homes of the people. Necessity does not wait for government to protect and to guide, but makes use of the most serviceable means for supplying wants. It is different when, as now, commerce carries to the remotest hamlets whatever can be more profitably bought than produced by the exertions of the people. By natural selection, so to speak, gradually the fittest occupation of the individual has become the surviving employment out of the manifold and almost unlimited industrial occupations which our early ancestors practiced by compulsion. Consequently, all these questions of occupation become questions of competition of employment, expressed in three words: "Does it pay?" From this standpoint alone can we consider these questions, not from that of mock patriotism, which only means serving a few at the expense of the many.

To properly see this in relation to the flax fibre it is necessary to examine the processes from the time of growth to the procuring of the pure fibre. The difficulties are many. At the start it is well to say that moist and moderate climates are best suited for the cultivation. The flax must have time to grow and mature in the stalk. It must be pulled at the proper time, before the seed has ripened. Hence, flax cultivated for the seed is not suitable for textile purposes. The fierce summer heat quickly following in America the long and severe winter makes the plant shoot up quickly to great height, thereby weakening the fibre.

This statement does not at all become vitiated by the fact that we have grown flax in the time when we made our own linen. It is one thing to grow flax for home purposes, spinning and weaving it at the fireside, far away from the roads of commerce, and quite another to have the power mill manufacture for us, able to choose the best suitable raw material from all the climes of the globe at a mere nominal transportation expense.

Not only is a proper, heavy soil required, but also an unremittent care is necessary from the time the flax gets ready to be pulled. When it has attained the proper height (three to four feet) it is pulled by the root. The root ends must be even, the stalks parallel and of equal length. Then the process of retting the flax takes place. Though other methods are in use, water retting is the only one giving satisfactory results, and therefore still generally applied to freeing the fibre from the resinous substance of the stalk. For the steeping, a pure, soft water is required, free from iron, lime, or any mineral substance which might affect the color or the tenacity of the fibre. The flax is tied up in bundles and immersed upright in ponds built four feet deep, after which the process of fermentation begins. This takes about ten or twelve days till complete. During the steeping the stalks must be examined frequently, and when ready for the purpose must be spread evenly on grassy meadows, frequently turned and watched so as not to miss the proper time for the gathering. Great care has to be taken in all these operations. Neglect in either of them makes a great difference in the value of the flax. Twenty-four hours of inattention may destroy the expected profit of a whole season's work.

Now, besides the toilsomeness of all these operations, there is not a little unwholesomeness connected with the proper management of flax cultivation. Standing in water away above the knees, and the endurance of the malodorous smell which the rotting stalks spread about, are some of the inconveniences.

Under these circumstances it will be seen that much toil and small compensation would be the result to the farmer. Flax cultivation is incompatible with our systems of extensive cultivation of land, the only one suitable where human labor is scarce and land is in plenty. What gives the greatest results with the smallest amount of labor here becomes choice and necessity. Hence so many industries are left untouched, although they would give splendid results, according to book farmers and political tinsmiths and political weavers, if our farmers only could be brought to do this thing, that thing, or the other thing. Cultivation of flax for the seed pays them well; cultivation of flax for the fibre does not pay them under conditions prevailing and illustrated. So long as labor is left free to choose its occupations it will certainly take up what is most remunerative and what is most inviting, and refuse to be lured into the other alternative. The views here expressed are supported by the fact that even European countries like Ireland and Germany, countries where small culture and the cheapness and abundance of farm labor conspire to make the industry a permanent resident, recede more and more as producers, and leave the honors to Russia, which now produces two-thirds of all the flax fibre of Europe. Germany, some twenty years ago, had over 200,000 hectares (about 500,000 acres) under flax, but has now not more than half that number. Ireland in 1867 had 253,257 acres under flax; in 1884, only 89,225 acres; in 1889, there were 107,000 acres.

Nor is the yield, after all the hardship the cultivator has to endure, so very dazzling. Some 300 to 400 pounds of fibre to an acre, according to the years, is the product in Ireland, and less in Russia. The yield here would certainly not be as high as in Ireland. The highly superior Irish flax is landed here at under ten cents a pound. Our inferior growth would bring to the farmer not more than seven cents, perhaps. A not very alluring prospect, considering all the hardships and risks of flax culture for the fibre.

Linen Manufacturers.

Probably in order to make the increase of duty by the recent act on household linen (from 35 per cent. the old, to 50 per cent. the new) more palatable to the farmer, the argument was most liberally used that an encouragement of the linen industry by the increase of duty would benefit him enormously. A market for his flax would thus be opened which he could not obtain otherwise. At the most superficial examination, this promise cannot be meant seriously. Nothing interfered heretofore with the use of American flax. But the flax raised went into the rope-making mills, and hardly a pound of it into the linen factories or the yarn mills. Will a higher rate of duty on linen make the flax more valuable to those manufacturing the higher grades when it is rejected on account of its unserviceability in the commonest grades? The question hardly needs answering. It answers itself. There is no market for American flax in American mills at the present time, and it is not a desirable consummation that there should ever be, considering all the changes in the farmer's condition this would imply.

But our linen industry has never, during the whole period of war-tariff legislation and protection inebriety, gone beyond the crash stage. We have never been able to make anything above common crashes, in the production of which the character and color of the fibre, the bleaching and finishing, play no such important part as in the higher numbers. And even here, with the exception of a few concerns backed by the wealth of their owners, the crash came back to roost in the other sense of the word. Many hundred thousands of dollars have been sunk in unsuccessful efforts, and failure is the general verdict of history. If this is the experience in the most rudimentary lines, the coarsest linens, what can be expected when we touch the damask and finer linens—up to one hundred threads to the square inch, which the new law assumes as the limit of ability of our manufacturers? To any one knowing the requirements of successful linen manufacturing, the proceeding seems so absurd that it becomes almost impossible to speak of it in serious terms. Not alone the external, but the internal conditions are wanting. The dryness of the atmosphere, the cold winters, the parching heat of summer, the absence of skilled help and capable technical management, except of foreign adventurers trading on the ignorance of mill owners and capitalists—all these are so many drawbacks, and very seriously interfere with spinning, weaving, and bleaching operations. The arguments advanced by would-be manufacturers and their advocates show that they are utterly unacquainted with the manufacture of any kind but political linen. The new tax is laid on the people. They will have to pay some millions more a year. But the manufacture of fine linen will remain, as before, a matter of longing. The few yards of linen produced before Mr. McKinley and his committee in demonstration of what could be done if the duty were raised "high enough" will be the last we shall see of American linen of a higher grade than crash linen.

Cotton Embroideries, Cotton Lace.

Increasing duties by a change of classifications is a trick. The law here does covertly what the authors have not the courage to openly promulgate. Otherwise why should cotton embroidery and cotton lace be brought in under the caption of flax and manufactures? But so the law decrees. A sweep of the pen could thus raise duties formerly 40 per cent. to 60 per cent., which is the new duty on all embroidery or laces, whether of cotton or flax. "They are articles of luxury." By no means. Some $10,000,000 worth are imported annually. Cotton lace, lace curtains, etc., are bought by the lowest wage earners, as well as by the farming and middle classes. Cotton embroidery has become an article of immense consumption since the so-called Swiss machine has pushed aside the human hand— the machine of former times. The cheapening has gone on from year to year in Switzerland and the Saxon district about Plauen. The result is a consumption more than double that of a dozen years ago. But cheapness is a curse, according to Mr. Harrison, Mr. McKinley, and others of the protectionist creed, a curse which has to be counteracted by legislation. Those who have to support a family on $1 to $1.25 a day, and they compose a good majority of our people, begin to appreciate the Republican axiom.

"Yes, but we can make them here and establish a new industry." Fortunately I happen to know something about machine embroidering in this country from personal experience. There were brought here from Switzerland in the course of ten to twelve years some two to three hundred embroidering machines. They are employed mostly on silk embroidery, fancy trimmings, embroidering of robes in silk and wool. Most of the work could be imported, duty paid, and sold cheaper than the American work on which they are employed. But a very strong protection of home industries exists, which is not found in the statute book. This is protection in the supplying of immediate demands by the agencies in touch with the variable tastes of this country. The risks of importations in such fancies are immense and powerful deterrents. Some six or eight years ago, when embroidered cashmere robes were in fashion, the early importations were bought eagerly. The machines in the country were kept busy to the utmost. Second importation orders became out of date, and a good many were brought over and had to be sold and slaughtered in the auction rooms. The home machines, feeling the pulse of demand, could easily be shifted to other work; the foreign goods had to carry the full loss under the whims of fickle Dame Fashion.

The men working these Swiss machines are all brought over from Switzerland. The machine is expensive and requires careful and experienced tending. In Switzerland some 30,000 machines are employed. The work is paid on the stitch basis. Competition has brought down the rate of pay to so low a point that 3f. a day would express a fair average of earnings. Yet I remember that, although the earnings of the embroiderers were as high as $15 and even $20 a week, it was difficult to resist their demand for higher pay whenever they felt their work was more in demand than ordinarily. It is a common experience that labor brought over from abroad for special pursuits is far more intractable than American labor, whether of native origin or of foreign, but, by long contact, imbued with American ideas. This is matter for serious consideration in more ways than one. I cannot enlarge on it here. In " cotton embroideries " it is a very formidable factor.

There is no risk attached to the importation of white cotton embroideries. Were there no other obstacles in the way, it can be seen that we cannot possibly engage in this new "infant industry," even under a 60 per cent. duty. But there are other obstacles. The cloth and the cotton for embroidery are about 40 per cent. higher than in Switzerland, all for the glorification of protection, which, as a matter of course, takes away with one hand what it gives with the other. The materials on which these embroideries are made are sheerer and finer than our general line of goods. They do not cost very much more to produce, at least not in the lower class of prices, than English goods, but are sold nearly up to the foreign price plus the duty, although inferior in character and finish. * The final finishing is a matter of no small importance, but I will waive it as one of the things attainable by study and application. The other objections must convince everybody, outside of a small charmed circle, that we are not able to produce these goods on commercial principles.

The same strictures, somewhat modified, according to the character of the branches, apply to cotton laces and to cotton lace curtains. The raising of the duties on these articles of large consumption by the poorer classes a full 50 per cent. is almost incomprehensible, even from the standpoint of the new departure in protectionism under the McKinley act. Here certainly no claims worth considering could have been brought forward that an industry " could be established "

---

* The English and Swiss manufacturers use almost entirely Egyptian cotton for their fine yarn goods. It makes an even thread, shown in the absence of knots and uneven places so abundant in the American goods intended to replace the former. Self-sufficiency, negligent and wasteful, opens the back-door, while protectionism anxiously keeps guarding the gate.

under the plea dealt with before. That an increase in duty means an increase in the selling price is proved by the fact that the importer's selling price of the franc under the old tariff was 30 cents less 7 per cent. cash discount, and under the new tariff is 36 cents with the discount. The consumer, of course, pays a greater difference still, as demonstrated in our cotton velvet example.

Embroidered and Hemstitched Handkerchiefs.

That we make no embroidered or hemstitched handkerchiefs of linen in this country need hardly be stated. That we cannot make them, even with the 60 per cent. protection so lavishly dealt out by Mr. McKinley in place of the former 30 per cent. on embroidered and 35 per cent. on other linen handkerchiefs, hardly needs emphasizing after what has been said above. All who have used linen handkerchiefs will have either to pay the increased price, or confine themselves henceforth to the use of American cotton handkerchiefs. The makers of these did not feel themselves able to prevent the importation of foreign linen at 30 and 35 per cent. and of cotton embroidered hemstitched handkerchiefs, neither of which they can produce. Nor can they prevent it now. But with them any exclusion, by whatever cause, is considered equivalent to an extension of market for their quite inferior goods.

The finer, sheerer goods used in Switzerland and Ireland for cotton handkerchiefs, embroidered and hemstitched, are seldom employed in handkerchief making here. The class of goods made here is of a rougher sort. The hemstitching in Ireland is done by machinery now, and the goods are woven so as to leave the threads open where the stitching is to run in, which makes this operation one of trifling cost.

Our goods do not show that even the manufacturers possess the best machinery for hemstitching, employed on the other side. The finishing and doing up also leave much to be desired. The increase of duty here shows most plainly the object of the new tariff to saddle the consumer with high taxes so as to give a greater margin of profit and room for experimenting to the makers of a very inferior class of goods.

It is not likely that American industries will be benefited much by this sort of legerdemain tariff increase in cotton embroideries, cotton lace, cotton lace curtains, and embroidered and hemstitched handkerchiefs. Our importations in 1890 were $13,000,000. The people will pay on these hereafter some $8,000,000 duty, or nearly $3,000,000 more than formerly, with not even the semblance of a showing that any existing (or even prospective) industries will be benefited, except in paltry and insignificant ways. On the contrary, many industries are injured by the high rates wantonly imposed on articles that cannot possibly be produced here. Branches of magnitude in America, which in Germany and England work largely for export, in which we show superior capacity, could be profitably extended and their products exported but for these duties. In these employment could be found for ten times the labor that will ever be employed in the additional manufacture encouraged by the increase of duty on cotton embroidery and cotton lace and kindred goods.

Thus it will be seen that an amount of ignorance on the one hand and recklessness on the other has been displayed in the formulating of new tariff provisions, which can only be explained by the fact, patent to all, that the makers of the law had only political ends in view, and that their considerations for the industries of the country were conditional on the latter, serving these ends.

CHAPTER VIII.

Science and Skill in Manufacturing Industries.—Silk Manufacturing.—Lyons and Paterson compared.—Labor Cost about Equal.—Superiority of Lyons Goods.—Lower Cost due to other Causes than Differences in Labor.

THE powerful effect which science exercises on prices, along with the skill of the workpeople, is well demonstrated by the silk industry as conducted in the representative centres of Europe and America. Here we can show most distinctly the popular fallacy that the lower rate of per diem wages causes the difference in prices, which is so manifest in the fabrics of the two countries. To do this with full clearness, we have to follow the industry from the fibre to the finished fabric.

Silk is a tender tiny thread as reeled from the cocoon. Perhaps for this reason it has at all times been considered a fit subject of government's protecting hand. From the time the first eggs were brought from China to Europe by Byzantine monks, governments have been anxious to provide hospitable homes, even under unfriendly skies. The worm, however, obstinately refused to prosper, except in Southern France and in Northern Italy. In America early attempts were made. The kings, from the Stuarts down to the time of the Revolution, spent much money and offered prizes to encourage the cultivation of silk. The legislatures and colonies followed in the wake of royalty, and left no attempts untried to get the people to leave or neglect remunerative occupations and turn to the raising of silkworms, despite repeated experience of barren results.

Attempts in the same direction were not given up, though. The legislature of California, a State whose climate is eminently fitted for the successful breeding of silkworms, early passed a law offering a bounty of $300 for every 100,000 cocoons raised, and one of $250 for every 5,000 mulberry-trees planted. The results did not prove more satisfactory than in colonial times, and the law was soon repealed. Agriculturists do not seem to take kindly to silk raising for the same reasons that they do not take kindly to flax raising. They seem to think that their labor can be more profitably employed than in the rearing of silkworms and cocoons in opposition to Chinese, Japanese, Hindu, and South of Europe labor. Were it not for this emphatic refusal of our rural classes to have themselves cajoled into silk raising, even by the aid of government bounties, we might now have a duty of some 25 or 50 per cent. on raw silk to pay, and thereby have prevented the growth of an industry which gives employment to far more hands in a year than could have found profitable employment in the raising of the raw material in a lifetime.

The industry is a most important educational lever when properly conducted, and for this alone would deserve the most serious consideration. It repays careful furtherance. But whatever the most effective means, high protective tariffs have not proven that they are able to supply the necessary qualification. The instruments mentioned in the preceding pages are far more important to industrial efficiency and—sufficiency. These ends can only be reached by the proper educational facilities, entirely wanting here, and neglected by the ruling passion for tariff protection. Science, art, individual skill, leadership of no common sort must combine in silk manufacture not to create a momentarily successful enterprise, but to carry it through good and bad report to more than ephemeral success. Whether silk manufacturing could have ever become the great industry which it is undoubtedly to-day without a high tariff (50 per cent.) is an academic question, and not necessary for us to inquire into. We do not deal with theories and suppositions, but with facts. It may be stated in a broad sense, however, that no amount of protective duty could have created a silk industry in America under the old method of manufacture, strictly one of hand labor. Neither 50 per cent. nor a higher duty could have enabled our home talent or provided us with the necessary auxiliaries from abroad to produce goods in quantity and of quality able to supplant the work of the old-time industries of Europe. Mechanics has taken a great part of the work out of the hands of the old-time plodders, and made the successful introduction of this great industry possible. Chemical science, on the other hand, has put obstacles in our way which again call our success somewhat into question. Production by the aid of machinery and power is the only possible method of production on a large scale in this country. This is not saying that it is the best method, in silk weaving at least. But by the aid of power, improved machinery, and complete mill organization, we have become able to produce, so far as price is concerned, goods that even under a very moderate revenue duty foreign goods could not be landed, if all other things were equal.

But here many other influences come in, which in a general way have been dwelt on before, but are of greatest importance in silks, chiefly on account of the costliness of the goods, and the susceptibility of the fibre, which enables the skilled worker to enhance its value to almost any rate above that which an inferior handling gives it. The dyeing, the weaving, the designing, the selection of colors, the finishing, all become matters of greatest importance. Skill and taste in all of these are essential to success. Their presence in the fabric does not increase the cost of production, but their absence detracts very materially from the value.

How well this principle is understood in Lyons is seen from the fact that in a specimen of work intended for the Paris Exposition of 1889, I found that every part was executed by the manufacturer himself, who happened to be the President of the Lyons Silk Manufacturers' Association. He would intrust no part to anybody else; the result was work equal to the very best that could be produced. To the hereditary skill distributed among all classes of silk workers in Lyons is due the fact that depression in the silk trade is seldom felt as severely in Lyons as elsewhere, in America, for instance. In Lyons every one concerned puts a certain amount of feeling into the work, if I may so express myself. In this country everybody concerned is bent on but one end—to grind out the greatest possible quantity in a given time.

It may be suggested that Europe could very easily adopt our methods and substitute power for hand-loom weaving. This is done to an extent. To those unacquainted with the economic reasons, it must seem hardly consistent with the spirit of otherwise progressive trade centres to cling mainly to the old mode. On examination we find, however, that for Europe the advantages are all with the old system; for us, on the contrary, with the new, because, as said before, we have no choice in the matter.

The advantages of the old system were explained in Chapter IV. of Part I. The power mill under these circumstances makes naturally but slow headway and takes up only the cheaper fabrics. These mills are usually situated in the country, and take the work from the Lyons manufacturers on the same terms, to wit: half of the piece rate to the weaver and the other half to cover the other items, such as winding, warping, power, expense, and profit, as explained.

Loading of Silks.

The loading of silk plays a prominent part in silk manufacture. Few who wear silks, especially black silks, know that they often carry more chemicals, salts of iron and tin, with them, than silk as reeled from the cocoon. Silk is an absorbent of moisture to a very high degree, and this quality has been taken advantage of by the profit-making propensity of man. With the aid of science he has found means to retain the absorbed material and thereby increase the weight and thickness of the thread. It must be remembered that the silk as reeled from the cocoon is of such great fineness that it takes from forty to eighty threads, according to the different kinds, laid closely side by side, to cover the space of a millimeter. A number of the filaments (from three or four up to twenty) are therefore united in the reeling to make one thread as it comes into the market as raw silk. When one cocoon is exhausted, the reeler puts a new one in its place, and so an endless thread of even thickness is produced by proper reeling.

In the throwing of silk, two or three strands of raw silk are spun into tram (the weft), and several of these twisted are made into organzine (the warp). Now science comes in and puts it into the power of the dyer to make a pound of raw silk weigh, when returned, all the way from a pound to three pounds in black. In light colors, weighted with vegetable matter (mostly sugar), and less injurious to the wearing quality of silk, 20 per cent. weighting in organzine, and 50 to 70 and even 100 per cent. in the tram is practised.

Now, it will be seen that when in this black art a pound of thrown silk (worth $5, to take a round figure) can be made to take the place of two pounds ($10), and by the gentler handling on hand-looms, heavier weighted and therefore more brittle silk can be used and produce even a sightlier fabric, a saving of a few cents in weaving the yard ceases to be a matter of the importance which it otherwise might have. Our high duties have certainly contributed to the causes which led to the practice of overweighting, by which silks have come to be regarded with suspicion. The low prices at which foreign silks were invoiced were frequently attributed to undervaluing, which low prices could, nevertheless, be distinctly traced to the disproportion between real silk and the weight of lustrous and beautiful silk fabrics. Weighting with metallic compounds, even, is required to give black silks the richness of hue which makes them so much more attractive than pure dyes. It is only the heavy weighting which is dangerous to the fabric.

But here the difficulty lies to make the manufacturer keep the safe line. It is easy for the buyer as well as for the appraiser to determine the rate of the weighting practised. Every species of silk has a specific gravity. By counting the number of singles in the thread the specific weight of pure silk can be easily ascertained. By comparing the result of the calculation with the weight of a certain quantity of the weighted fabric it can speedily be determined what percentage of weighting matter has gone into the goods and swelled up the fibre sufficiently to make the silk feel as heavy and stocky as a much greater number of filaments in the thread of pure silk. With these explanations it is perhaps easier to understand how so much cheap silk is brought into the market, and also the difficulties which have beset our silk industry as well as that of other nations. Of this I shall say a few concluding words, and deal now with the general question of comparative cost of production.

Comparative Cost of Spinning.

In America the fierce competition among the throwing mills has in a very few years brought about such improvements in machinery that, whereas in 1885 I found machinery spinning at the rate of 6,500 revolutions, I found in 1887 and 1888 a mill in Bethlehem, Pa., running at the rate of 9,500, and one at Paterson as high as 12,500, and new machinery in view of being put up, to run 15,000 revolutions a minute. In Macclesfield I was informed by silk throwsters that if they attempted to run above 3,000 to 3,500 revolutions their girls would run away.

In a product per month of 3,300 pounds of tram and 3,500 pounds of organzine, which, at the rates at which the throwing was done by these mills for silk manufacturers, would net $4,120, the labor stood $2,600 (120 hands, 60 per cent. of which are women), and the remainder of $1,520 would stand for other expense, such as power, rent, interest charges, and profit. This is an average of 37.6 cents for the tram and organzine. The silk taken in this is Japanese for the tram, and for the organzine three-fourths Japanese and one-fourth Italian.

Now, in making a comparison with the English cost, it must be noted that we take in America the best reeled Japanese silks, which are exceptionally good winders and require little or no cleaning. The English throwster takes the same silk, but of the second or even third grade. I therefore leave out of the English labor statement the items for cleaning and recleaning, and take the winding cost from a superior Italian silk, so as to obtain an even basis. This gives us an average labor for tram and organzine as 1s. 8d. per pound, or 40 cents, as taken from the mill statement of one of the leading silk mills. The weekly wages in winding are from 6s. to 9s. ($1.52 to $2.18); for spinner girls, etc., 10s. to 12s. ($2.43 to $2.92); and for men, 18s. to 24s. ($4.44 to $5.83) a week. In Bethlehem a mill with an output of 2,000 pounds per week employs 200 hands and has a weekly pay roll of $600 to $650. This gives us $32\frac{1}{2}$ cents as the labor cost, and an average of $3 to $3.25 per hand employed. In Paterson the average monthly earnings stand 2,600-120, or $21.66, or per week (counting 26 working days in the month) $4.98. A mark of greatest significance—Bethlehem against Paterson—$3 to $3.25 against $4.98 in weekly wages, and only 5 cents difference in the cost of production. England's average of weekly wages (12s. 9d., $3.10) rates on a par with Bethlehem, but the throwing labor cost is higher by about 20 per cent. We can understand very well why, upon trial, American manufacturers do not find it profitable to transfer their mills from a manufacturing centre like Paterson to country towns like Bethlehem, Allenton, or Boonton in the run after cheap labor.

Even in silk spinning, skilled and well-trained labor stands for something in the battle for industrial pre-eminence. The lower the day wage, the smaller the rate of improvement in labor-saving methods and machinery. In Italy, where labor is cheapest, the progress is the slowest. They do not find it profitable to employ improved machinery. They stick to their hand methods. They can do the work by the cheap labor of peasant girls as cheaply as if they employed the new processes with all the expense and capital involved in them.

The Dyeing of Silk.

Dyeing is done cheaper in America than in Europe on account of the greater quantities sent to the dye-houses. Some of our large mills even do their own dyeing. But the dyeing done in Lyons and in Zurich is far superior to our dyeing, if the richness and softness of color presented in their fabrics can be considered valid proof of the assertion. The dyeing establishments, as a rule, have an expert chemist at the head. It is a common saying among them that they understand dyeing, and certainly loading, far better than we do. In this, too, they are correct. We have practiced this art far more extensively of late, and have to a good degree injured the reputation which American silks used to enjoy on account of their greater purity.

In Lyons the charge to manufacturers was at the time of my visit 4.50f. to 7f. a kilo, 42 to 66 cents a pound, for pure dyes, and in black up to 12f. and 15f. a kilo, or $1.05 to $1.26 a pound, weighted to 24 ounces, or 100 per cent. In Zurich the charge was 10f. for black, weighted 50 to 60 per cent., 88 cents per pound; and if weighted 100 per cent., 13f. the kilo, or $1.14 the pound.

In America the dyeing charge stood then (1886–7) for large lots, unweighted, 35 cents; weighted black (100 per cent.), 85 cents. This price was increased after a strike of the dyers on March 1, 1887, to stand 40 to 50 cents for pure colors and 50 cents for pure black, and $1.10 for black weighted 100 per cent., with a discount under the depression ruling in the silk trade. It is not to be assumed that the increase prevails now.

We have here the two most important preliminary labor processes in silk manufacturing, spinning and dyeing, on a nearly even basis with the cost of European countries, where the lowest wage rates are paid. If there are differences in cost, they incline favorably to the American side with its highest wage rates. We have now to examine the weaving part in order to determine our standing in the matter of cost in silk manufacturing.

Weaving.

For comparison I took a colored silk, *faille française*, from one of the best American manufacturers. Having given already the cost of throwing and dyeing, it only remains to speak of the relative manufacturing cost, from the weaving and connected parts up to and including the finishing of the product.

The silk is 54 centimeters (21 inches wide). The American piece, calculated on 80 yards length, came in the winding to $1.46, the warping $2.50, the weaving 10 cents the yard, the quilling at $2.50, and the finishing and general expense, including all mill charges, was given as $6, then a rather high estimate. This brings the piece up to $20.50, or 25.62 cents per yard. Under pressure of dull trade and the consequences of tariff-bred congestion the labor price in the silk trade has come down considerably. Later inquiries show that for the labor processes quoted above the rates are now: 1. Winding, $1.46; 2. Warping, $2; 3. Weaving, 7 cents per yard, $5.60; 4. Quilling, $1.50; 5. Finishing and other expense, $3 to $4; in all, $14.50 the piece, or 18 cents the yard.

The same silk, calculated on the basis of a hundred-yard piece, costs in Zurich: 1. Winding, 12.90 f., $2.48; 2. Warping, 3.05 f., or 60 cents; 3. Weaving, 46 f., or $8.90; 4. Finishing and other expense, 10 f., $1.96; in all, $13.94 the piece, or 13.94 cents the yard.

This is on hand-looms. The weaving, it will be noticed,

is at the rate paid in America, if we include the incidental operations which are done or paid for by the hand-loom weavers, but in power mills paid by the mill. The general expense is naturally higher in power mills. In America warping and winding are done by machinery, while in Europe hand labor is still practiced. The cheaper labor in Europe enables them to do the work at less expense than hand labor could do it here. But machinery comes to the rescue. Yet there is only a difference in the finished yard of a silk worth 85 cents, manufacturers' cost, of 3 cents in the labor between Zurich and New York. For Lyons the calculation is more simple. The manufacturer pays a specified price, which includes all operations from the dyed tram and organzine up to the finishing. The finishing is done separately by finishers at the rate of 5 centimes the meter, about ¾ cent per yard. For this class of silk 80 centimes is paid per meter, or 14½ cents the yard. The weaver gets half, or 7¼ cents, and for the other 7¼ cents the master furnishes all the rest—shop, rent, harnessing the loom, winding the tram, and all incidental factory expenses. The total cost, therefore, is a trifle over 15 cents per yard. The power loom work is given out on the same principle. The owner of the mill, situated away in the country, to avail himself of the cheap labor of peasant girls, pays one-half of the price he gets to the weaving girl, and the other half supplies the incidental labor expenses and profits.

In Crefeld some power mills have been started. They pay at the rate of 3 marks or 72 cents a day. For this pay the weaver has to turn out a certain number of meters, according to the number of shoots to the inch. If he does less than the regulated quantity a corresponding deduction is made from his wages. Of a quality like the one under discussion he would have to do about 12 yards a day, which would bring the weaving wage per yard to 6 cents, not very different from our price per yard. But here the weaver has two looms, while in Crefeld, as well as in the southern centres, one loom is the rule. The American weaver turns out 20 yards a day, and earns for this reason his higher wages in silk weaving, the same as in other employments which we have traversed in our journey over the world's industries. How small the differences in the labor cost, after all this clamor of selfish interests.

But what savings are effected by the other agency is illustrated in our sample, too. In America the silk consumed in a piece of 200 yards as given by the manufacturers is 10.27 pounds. Organzine pari (not loaded) and 12.17 pounds of tram loaded to 20-22 ounces, or about 65 per cent. In Lyons the experts at the consulate, to whom I submitted my sample for analysis, stated that this silk would be loaded more heavily in Lyons, and would consume 7.68 pounds of organzine and 10.20 pounds of tram. The saving is therefore 4.56 pounds of silk in the piece, equal to 20 per cent. Besides this, that the silk would be some 40 to 50 cents cheaper per pound than the silk we are using in America. This is only putting the heavier loading against a lighter loading, leaving a much greater margin from lighter weighted down to pure dyes. But as it is, the two silk accounts stand as follows per yard:

	Lyons. Cents.		America. Cents.
Value of silk	44.7		60.7
Dyeing of silk, 85 cents per pound	7.7	(65 cents per pound)	7.15
Labor, etc	15.25		18.00
Total	67.65		85.85
Manufacturing cost differences (labor) over Lyons			+ 2¾
Differences due to heavier weighting of silk			+ 16
Total difference			+ 18¾

We see by this practical demonstration how much greater the cost differences wrought by invisible than by visible causes.

General Conditions of Silk Manufacturing in America.

Weavers under the old rates could make considerably higher weekly wages—from $14 to $16 where they earn from $8 to $9 now. The high pay formerly given attracted a great deal of help from European countries. The high profits obtainable under a 50 per cent. tariff (which covers the duty-free silk as well as the labor cost in the goods) started people in silk manufacturing who had little understanding of its requirements and character. Manufacturers paid willingly whatever price capable labor could be got for. This to an extent depleted the European labor market and somewhat raised the cost of weaving there. But the tide turned. The abundance of weavers thrown over here, under stagnating trade, soon enabled the manufacturers to reverse matters, and to dictate terms to the weavers instead of being dictated to by them. The increased supply and lessened demand from change of fashion reduced wages, of course.

Silk manufacturing cannot be established in a rush and be a lasting success. It wants closer study and greater knowledge of a greater variety of detail than is required in most other industries. Here, however, less is brought in under the artificial stimulus given it than in most other industries. The waste in American mills is greater on this account. Profits are realized by American manufacturers thoroughly understanding their business, while loss is marked where this qualification is absent. Truly it can be said that the industry suffers from indigestion. As a manufacturer, having mills here and in Europe, told me recently, "People go into manufacturing without any previous knowledge and understanding. A man came to me not long ago, saying that he had a capital of about $30,000 which he wanted to employ in silk manufacturing. He wished to start in the business, and wanted me to tell him what machinery he would require and how to go about it. He had not the first idea of silk manufacturing, and still was ready to embark in an enterprise so costly and risky. I advised him to keep his money and put it in a safe deposit company, and he would make more out of it than out of the silk manufactory if he asked me such questions."

I only repeat what capable manufacturers have stated, when I say that the silk industry would be in a far healthier condition to-day if the tariff had never exceeded 25 to 35 per cent. *ad valorem*. The class of men of whom the above-described enterprising capitalist is a typical example would certainly have been kept out of the business and have devoted itself to more congenial occupations; as it is, more such men than a few are silk manufacturers. As in all tariff-bred industries, the pressure comes from over competition at home and far less from foreign countries, and least of all from France, the world leader in taste and fashion.

CHAPTER IX.

Silk Plushes.—Increased Duties to Foster Non-existing Industries.—Marked Decline in Silk Manufacturing in General.—Tariffs cannot supply the Absence of Skill and Knowledge.

WE imported for the fiscal year 1890, $38,686,000, and for the year 1891 (nine months of the new tariff), $37,880,000 of silk goods, a falling off of $800,000. That this slight reduction is due to other causes than our improved ability to keep out of our markets the fabrics of Europe under the tariff is seen from the far greater falling off in importations of raw silk. We imported in 1890 to the value of $24,325,000, and in 1891 to the value of only $19,077,000, a falling off of $5,250,000 in raw silk, inclusive of waste silk.

The value of manufactured silk, however, is fully double that of raw silk, considering the increased product which is turned out of a pound of pure silk nowadays, under the processes already described. This decrease of $5,250,000 in the consumption of raw silk is therefore equal to a falling off of some $10,000,000 in the production of silk goods. "The tariff was not increased in plain silks," I shall be answered, "hence we do not see how the McKinley act could have contributed to the depression in silks." True, but we cannot but see that tariffs cannot force people into buying what they do not find to their taste. We have seen that American goods, so far as regards cost of production, can easily keep out of the country foreign duty-paid goods. But this is not sufficient. The great falling off in the

American product, compared with the small decrease in importation, shows that we have to look for relief to some other remedial agency than a high tariff; to wit, excellence, through whatever may be the means required to reach it.

The manufacturers, whose position as pioneers of the trade makes them the fittest judges of its requirements, deprecated any increase of duties. Still, some pushing outsiders, mostly engaged in other lines, succeeded in getting their specialties, present and prospective (but more the latter than the former), taken care of. "Velvets, plushes, or other pile fabrics," as in other textiles, were singled out in silks for special legislative favors. The tariff, formerly one of 50 per cent., was changed into a compound tariff as follows:

1. Goods containing less than 75 per cent. in weight of silk to pay $1.50 per pound and 15 per cent. *ad valorem*.

2. Goods containing more than 75 per cent. in weight of silk to pay $3.50 per pound and 15 per cent. *ad valorem*. "But in no case shall any of the foregoing articles pay a less rate of duty than 50 per centum *ad valorem*." No danger. Few goods, except all-silk velvets, cost over $10 a pound. Most of the goods coming under this clause have a heavy cotton back; the silk is schappe, or waste silk, and would average nearer $3 than $4 a pound. All of them are necessaries and not luxuries. Our higher standard of life makes the working girl, the servant girl, and the farmer's wife and daughter the principal consumers of these fabrics, which are used for millinery, as well as for cloakings and trimmings. No American woman would go bareheaded or without a cloak or mantle, whatever the fashion, on a holiday excursion or to her daily work, as her sisters do all over the continent of Europe. We live on a different plane, on a higher level. With us things have become necessaries which in other countries may well be called luxuries. To

call them so here is rank nonsense. To use the plea as a cover for filching higher taxes out of the slender incomes of our female wage earners is perfidious, and adds insult to injury.

How the new imposition acts on prices can be seen from a comparison of the importer's selling prices of velvet and plushes under the old 50 per cent. duty and the new compound duty, foreign price and measure reduced to cents and yards:

PRICES OF COTTON-BACK VELVETS, EIGHTEEN INCHES WIDE.

	Cents.	Cents.	Cents.
Foreign price	32	40½	47
Price in New York under old tariff	52½	75	85
Price in New York under new tariff	70	86	95
Increase per cent	33½	15	12
Difference foreign and present American	38	44½	48
Difference per cent. over foreign price	120	110	102

PRICES OF PLUSHES FOR MILLINERIES, ETC.

	15 in. Cents.	18 in. Cents.	18 in. Cents.	18 in. Cents.	24 in. Cents.
Foreign price	18	23	24	26	34
Under old tariff	31½	39	41	50	60
Under new tariff	45	55	57½	65	80
Increase per cent	40	40	40	30	33½
Difference, cents, foreign and American	27	32	33½	39	46
Difference foreign and American per cent	150	140	145	150	136

The increase is heaviest in plushes, because the relative weight is greater of cotton in the fabric. The cotton back in plushes is of a heavier, coarser yarn than in velvets. We have never made velvets. Our manufacturers understand the difficulties, and have not attempted an enterprise which has offered small prospects at best. If a protection of 75 per cent. (practically this is the rate of protection, the difference between the foreign shipping prices and the American importer's selling prices) gave no stimulation, the increase will not supply the want of ability—the main cause of our neglect. These cheap velvets and plushes are made on power looms to a considerable extent now in the Crefeld district. The cheapest grades of schappe and waste silks are used. In the handling of these we are very deficient, while in Crefeld they are very expert. These goods, with cotton-back satins, form the principal industry there, and give employment to multitudes of weavers for twenty and thirty miles into the country.

They know how to make a little go a great way. When the Crefeld and Lyons cotton-back satins come out of the finisher's hands they have a brilliancy of face, softness of touch, and richness of color tint far ahead of that which goods of the same composition would have here. Even a larger percentage of superior silks in the American satins show lack-lustre, dull, leaden colors compared with the foreign product, while the finish usually gives a hard sizing which leaves creases when handled. In plushes the outlook at the first glance seems a more promising one.

The goods are woven in two layers, and the pile is cut automatically. On power looms two widths are stretched, and two lower and two upper pieces are turned out in one operation. But the reasons which stay our hands in velvets must stand for something in plushes, else we could have made them successfully under the old tariff. The protection was ample, the inducement sufficient for starting any number of mills. But we did not make any. The demand for these goods is a fickle one, as every manufacturer and dealer knows. The inducements are not great enough to counteract the risks of starting a mill with machinery for the manufacture of goods which might be blocked up in the storehouses on a change of fashion from velvets and plushes to flowers and ribbons. The heavy decline in the importations of plushes is taken in some quarters as a realization of the early promise that after the passing of the McKinley act we should make our own plushes and cotton-back velvets.

The reduced importation of waste silk, however, tells plainly enough that this cannot have been the case. To make the goods here on a basis of importations of previous years would have required an importation of waste silk of many millions of pounds. But actually we imported less in 1891 than in 1890 (1,300,000 pounds against 1,404,000 pounds).* In point of fact, fashion has changed so quickly, that but few velvets and plushes are bought as compared to a year ago. For all these reasons it is easy to understand why old-established manufacturing houses did not feel interested in and even advised against the increase. But to quote Pope: "Fools rush in where angels fear to tread."

The impetus came from quarters where silk was only an incidental industry. The aim was to get a greater profit and experimenting margin for manufacturing seal plushes, then in large demand for cloaks, than under the 50 per cent. tariff, or rather to exclude the English plushes by putting the price up so high that people would be forced into buying the American substitute. Furniture plushes had been very successfully made by some of these parties; so success-

---

* For the eleven months of the fiscal year of 1891–92, just past, the outlook for these new national wards, waste silk plushes and velvets, is a more dismal one yet. The importations compare for a like period of the preceding year as $575,026 against $955,100. In weight 1,033,730 pounds against 1,190,486 pounds of the preceding year. This is the more remarkable, because the importation of reeled silk has increased again to the old position, under a better demand for the plainer silks, where we are able to hold the field, as shown in the preceding chapter.

fully, that for quite a number of years foreign goods were entirely excluded from our markets. Under the old duty (an *ad valorem* one, too) the manufacturers made very handsome fortunes. But this must have whetted the appetite for the great seal plush trade. They obtained their morsel, but, alas! the expected revel turned out a Barmecide feast. The great increase of tariff duties induced English manufacturers to bring over their machinery and their help to transfer the manufacture from foreign to American soil.

This could have been foreseen by any but greedy would-be manufacturers. Under a declining demand and increasing production, the increased home competition would have at once taken the advantage to be derived from the increased tariff out of the hands of the American manufacturers. English friends of mine came here last winter for the purpose of prospecting the field. I advised against their transfer. They said that these goods had been made of late years only for the American market. The machinery was on hand, and it would cost little except the duty on old machinery to transfer the manufacturing plant entire; otherwise the machinery would prove a dead loss. This party did not come over. Others, however, did. But they did not make much out of the venture, and will probably regret not having stayed at home.

The industry was started, but the results of a year's operations are not very brilliant. The demand for the article was on the decline previous to the enactment of the McKinley bill. "At the end of 1890," I am informed by one of the leading cloak manufacturers who knows the market most thoroughly, "there were probably 5,000 pieces in the hands of manufacturers and importers to supply the demand for 1891. When the various domestic factories were established, they received orders for fair quantities, but hardly any of the broad goods (fifty to fifty-two inches wide) made in this country were satisfactory; they were inferior in color and finish even to the poorer qualities of English goods, so that they had to be sold at cost or below. The narrow (twenty-four inches wide) domestic goods were better, and a fair quantity was sold; but the demand proved to be much smaller than was anticipated, and did not equal that of former years by perhaps 50 per cent., so that, it is stated by competent authority, there are now quite large stocks in the hands of manufacturers and commission merchants.

"But there is a worse side than this in the way the working people are affected by this system of establishing industries by act of Congress. In order to manufacture these goods here, a large portion of the factory hands had to be imported from England, while, at the same time, quite a number of resident working people found employment in these mills. As it is, most of these imported hands have been thrown out of employment at the beginning of winter; they intend to return, or probably by this time those able to defray the expense have returned, to England, where things have changed to the better for them. The demand for English plushes, slacking here, has largely increased on the Continent, so that, after all, we have not succeeded in causing great injury to England, which, from utterances cast about freely at the time, seems to have been the main object of the McKinley bill. Those who elect to stay along with the resident American help will scatter and look about for other occupations, as hardly any of the newly-established plush factories can either continue to work at present or resume operations for months to come at the best."

The benefits which the new industries established under the McKinley bill brought to labor are not very prominent. The account which the enterprising manufacturers may yet have to score may prove more costly in the end than the loss on the sale of undesirable surplus stocks left on their hands. That the goods needed no extra tariff stimulus to make the enterprise remunerative, if conducted with the skill and technical knowledge required, will become evident from an examination of the English cost of production, which I have obtained from a prominent manufacturer there. I have two qualities of 50-inch width. The cheaper quality weighs 24 ounces a yard, and is sold at 10s., or $2.43. The old duty equalled $1.21½; the new duty is $1.50 per pound, or $2.25 per yard, plus 15 per cent., or 36½ cents; total, $2.61½, or 108 per cent. The importer's selling price under the old tariff could not have been less than $4.50, allowing for 7 per cent. discount (the usual rate) and a 10 per cent. profit. This left a margin of fully $2 to pay the difference which American labor usually gets as its share above foreign labor. But what is the foreign labor cost?

(1) Cost of yarn per piece of 28 yards.
No. 2-40 cotton warp, 6 pounds 3 ounces, 15½s........$2.27
No. 2-14 weft, 13 pounds 7 ounces, 10s.............. 2.69
No. 2-17 spun silk (Tussar), 21 pounds 12 ounces, 8s.. 43.21

    Total................................. $47.17

This is material per yard........................$1.69
(2) Weaving....................................... 8
Incidental labor, etc............................. 4
Dyeing and finishing, 8½d........................ 17

    Total................................$1.98

Leaving 45 cents for general mill expenses and profit.

The better quality weighs 25 ounces and is sold at 14s., or $3.40. The new duty on this quality stands $\frac{24}{16}$ × $1.50, equal to $2.34, and adding 15 per cent. *ad valorem*, 51 cents; total, $2.85, or 84 per cent. The importer's selling price came under the old duty to $6.50, which left a very considerable profit to be divided between labor and capital to any enterprising manufacturer (which is always a fixed quantity—90 per cent. labor and 10 per cent. profit).

The materials in this quality were:

No. 3-60 warp, 9 pounds 7 ounces, 44 cents	$4.15
No. 2-30 weft, 8 pounds (14s.), 28 cents	2.24
No. 2-35 silk yarn, 26 pounds (10s.), $2.43	63.18
Per piece of 28 yards	$69.57
or $2.48½ a yard.	

A margin of $4—sufficient, one would suppose, to satisfy the most exorbitant demands of both labor and capital without a raising of duties.

In this quality the weaving rate is 1½ d., or 3 cents, above the lower quality. The other elements of cost are about the same. The dyeing and finishing include all incidentals belonging to the two operations. The direct labor cost in these would not exceed one-third of the price quoted for dyeing and finishing.

The cotton yarns do not cost more here than in England. The labor cost in these is not above the English. That we have the proficiency of the English for spinning spun silks may be doubted, generally speaking, but the mills that were making these goods are certainly proficient in the handling of the silk in their furniture plushes. They make their own yarns, and what they pay in their spinning department more than is paid in England, would not add much to the labor expense of a yard of seal plush. The weaving cost, if it were double and treble the English rate, would not have cut a deep hole in the margin left over the English cost.

The difficulty in successfully making seal plushes could at no time have been in the difference in labor cost.

The old duty gave to the manufacturer here in the lower quality a margin of $2 over the English cost, inclusive of charges and profit. In this $2.43 of the English price, the labor cost is 29 cents, including dyeing and finishing expense. The dyeing and finishing done in England by outside parties contains the cost of supplies and dyes plus the profit, which in American mills is not included in the mill account, but goes into the general profit. Allowing, therefore, double for all this, twice 29 cents, or 58 cents for manufacturing in America (of which at least 18 cents ought to go to dyeing materials, etc.), it will be seen that a certain profit of $2 was in store for the American who could give to the trade goods in every way as satisfactory as the English plushes.

In naming this margin of profit I set the increased cost on account of labor against the profit of the English manufacturer, which, of course, is included in the price of $2.43.

In the second quality, the profit to the American manufacturer would have been as high as $3.08 over the English shipping price. The labor cost is but a few pence higher than in the lower quality. The margin of profit, however, is considerably above that what it is in the lower quality. On a basis of net cost, i.e., minus the profit of the English manufacturer, the American, under the old duty, had a profit guarantee of $2.25 a yard, and in the finer goods of $3.50, or 100 per cent. and 150 per cent. respectively.

From this it must be plain that under the old duty the goods could have been made as well as under a higher duty. What is required cannot be supplied by protective duties. It has been stated above that Germany, with all the advantages it derives from its many universities and technical high schools, could not equal England in the dyeing of seal plushes, and less yet in the finishing, where the difficulties are equally great.

The Germans as well as the French are drawing their own supply from England. A demand springing up from these highly developed manufacturing nations means an immediate activity in English mills. Our people had to learn for the hundredth time the same old lesson, and pay dearly for it, that an ounce of foresight is better than a pound of hindsight. But experience must be bought at a high price to be of value as a lesson.

America has found out, too, that the main difficulty lies here also in the dyeing and the finishing. Many of the goods that were cut up proved well-nigh worthless. Many of these goods, looking well enough in the piece, when made up and worn and subjected to the influence of perspiration, changed color and became rusty-red and rather undesirable luxuries. Goods gaining an unenviable reputation through such vital defects cannot easily come into favor again, and so this industry, too, has become extinct after a brief *début*, and will be known to posterity only from the fame it received as being one of the remarkable industrial creations of the McKinley act.

These creations are a fine sight, to be sure. Advertised far and wide with great flourish of trumpets as the solution of the question how to employ our surplus labor, they one and all have either not been able to start, or when started have been doomed speedily to wither and sink into an early grave. Like Potemkin's painted prosperity, villages and towns, they fill the prospect for an hour, and disappear as soon as the royal *cortége* has passed.

CHAPTER X.

Wool and Woolens.—Protection frustrated by its own Excesses.—Wool Artificially Dear limits Consumption.—Decrease of Sheep.—Increase in England.—Decline in Wool Manufacture traceable to the Tariff.—Great Increase in the Use of Wool Substitutes.

ARIADNE'S thread is required to lead us through the maze of the tariff in its relation to the woolen industry. The industry is so complicated and comprises so many subdivisions that, without a systematic treatment of its most important branches, the space here available would not permit me to give an adequate idea of the importance of the subject. Not alone is a greater line of industries affected by the wool tariff, but the very health of our people pays tribute to it. The raw wool, varying as it is, is but a uniform article compared with the variety of manufactures wrought of it. Wool and shoddy, cotton and wool, woolens and worsteds, dress goods and clothes, knit goods and knit "fabrics," all are covered by the one general name. Each implies such differences in manufacturing and in work, that all similarity disappears outside of the fibre and of the common name. The name, even, is no guarantee for the possession of the quality. Some fabrics contain so little wool, that it is an abuse of language to call them woolens. Cotton and ground woolen rags form the material upon which much good labor is wasted. We have to treat seriatim the leading branches. But if dissimilar in all respects, they have this in common, that they all proclaim the unavoidable necessity of free wool for the consumer's interest, as well as the producer's.

The Wool.

It is conceded by all whose opinions are worth considering, that in a climate like ours wool is, of all materials used for clothing, the most conducive to health. Our cold winters and the frequent, sudden, and great changes in our temperature make woolen clothing of as great importance to health as pure drinking water and unadulterated food. Fortunately wool has become so cheap that nothing could prevent a vastly greater consumption in America if things and prices were left to find their own level. But here again the Republican lawmakers say cheapness is a curse, and must be prevented in the interest of the producer, which means—so many electoral votes from Ohio, etc. "We'll put on a specific duty of 11 cents a pound for the wool, and 11 cents for each pound of grease, sand, and dung that may be found mixed with or contained in each pound of absolutely clean wool as it goes in the manufactured state into clothing." But how will this wool producer stand if outside prices keep dropping, dropping, dropping, to which fact our own meddlesome laws have contributed not a little, and the buffer only helps make a breach in the wall for foreign manufactures and shorten the market of American woolens made of American wool? Wool, as a fact, has become provokingly cheap. How cheap can be seen from a brief history of prices.

England was all through the Middle Ages, as she is now, the great wool-producing country of Europe. The price of wool in the fourteenth century averaged about 4s. 6d. a stone, or 4d. a pound, which, money at only twelve times the present value, is equivalent to 4s. (97 cents) a pound. A nearer appreciation of this we get when we consider that the price of wheat averaged about 5s. a quarter, or 7½d. a bushel. A pound of wool was then worth half a bushel of wheat, or a day's wages of a master carpenter or a master mason. At the present time, wool worth about 20 cents and wheat one dollar, a bushel of wheat buys five pounds of wool. One pound of wool buys now only one-sixth to one-eighth of an English carpenter's, bricklayer's or mason's workday. Wool was the chief article of importance; almost the only article of export, it was also the only one which gave revenue to the crown. Agriculture was the principal occupation then. The produce of the land alone could yield revenue. Wool manufacturing barely existed as an industry. Flanders, however, was the seat of a great woolen industry, and raised little wool. Hence the great demand for English wool, even at double the price ruling in England, and the facility of collecting an export duty as high as 100 per cent. from it.

In the seventeenth century, woolen manufacturing became a great industry in England. The manufacturers wanted cheap wool. In consequence, the exportation of wool was prohibited and made a felony in 1662 in England and Ireland. In 1690 a law was passed, practically closing the English ports to Irish woolens, thus ruining the industry formerly flourishing there. The Navigation act had previously excluded them from the colonies. Arthur Young declares it one of the most infamous statutes that ever disgraced a legislature.

Under the sway of these laws, English wool was worth about 25 cents a pound.* But Spanish wool, which up to

---

* Arthur Young, in "The Question of Wool Truly Stated," gives very interesting details, which are worth quoting, if only for the moral they convey, and to show that legislative interference with trade has never the desired effect : " In 1660 the laws first seriously avowed the absolute prohibition of exporting wool. In 1662 it was made a felony. But the severity answered so ill the intention, which was to encourage the manufacturer, that in 1665 the act passed, directing all persons to be buried in

the middle of this century occupied the position that Australian wool holds to-day for fine wool, was worth from 60 to about 80 cents a pound. After this policy was abandoned, a small import duty was put on wool. But under free wool in 1850, English wool had become worth about 45 cents, and Spanish wool commanded about the same price. Free trade in wool evidently did not depress the price of wool, but, in extending the markets of the manufacturers, extended the market of the farmer for his fleece, and so benefited him to a greater extent than any protective duty could have done. These high prices for English wool remained up to about 1875. Fashion favored the demand for English wool,

---

woolen, by an extraordinary policy forcing the dead to consume what the living were inadequate to purchase. In 1688 the prohibition was repeated, a sure proof that it had not answered ; which was more formally avowed by the statute of the 7th and 8th of William, which repealed the felony of 1662, declaring it to be too severe to be executed. In 1699 the law passed, that subjected Kent and Sussex to those restrictions which the bill of 1787 proposed to extend to all the coasts of the kingdom. In 1699 the Irish woolen fabrics were destroyed by one of the most infamous statutes that ever disgraced a legislature, manifestly proving how little the new system had answered. In 1717 the act passed, that made the non-payment of the fine punishable by transportation, marking decidedly enough that smuggling was then as much complained of as ever. In 1732 the Boards of Trade made a report to the House of Commons against the plan pushed by the manufacturers for a general registry of all the wool grown in England. In 1739 the general Wool act passed, the preamble of which declares that the clandestine export is great and notorious, etc."

" From this deduction it appears clearly, through the long course of 128 years, that severity and restrictions are not the means of putting a stop to smuggling." A further good illustration how the farmer fares in the partnership of protection is also given by Young. In a speech he says : " The manufacturer says to the farmer, ' I will have your wool 100 per cent. cheaper than you could sell it for abroad.' ' Very well,' replies the farmer, ' then you will let me buy my coat at the cheapest market.' ' Not at all,' returns the other; ' you shall buy it of no one but me, let the price be what it may.' "

and long after the fine wools had become depressed in price, English wool held its high price of twice the value of colonial wool. The unparalleled increase in the supply from the antipodes (in 1860, 189,000,000 pounds; 1875, 619,000,000 pounds; 1885, 880,000,000; and now about 1,000,000,000 pounds) did not alter this until fashion pronounced her unalterable decree, which shows, aside of all other points to be deduced from a consideration of these facts, that demand makes prices for commodities, and that wool and wool are different things.

American Wool.

English wool has rapidly declined since, and is now barely worth more than Australian wool. A long and strong staple, formerly the principal combing wool, it finds now, with the improved combing machinery, a formidable rival in New Zealand, Botany, and other similar wools. Still, the flocks of sheep increase in England. The present number is stated to be 33,000,000 to 34,000,000 head. Per capita of population, this is more than in America. In America sheep raising for the fleece recedes with the growth of population. The Territories, even, cannot keep it up long as a paying enterprise. The inferior quality of the fleece precludes a high price for wool, protection or no protection. The losses from all causes, principally from winter exposure, are extremely heavy. In 1889 the loss in the new Western States and Territories, including California, amounted to 15 per cent. (2,500,000 in about 17,000,000, in some of these reaching as high as 21, 23, and even 34 per cent.).

The farmers of the older States show their real appreciation of the American sheep by letting him die out by gentle diminution. Even Ohio goes back on the poor sheep which has been such a mainstay in politics. But politics knows no friendship, either in sheep or man. Except for the mutton, sheep raising in the States would become a lost art, despite all the efforts of our political shepherds. This is shown by the following tables for the years 1870 and 1889, taken from the Reports of the Department of Agriculture:

NUMBER OF SHEEP IN THE OLD SHEEP-RAISING STATES.

	In Thousands.	
	1869-70.	1889.
1. Maine	551	542
2. New Hampshire	466	193
3. Vermont	976	362
4. New York	4,350	1,548
5. Pennsylvania	2,850	945
6. Virginia	557	444
7. North Carolina	325	415
8. Georgia	275	412
9. Tennessee	866	511
10. West Virginia	827	508
11. Kentucky	942	806
12. Missouri	1,579	1,198
13. Illinois	1,091	688
14. Indiana	2,160	1,278
15. Ohio	6,250	3,943
16. Michigan	3,340	2,240
17. Wisconsin	1,670	809
18. Iowa	2,003	475
Total	31,582	17,317

Number of sheep in all the States and Territories in 1869-70, 40,853,000.
Number of sheep in all the States and Territories in 1889, 44,336,000.
Increase in population, 50 per cent.
Total increase in sheep, 8½ per cent.
Percentage of total in the old States in 1869-70, 77 per cent.
Percentage of total in the old States in 1889, 39 per cent.
Decline in number of sheep in the old States, 14,250,000.
Decline in number of sheep in the old States, 45 per cent.

But to make the lesson to be taken from this comparative statement more conspicuous yet, it is only necessary to show what progress has been made in the status of other live stock in these agricultural States, foremost in sheep raising twenty years ago.

COMPARATIVE STATEMENT OF OTHER LIVE STOCK (IN THOUSANDS).

	Horses.		Oxen and Milch Cows.		Hogs.	
	1869-70.	1889.	1869-70.	1889.	1869-70.	1889.
Maine	87	91	385	333	45	62
New Hampshire	48	52	228	219	31	52
Vermont	65	84	333	404	44	70
New York	600	674	2,116	2,336	095	686
Pennsylvania	501	607	1,450	1,791	1,014	1,193
Virginia	220	259	535	692	904	1,009
North Carolina	125	154	501	671	850	1,292
Georgia	108	116	651	935	1,335	1,627
Tennessee	317	303	541	862	1,503	2,242
West Virginia	90	147	311	466	357	486
Kentucky	321	391	630	841	1,955	2,255
Missouri	460	790	1,060	2,290	2,300	5,096
Illinois	881	1,124	1,583	2,786	2,005	5,433
Indiana	555	668	1,002	1,560	2,025	2,845
Ohio	724	772	1,502	1,778	1,700	2,611
Michigan	259	477	685	1,002	462	979
Wisconsin	275	438	813	1,480	427	1,087
Iowa	514	1,095	1,162	3,900	2,500	5,805
Total	6,150	7,842	15,488	24,355	20,464	34,855

These figures tell the story. The decline in sheep raising is evidently due to the fact that the farmer long ago found out that his farm, and, along with it, his income, are benefited more by the raising of live stock than of sheep. The shepherd and the agriculturist soon part company. The myth of Cain slaying his brother Abel gives early emphasis to an old historical fact. The myth is the epitome of history.

The United States emphasize this historical commonplace by the decline of sheep from a status of 31,000,000 in 1869-70 to one of 17,000,000 in 1889. When agriculture expands, the wool sheep becomes an unimportant incident. The chief value centres then in the mutton. But as the more desirable mutton sheep carries a different character of wool from our wool breeds, it is the more apparent that the wool tariff cannot help the farmer, but work only injury to the manufacturer. That the number of the English sheep is not allowed to decrease is due to the fact that he carries under his wool what in time becomes most excellent mutton. Though our mutton is inferior to English mutton, yet it brings equally good returns, and so do the tallow and the skin. But advocates of a wool tariff would have us believe that the only salable value is in the wool, and that a possible loss of 60 cents in the entire fleece would ruin the farmers, a majority of whom do not own a single sheep, and nine-tenths not above three sheep on an average. Still they keep on paying fifty times that amount each year on their woolen goods in order to keep up the sixty-cent protection on the sheep. The Irish statutes referred to above prompted Dean Swift to say: "Ajax was mad when he mistook a flock of sheep for his enemies, but we shall never be sober until we have the same way of thinking." And this sentiment very fitly applies to the situation created in America by the high wool tariff.

Other Disastrous Effects of a Wool Tariff.

One of the greatest disadvantages to the manufacturer, and to the grower, reversely, is the exclusion of foreign wools. He cannot mix his wools properly, and seldom has the right wool in the right place. Unless fashion gives him a chance for profitably using his favored American brands, he will continue to see foreign wools imported in the manufactured state and given a preference over his own. The manufacturer, by protection, has become an exclusionist. This is more the case in wool and woolens than in any other branch. He does not study the progress made in Europe, principally in England and Germany, with as keen an eye as he would if the pressure of competition were brought nearer home to him. But worst of all, he is deprived of the chance of a fair selection, because many most desirable wools never come to him. They are excluded by the tariff or neglected by the wool importer. But to the English manufacturer they are a very profitable material, either for the back, the filling, or the entire fabric. Despite their cheapness they have a spring and elasticity which ever give cheap English goods so much life and character. The absence of these features in our wools, their dryness and dulness, make our goods appear quite dead and uninteresting by the side of English corresponding fabrics.

A dense ignorance seems to prevail as to the character of the different classes of wool so essential for giving the fabrics the stamp of genuineness, without which they cannot pass the critical eye of trade. Neglect and ignorance are the worst enemies of industries, but they become rampant under protective legislation. It would be strange if woolen manufacturers made an exception to the rule. A duty averaging some 75 per cent. made them believe that they had fullest control of the home market. The duty on wool, neutralizing this to a very large extent, took away much of their chance, and besides made them look to the home growth as the only source of supply (except as to the carpet wools, not grown in America). The quantity of clothing and combing wools imported is ridiculously small, considering their greater desirability at nearly equal prices, duty added, than the corresponding home product.

But some of these wools are practically excluded by the tariff taxing the grease and dirt the same as wool, so that high shrinkage wools cannot be imported at all, and, of course, remain unknown. Others again could be very advantageously brought in on account of light shrinkage, but remain unknown on account of the stream of foreign supply not running our way. Hence, an ignorance of the particular merits of the various kinds has become all but universal.

This was brought home to me very forcibly in wools used for sackings in England (6-4 sackings, flannel weave, used for ladies' dress), on which I sent a report to the State Department. The wool used in the English fabric I described as "Cape or Sydney wool, for which they pay $6\frac{1}{2}d.$, or 13 cents, a pound. The wool shrinks 50 per cent. in scouring, with an additional loss in manufacturing, and yields $6\frac{1}{4}$ pounds of cloth to 16 pounds grease wool. The wool would then stand at $16d.$, or 32 cents, per pound in the cloth." Another mill used in similar goods "New South Wales greasy lamb, pieces and locks, of which the present price is $5\frac{1}{2}d.$, or 11 cents, per pound." This wool was much greasier, and yielded only 25 per cent. of cloth to the pound of greasy wool—hence dearer in the cloth, though cheaper in the wool price. No one would think of importing this class of wool and paying 44 cents duty, or 100 per cent. on sufficient wool to make a pound of cloth. The editor of the Boston *Journal of Commerce* gave expression to doubts considering these prices quoted in my reports. He said: "The comparative cost of stock is evidently wrong, for if Sydney or Cape could be bought in England at 13 cents per pound, shrinking 50 per cent., the American manufacturer would certainly pay the duty of 10 cents a pound, and get his wool at 46 cents clean, instead of paying 70 cents." The matter seemed to me somewhat questionable too, and I expressed my surprise to the manufacturer from whom I got my information first, at his office in Leeds. He invited me out to his factory, and there took me through the different departments. The wool in question was very fine, but very short and burry. It was not more than from half to three-quarters of an inch long, and some parts did not measure that. The burs were extracted by the acid process; that is, the wool is subjected to an acid bath to eat out the burs, and then carbonized to kill the acid. This I witnessed with my own eyes. Why our manufacturers do not make use of these wools of lighter shrinkage can only be explained on the above premises. On the other hand, it must be admitted that what our goods of this character lack in brilliancy and lustre they gain in strength. So far the long fibre of Ohio wool, as represented in an American sample which I used for comparison, was superior in wearing quality to the short staple referred to above. In this instance the short staple and the difficulty of extracting the burs may offer an explanation, though by no means a sufficient one, for their exclusion. But this would not at all explain why our manufacturers do not use Scotch wools and Irish wools for flannels and for tweeds. They are of very low shrinkage, and would give an article vastly superior to our inferior looking substitutes.

At Inverness the best cheviot wool, with very light shrinkage, sells at 22s. 6d. to 24s. the stone of 24 pounds. This is equal to 24 cents a pound. The ordinary Scotch wool sells at about 10s. the stone of 24 pounds, or at about 10 cents a pound. The price at Leeds is about 12 cents.

Nothing makes a more desirable article for outside wear, men's suiting, ulsters, and wraps for hard weather, than Irish wool. It is suitable for all purposes. It is worked into tweeds, friezes, worsteds, knitting yarn, etc. Irish wool has always ranked high, and when it was a felony under the old English law to export wool, the most lively contraband trade with France was conducted along the whole south and western coast of Ireland. Now the best Irish wool sells at 11s. the stone, or about 17 to 18 cents a pound. This wool shrinks from 10 to 12 per cent. in scouring. Knitting yarn made of it is sold by the mill at 16d., or 32 cents a pound. Against this our corresponding wools cost near 30 cents, with a shrinkage in scouring of from 35 to 50 per cent. I have kept samples of all the fabrics in which these wools are used. The most superficial examination would convince any one of the superior character of these wools, and that it would be profitable to employ them in our tweed, serge, cheviot, and worsted mills. The crispness and spring of an Irish tweed before me, 54 inches wide and 23 ounces in weight, at 3s. 9d., less cash discount, 85 cents (all pure Irish wool), and the dull, cottony appearance of an American tweed, 22 ounces in weight (the filling wool and shoddy), and selling at the time at $1.25, less the discount, would convince anybody that these wools would give character to our goods and make them more desirable than the spurious ones going under that name, without increasing the cost.

Many other kinds of foreign wools could be mentioned, equally low in price as these, and cheaper than American wool of corresponding character, duty paid, on account of their lower shrinkage in the scouring. I submitted some wool samples of American growth to Mr. Bowes of Liverpool, an acknowledged authority in all matter concerning wool, for comparison with foreign wools used in England. He selected the corresponding brands and sent them to an expert in Leeds for analysis with these results:

1. Ohio XX.
2. Fine, year's growth, Texas.
3. Fall shearing, Texas.
4. Medium Colorado.
5. Spring California.
6. Coarse Colorado.

7. Superior New Zealand, unwashed.
8. Average New Zealand, unwashed.
9. Ordinary New Zealand, unwashed.
10. Ordinary Cape, unwashed.
11. Montevideo, unwashed.
12. Georgian, unwashed.

They stood after scouring as follows:

Numbers.	Prices Unscoured.		Scoured Prices.		Per Cent. Loss in Scouring.	
	American.	English.	American.	English.	American.	English.
	Cents.	Cents.	Cents.	Cents.		
1 and 7........	33	22	67.5	35.9	51.12	38.67
2 and 8........	23½	15	61.4	33.0	61.71	54.57
3 and 9........	21	13	65.6	23.4	68.00	44.05
4 and 10.......	20½	10	48.8	23.5	58.00	57.31
5 and 11.......	21¼	13	70.7	24.7	69.70	47.39
Carpet wool....						
6 and 12.......	14½	11¾	14.0	14.0	27.81	16.74

We have here three numbers of colonial growth (7, 8, and 9), at 13 cents, and below and at even a lower shrinkage than the one referred to by the editor of the *Journal of Commerce.* The fact, as he states, that "the manufacturer does not pay the duty and import these wools," does not at all disprove their existence, their profitable employment by foreign manufacturers, and their importation in the form of manufactured goods. By their aid, more than by the cheapness of the labor, can so many goods be brought in under the present high tariff, and much to the astonishment of our manufacturers.

Decline in Wool—Increase in Shoddy.

But if sheep and wool have not increased, despite an increase of 50 per cent. in population, the importations of wool and woolens have by no means been proportionate to the gap to be filled. Our wool imports for 1870 were 49,000,000 pounds, and for 1890 105,000,000 pounds, 81,000,000 pounds of which were carpet wools, leaving only 25,000,000 pounds of clothing wool. The increase in clothing and combing wool importation is slight, relatively speaking.

The woolen importations for 1870 were $34,500,000, and $56,000,000 for 1890. Much of this large importation of woolens is traceable to the tariff on wool. These woolen imports show a considerable falling off for 1891, but they are by no means made up by the increase in raw-wool importations of Class 1 and Class 2 (an increase of $3,000,000, against a falling off in woolens of something like $15,000,000 to $20,000,000). It is admitted that the woolen industry of the country had for some time not been in so depressed a condition as in the two years following the passage of the McKinley bill. Combining all these facts, it will be seen that neither wool nor woolens based on the consumable quantity of wool are produced in anything like the quantities of 1870, considering the increase in population.

At the same time we cheerfully chronicle the fact that we have not gone back to paradisaical conditions, but that our people apparently wear woolen clothing. The supply was never so abundant, if the trade aspects (depression in woolens) reported by trade papers far and wide have any meaning. More machinery is employed and more backs are covered. Mr. Porter says that we manufactured $344,000,000 in 1890, against $276,000,000 in 1880. But where does the wool come from? Well, can woolens be made of wool only? By no means. We live in a progressive age, and if wool is made artificially high, we help ourselves by recourse to art, and substitute "art wool" (the German term "Kunst-wolle"), shoddy, for real wool, more and more from year to year.

A comparison of the quantities of wool and wool substitutes entering our mills in the two census years will make this plain.

QUANTITIES OF RAW MATERIALS CONSUMED IN 1880 AND 1890 IN WOOLENS AND WORSTEDS (IN THOUSANDS).

	Wool scoured. lbs.	Shoddy. lbs.	Camel's-hair and noils. lbs.	Mohair and noils. lbs.	All other hair. lbs.	Cotton. lbs.	All other materials. including yarns.
1890	155,236	54,470	6,192	2,098	10,702	41,040	$33,500
1880	135,095	46,773	1,441	115	4,498	26,501	21,480
	19,141	7,697	4,751	1,983	6,204	14,539	$12,020

The reader can draw his own inferences from this parallel. Wool has increased 19 million pounds, about 15 per cent. Wool substitutes, shoddy, hair, and cotton, have increased 35,000,000 pounds over the 79,000,000 pounds consumed in 1880, or about 40 per cent. This does not take into account the great proportion of cotton warps contained in the item of "All other materials." Nor do I draw into this comparison a similar decline in the proportion of real wool to substitutes which took place in the decade from 1870 to 1880.

In 1870 the consumption of shoddy in our woolen mills was 17,500,000 pounds; in 1880 it was 46,000,000 pounds. Exclusive of carpet wools, we consume in woolens and worsteds some 260,000,000 to 275,000,000 pounds of grease wool, home growth and imported. This wool shrinks more than is

THE ECONOMY OF HIGH WAGES. 309

given in the census report. If we assume the shrinkage in the scouring to be only 50 per cent., there would be left 135,-000,000 pounds of clean wool to be put against 112,000,000 of substitutes, shoddy, hair and cotton. Such facts in their brutal, massive force point out a state of decadence under oppressive tariff taxation, principally taxation of raw materials, far more graphically than any dissertation could.

CHAPTER XI.

Woolens and Worsteds.—Method pursued in Comparative Inquiry.—
Inadequacy of Inquiry of National Bureau of Labor.—Labor Cost in
Worsteds in America and England.—Failure of America in Spite of
Tariff Increase.—Reasons.—All the Benefits reaped by Great Cor-
porations.—General Depression in Woolens and Worsteds following
the Tariff Increase.

IN an industry as varied as "Woolens," it will readily be admitted no satisfactory evidence could be gained for comparing cost of production, except by the plan here adopted: to select American samples of products of leading branches of the industry, find the places in England where corresponding goods are manufactured, and there obtain all available information for comparison with the American data. Nobody at all conversant with manufacturing, or commercial matters, even, could possibly think of any other method. There are dozens of different articles, and as many qualities in each leading branch. Each article bears a different percentage of labor to material. The finer tissues have more yards to the pound of wool, hence higher spinning cost and greater weaving expense than the coarser or heavier goods. In mixed goods, in shoddy and cotton, etc., the labor cost would be rather more than less than in the all-wool article, on account of the greater difficulty of working poor yarns than good, sound ones. Yet the ratio of labor to material, equal in the shoddy or mixed goods, would under the same labor cost be 1 to 2 or 3 in the all-wool fabric. But still so plain and natural a method has never been followed, while others which could not lead to any but spurious results were pursued for want of better knowledge, showing again that the most commonplace truths are most liable to be overlooked in the theoretic treatment of economic questions. Taking 50 for wool and 25 for labor in a pound of all-wool cloth in England, the relations are 2 material and 1 labor. In the shoddy article we should have, let us say, 20 for material and 20 for labor, and get relations of 1 to 1. Finer goods, requiring more labor, would perhaps stand: wool 60 and labor 90, or 2 to 3. This is the case in a great number of the higher grade fabrics. Adding these three representative formulas, we get 5 for material and 5 for labor: cost of material and cost of labor would be equal in such classification as pursued by the census, though the items be as different as has been shown. Upon such statistical data our economic deductions are based. Adding up columns of unrelated parts and drawing averages from them has been the chief employment of official labor statisticians. Recent publications show that this is not an exaggerated statement. For comparison with other countries such methods would become still more hazardous. In America, with the high cost of materials, any given ratio of labor to material would express conditions entirely different from those expressed by the same ratio in countries where the raw material is untaxed, and therefore represents not more than one-half or two-thirds the American cost.

For example, if we take the ratio of England in the three kinds of goods named, and translate the formula into American prices of wool, with equal cost in labor as paid in England, we should obtain the following relations:

(a) ENGLISH COST.

	Material.	Labor.	Ratio.
1	50	25	2 : 1
2	20	20	1 : 1
3	60	90	2 : 3
			5 : 5

(b) AMERICAN COST.

	Material.	Labor.	Ratio.
1	90	25	9 : 2½
2	30	20	3 : 2
3	100	90	10 : 9

The total here reached would be $22 : 13\frac{1}{2}$, or about 63 per cent. material against 37 per cent. labor. Labor, though at the same cost as in England, would be quoted as less in the cost of the fabric, a fact of not infrequent occurrence in deductions and debates based on statistical tables. So without going much farther, it will be seen that comparisons on averages and percentages are out of the question. For the same reason a comparison between European and American cost on the basis of the pound weight "in woolens," as has lately been attempted, will be equally impracticable. Another method pursued is the subject of the report of the Commissioner of Labor at Washington. His report covers not less than 237 numbers of woolens, worsteds, dress-goods, flannels, etc. But strange to say, though quite a number of the bureau's agents were scattered over Europe for the last two or three years to collect data, none of the foreign goods reported on resemble either in name or character any of the goods classified as from America. Comparing an article with itself does not impart much information. But even percentage calculations or pound comparisons from this report would be entirely impossible aside from the strictures made above, because in the English materials we have the yarn as the basis, in the American, the wool. In

THE ECONOMY OF HIGH WAGES. 313

the English the dyeing, done outside, is an entirely different coefficient than in America, where it is done in the mill. In America it is part of mill labor; in England it appears under a different heading. Comparisons must be based on commercial realities, figures, weight, and measure of identical objects, and report facts which can at all times be proven or disproven. Subject to the dissecting criticism of political and industrially interested opponents, their accuracy must be considered established if they stand this severest of all tests.

Worsteds and Combed Yarn Goods.

People have of late years become familiar with worsteds, by the attention the article received in the press through the discussions in Congress and litigations in the courts. The tariff was increased from 35 cents a pound and 35 per cent. *ad valorem* for goods over 60 cents and under 80 cents a pound (the goods forming the bulk of importations) to the new duty of 44 cents a pound and 50 per cent. *ad valorem*. The manufacturers obtained four times the duty of grease wool in the pound of cloth, though it barely takes 3 pounds of Ohio wool to manufacture a pound of worsted cloth. A worsted mill whose accounts I was permitted to make extracts from had used 275 pounds of wool in 100 pounds of yarn. Bradford manufacturers in a recent statement declared that when using Botany wool in warp and weft they require 34 ounces of grease wool in every 16 ounces of cloth. This would be $212\frac{1}{2}$ pounds of grease wool only in 100 pounds of cloth. With a full 11 cents extra protection in the cloth (allowing 3 pounds of wool even to the pound of cloth protected by 3x11=33), and 50 per cent on the total value, all difficulties ought to seem removed, the foreign imports to be stopped, and satisfaction and quiet to rule supreme among the manufacturers of worsteds. But no. By their own admission things are not as expected when they obtained their full allowance in the McKinley act. It will be an interesting object lesson to go hunting for the causes of failure while outside appearances all seem to be favoring success.

The Labor.

The first consideration is the labor. We are willing to concede its higher cost in worsted manufacturing. In Philadelphia, especially, the worsted mills have to pay higher rates than in the country near by, or in Rhode Island and Massachusetts. Labor is scarce, and, on account of the great variety of kindred industries, in constant demand there. But still it is a determinable quantity. I made an inquiry into the relative labor cost of a yard of sixteen-ounce black worsteds (so-called corkscrews) from the wool up. I took an American sample of the goods, with all the details of cost of the various divisions, and made comparisons on the same article in Bradford. It must be understood that Bradford is the lowest place in England, and Philadelphia the highest in America for the manufacture of these goods. At Huddersfield the cost would be higher for England, in Rhode Island lower for America.

There are differences in the manufacturing methods, as in almost all other manufacturing branches treated in this inquiry, relative to America and England.

The American mill manufactures the cloth from the wool. The English buys the yarn, weaves the cloth, and has the dyeing and finishing done outside. The supplies and general expense account in the American mill are distributed over the whole cost from the wool to the cloth. In the English account the spinning mill as well as the dyeing and finishing establishments had to be investigated separately. Each of these three stands in the nature of commission spinner, commission dyer, or commission finisher toward the weaver or manufacturer or the commission merchant, who frequently employs all four. Each of the four, of course, charges a profit on the product of his own works. The labor, however, is net expense in every item.

In the cost of spinning, doubling, and twisting, no difference exists. Nor could I find any in the combing, which is a separate branch in England. A difference only exists in the sorting cost, being hand labor. The comparison will show this:

1. The cost of spinning a pound of No. 2-40 yarn:

	PENNSYLVANIA.		BRADFORD.	
	Labor.	Expense.	Labor.	Expense, etc.
	Cents.	Cents.	Cents.	Cents.
Sorting.....................	3.00	....	1.5	....
Scouring and carding.........	1.13	....	3.5	3.5
Combing.....................	2.48	....		
Spinning....................	2.63	....	4.5	3.5
Doubling and twisting........	2.29	1.32		
	11.53	1.32	9.5	7.0

The total cost of the yarn is higher in England, because of the profit of the woolcomber and the spinner, contained under expense, which is not contained in the American mill account.

2. In the weaving I found the labor and expense:

	PENNSYLVANIA.		BRADFORD.	
	Labor.	Expense.	Labor.	Expense, etc.
	Cents.	Cents.	Cents.	Cents.
Weaving.....................	16.2	....	7.17	....
Warping.....................	3.7	....	1.8	7.17
Mending and burning.........	4.5	....	1.8	....
	24.4	....	10.77	7.17

3. In the dyeing the account stands:

	PENNSYLVANIA.		BRADFORD.	
	Labor. Cents.	Supplies and Expense. Cents.	Labor. Cents.	Supplies, etc. Cents.
Dyeing	1.0	4.3	2.7	2.9
Finishing, etc.	3.1	1.0	2.0	4.0
Total	4.1	5.3	4.7	6.9

The 4.3 cents in the dyeing includes soap and coal besides the dyestuff. The mill used water power besides. In recapitulating, we obtain the following collective data:

	PENNSYLVANIA.		BRADFORD.	
	Labor. Cents.	Expense. Cents.	Labor. Cents.	Expense. Cents.
No. 1. Sorting, scouring, and carding, combing and spinning.	11.53	1.32	9.5	7.0
No. 2. Weaving, etc.	24.4	....	10.77	7.17
No. 3. Dyeing and finishing.	4.1	5.3	4.7	6.9
To the expense has to be added, weekly wages and salaries	....	2.70	....	....
General expenses and sundries.	....	1.32	....	....
Total	40.03	10.64	24.97	21.07

A difference of 15 cents in labor, mainly in the weaving, while in all other departments the labor cost is nearly the same. And this is all the labor difference in worsted coatings. The cost difference, however, is only one of 5 cents between the goods leaving the finishing room in America, and the English goods re-entering the office of the manufacturer or the commission merchant, when returned from the finisher's shop.

The cloth in England was then worth 4s. 2d. net, or $1 a yard. The labor and other associated items given above as 46.04 cents bring up the cost to 94.04 cents. Landed in

New York with duty at 35 cents a pound and 40 per cent. *ad valorem*

Brings the cloth to cost	$1.75
Add 7 per cent. discount	16
Add importer's profit	25
These goods could not be sold at less than from first hand.	$2.16

The asking price of the American goods was $2.25, less 5 per cent., and 7 per cent. cash discount, which is $2.13¼, less 7 per cent., or $1.98 net. From this we have to deduct the selling expense, 7 per cent. to the commission merchant, and other possible charges, say 10 per cent., and we have net $1.78 to the manufacturer's credit. The goods cost in

Labor, etc., as shown above	40.03
Supplies and other expenses	10.65
The wool stood	84.10
Total	$1.34.78

leaving under the old law 43 cents for profit and to whatever capital charges. The difference in the labor and general manufacturing cost is 5 cents, but in the cost of the wool 36 cents, or 10 per cent. more in the former and 75 per cent. more in the wool.

In order to be able to test the general applicability of this account, I obtained a corroborating statement from a Philadelphia manufacturer who buys the yarn. He stated the weaving price in his mill to be $19\frac{6}{10}$ cents, or $3\frac{4}{10}$ cents more than paid in the mill cited above. The Philadelphian's admission of paying higher rates than elsewhere fully corroborates the above. This manufacturer is an importer as well. He has the yarn bought, the worsteds woven, and frequently imported in the gray, and dyed in Philadelphia. He finds labor in dyeing cheaper in Philadelphia than in

Bradford. At any rate, he can get worsted coating dyed in outside establishments at 6 cents. Hence the dyeing rates are not different in his finding from those stated in the comparison. The other parts in the weaving department he covers by 40 per cent. of the weaving rate, and this part, along with general and finishing expense, supplies, etc.—in fact, every item of getting the goods ready for the market—would be fully covered, according to their rule (the rule of the Bradford commission weavers) of reckoning, by the additional charge of the weaving rate.

Hence the two compare:

	Philadelphia. Cents.	Outside Philadelphia. Cents.
Weaving labor	19.6	16.3
Other labor in weaving and finishing, weekly wages, salaries, and supplies	19.6	16.32
Dyeing	6.0	5.1
	45.2	37.72

The Yarn.

The spinning cost, as has been shown above, is not different from Bradford rates. The American mill from which I got the above data turned out 6,500 pounds of yarn a week, woven into cloth on the premises. Here the spinning cost is 12.85 cents and the wool 84 cents—a total of 96.85 cents. That this is a substantially correct net cost statement for yarn spinning is proven by the fact, that the Philadelphia house referred to, and whose reputation for ability and fair dealing stands second to none, imported Bradford yarns of the same numbers and corresponding quality of wool at 30 pence, or 60 cents, and paid duty on yarn, 18 cents a pound; 35 per cent. *ad valorem*, 20 cents; charges to land, 5 cents; a total of $1.03.

As domestic yarns are always held somewhat below English yarns, the two come remarkably close. The American yarn could certainly not cost the spinner, then, above the price stated and find a market among manufacturers of worsteds, who are but sparingly supplied with machinery for combing and spinning worsted yarns. An additional cost is probably to be added to the yarn for loss in the weaving. But this would not exceed 10 cents in the pound of cloth in our calculation. Making allowance for all the contingencies, under the old law the manufacturer who made his own yarn had a profit of 35 cents, and if he bought his yarn, of 20 to 25 cents, a yard. It must be said, however, that American worsteds never ranked with English worsteds. It is, therefore, by no means to be taken for granted that the above-quoted selling price at all represented the price generally realized. Still the margin of profit was large enough under the then existing tariff to give ample protection to competent manufacturers. But an increase of protection was asked for under many misrepresentations at the time. Under the new tariff the duty on these same goods is four times the duty of unscoured wool, or 44 cents a pound and 50 per cent *ad valorem*. This brings our 4s. 2d., or $1, cloth up to $1.94, instead of $1.75, as above—an additional 20 cents, even where not necessary from the producer's standpoint. He ought to be satisfied surely from the face of the thing. But he is not; and, what is more, he has reason for his dissatisfaction. He probably knows by this time that protection cuts both ways. We have here a most forcible illustration of the neutralization of protection by the burdens it creates. Yarn has been increased in duty from 18 cents a pound and 35 per cent. *ad valorem* (in this quality) to three and a half times the wool duty, or $38\frac{1}{2}$ cents and 40 per cent. *ad valorem*. The manufacturer who used to import foreign yarns at $1.03 a pound would now have to pay 60 cents plus 38½ plus 24 plus 5 cents, or $1.27½, a clear 100 per cent. duty on yarn. In reality, No. 2-40 worsted yarn, made of Australian wool, is worth in the Philadelphia market from $1.22½ to $1.25, and of American wool about $1.17½ to $1.20. Great profits are made by the yarn makers to the detriment of the cloth industry. The manufacturer who has to buy his yarn, and the majority of the makers of worsteds are in that position, is now worse off than before the increase.

On the cost of the worsted cloth in reference, the results are as follows:

Protection before the advent of McKinley, 75 cents.
Protection after the advent of McKinley, 94 cents.

Yarn..	$1.03	$1.27¼
Dyeing, shrinkage of yarn in manufacturing, etc.	15	17
Manufacturing cost, including labor and expense..	39	39
Total.....................................	$1.57	$1.83¼

He has 19 cents extra protection, but has to pay 26½ cents more, or 7½ cents in excess of what he got in the great bargain he brought home from Washington Fair. But the troubles invited by the tariff increase are not ended here. Of course, the foreign manufacturer will not let his best market slip from under his fingers. He improves the opportunities which the incapables who framed these laws offer him so freely. He has the free choice of all the wools of the globe. We have seen how he profits by it. He makes the sixteen-ounce summer article to weigh fourteen or fifteen ounces; the twenty-two-ounce winter cloth to weigh twenty ounces, and thus saves first one-eighth pound, or one-eighth of 44 cents—5½ cents. He reduces the cost a few cents here and a few cents there—and there is always some margin in manufacturing for economy, when closely pressed—and, by practicing these and by the savings in duty, is enabled to sell his all-worsted cloth even at a little less than the price before the new law went into effect. Of course, we know that this is not fair in our cousin on the other side of the water. He ought to have given warning to our Philadelphia friends. But we are not moral teachers, and have to regard the depravity of human nature in trade matters as a fact to be accepted without discussion. Our manufacturers endeavor to meet this. But how? An analysis recently undertaken by the *Dry Goods Economist* gives the following facts:

A worsted fabric, weighing twenty-two to twenty-three ounces, varying in price from a piece-dyed, solid black at $1.50 to fancy weaves from $1.62½ to $1.75, was found to be made up of a worsted warp, which only composed the face and constituted 28 per cent. of the weight, and the filling making the balance of 72 per cent., and entirely cotton and shoddy, in the proportion of 92½ per cent. of cotton and 7½ per cent. of shoddy. A finer fabric, selling at $2.42½, was to all appearances a solid worsted fabric, both face and back. An examination, however, proved these appearances deceptive. The worsted of three-eighths and delaine stock, yet every alternate pick of filling was cotton, as also the warp between the filling cord and the back warp. Thus we have a cloth which every one but an expert would call an all-wool worsted cloth, containing 21 per cent. of cotton and 79 per cent. of worsted.

A third example shows that the percentage of worsted to the rest of the fabric varies from 35 to 40 per cent., according to the pattern. The remainder of the cloth was cotton. Another fabric, a worsted-faced suiting cloth which sells at $2, was composed of 58 per cent. delaine worsted, while the back, composing the rest of the piece, was entirely cotton.

Another cloth was a cotton-filled, piece-dyed worsted, three-fourth width, ranging in price from 38 cents to 52½ cents per yard. The worsted warp is chiefly composed of quarter-blood, and comprises from 20 to 45 per cent. of the total weight of the cloth. The filling is entirely cotton, and makes up the balance of 80 to 55 per cent. of the weight.

From these cotton and shoddy and part-worsted fabrics we rise to the better and best grades. But even these are only half worsted yarn and half wool yarn. The consumer has to be content with three-quarters cotton and shoddy, and one-quarter worsted, at prices for which he could get all-worsted fabrics if wool were free of duty. He has the choice between wearing heavy and baggy cotton-and-wool suits, or paying the difference and keeping to the foreign article. In the lighter weights he has selected this latter course, and appearances seem to indicate that he will incline to this even in a large measure in the heavier weights so long as worsteds will keep in good demand. But in either way he gets cheated. He either gets for his dollar's worth of worsteds more cotton and shoddy, or less weight of wool in the yard than before. A clear blood tax, take it as you please.

That under such conditions large importations would continue is but a matter of course. In no year was the depression so deep as in the year and a half following the McKinley act. That the importations fell off considerably in this line is due entirely to the change in fashion from worsteds to cheviots and other soft wool fabrics, and not to the duty increase, as is manifest from the above comparisons. The real worsted cloth is brought from abroad, and is not to any greater extent interfered with by the home product than was the case before the enactment.

Italian Cloths

were not very successfully brought out as articles of manufacture in America, though the duties ranged way up in the eighties and nineties.

Some $5,000,000 worth of Italian cloths were imported annually under these rates of a compound duty: For goods under 20 cents per square yard, 5 cents per square yard and 35 per cent.; and above 20 cents, 7 cents per square yard and 40 per cent.; and if weighing over 4 ounces, 35 cents per pound and 40 per cent. *ad valorem.* This has been changed, and stands now as follows: For goods not exceeding 15 cents per square yard, 7 cents per square yard and 40 per cent. *ad valorem;* for goods exceeding 15 cents per square yard, 8 cents per square yard and 50 per cent. *ad valorem;* and for goods weighing over 4 ounces per square yard, 44 cents a pound and 50 per cent. *ad valorem.*

In the place of explaining what these increases signify, I will give the cost under which identical goods were landed before the new tariff went into force and what they cost now. The goods are imported by a leading house in the line of worsteds and Italian cloths. There is an additional charge on the goods of 1 cent per running yard to cover expenses, and 10 per cent. to cover discount and interest to carry stock. Otherwise net.

LANDING COST OF THIRTY-TWO-INCH ITALIANS

WEIGHING UNDER FOUR OUNCES.

	Foreign Cost per Yard. *Cents.*	Old Tariff Cost. *Cents.*	Ad Valorem. *Per cent.*	New Tariff Cost. *Cents.*	Ad Valorem. *Per cent.*
1.	12¼	24⅞	103	27½	125
2.	17½	32¾	87	37½	120
	OVER FOUR OUNCES.				
3.	15½	29¾	92	40¾	163
4.	17¼	32⅜	87	44½	158
5.	28½	52⅝	84	72	159
6	34½	66¾	93	82¼	139

With the addition of the importer's profit, these goods stand the wholesale clothier or dealer at the closest:

	Foreign Cost. Cents.	Old Price. Cents.	Ad Valorem. Per cent.	New Price. Cents.	Ad Valorem. Per cent.
1	12¼	27·	122	30¼	150
2	17½	36	108	42½	140
3	15¼	33	108	45	190
4	17¼	36	108	50	190
5	28¼	60	112	80	180
6	34¼	75	118	92	167

The lowest quality of home-made Italians was protected by 122 per cent., and none of these qualities could be sold at less than 108 per cent. above the price at which any cloth house or clothier could buy these goods in England. Now the consumer has to pay from 30 to 50 cents for an article which costs in England from 12¼ to 17¼ cents a yard, and in character of goods, color, and finish is superior to what has ever been produced in this country. The history of the manufacture of Italian cloths in America is not a very bright one. Many tried the manufacture, none succeeded in giving satisfactory goods to the trade. One mill kept up the struggle and turned out fairly good cloth, but even their goods were always sold under the price which the English goods brought. Italian cloth is one of the most difficult articles to manufacture. The English take the finest and best Botany wool and Egyptian cotton for the warp yarn. Egyptian cotton has advantages barely known to our people, judging from the limited quantity in which it is used. For fine yarn goods and fine warps it is far superior to American, though in price not much above our good middling cotton. It makes a silky thread and takes the dye far better than American cotton. Hence the English are very eager purchasers of it. By the lowness of materials and intelligent selection they are able to furnish now a better cloth than

THE ECONOMY OF HIGH WAGES. 325

ever before, at prices that seem hardly credible from our standpoint. We are so debauched in our ideas of wool and woolen prices, that our standard of measurement has come to be entirely out of relation with that of the rest of the world. We force the people to either pay 150 or 200 per cent. above the foreign price of so useful and common an article as Italian cloth, or to forego its use and use cotton instead. The beneficiary of this policy is at present one very large corporation which has now a greater margin for profit making as well as for experimenting.*

The profits which these corporations reap are enormous, though the labor is not paid more than the rates usual in Massachusetts and Rhode-Island in woolen mills, rates lower than in almost any other industrial employment. One of these corporations in its own report showed a profit of over $900,000 on a capital of $2,000,000, or about 45 per cent. The treasurer of this corporation is the originator of the woolen and worsted clause in the new tariff, and has for years urged the tariff increase for the better protection of American labor. The false pretense cannot be more clearly shown than by an occasional reference to the proceedings before the Congressional Committee on Ways and Means on the one hand, and the facts as revealed from the mill and the counting-room on the other hand.

Mohair and Other Combed-Wool Dress Goods.

The same tariff clause applies to dress goods with cotton warp—cashmeres, mohairs, siciliennes, alpacas, etc. Cash-

---

* The Italian cloths made here were deficient in the finishing, not to speak of other defects. The sizing and color run more to one side, gave lustre unevenly divided. In manufacturing them into garments they had often to be returned after being cut up, as the shadings in the parts would injure the salability of the finished goods.

meres, except in all wool, prospered well enough under the old tariff. It seemed for a time as if lustre goods would come into great use again for dress goods, but this proved deceptive. As linings for men's wear they have come quite in demand of late, however, which fact furnishes an explanation of the duty increase.

COMPARATIVE STATEMENT OF COTTON WARP, LUSTRE DRESS GOODS.—FOREIGN COST AND IMPORTER'S SELLING PRICE UNDER OLD AND NEW DUTY.

Mohair Brilliantine.

In.	English Cost. Cents.	Old American Price. Cents.	Above English. Per cent.	New Price. Cents.	Above English. Per cent.
27	13	27	108	32½	150
27	15	30½	102	36	140
38	17	36	112	43	154
38	19¼	40	108	48	150

Mohair Sicilienne (over 4 Ounces) largely used for Linings.

In.	English Cost. Cents.	Old American Price. Cents.	Above English. Per cent.	New Price. Cents.	Above English. Per cent.
27	11¼	25	118	34	195
..	19	40	110	48	152
42	22½	47	108	62	180
..	29½	62	110	73	148
..	40½	80	98	97	140

Whatever is produced in this class of combed-wool dress goods, linings, etc., is made by a few powerful corporations. Their manufacture is so risky, and requires so great an outlay for machinery, principally combing machinery, that the makers of carded-wool dress goods—and they are the mass of our manufacturers—could not, even if they would, take up these lines. Hence these few concerns have everything their own way. It is they who managed and carried the increase of duty in these branches. It is they alone who reap the benefits under the tariff, limited only by their ability of turning out goods satisfactory to the trade. In this, however, they have rarely succeeded, except in the lower numbers.

But it is always the few great capital concerns who reap, while the many hundreds of smaller manufacturers are excluded from the benefits. They have to plot and to grind at the wheel, or are ground under the wheel, and the people have to pay these tremendous taxes on dress goods, linings, and necessaries of life. I hope nobody will dispute their being necessaries of life.

CHAPTER XII.

Carded-wool Goods.—Labor not Higher than in England.—Flannels and other Fabrics would be Exportable but for the Wool Tariff.

IN carded-wool goods American manufacturers are in much safer position. The nap of the cloth covers up a great deal which in worsteds and combed goods is provokingly forward in making a display of itself. Still, they do very well in flannels, sackings, and cloths, so long as they stick to the genuine wool and keep to the standard both in wool and in the goods, a thing not always practiced in woolen manufacturing.

Whatever foreign importations are brought over are brought on account of the superior character, and independently of the American substitute as to price. This has been so under the old tariff, and will remain so until we learn to build upward instead of downward, which again cannot be done unless we have the wools necessary for the desired effects. The class of goods of which we treat now under the old tariff would have paid 24 cents a pound and 35 per cent., an *ad valorem* equivalent of 68 per cent. Under the new tariff they pay like all-wool dress-goods, Italians, etc., made of combed wool, 44 cents a pound and 50 per cent., an *ad valorem* equivalent of 110 per cent. None of this class needed extra protection, as will be seen in the sequel. None of this class could be imported or were imported under the old duty, except fancy fabrics of better styles and superior workmanship, and better selection of wools. They do not militate against our own goods. On the contrary, these importations are the only healthful stimulation which our manufacturers receive and of which they are certainly very much in need.

Dress Goods.

In dress goods a change has taken place in favor of the softer goods, the same as in men's wear, against cashmeres (made of combed wool) which had a run for quite a number of years. The trouble in dress goods is that one can seldom say from one season to another what class of goods will be in demand. Hence, the domestic manufacturer with his limited market is always tossed about between the rocks of over-production and of inability to supply the goods just in demand. In this the foreign manufacturer has an advantage. He originates fashions and designs for America as well as for the rest of the world. He can turn his looms with ease and more readily than our manufacturers, partly because he works on a smaller and more scattered basis (in Germany * and France a very large number of hand-looms are still in operation) than our big concerns, and partly because he has the world's nations as his customers, and is, therefore, not engaged with his entire force on one and the same class or style of goods.

Importations will for these reasons always go on, whether we continue advancing the tariff or not, and the bulk will continue to be made here after increase or reduction of tariffs. Whether with a profit or without, depends entirely on whether manufacturers happen to hit the things in demand or not. That the labor cost plays no great part in this can be seen from a statement of comparative cost re-

* See page 157.

330   THE ECONOMY OF HIGH WAGES.

lating to dress goods of carded wool, so-called sackings. These goods are very extensively manufactured, and at present are in good demand. They are of the flannel kind, and what applies to these in the manufacturing and cost is applicable to sackings, too, as also to stripes or plaids. The principal difference is that sackings are dyed in the wool or in the piece, plaids in the yarn. But even this is an infinitesimal quantity in cost, as will be seen farther on. The shuttle, of course, carries with equal speed and equal good-will, whether freighted with yarns of one color or of many colors or yarn in the gray.

The goods in America are made from the wool up, carded, spun, woven, dyed, and finished in the mill. The English goods, to which the comparison relates, are made complete in the mill except the dyeing and finishing, which is done by outside parties. I found the relation to stand thus:

Comparison of cost (in cents) of 6-4 sackings, 6¾ ounces to the yard, calculated on the pound basis in

	MASSACHUSETTS.			ENGLAND.		
	Labor.	Sup-plies.	Total.	Labor.	Sup-plies.	Total.
Scouring, carding, and spinning...	4.8	1.1	5.9	4	1.5	5.5
Weaving, beaming, burling, etc...	9.62	.85	10.47	7.4	...	7.4
Dyeing...........................	.8	1.1	1.9	...	...	8
Fulling and finishing.............	2.6	....	2.6	...	...	4
Charges, etc.*...................	...;	....	11.4	...	...	13
			32.27			37.9
Wool.............................			70			32
Total........................			$1.02.27			69.9

The general cost outside of the wool was stated by the

---

* The charges for the American goods cover the following items : Wool expense, $836 ; general expense, $10,106 ; rent, $2,884 ; insurance, $352 ; taxes, $1,009 ; interest, $3,461 ; and cover half a year, with a product of 163,614 pounds of woven goods.

manufacturer as being covered by 33 cents a pound. In England the dyeing and finishing is higher, being done outside. The American dyeing cost has to be corrected, being higher than given in my report on these dress goods. I intimated then, that some corrections might be necessary. The American goods are dyed in the wool. The mill manufactures, besides the all-wool goods, a considerable quantity of cotton mixed goods, and has the cotton dyed outside before it is carded in with the wool. This item of cost has to be added. An additional sum of 1.9 cents would amply cover this, as by the account of the mill rendered to me subsequently.

Goods of the same weight dyed in the piece, in all colors except navy blue and myrtle green, cost 4.6 cents the pound by the account of the mills to the commission merchant, who is the selling agent for the goods in question.

Allowing for this difference, there is still sufficient margin in the general cost to make American flannels and carded-wool dress goods independent of foreign competition were there no tariff whatever. The American weaver gets 2.65 cents per yard of these goods, turns out about 300 yards per week, and earns, accordingly, $7.95. The English weaver gets (7s. 8d. per piece of 72 yards) 2.56 cents per yard, turns out 105 yards on an average, and earns $2.71. Both are paid by the piece at nearly the same rate. The American operator handles two looms, works harder and longer hours. The Yorkshire girls handle one loom and are satisfied with earning 12s. a week. "Higher than 15s. their ambition seldom goes," a manufacturer told me. This is the Alpha and the Omega, the question and the answer, in the problem of to-day. This class of goods needs nothing so much as free wool to make it exportable. Manufacturers know this very well, and have been very outspoken at times about it.

How could it be otherwise? The general cost of production aside from the wool is somewhat below foreign cost, but the wool costs more than twice as much as abroad.

It was pointed out at the time by the editor of the Boston *Journal of Commerce* that I had allowed 20 per cent. for shrinkage in the manufacture of the clean wool in the English cost and not in the American cost. My aim at that time was more to get at the manufacturing differences than at precise wool cost, which, as I stated then in my report, could be corrected. With the 20 per cent. added, the relative wool cost would have stood as 84 American against 32 cents English cost. Hence, the smaller price seemed the safer to accept in consideration of the selling price of the goods. As to the objections raised against the price of the English wool, I have answered them on page 303. The statement made there, in reference to the wool question in general, found emphatic support from an American manufacturer and commission merchant. He writes to me on the subject:

"English goods are invariably made out of a blend, and in this blend there are all the way from five to twenty different qualities of wool, each of which is associated with it to give some desirable quality to the goods, either of texture, finish, or price. . . . I am obliged nearly every week to refuse profitable contracts to make goods which would occupy considerable quantities of American machinery, simply because the raw stock and the experience of handling the same do not exist in this country. The importation of the former is prohibited by the tariff and the tariff, is likewise responsible for our inexperience in handling certain raw stocks, which have been excluded from this market for upward of twenty-five years."

Here we have the whole difficulty. We have not the experience in handling raw stocks, nor have we the stocks of wool required for the blending, because they have been excluded from the market for upward of twenty-five years. Otherwise we could employ our cheap labor and working methods very profitably on orders now going constantly to foreign countries. It needs no emphasizing that this gentleman asks for no other favors than free wool.

Answering by "If."

That the statement of the hard fact that the cost of production, irrespective of wool, is not higher in America in the labor, and in the total even lower, than in England, should be assailed, and its refutation attempted by those who were for years scrambling for higher duties on woolens, was to be foreseen. Hence it can be well understood that I took especial care to satisfy myself of the correctness of my information. This explains why I acquaint the reader with the manner of the investigation. As in our fight for open markets and lighter burdens so much depends on the facts, it is certainly necessary that facts like the above, upon which the case is rested, should be unassailably correct and be safely depended upon as absolutely correct, and, therefore, if they are challenged by what appears competent authority, it also follows that the challenge should be answered.

The report on this subject found wide discussion at the time. The leading papers commented on the evident lessons. Some one had to reply so as to save the theory that protective duties were required on account of the wages, and the treasurer of the Farr Alpaca Company was good enough to assume this duty of chivalry. The head of so large a corporation principally engaged in the manufacture of "dress goods" would certainly be the fittest person to silence all who accepted, and possibly in argument made use of the statistical facts and comparisons. And so he did, judging from the quiet that reigned ever after. It escaped notice, however:

First, that the Farr Alpaca Company, as the name, even, would indicate, makes goods of combed wool only, such as cashmeres, Italian cloths, and mohair and alpaca goods, and that I had distinctly stated that "they are made of carded wool, and are of plain flannel weave. They represent, therefore, manufacturing flannels as well as sackings or ladies' cloth." The two kinds of goods are so essentially different, and are manufactured on such different bases, that it would show either great ignorance or great disingenuousness to substitute one for the other.

Second, it escaped notice that the treasurer of the Alpaca Company offered no data from his own mill. He proceeded by ifs and innuendoes and by statements obtained from dyeing establishments in Philadelphia. In regard to the yarn, he says that, if the wool price were as low in England as stated against the price here, the yarns could be imported, and, with the manufacturing and dyeing done as cheaply as appears from the mill account, "they [the American manufacturers] would not only monopolize the home market, but be able to export under the tariff clause, for a drawback of duty on goods exported when wholly manufactured of material imported." Precisely. But who has ever heard of flannel yarns or carded wool yarns as an article of export in England? Our flannel mills make their own yarns, the same as in England. For combing yarns the short wools in the English goods are entirely unsuitable, as the gentleman undoubtedly knows. But combed yarns were always imported in large quantities until the new tariff, as the gentleman must likewise know, gave a monopoly to the American spinners and to the Farr Alpaca Company and a few other large corporations, the Arlington Mills, etc. They undoubtedly know the reasons why the tariff on yarns was put up so high, as they were the parties who prepared the tariff clauses relating to these points so profitable to them and so disadvantageous to all other branches.

It would be very interesting to get a detailed statement of the cost of the company's goods; but upon this subject the treasurer is eloquently silent. Upon the cost of flannels or sackings he is hardly a competent person to speak. Yet he creates the impression that he is treating identical goods. Not a very creditable method, to controvert by substitution of different articles and by befogging the people. That he had cashmeres in view, and not sackings, when he spoke of "all-wool dress goods dyed black" is seen from the weight of the goods, for which he obtained the price from "a job dyer in Philadelphia." * They are 35 inches wide, six yards to the pound, or two and two-thirds ounces to the square yard—about one-third the weight of sackings or ladies' cloth, which are about two yards to the pound. Cashmeres are certainly a more expensive article to dye on the pound basis than flannels or sackings. One may send them to dye-houses, and importers and others frequently do so, but manufacturers of flannels and sackings are certainly not in this habit. The job dyers make a good profit out of their advantage on the cashmeres, which the manufacturers of flannels and sackings find it useful to keep for their own benefit.

The job dyers pay freight, general charges, and a number of expenses which the manufacturers either do not figure or classify with the total general expense. The job dyer also expects to make a profit, and I am informed by a manufacturer who occasionally sends goods to job dyers that these items amount to about 40 per cent. of the total price asked by the job dyer. Accordingly what would stand on the

---

* The Farr Alpaca Company's mills are in Holyoke, Massachusetts.

books of a mill dyeing its own goods as 6 cents, would be charged as 10 cents by the job dyer.

The dyeing charge of this Philadelphia job dyer is stated to be $16\frac{1}{2}$ cents a pound, but with six yards to the pound. Hence, the treasurer of the Farr Alpaca Company insists that the dyeing of sackings ought to be charged at the same rate, and other things in proportion.

The cost of labor in dyeing depends largely on the quantities put into one dyeing. A job dyer doing work for all comers and in varieties of goods cannot do the dyeing on the plan on which a mill does its own dyeing, where one class of goods is dyed one color at a time, let us say for a day, without a change of vats. How cheaply the dyeing is done by large quantity dyeing, is proved by other accounts collected by me at the same time. A mill in Massachusetts making heavy 6-4 indigo blue sackings for men's wear, weighing from 10 to 18 ounces a yard, gave me 6,500 to 7,000 pounds of wool dyeing as a day's work. They employ from 45 to 50 men at $1.15 a day in the dyeing. Including the foreman they get $60 a day in wages. This is six-sevenths of a cent in labor per pound. But the same hands do the scouring of the wool likewise. As the accounts of the two operations are not separable, we have to take the labor cost of scouring from a mill in Rhode Island, where wages are on a not very much higher level. This is three-eighths of a cent, and leaves $.47\frac{1}{2}$ cent, about half a cent, for the dyeing labor. Now, I hear it said that wool dyeing may involve less handling than yarn dyeing or cloth dyeing. Well, I have here an account for yarns from a Philadelphia dye-house, who pay much higher wages than are paid either in Massachusetts or Rhode Island. A week's work is about 35,000 pounds of yarn. For this work are employed:

Five sets of kettlemen at $12 a week $120
One set of kettlemen at $13 a week 26
Two polers at $10 a week 20
One carrier up at $10 a week 10
One whizzer tender at $13 a week 13
Three scourers at $13 a week 39
One fireman at $14 a week 14
One driver at $12 a week 12

  With a total pay roll of $254

or 0.725 a pound, barely three-quarters of a cent. These men get fully 100 per cent. higher wages than is paid in Yorkshire, but we can safely challenge dyeing being done there as cheaply as .362d. a pound.

Of wool dyeing in the piece I have said enough under worsteds. I am informed that, with the new kettles and appliances now in use, from six to twelve pieces are dyed in a kettle where formerly only two were put. All that is required is a good quantity of the same goods and dye to make the cost of labor a matter of small consequence indeed. This is here as in all other manufacturing branches, and wherein America distinguishes itself.

The Proof is in the Selling Price.

But we have most complete proof of the statement in the selling price of the goods. Six-quarter width sackings, weighing eight ounces, were sold in 1886 at 66½ cents, and in 1887 (the time at which the mill statement was taken) sold as low even as 65 cents, less 5 and 2½ per cent., or 60.21 cents, regular terms; i. e., 7 per cent. cash discount. They netted the manufacturer, deducting 7½ per cent. commission, interest for carrying goods, etc., 57.21 cents and 51.80 cents, respectively.

The 6-4 sackings, weighing 6.6 ounces, the goods in reference, were 55 and 50 cents at different times, and netted 47.41 cents and 43 cents respectively. Extending the yard price to the pound weight, the mill realizes for 8-ounce goods, $1.14¼ and $1.03½, and 6.6-ounce weight, $1.15 and $1.04¼. (In scarlet flannels the same price relations could be shown to exist.) In these sackings 11½ cents marks the difference between cost and selling price of the heavier, and 12 cents of the lighter weights, at the higher prices realized. Under the price declines resulting from the different phases of trade, this profit frequently disappears, almost entirely. Certainly not an excessive average rate, under nearly uniform wool prices (1886 and 1887). How these manufacturers would fare if they sent their goods to job dyers in Philadelphia is needless to say. They could neither afford to have their dyeing cost exceed 4 cents a pound (inclusive of dyestuffs, etc.) nor the wool to exceed the price of 70 cents in the pound of finished cloth. Wool at 35 cents, shrinkage in scouring at 50 per cent., and an additional shrinkage in manufacturing of 20 per cent., and a total wool cost of 70 cents was due to the fact, as ascertained later, that a certain percentage of noils (costing 45 cents then) was mixed with the wool. The correctness of these accounts is abundantly proven by the fact that nothing could be put against their correctness except the above—shall we say, absurd—attempt at controversion.

All-Wool Kersey Cloth.

I found the same relations to exist in heavier woolens. I did not select fancy articles subject to fashion prices and demands, but plain staples. Here I subjected to comparison a plain, army-blue kersey cloth. It is used in America and England for the army, and here, as well as there, submitted to bidders for army contracts, hence usually worked on a close margin.

The cost of labor in scouring, carding, spinning, dyeing, finishing, and other expense in America, I found to be 11.54 cents, and in England to be 9.376 cents, a difference of only 2 cents in favor of England. But in the weaving part, including warping, etc., the difference is greater—10.46 cents in America and 5½ cents in England; altogether a difference of 7 cents a yard. The difference in the weaving between the dress-goods' account given above and the different cloths mentioned here is due to the fact that in the heavier goods only one loom is managed by an operator. But while the English weaver girl turns out in this class of cloth 65 yards per week on her loom, the American averages 100 yards. Hence the earnings of the latter are considerably in excess of what the difference in the piece-price of weaving would indicate. The difference of 7 cents in the total of labor cost is, however, reduced 3.43 cents by the lower general cost in manufacturing, which is 14.2 for America and 17.63 for England. It must always be remembered that difference of manufacturing methods implies differences in bookkeeping and accounting. Labor items are contained in the English general expense accounts, which in American accounts appear directly as labor expense. Carding, spinning, and dyeing accounts contain items of charges and profits, which in America are charged on the general output. Hence, the total cost difference outside of the wool price in a six-quarter indigo-dyed kersey cloth (all-wool) is the difference between 36.2 cents, the American cost, and 31.25 cents, the English cost, equal to 5 cents.

The goods consume 28 ounces of scoured wool, and weigh when finished 22 ounces. The wool costs 24 to 25 cents in the grease, and loses about 50 per cent. in the scouring,

340   THE ECONOMY OF HIGH WAGES.

which makes the wool cost in the yard of cloth come to 84 cents. But the English cost is only 52 cents, which makes 32 cents more cost in the wool alone, against only 5 cents difference in the labor. The charge for weaving was taken rather high compared with similar goods made elsewhere, or the approximation would have been still closer to the English cost.

6-4 Cheviots.

The mill which made the above goods manufactured 6-4 cheviots very largely. These were only 35 per cent. wool and 65 per cent. shoddy in the warp and in the weft. The manufacturer said that they were driven to this by the high price of wool, and that they would be glad to use pure wool as being easier and cheaper to manufacture. On account of the mixed character of the material and the difficulty of fixing upon the same component parts in the fabrics of the two countries, I leave out the comparison of the cost of materials, and only state the manufacturing items of cost. They compare as follows:

	America.			England (Dewsbury).		
	Labor.	Sundries. Expense.	Total.	Labor.	Sundries. Expense.	Total.
1. Preparing, carding, spinning	3.97	1.34	5.31	4.00	3.40	7.4
2. Warping	0.96	..	.96	0.75	1.25	2.0
Weaving	7.00	..	7.00	4.40	..	4.4
Additional	1.50	..	1.50	0.60	..	0.6
3. Dyeing, finishing, etc.	4.64	11.01	15.65	3.00	12.60	15.6
Total	18.07	12.35	30.42	12.75	17.25	30.0

We have here the same total cost in both countries for labor, sundries, and expense and charges incidental to getting the goods ready to the mill's door. The weaving wages are only 2.6 cents higher. In the finishing, dyeing, and additionals in American labor account, items are contained which in the English account are classed in the column for sundries and expenses. Closely analyzed, the American labor would not stand more than 3 to $3\frac{1}{4}$ cents above the English cost. It is unnecessary here to give an account of every detail. In the dyeing and finishing account for America the scouring expense of wool is included, which in the English part is contained in the spinning items. With these explanations, the statement here presented will be precise enough to convey to the general reader the substantial basis upon which these comparisons of manufacturing cost rest.

That these statements of labor cost in America are rather over the general average than below can be seen from the weaving wages paid for 6-4 twilled sackings for men's wear in a large mill in Massachusetts. These goods are somewhat finer, hence have a greater number of picks to the inch. The girls are paid at the rate of $6\frac{1}{4}$ cents per yard, and, averaging about twenty yards a day, earn $1.25, against 7 cents paid for coarser goods in the mill quoted above. The help is more expert, too, in the Massachusetts mill than in the cheviot mill, which is situated in an isolated position in the country. The average output in the latter is given as 116 yards a week, in the Massachusetts mill as 120 yards, but in England as only 80 yards in a somewhat coarser fabric than the quality under discussion. Wherever our examinations turn, we find that differences of cost in labor and in the other general manufacturing items are either entirely absent, or at the most so trivial that they hardly deserve notice, especially when held against the wild assertions dealt out so freely by protectionists and "authorities," of which the party quoted is a very fair sample.

CHAPTER XIII.

Strange Bedfellowship made by the Tariff.—Doubling the Rates by Classification.—Plushes, Pile Fabrics, Knit Goods classed with Clothing.—Carpets.—Lower Cost of Labor than in England.—Great Trade Depressions at Home.—High Wool clogs the Market.

THESE goods have been taken out of the company with which they were associated under the old tariff and thrown in with ready-made clothing. A strange friendship. Not that the duty was not, considering the low foreign price, a very high one heretofore, but that, clothing paying the highest rates in the woolen schedule, the division of clothing was considered best fitted to serve as an infirmary for the infants in the tariff asylum, even the small supply of fresh air let in here and there in the general wards seeming to the tender-hearted tariff doctors too strong and dangerous. Some goods of this class are made with a cotton back and a face or pile of wool, mohair, and, in the cheap fabrics coming under this clause, of cow's, goat's, and other similar hair. Under this heading come carriage robes and lap robes, travelling rugs, plushes made of wool and mohair as well as of cow's hair. Imitation astrakhan and similar fabrics are likewise assigned to this class of goods. They have of late become very favored in the eyes of our sisters for outer coverings and for trimmings.

But no sooner did this become apparent to some manufacturers than they laid claim to the industry and lodged their modest demands with Mr. McKinley, who submissively did as he was bidden to do. And no sooner was the prize carried home than mills set to work to manufacture astrakhans. The term "pile fabric" was not meant, perhaps, to cover this class of goods, but it at all events was a good enough Morgan to do the desired service. Here was an article coming into fashion, the protection of which was suddenly raised from 100 per cent. to something like 200 per cent. What an opportunity did this offer for enriching ourselves, establishing an infant industry, and preventing the money from going abroad! Some hundreds of pieces were made by two of the most capable manufacturers in the country. But the goods had to be sold under the cost of production; the trade had declared them unmerchantable fabrics. They were failures, with a carpet-like back, and a face of a hairy-woolly appearance, instead of being a supple, pliable fabric with a crisp, curly face, as the imported article undeniably is.

It was not difficult to get the duty raised to almost any height, but no amount of duty suffices to supply the qualities necessary for turning out goods satisfactory to the buyer, who is the ultimate arbiter, and determines the value of a fabric regardless of the cost of production or of the suffering of incompetent infants. He is a cold-blooded, selfish creature, without enthusiasm, and guided only by his senses and his sense. But if he wants proper goods he has to pay duties of four and a half times the duty on a pound of unwashed wool, or 49 cents (in some of these fabrics there is no wool at all; in most of those containing wool, not a third of a pound of clean wool to the pound of finished cloth) and 60 per cent. *ad valorem.*

Some of these duties, chiefly in the lower grades, are beyond any thing in the experience of our people even under the present tariff, which is saying a good deal.

Under the old duty most of them, as valued under 30

cents a pound, paid 10 cents per pound and 35 per cent. *ad valorem*. These pay now as follows:

First.—A seal plush made of cow's hair, but a very sightly fabric for cloakings and trimmings, largely used in England for jackets of working girls, 49 inches wide, 25 ounces in weight, costs there 1*s*. 5*d*. per yard less 6¼ per cent. discount, or 31.79 cents net. This paid a weight duty of 15.7 cents and an *ad valorem* duty of 11.12 cents, or 26.82 cents—equal to 84½ per cent. This article pays now:

```
Weight duty ................................................. 78 cents.
Ad valorem duty ............................................ 19 cents.
                                                           ---------
         Total ............................................. 97 cents.
equal to 305 per cent.
```

Second.—An English article called "Polaris," and in the nature of astrakhans, costs 44.88 cents net, and weighs 28 ounces, which is 25.65 net the pound. These goods paid formerly weight duty of 17.50 cents and an *ad valorem* duty of 15.90 cents, a total duty of 33.40 cents, equal to 75 per cent. Now note the difference on the same value: Weight duty, 87½ cents, and *ad valorem* duty, 27 cents; total, $1.14½ duty on a foreign cost of 44⅞ cents, a compound duty of 255 per cent.

Third.—A German astrakhan, 50 inches wide, costs 80 cents a yard and weighs 23 ounces. This class paid formerly 18 cents a pound and 35 per cent. *ad valorem*, hence in weight duty 25¼ cents and *ad valorem* 28 cents, a total of 53⅜ cents, equivalent to 67½ per cent. *ad valorem*. Now, these same goods have to pay in weight duty 34 cents and *ad valorem* duty 48 cents, a total of $1.32 on 80 cents cost, or 165 per cent.

Fourth.—Travelling rugs, of which the Berlin price is 15 marks, or $3.60, were sold under the old tariff at $6.25 wholesale, and retailed by the large retail houses at $7.50 under the old duties. They cost now $10.50 wholesale, and have to be retailed by the same houses at $12 apiece. Formerly the consumer paid 108 per cent., and now he has to pay 233 per cent., above the foreign price.

This, indeed, is tariff reform with a vengeance. But if the good people of America do not like the Republican way of lightening taxes, they have but to use the remedy as laid down in 1 Kings, chapter xii., verses 16 to 18, *i. e.*, change rulers and undo this vicious system of taxation.

Knit Fabrics.

Knit fabrics were formerly called by an honest Saxon name—"knit goods." Under this homely name everything made on knitting machines and frames and composed wholly or in part of worsteds, etc., paid a duty (1) on goods not exceeding 30 cents a pound, 10 cents per pound; (2) above 30 and not above 40 cents, 12 cents per pound; (3) above 40 and not above 60 cents, 13 cents per pound; (4) above 60 cents, 24 cents per pound, and in addition on all these grades, 35 per cent. *ad valorem;* (5) on goods above 80 cents a pound the duty was 35 cents per pound and 40 per cent. *ad valorem.* The duties averaged about 70 per cent.

But now on "knit fabrics" and "all knit fabrics made on knitting machines and frames" the duties are on goods (1) valued at not more than 30 cents a pound, 33 cents per pound and 40 per cent. *ad valorem*, equal to some 140 per cent.; (2) valued at not more than 40 cents, 38½ cents per pound and 40 per cent. *ad valorem*, and (3) valued above 40 cents a pound, 44 cents per pound, and in addition thereto 50 per cent. *ad valorem*, or 150 per cent.

Mark the difference. The fourth and fifth clauses are omitted, and the highest rates are imposed on the 40-cent value limit, instead of the 80-cent limit, as under the old law. This is honest work. Brutally realistic. But we know what it means when applied to knit goods.

But this was not enough for the law makers. One cannot so easily cheat the people under Saxon names of things, so if you have sinister designs you have recourse to the old lawyer's trick and dive into Norman-English. Hence they said, "Let us call 'knit goods' 'knit fabrics.'" Under this change of name the common folk will not see what you are after." They soon learned it when the Board of Appraisers of New York decided that the goods heretofore imported as knit goods are not knit fabrics at all, but must be rated as wearing apparel and clothing, and pay duties at the rate of 49½ cents a pound and 60 per cent. *ad valorem*.

It is not my province to analyze minutely the error in the judgment of the wise Daniels, nor to find fault with them, as they may possibly not have had the case brought before them with the full array of facts that ought to accompany cases involving a good deal of technical detail. We are here concerned only with the tariff and the cost of production for the protection of which American consumers are made to pay two and three times the entire value of the goods in duties. It suffices to mention that what has been said concerning cotton hose applies here also. The goods we manufacture in America are of an entirely different kind from what we import. I doubt—and I base my doubts on very substantial grounds and figures—that any of these goods which we manufacture successfully could be imported even if all duties were removed. What we import is a higher class of regular-fashioned half hose, hose, shirts, and drawers. The knitting on circular frames, on which the material is made for our shirts and drawers, is done so rapidly and so cheaply that we can dismiss the question of labor in the product of knitting at once. A knitting machine which I saw in operation in Philadelphia, which made jersey cloth 60 inches wide and weighing 10 ounces per yard, turned out 120 pounds a day. We can judge from this what the much heavier stock will be, out of which shirts and drawers are cut.* The making up is a very

---

* The heavier and coarser goods going into undershirts and drawers would be turned out at double the rate of yards to the pound of yarn. It is safe, therefore, to estimate that, taking 1¼ yards, roughly speaking,

simple affair and of trifling expense, as it is all machine work.

It is different with the so-called regular made goods. I made comparisons of cost in Nottingham and America, and behold! the wages by the piece are pretty nearly the same in the two countries. I will not go into the details of comparisons of machinery, output, and cost of production. It will suffice to quote from an American manufacturer who wrote to me after we had gone through his mill and had compared notes:

"I think that as far as our industry is concerned you should modify the statement that the labor cost by the piece is not so very different abroad from what it is here ; viz., that while the cost of knitting is about the same here as in England, the cost of seaming and finishing is more than double here."

I accept this modification as perfectly correct. I want those standing on the other side of the controversy to draw every possible advantage from this substantial fact, whenever a new and, let us hope, rational tariff shall be enacted.

In America 50 cents a dozen was paid in 1887 for seaming regular made shirts and drawers. In England 18d., or 36 cents, was paid for hand sewing, and 12d. (24 cents) for machine sewing. For finishing men's shirts 85 cents, and drawers $1.10, was the American average. This includes hand sewing on the neck, the bands, buttons, and buttonholes, pieces set in, and all finishing labor. In England this work is given out to be done by outside workpeople. But allotting one-half only of the American expense to the English workingwomen, we have in all the making-up expense

---

to make a pair of drawers or an undershirt, one knitting machine tended at the rate of less than $1.50 a day would turn out material sufficient for 6 dozen shirts and 6 dozen drawers.

of a dozen regular-made shirts a difference of 60 cents, and on a dozen of drawers of 75 cents. What formidable measures were adopted for the protection of such trifling labor differences! Truly, "diving into the ocean and bringing up a potsherd." Of course, there was some other motive than all this, the motive of the McKinley act, with which the reader is familiar already, to wit: To exclude, wherever feasible, foreign importations, as we might possibly at some undefined time become expert enough to make "everything at home," and in the meantime to be free to charge the consumer whatever home producers may agree on.

Carpets.

A review of the woolen industry and the wanton character of recent legislation would not be complete without an examination of the carpet industry. As the strength of a chain is determined by its weakest link, so is the absurdity of tariff legislation shown by the strain it places on our industries.

Carpets are made at a lower cost here than even in England, at least in the lower grades, such as ingrain carpets, and as cheaply as there in Brussels, etc. A comparison of the cost and manufacturing methods of two-ply ingrains shows the following:

	PHILADELPHIA.			LEEDS.		
	Labor.	Expense.	Total.	Labor.	Expense.	Total.
Yarn..........	—	—	38.75	—	—	28.75
Weaving......4 to 5.25		—	7.92	4.5	—	8.26
General labor .. 2.67				3.76		
General expense	—	2.4	4.4	—	5.0	7.5
Selling expense.	—	2.0		—	2.5	
Total......	7.92	4.4	51.07	8.26	7.5	44.51

In England much of this class of goods is still made on hand looms. The rates quoted above are from a power mill near Leeds. The hand-loom weaver gets 10 cents a yard (5 pence). He obtains the yarn and returns the finished carpet. The labor cost is calculated at the same rate in the two methods of work. What the hand weaver gets more (10 cents against 8.26 cents for the power-loom work) is taken from the 5 cents charged in the above comparison under "General Expense," which, of course, is considerably higher in power-loom weaving than in hand-loom weaving.

After my report had been published, an English carpet manufacturer wrote me that it would be erroneous to assume that ingrain carpets were manufactured to a large extent on hand looms. But, curiously enough, he insisted that I had stated the manufacturing cost too low; that burling, warping, finishing, and general expense would not be covered by what had been stated. This by the way only. The comparison between English and American cost shows that the labor cost, from the yarn up, is somewhat higher in England. The lower American cost of "general labor" on the yard price is in this instance due to the fact that it is distributed over a much larger output. The same refers to the general expense item. The higher cost of yarn is due entirely to the higher cost of wool in consequence of the wool tariff. Without this tax we could easily export carpets, as can be seen from the foregoing comparison, and from the selling price of carpets. This at the time barely covered the cost of production, and certainly would hardly do so now, under the McKinley blessings (so assiduously invoked by certain carpet manufacturers), culminating in the recent forced sales of 2,500,000 yards of carpets at one auction sale—and the continued stagnation in the trade.

But the public was informed by a gentleman in Philadelphia, one of the largest carpet manufacturers there, that I had considerably understated the manufacturing cost; that he had given me figures which I had seen fit to disregard, and adopt figures given me by others. He said that it cost him 12.21 cents in labor to make a yard of ingrain carpet from the yarn up, instead of 7.92 cents, as stated by me, and that the yarn would cost another like amount of 12.21 cents in labor to prepare from the wool up. (This I need not discuss, because I took the yarn cost in the amount.) He further stated to the world that where he pays 12.21 for the weaving part, the English pay only $5\frac{1}{2}$ cents. Yet with all this the English manage to get 2s. 2d., or 52 cents a yard, for what the American manufacturer gets 50 cents a yard, or $47\frac{1}{2}$ cents net.

According to Mr. Dobson, the gentleman in question, not unknown to those who have followed the history of the tariff enactments under plushes and pile fabrics in wool and silk, the 50 cents worth of carpet costs him twice 12.21, or 24.42 cents plus 4.4, or 28.82 cents, which leaves for the cost of the wool contained in one and one quarter pounds of yarn less than 20 cents, which he says (and I had admitted it in England) is of better quality than the English wool. What tremendous profits these Englishmen must be making! Paying one-third less for their wool, with labor and other items of cost, only 40 per cent. of ours, and selling their goods at a greater price than we obtain in au entirely reserved home market.

Mr. Dobson has to pay, according to his own statement, an average of 100 per cent. more, counting labor and wool, and cannot get a jot more in return than the English free-trade manufacturer. Does he not see that he paints in the most glaring colors the utter breakdown of the beloved system? I must state that Mr. Dobson gave me the price for weaving at 5 cents for plain and 5½ cents for the shaded work. This he will undoubtedly find correct and in keeping with pay rolls and trade facts. He gave me 47½ cents as the prices netted to him from the sales, and a lot of other data which would make interesting reading if set side by side with assertions made in the fall of 1888. But then there was a political campaign in progress, for which charitable allowance must be made. The results of the campaign did not prove very profitable. With the shepherds he went to shear and came home shorn. Yet anybody could have foreseen it except a political manufacturer. I quoted 5¼ cents for weaving wages, taking Mr. Dobson's average figures, and an output of thirty yards per day; though on the new Knowles and Crompton looms a lower rate of only 4 cents is being paid, but an output of forty yards keeps up the earnings to the same standard.

These facts and the quoting of the respective selling prices alone would prove that with free wool and free dyestuffs we could export largely. Why, then, those extraordinary efforts to silence the fact that the higher working capacity of our operative, the better organization of our mills, and the more extensive use of improved machinery make high earnings possible, while at the same time they produce goods cheaper than in countries where opposite conditions prevail?

Summary of Comparative Cost in Woolens and Worsteds.—What is the Cost Difference under Free Wool?

Having reviewed the positions which wool and woolens occupy in England and in America, methods of manufacture and cost of production of identical articles, representative in their nature of great branches, we can now answer a question frequently asked; viz., What is the relative position of American labor cost in the fabric if the English is represented by 100? The question, as frequently asked, is "On woolens," as if woolens were a uniform article like steel rails or pig-iron. In this form it no more admits of an answer than if it were on "a pound of machinery." But in the form prepared by this present inquiry we can define the relative positions in equivalent fabrics and leave to others the drawing of conclusions. Whatever the ratio of labor to material, it must be plain that where material is free, the same percentage of labor cost would express a value entirely different from that expressed where the raw material is taxed. Furthermore, it will be remembered that, while many labor items are considerably above English cost, chiefly in the weaving, the general cost differences are almost equalized by the difference in manufacturing systems, etc., as fully explained above. I will, therefore, summarize the comparisons under equal wool cost in both countries, and unequal cost (taxed wool in America and free wool in England), and compare these with the net labor cost, as also with the general manufacturing cost. As this latter makes up the cost of the goods and represents the commercial aspect of the case, the only one of value in this demonstration, it is necessarily the one to fix our attention on.

ARTICLES REPRESENTING "NUMBERS."

Worsteds as No. 1.
Carded Wool Dress Goods as No. 2.
6-4 Cheviots (Shoddy and Wool) as No. 3.
6-4 All-Wool Kersey Cloth as No. 4.
Two-ply Ingrain Carpet as No. 5.

THE ECONOMY OF HIGH WAGES. 353

RATIO OF LABOR AND OF THE TOTAL MANUFACTURING COST IN AMERICA TO WOOL TAXED, AND IN ENGLAND TO FREE WOOL.

	Wool Cost.		Labor.		Total Manufacturing Cost Exclusive of Wool.		Ratio, England being 100.	
	England.	America.	England.	America.	England.	America.	Labor.	Mfg. Cost.
	Cents.	*Cents.*	*Cents.*	*Cents.*	*Cents.*	*Cents.*		
1.....	44	84	25	40	46	50	107	73
2.....	32	70	14.4	18.6	38	33	88	61
3.....	25	35	12.8	18	30	30.4	120	84
4.....	52	84	15	22	31	36	100	80
5.....	28.7*	38.7	8.3	8	15.8	12.3	84	68

The reader will observe by this statement the fallacy of statistical demonstrations of ratios if the co-efficients are not of equal values. The labor expense in a pound of cloth is higher in the five species of woolens (varying from −3 in carpets to +60 per cent. in worsteds). In percentage relation to the total cost, the difference almost disappears, and if averaged the ratio is the same as in England. The general cost of manufacturing, exclusive of the wool, is nearly the same in the two countries. The ratio of percentage, however, is 61, 68, 73, 80, and 84 against 100 in England. An arithmetical absurdity, but statistical reality. The classification of unrelated parts and the comparison of unequal denominations lead to results as faulty in statistics as in ciphering.

The only valid comparison, then, is of like and like: material at even cost, and the labor cost, and the manufacturing cost.

---

* Yarn cost.

The relations then are:

Wool Cost Equal.	Labor in		Manufacturing Expense.		Ratio, England being 100.	
	England.	America.	England.	America.	Labor.	Mfg. Cost.
Cents.	*Cents.*	*Cents.*	*Cents.*	*Cents.*		
1...... 44	25	40	46	50	150	104
2...... 32	14.4	18.6	38	33	136	92
3...... 25	12.8	18	30	30.4	141	101
4...... 52	15	22	31	36	139	108
5...... 28.7	8.3	8	15.8	12.3	105	85

In these tables we have compared the single factors of labor and of manufacturing expense. In the final value the cost of the material is included, and this added to the other elements of cost, of course, changes the relations of values.

Then the two positions are changed to this:

VALUE OF GOODS IN ENGLAND AND IN AMERICA WITH FREE WOOL.

	England.	America.	Ratio to England, 100.
	Cents.	*Cents.*	
1............	90	94	104.4
2............	70	65	93
3............	55	55.4	100.8
4............	83	88	106
5............	44.5	41	92

But it may be said that if the factory methods of America were employed abroad, and there lowered the cost of production, outside of the direct labor expense, to that of America, the difference calling for the intercession of the protective tariff would by no means be so low as the last column, representing the manufacturing ratio, indicates.

In that case even the American ratio against 100 of England would be expressed in the following:

THE ECONOMY OF HIGH WAGES. 355

Wool.	English Labor.	Additional American Manufacturing.	Total Ideal English.	Present Actual American.	Ratio American to English.
Cost.	Cost.	Cost.	Cost.	Cost.	
1.....44	25	10	79	94	119
2.....32	14.4	14.4	60.8	65	107
3.....25	12.8	12.4	50	55.4	110
4.....52	15	14	81	88	109
5.....28.7	8.3	4.3	41.3	41	100

We cannot even here discover an impending doom. All that "the enemies of American industries," the tariff reformers, have so far proposed in reference to woolens has been in the extremest case—free wool and a tariff of 35 per cent. *ad valorem.* The above demonstration of facts proves that the actual differences of cost in the ratio of 100 are expressed by the counter figures of 100.4, 93, 100.8, 106, and 92. Even under the complete approximation of English cost to American methods and cost, the difference would be—ratio of 100—119, 107, 110, 109, and 100 in the order followed above.

But practically this is a non-existing condition, not likely to become a reality under the principles governing production, as explained in the first part of this book. In fact, the differences would be covered, as seen from the showing of the real cost of production, by less than 10 per cent. The cost differences are so small that they would not weigh in the balance in a question of tariff reform. The difficulties in the way of our woolen manufacturers have been great. But the dearness and isolation in raw materials by tariff exclusion alone have handicapped them, and this to such an extent that woolens form now one of the weakest links in our industrial chain. They will be one of the strongest when we have removed the impertinent barriers which paternalism in government has interposed to their free development.

CHAPTER XIV.

The Making-up Industries.—The Berlin Manufacturing System.—Industries protected, but not by Tariffs.

A REVIEW of the development of textile industries would not be complete without an examination of the making-up industries. Beginning with the methods of the old countries, the tailor in his shop, or, like the seamstress, in the customer's house* and the shoemaker at his bench, we have here, in America, gone through a most thorough process of evolution, and arrived at a stage at which the wholesale manufacturing and distributing system has absorbed the old trades and the means formerly employed in making up the clothing of the people. We were driven to it by the irresistible force of circumstances—the rapid growth of population, the rush westward into the untrodden wilderness, the sudden appearance of States with millions of inhabitants (for what are ten or twenty years, which mark the time of their life and phenomenal development?). All this put it out of the question, that the old ways could prevail.

Most of the labor required is agricultural. Outside of this, the multitudes attracted are the trading classes, who supply the country with necessaries not raised on the farm,

---

* The practice prevailed, from my own recollection, in the larger towns even, some thirty years ago in Germany. In the smaller towns and in the country it is the practice known to-day for the tailor to come to the customers to make up the men's clothes. He is paid by the day or the job, and takes his meals at the patron's house.

and, in exchange, take the produce of the soil to the hungry millions eastward.

It would be impossible to find skilled help at all adequate to the wants of a population rapidly growing in numbers and prosperity. The population is far too energetic, the labor of men and women too much engaged on other more engrossing work, to allow the use of time in the making of homespun and of clothing as of old. Further, the necessity has ceased to exist. The railroad follows, or rather goes ahead, and marks the location of future settlements. Hence, nowhere except in remote mountain districts do any of the old methods prevail. Domestic industries have no footing in our whirling, rapid, pushing life. Even in our old States, similar causes have led to the same condition of things. The "art tailor" and the "pedal artist" hang out their gilded sign-boards and are patronized by the fastidious, but the masses look to the stores for what is required to cover their nakedness.

Indeed, take the male of the species, and you find not a single article of clothing which he can not and, with few exceptions, does not supply from a store. With the female it is becoming more and more so from year to year. This implies a complete transformation of industries. It implies, also, an equally complete transformation in the distributive trades of the country. In some lines it affects even the question of exports of fabrics. It has been said before, that the cause of England's heavy exports in cotton goods is not her cheaper labor, but, by the use of finer yarns, her saving of cotton, and filling up by heavily sizing with clay and other sizing materials. Now, we make our cottons with very little sizing, because most of them, or so large a proportion of them that they determine the character of the output, go into the clothing or underwear factories, where, under the sewing machines, heavily-sized cottons would not be workable at all.

The number of hands employed in the wholesale manufacture of clothing for men and women in 1880 was 185,000, against 103,000 engaged in woolens and worsteds. In boots and shoes 138,000 hands were employed, while all the leather made in the United States did not give employment to more than 40,000 working people. Yet the value of leather tanned, curried, and varnished is $200,000,000 and of boots and shoes $207,000,000. This shows how the ratio of employment increases in the progress of industries from the crude materials to the finished article of wear. The total of employment given in all the different making-up industries in textiles and leather is some 435,000 to 440,000 persons, while all the woolens, worsteds, mixed goods, carpets, cotton goods, silks, and leather employ only 420,000 people. The new census will undoubtedly show a very great increase in the ratio of ready-made goods to piece goods, as the tendency has all the time been in the direction of the wholesale manufacturer absorbing more and more what remains of the old isolated shop. The cloak industry had a most phenomenal rise in the eighties, to the nearly entire extinction of the once very extensive shawl trade.

Now, strange enough, none of these trades has had much to say for an increase of protective duties in the different tariff deals through which our generation has passed. At times they did raise their voices for a decrease of duties on the materials which they consume. But of what avail is the cry of the clothing manufacturer, the cloakmaker, and the shirtmaker against the well-supported woolen or shoddy manufacturer (the latter the most vigorous opponent of free wool)? The former do not threaten destruction to the party when their interests are not taken care of, as the political shepherds of Ohio do when the wool tariff's existence is threatened, nor prophesy the extinction of an industry on a reduction of duties equal to the compensatory wool duty in the tariff on woolens, as many wool and shoddy manufacturers have been doing during recent campaigns. They show, perhaps, less regard to politics than would be useful to them in a business world whose aspects and prospects are so largely at the mercy of ignorant legislators. They attend strictly to business; make money or lose money—mostly make. But, certainly, if the claim that the American laborer and manufacturer cannot exist without high protection is true, then the protection remaining over for these workers, after the subsidiary industries have taken their slice out of the all-round allowance, must be insufficient. The low day wages paid to the sewing women of London in the clothing, and to the female workers in Berlin in the cloak trade, would make it seem easy for England and Germany to flood us with their ready-made clothing, certainly with their surplus stocks.

But even the importation of cloaks from Berlin, now doing the principal exporting trade of the world in that line, cuts but a small figure; smaller and smaller from year to year, though we still get a good many first importations for fashion and style. Our whole importation of ready-made clothes, about half of which are cloaks, does not exceed $1,750,000. The reason is plain—the actual labor differences are trifling in the end, though the daily earnings of some of the workingwomen in the East End of London, whom I visited to inquire for myself into their condition, were so low that no American woman would find it possible to sustain life on the pittance. The main cause, however, lies in the impossibility of satisfying from foreign countries the tastes and wants of so whimsical a market as ours. The difficulties increase as the manufacturing stages become more and more removed from the raw material. In ready-made clothing the difficulties are insuperable. Few persons in America would wear, even if offered at a few dollars less than a corresponding home-made article, the product of the London or Leeds ready-made clothing industries, far less the clothes which make the breast of Hans or Jean swell with honest pride when he dons them on a Sunday afternoon. So we need not fear an extinction of our civilization from that quarter.

In cloaks this could be done more easily. They have in Berlin great advantages over us in the selection of materials, especially woolens. Their cloakings are much softer and drape better. Even their mixed, shoddy-filled goods are more pliable and hang better in the folds. Their styles are all that can be desired, and furnish the patterns that ours are formed on. Taking the difference between our high-cost woolens, satins, and trimmings, it was easy to import foreign cloaks under the old tariff, and is so still under the new. Taxing the materials excessively neutralizes—confiscates, so to speak—protection on the finished garment. American dry-goods dealers, as well as cloak manufacturers, were not slow to perceive this and avail themselves of the opportunities. Berlin-made garments were for some time quite a feature in trade, and were advertised as articles of particular attraction. American houses established factories in Berlin, and, by consigning the products of their factories there to themselves here, had the advantage of entering the goods on a lower rate of valuation than houses that bought their supply from Berlin manufacturers. They could even obviate the great difficulty mentioned above, inasmuch as they were to the manner born, and knew what the American trade would want and what not.

The Manufacturing System of Berlin.

But easy as it seems, pencil in hand, calculating the cost —the savings and the sure profit—to order accordingly, it is not a safe operation after all, as many have found out. The difficulties are not very great; quite the contrary. Everything in the Berlin market is so habitual and in customary trim, that any one who knows what his trade wants, and whose individual requirements are of enough magnitude to spend sufficient time in Berlin, or to have a reliable and expert man to represent him, can go to work and be a cloak manufacturer. The system is a remarkable one. It shows how the old, ingrained, domestic industry has persevered. It has been greatly extended, but has not changed in character. The shop may be larger, it may employ more hands, but it has not lost its distinctive feature. The shop may subdivide its labor, but alongside and in large numbers are the operators who take the garment home from the contractor and complete it, with the exception, perhaps, of some finishing touches. The factory has not absorbed or transformed an old system; the cloak manufacturer has left it intact, as the best fitted for the people, and has appropriated it to his purposes. He is more of a merchant than a manufacturer. Berlin cloakmakers, in a way, get their styles from Paris. They willingly pay a high price for the brains in the ideas of the French fashion makers. These are fully aware of the salable value of taste, and govern themselves in their charges accordingly. A costume from Worth is paid at the rate of $200, let us say, which from the sewing woman's point of view may not contain more labor than one for $20. These patterns, however, are not copied exactly, but they give ideas that lead to numerous applications and adaptations in other patterns and styles, as turned out in the Berlin establishments.

When the season opens, the manufacturers have a large assortment of patterns ready for all countries and tastes. The buyers come, place their orders, with changes here and there, or with other combinations and selections of materials. Unless he is sure of his cases, the manufacturer makes no stock ahead. When he has booked his orders, he buys his stock, unless he purchased at reduced prices ahead of time from holders needing the cash. But quite frequently he gets the goods made by the large mill, or the large number of small manufacturers and weaving masters. If he has the stock on hand, or as soon as he has it delivered, he gets his cloak-makers, who take the goods, trimmings, and belongings to their shops, where they have to do all the incidental and preparatory parts and deliver the goods ready for shipment. If there are any defects in the work, the cloakmaker has to make them good. The manufacturer has no further responsibility, except to pay the man the stipulated price.

This system prevails with the largest houses. One acknowledged as the largest manufacturer in the line told me that the only cutting he did on his own premises was of jerseys, then (1887) manufactured and exported in large quantities; that, except for this, he employed not a solitary cutter, and that most of his patterns were furnished by the cloakmakers. It is the common custom that cloakmakers make the patterns and furnish the cloaks at a stipulated price for the making, and that the manufacturer has no other function than the furnishing of the requisite number of yards of goods, trimmings, etc.

Now, with all these advantages, it can be seen how easy it becomes for Americans to supply their home market from so inviting a manufacturing system. But the risks and losses were soon found by many to be greater than the profits. When long garments were brought over, a tendency to medium or short styles manifested itself, or *vice versa;* a question of loose or half or wholly tight fitting, or some other similar discrimination would determine whether the enterprise was a paying or a losing one. Then the question of materials and trimmings is not less grave, and has to be taken into consideration along with the other risks. So it was soon found that even an unprotected industry could stand the onslaught of fierce foreign cheap labor, always anxious to keep its grip on the American market. The business has gradually dwindled away, and the American cloakmaker holds well-nigh complete control of the field. Whatever the importations may have been heretofore, now they are too inconsiderable to interfere with his trade, his profits, or the wages of the working people.

The Sweating System.

The world has of late heard so much of the sweating system, that a general interest is aroused by the mere mention of it. The first question is, What is sweating? The House of Lords' Committee made a profound investigation. Some three or four volumes, thousands of pages folio, were printed, containing the questions of noble lords and the answers of common people (manufacturers, merchants, and working people). But after going over all the evidence we still ask, What is sweating? Of course, we know it means the taking from working people a part of their earnings and the appropriation of it by others, not workers in the strict sense. The man who takes the work from the manufacturer would then be a sort of middle-man, appropriate a certain portion, an unearned increment, and be the sweater. So we have the sweating and the sweater easily defined. It is just as easy to locate the victim and the tyrant.

The next step, then, is to propose a remedy—somewhat more difficult—even to legislative committees. The system finds a foothold wherever distributed industries exist as against the factory system. In England, even the furniture and upholstery trades, as well as the boot and shoe trades, and, as we have seen already, the nail and small chain making trades, besides the clothing and cloak making trades, are to a large extent conducted on this system. In America the system of giving out work through the medium of what we may term "sweating" until we shall have found our own definition, has maintained itself as against the factory in no line except ready-made clothing and cloaks. The middle-man takes the work from the manufacturer in larger or smaller quantities. If the goods were distributed to individuals and finished by them, and the middle man or woman appropriated part of the wages for no other but mandatory services, this would properly be "sweating." This sort of business is practiced frequently by cutters in the trade or by department men, so far as the English commission's evidence goes to prove. The system of taking commissions for preferences has grown rank, and has become one of regular practice for levying toll on all work taken home or letting poor people, who come from distances, go without work. A working woman, doing work for a certain firm, the principal partner a member of the County Council, told me that she had often to stand for half a day vainly waiting for work, and then to walk home empty handed, without work and without money. If the poor white slaves should complain to the firm, generally concerned only in getting the work at the lowest possible price, it would be worse for them yet. Then they might never get any work from the contemptible, petty despot. The nefarious practice may not obtain in America now, but I remember that in former times complaints were not infrequent. But this is not "sweating," in the meaning in which the term is applied, though it be the genuine bloodsucking and grinding of the faces of the poor workingwomen.

It may seem stranger yet when I say that the sweater who follows his vocation honestly and openly has even been the instrument to make the other practices gradually become extinct, or at least less harmful. The "sweater," as we see him brought under public notice, is nothing more nor less than a contractor, a *contre-maître*, or foreman, a superintendent—in fact, the manufacturer proper. He stands in the same position in which we have found the weaving masters in Lyons. He takes the work from the firms, subdivides it among his hands, has to superintend the progress as well as to examine the work before delivering it, to furnish the shop light and fuel, and, as we learn from the English proceedings, tea and sugar for the afternoon tea.

What these people keep over is not usually a very large sum, if the shop is not large. One whom I visited in the East End of London, and whose statements before the Lords' Committee I could thus verify in every respect, was a coatmaker. He had good medium quality work for a well-disposed house, with constant supply of goods. He employed thirty-eight hands, eighteen men and twenty women, in a well-lighted shop to the rear of his dwelling house. In fact, what we read of the squalor and darkness of East End London is more atmospheric than architectural. With miles and miles of streets of small two-room, two-story houses (I have been in houses with one room on each of the two floors, the lower floor level with the street, and whole streets of these houses exist), air and light, if there are any about, are by no means the rare luxuries which they are in the tenement houses, and principally the rear tenement houses, of New York.

The "sweater" pays his hands by the day, except the buttonholers, who are paid by the piece. The buttonholers furnish their own silk and cord, while the "sweater" furnishes the thread, silk, and findings for the rest of the help. He pays the following rates per working day, from 8 to 8, with an hour for dinner and half an hour for tea. First machinist, 8s. ($1.93); second machinist, 6s. ($1.46); third machinist, 4s. 6d. ($1.09); improver, 3s. (73 cents); first presser, 7s. 6d. ($1.83); second presser, 4s. 6d. ($1.09); first baster, 6s. ($1.46); second baster, 4s. 6d. ($1.09); female hands, 2s. 6d. to 4s. (61 to 97 cents); the latter are buttonhole makers, and are paid ½d. or 1 cent a buttonhole. Four shillings is an average of net earnings of good buttonhole makers.*

This man made overcoats for which he got 3s. apiece, or 73 cents. If the man has a fair profit left over, it is certainly not by paying poor wages. It will be admitted that they are high in consideration of what we usually glean from reports about East End of London labor. I could not see any evidence in the report of the committee that compe-

---

* In America 80 cents is paid on contract for a hundred cloak buttonholes. The contractor owns the machine, furnishes the silk, and pays the workmen, of course. The direct pay to the workman is not more than half a cent, about half the English rate. Yet the workman earns between $10 and $12. Another illustration, from personal knowledge, of the subject of the absurd claims advanced and "the facts" on which they are based. Even in the sweater's shop the English get higher pay by the piece, though they may earn less money than their American brothers and sisters.

tent labor can be obtained at a reduction from the above. Here, again, the subdivision and intelligent direction of labor pay good wages, and give the contractor a profit at so low a price as 3s. for an overcoat. I bought one of these overcoats, paid 15s. 3d.—$3.86—for it (the wholesale price), brought it home, gave it to a young friend to wear, and after a winter's usage in rough weather, I find it in excellent condition. The lining is a good, real Italian cloth (not cotton Italian), and the cloth of good texture and face. Now, this contractor is certainly entitled to compensation for his work, and if he makes a profit in excess of what would be a fair allowance for the work, etc., which he puts in himself, it is only by the larger operations, the more constant work he has command of, and the greater number of hands he can employ. He does not take it out of his working people, because he pays day rates. He even pays top prices for the class of work he turns out. Yet this man is a "sweater." Mr. Burnett, the Labor Correspondent of the Board of Trade, says of this class: "They, as a rule, have good regular work, fair prices, cheap labor, and large profits." Mr. Burnett, then referring directly to my informant, gives substantially the rates which I have quoted above from a statement written out for my use. If this is "sweating," then by all means give us more of it. The horrors are certainly not as we imagine when we hear reports of it. And still they are bad enough, in the general way. But they are due to scarcity of work, whimsical supply, the capriciousness of the men who give out the work, long hours lost in waiting and then a rush for an immediate filling out of lost time—all the sad results of labor unorganized and at the mercy of anybody who wishes to impose on it. All these evils are excluded from the factory system.

A poor Englishwoman carried on for some years, on her

ground floor, a shop where she employed a number of machines and workingwomen making trousers and common shirts for a wholesale house. She told me, and it was corroborated by the woman who occupied the floor above, that many a week she had not two shillings over after paying her help.

These "sweaters," in the absence of any other and perhaps better organization, are the best protection the working-people in these industries have. They stand as buffers between them and the employers. They resist the grinding-down process successfully. They are organized to an extent, and cannot be dispensed with by the wholesale firms. They are responsible, and can be relied upon to turn out satisfactory work in quantities and in uniform condition. While labor in the larger " sweater " shops is well paid for, and good earnings and bad earnings are questions of time worked and employment found, the same cannot be said of the workers who take the work directly from the firms to their homes, and are not "sweated," as the term goes. I found several poor women who made pantaloons for leading English wholesale firms. They got 5*d.* per pair. Two sisters worked together; one did the machine part, for which she got 2½*d.*, and the other the finishing, the buttonholing, and the sewing on of buttons for the remaining 2½*d.* They could make eight pair a day, and earn about 40 cents each. But they did not always get full work, frequently not more than four pair a day. These are the cheapest grades. For the same work "sweaters" testified that they got 6½*d.*, or 13 cents, from the wholesale houses. This shows how things appear when freed from the conventional coloring which sentiment has laid upon them.

That the factory system is an improvement on these older forms will be seen later on. But under this system, and largely by the aid of the much despised and decried pauper-immigrant labor, an enormous exporting industry has been built up, which gives employment to an army of native workers in the cloth and allied industries. Work begets work. One employment puts another employment in motion. Labor consumes the product of other people's labor, and so prosperity is heightened all around, though occasional hard rubbing may occur, even by an influx " of foreign cheap labor " and of the downtrodden of other and more unfortunate countries. Liberty attracts, and is the spring to exertion, progress, and prosperity.

CHAPTER XV.

Improved Methods and Division of Labor.—Labor in Ready-made Goods here and abroad.—Great Export Articles.—Foreign Commerce restricted by the Tariff.

IN the rates of wages paid by the contractor referred to in the preceding chapter, we have a fair instance of the shop rates in the clothing trade in general, as evidenced by the testimony of the Labor Correspondent of the Board of Trade. The wages are high, though the piece-rate is low. In Berlin the cloak trade by far outweighs in importance the men's clothing trade. In fact, as an exporter of men's clothing, Germany plays no part at all. The day rates there are far below the English. The general mode of living is lower, and, knowing by long training how to make a little go a great way, the workers subsist on earnings which ruled in England a hundred years ago.

The average for female help is $1\frac{1}{2}$ marks; for male help, 3 marks. Not that certain occupations do not pay higher wages, but a great portion of workers also earn less than the above. A white-goods factory in Berlin, operating with steam power, and employing about 1,000 hands, had a weekly pay roll of 15,000 marks. Now, we must consider that this is a factory with all the modern accessories and its complement of profit-eating, stationary expenses and capital charges. The works must be kept going, the hands must be kept working, or the fixed charges, etc., make sad havoc with the profits and, ultimately, the capital. Hence, it follows that an even employment for the best help obtainable is guaranteed by this modern system.

The proportion of female help to male is greater than in most other industries. The male help here exceeds largely in its earnings the general rate for male help. Cutters get as high as 40 marks, and average about 30, so that the average of female wages in this factory would scarcely exceed 12 marks a week. Still, it did not strike me that they turned out work more cheaply than we do here, though the earnings here are higher.

The clothing industry in America is mainly conducted on the same system as in England. Many large shops are run by contractors who take the work from the wholesale firm to their own premises, and return it completed with the label sewed on, "Custom-made," etc. Small shops abound, too, with all the evils connected with their London prototypes. The wages paid both men and women do not so much exceed those paid at the best English shops that the contract price or selling price would thereby be materially enhanced. The goods are all cut on the premises of the wholesale firm and delivered to the outside makers, with all the belongings cut and ready for the workers.

The same holds good in the cloak trade, except that a very large percentage of help is directly employed by the wholesale houses. These do the finest work and earn the highest wages. Excepting the finer work, where a difference of 25 or 50 cents or a dollar in the making up of a high-priced garment would not tell, I found the labor cost did not differ very materially. In many of the operations, as they pass through the different hands, and where comparisons could be made, I found the rates below London and Berlin. The work is conducted on different principles here, largely with the aid of labor-saving machinery, while abroad it is still turned out by hand processes in the main, and what machinery they use is decidedly inferior to ours. More goods are turned out in a given time by one operative here than by three or four in the old countries. Cutting is done here largely by the aid of machinery now. But even where cutting is done by the cutting-knife, as in white cottons for ladies' underwear, I found in the Berlin factory mentioned that they have short cutting tables on which they lay the cloth and consider 24 thicknesses an achievement. The cutters, as I observed, set on several times until they got the knife through the layers, and finally brought out the pieces with uneven edges and hanging threads. Here at that time they put 72 thicknesses on the table, spread the cloth the whole length of the piece, some 45 yards long; the cutter passes his knife through with the greatest ease, and, with steady strokes through the whole thickness, he brings out the work smooth-edged. The same factories were then getting tables made with grooves for the cutting-knife to go through, by which to cut 120 thicknesses in one cutting.

I will not go into further details. The results may be summed up in one example: For the making of a jersey waist, the cheapest quality, given out all cut and ready for the workers, the Berlin house paid 60 pfennigs, or about 15 cents apiece, including buttonholes, etc. Starvation prices, people would cry, if 15 cents were named here as the price paid to sewing women for making a jersey waist, with 16 buttonholes, and buttons sewed on. Yes, in the Berlin way it would be so. But a large producer in Philadelphia turned them out in this quality at 12 cents—or 10 cents, taking off the cutting expense, as ought to be, in comparing with the Berlin labor cost. The work is subdivided, and paid thus: Two cents for running up the seams, 4 cents for making up, .

2 to 3 cents for buttons and button-holes, and 2 cents for pressing. The buttonholes, of course, are machine-made (self-finishing), and calculated at the rate of 15 cents a hundred, though they cost less in labor, as a girl turns out easily 1,200 a day. The buttons are sewed on by machinery, too. The girls average $6 a week, while in Berlin, at the same piece-price, their competitors would have to work long over hours to earn $2 to $2.50 a week.

Boots and Shoes.

I presume it is now conceded that boots and shoes are turned out in our factories at less cost of labor than in either England, Germany, or Austria. Yet, when I brought out the facts in a report to the State Department strenuous efforts were made to impugn them.* Our methods of manufacturing are as different as the results are startling. Ladies' button gaiters, on which I based my comparisons, cost, in the combined operations, from the leather to the packing in boxes, at Lynn, Mass., 35 cents; at Leicester, England, 64 cents; at Berlin, 57 cents; at Frankfort, 61 cents; and at Vienna, 71 cents. Yet the earnings in the

---

* For further details see Consular Reports No. 96, August, 1888. The report treats exhaustively the comparative method and cost of labor, etc., in the different parts of work in the different countries. I stated plainly what the boots were on which my comparisons were based. Yet a manufacturer was put in requisition by a protection paper in Boston to declare that I had taken American common brogans and compared them with fine goods of European make. By such tricks and devices the protectionists would only injure their own cause, but for the fact that the general public is usually unacquainted with the points really at issue. Hence, I think it is not more than a part of the duty imposed on the author by his mission, to call attention to the nature of the " contradictions " which his reports have received.

different places stand in an inverse ratio to the cost of production.

We are certainly justified in saying in regard to this industry that a low cost of production and a high rate of earnings go hand in hand, and are the result of the most intelligent application of the most improved methods and labor-saving inventions in the economy of production. Applied to the test of foreign competition, this is proved with most convincing clearness by this statement of comparative cost and comparative earnings:

	Cost of Labor.	Weekly Wages. Male.	Weekly Wages. Female.
	Cents.	$	$
Lynn, Mass	85	12.00	7.00
Stafford, England	63½	5.76 to 6.24	2.83
Leicester, England	64	6.72 to 8.40	3.60 to 4.32
Berlin	67	4.80 to 7.20	
Frankfort	61	4.32 to 7.20	2.16 to 3.60
Vienna	71	4.30 to 9.60	4.40

This is not, on a general question, based on averages, but on a closely-defined article. An American sample, procured from a Lynn factory, formed at each place the subject of a personal inquiry, so that no doubt could be legitimately raised.

The differences in the cost of production and in the relative earnings are all due to differences in the labor methods, the results of the habits and trade conditions of the peoples. They all employ machinery. The goods are everywhere factory products. The machinery is nearly all American or of American origin, with foreign improvement or adaptation. Yet these are the results. The application differs under the varying conditions imposed by national peculiarities and trade requirements. The facts collected on this particular branch, if fully brought out, would in themselves be a complete portraiture of the stages in the process of industrial evolution, and be an explanation of many knotty points in the labor question. The plan of this review does not permit more than a glance at these facts.

Briefly outlined, I have stated the positions in the ready-made industries in textiles and leather. I had to show how other nations conduct this important business of covering the descendants of Adam and Eve with clothing. I feel certain that henceforth the assurance will prevail that, whatever the tariff, the monopoly cannot be wrested from us by the foreigner and his "cheap labor."

The Foreign Trade Aspect.

The industries here mentioned have become large manufacturing industries in the Old World, more by a catering to foreign markets than in response to an urgent home demand. The foreign demand on the three leading countries is a constantly increasing one.

The principal exports, for 1890, from Great Britain, and for 1888, from Germany and France, show the following figures:

	In Millions of Dollars.		
	Great Britain.	France.	Germany.
Wearing apparel	25	18	26
Boots and shoes, etc.	11.2	14	26*
Haberdashery— Millinery	10.5	..	..
Hats and caps	6.2	2.6	2
Hosiery	8	10	24
	60.9	44.6	78

Millinery and gloves are leading export articles of France. I have at present on hand no data to specify them. It is a

* Including gloves and other fine leather goods.

safe estimate to place them at $20,000,000. Adding this, the total of the three countries would be over $200,000,000.

Our own contribution to the foreign trade of the world is slim, so slim that it is hardly worth mention. But, as we have to hang a very important argument on this tiny peg, we have to exhibit the figures to public gaze, patriotic feelings to the contrary notwithstanding. They were for 1890:

Wearing apparel, cotton	$278,000
Wearing apparel, wool	424,000
Boots and shoes	651,000
Total	$1,353,000

This is the more remarkable, as in the different branches of wearing apparel our labor is as cheap, and in a variety of operations it can be shown that it is considerably cheaper even than in England, Germany, and France. In ladies' underwear the work is not alone cheaper, but the goods are turned out in better style than in Germany or England. French lingerie, being chiefly hand-sewn, does not come within this category. In boots and shoes our greater cheapness is hardly a matter of contention. Yet how small a figure do we cut in the foreign trade!

The most remarkable thing about the figures given is the fact that a very large portion of these exports of Europe goes to countries from which we are so anxious to exact special favors by means of reciprocal treaties under the McKinley act. France sends nearly one-half of her exports of apparel and of boots and shoes to the countries to the south of us. Almost all of these exports of the three countries go to the Americas and to the colonial possessions of England. We are excluded from participation in a paying trade by the primary cause of high tariff duties. Whatever other impediments may exist in other branches, such as plain or colored cotton goods, in these this cause is vital, and it is hardly worth while to enumerate others, seeing that all efforts are useless so long as this one is not removed. There can be no possible success in an effort to sell articles abroad, of which wool is a component part, so long as we pay 11 cents a pound on wool which costs now in the London market 8$d.$, or 16 cents (the latest quotations of Australian wool were as low as 7$\frac{3}{8}d.$), and of which it takes at the least 3 pounds to make a pound of cloth.

But, waiving this, the McKinley tariff has raised the commonest supplies and ornaments to such a height, that the duties levied amount to as much as the value of the labor contained in the articles. On pearl buttons the duties are so high that none but the upper ten can afford to make the lavish use of them which can be made in the Old World of the untaxed article. If we wish to compete, we have to do for our customers as well as our competitors do. It would not help much to use the "sour grape" plea so frequently made use of by protectionists, that china, bone, or cloth-covered buttons are better or more serviceable. This article of common use has to pay now, in the lower grades, as high as 200 to 300 per cent. A certain importation of a low grade of pearl buttons, amounting to some $400, and still brought in under the old rate last year at 40 per cent., would have had to pay under the new tariff about $1,500, or well-nigh 400 per cent., as brought to my attention by the importing firm. If a lady's waist or a boy's shirt had pearl buttons, and they generally do have them—at least so far as foreign markets purchase them, the duty on buttons would balance and even exceed the labor cost. In white goods, lingerie, where we do excellently, France exports $7,500,000 to $8,000,000 worth, and Germany a very considerable amount, too. In this class of goods, Swiss embroideries and laces, used for ornament and trimming, form a greater part of the value than the materials of which the goods are composed. Our cheap labor and our excellent cottons will avail us little when we have to pay 60 per cent. duty on embroideries and from 200 to 300 per cent. on pearl buttons. I have found that in men's shirts we do as well as in Berlin; so in linen collars and cuffs, as far as the labor expense goes. But who would venture on an export business with linen duties of 35 per cent. in the fine and 50 in the medium grades, when competing countries have all these articles and materials duty free?

Protectionism overreaching itself becomes self-destructive. Tax the material and you limit production.

We may be told that in boots and shoes this does not now apply, as we export leather. But it does apply, and very strongly, too. A great many findings, kinds of leather, and materials used in the foreign boot and shoe trade are not those used or made in the United States. Whatever of foreign make enters into the boot or shoe has to pay high duties, and, if used to any extent, would soon outweigh the advantages of the cheaper labor cost demonstrated above. In hot countries lighter goods are worn. To these countries our longing eyes are directed when we speak of our trade possibilities under the famous reciprocity treaties. But we neither should have the materials, nor could we supply them at proper prices, so as to build a suitable shoe for hot climates. The people of these countries are fastidious, and those who are not wear some country made foot-gear, or buy no shoes—they go barefooted. So it is idle to speak of an expansion of trade in these lines under the treaties which are to open a new era in trade.

Reciprocity Treaties.

In Part II., Chapter VI., I gave a statement of English exports in colored cotton goods to the different American States with which we are negotiating these treaties, and our own insignificant exports, hardly more than 12½ per cent. of England's trade. But in all species of cotton fabrics England's South American trade is about $40,000,000 and ours about $4,000,000—about 10 per cent. The Brazilian markets took $12,500,000 from England and $620,000 from us. A bare 5 per cent. I stated the principal reasons, and need not dwell on them further. That they are sufficient to prevent any considerable expansion till we have adapted ourselves more to foreign trade requirements is seen from the facts of commerce.

The treaty with Brazil, the reduction of the Brazilian tariff in our favor by 25 per cent., was to do wonders for our cotton manufacturers.* Yet what are the results? The treaty has been long enough in existence to show what advantages can be realized under it. They are *nil*. There was even a decrease reported in cotton goods for the first six months in which the treaty was in force, as compared with the same months of the previous year. A considerable increase is reported to have taken place in the export of locomotives, steam engines, and cars for tramways and railways. But the shipments from England in all kinds of iron and manufactures of iron up to December 1, 1891, were

---

* The simplest economic facts are ignored in these speculative expectations. The Brazilian tariff is on the weight. The English cloth weighing by 20 per cent. lighter to the square yard than American cloth alone would counterbalance any possible advantage America might derive from one held in this remarkable treaty, not shared by England under "the most favored nation" clause.

£1,750,000, against £1,410,000 in the same months of the preceding year, the more perfected forms leading. This shows that the enlargement of our own trade in these articles was not caused by diplomacy, but by a naturally increased demand for them. The reductions amount to little, and by no means equal the cost increase which our high-priced iron causes in the cost of construction as compared with English cost. But even when the differences were far greater in the cost of iron and steel than they are at present, these goods formed the chief articles of export in manufactured goods to the American republics. As far back as 1883, when the Spanish-American treaty was under discussion, I compiled a table of exports, in which the United States figured as sending $10,600,000, Great Britain $21,000,000, Germany $1,000,000, and France $1,800,000 of iron products to these States. In 1890 our exports in manufactures wherein iron is the material of chief value to these countries were $15,500,000, constituting nearly one-half of all our exports of manufactures of the same class.

It is a matter of first importance in the consideration of our problem that only those articles are exportable in which the material forms the smallest part of the value, and labor the largest. It is a common saying among manufacturers that this ability to export increases with the ratio of labor to the cost of the material. Labor must exceed 40 per cent. in the cost of production before their manufactures become exportable. The articles of which our exports are chiefly composed prove this as fully correct. A great proportion of the English exports consist of railroad iron, castings, and supplies in crude forms. We cannot export these; our exports are entirely of the other category. We may safely deduce from this that we have in the metal and iron industries the cheapest labor and the dearest materials of any country in the world, and that treaties of commerce, such as can be framed under the act, will not be very effective in changing conditions so long as this great obstacle of highly-taxed materials is not removed.

Great promises were made to agriculturists of the advantages that would accrue to them from the treaties. These are as illusory as those given to our manufacturers. These countries are all pastoral and agricultural. The chief imports are manufactured goods, which they get from Europe in exchange for their products. Climatic and other causes force the countries under the tropics to import many products of temperate zones, wheat flour, salt provisions, etc. But nearly all of this trade had been safely in our hands long before any treaty was thought necessary for finding a market for the barrel of flour and the barrel of pork, so sadly neglected in the McKinley bill until Mr. Blaine made his dramatic effort in their behalf. All the salt pork, lard, and other hog products entering these domains came from the United States. All the wheat flour came from America. Austria shipped some to Brazil, but not enough to make much of a ripple. On the other hand, Argentinia is beginning to dislodge us in Brazil, as being nearer to her borders and ports. With these exceptions we held supreme control of the field before the treaties. The same with Cuba, which enters the charmed circle now. A great market for our flour is to be opened, we are told. But I cannot well see that what we did not already hold of this trade can be very large. The principal competitor of the United States in the flour trade of Cuba and Porto Rico, up to now, was Spain. Under the advantages granted to us we shall not any longer have Spain deprive us of our rights to supply the Spanish Antilles entire. Now the Spanish exports of wheat flour in 1880 amounted to

18,000,000 pesetas, or about $2,500,000. This gradually dwindled down to 5,700,000 pesetas, or about $1,100,000, in 1888. I do not know the figures of the last year, but the amount, the one of 1880, or 1888 (take the highest of the decade), will not make our agriculturists very prosperous.

It is an idle fooling of the people. A mere examination of the trade lists, a comparison of the imports of Central and South America from all countries with our exports to them in these commodities, will show that not one of the promises that have been made the chief article of glory in the Republican programme can be fulfilled. It is a trick from beginning to end. Our agricultural classes would have fared far better had the McKinley bill never been enacted. To the south of us, English capital is rearing the most formidable rivalry which they have yet had to encounter. The great financial breakdown of a year ago has not at all interfered with the material progress which the Argentine Republic has been making. Her wheat and her live stock will in the near future become most important factors in the competition for European markets, and the increased competition will be most keenly felt by the American farmer.

CHAPTER XVI.

The Tariff in its Relation to the Industrial Problem.—Summary.—Comparative Labor Cost in Principal Industries in America and England.—Treatment of the Labor Question by Economists in Entire Ignorance of Facts.—Resulting Chaos and Strife.—Wages paid by the Piece.—High Wages and Reduced Hours resulting from Improvement in Economy of Production.—Conclusions.

WERE our tariff one for revenue with incidental protection, such a one as we enjoyed before the war, of moderate *ad valorem* duties, or of specific duties on a basis of free raw materials for industrial purposes, such as Germany's tariff is, a reform or change of the tariff would not meet with many technical difficulties. Whatever the impelling causes for making it so, our tariff has become so cumbersome and intricate that any one object of taxation directly affects a variety of other objects, and a change in one would alter the relations of a great many connecting interests.

This artificial system has finally culminated in the McKinley act. Here we find all disguises thrown aside, and meet with the bold declaration that the object of tariff taxation is not the raising of revenue for the support of the Government, but, on the contrary, the reduction of revenue, and ultimately the extinction of revenue, by the exclusion of imports by duties to be raised to a height sufficient for the accomplishment of this end. The rates were left to the manufacturers and other interested parties to prescribe. We have seen how signally these extreme rates have failed to do what they promised. We have seen that the reasons for the failure are organic, and that the grossest perversion of the taxing power cannot succeed in supplying what is internally wanting.

But, be this as it may, the inflating causes remain. The war tariff and its late extension has so impregnated all values and so deeply affects industrial pursuits that it is not an economic political question, but, more than anything else, an industrial question, closely interwoven with all the most intimate relations of labor and capital. On this account it is clear that greater attention has to be given to the industrial side of the tariff than to any other. We are all agreed, except those who believe, or profess to believe, that the duty is paid by the foreign shipper, that the tariff is a burden. The consumer, apart from the industrial producer, has been taught to bear the burden as a patriotic duty, so as to give the producers of manufactured articles a chance to exist in competing with the products of foreign cheap labor. This, therefore, has become the salient point. No data existed for a verification of either an affirmative or a negative opinion, except general statistical compilations. It was necessary to establish a basis upon which so important a work could be undertaken, a reform of the tariff without injury to the producing classes. A comparison of the cost of production by the piece in the principal industries, the means and methods employed in production, the economic conditions which underlie and determine production in this country and in competing countries, would alone give a satisfactory basis.

We all remember that in all campaigns in which the tariff formed an issue, the difference in the rate of pay by the day was presented as the impregnable wall before which all efforts would have to cease. A reduction of the tariff would imply nothing less than the tearing down of the homes and firesides of hundreds of thousands, even millions, of artisans and laboring men and women. Here in America day wages were shown to be 200 per cent. above those ruling on the Continent, and 50 to 100 per cent. above those ruling in England. Exaggerated as the statements were in most instances, the actual differences were high enough to impress many a doubting mind. The reverse of the medal was withheld from view; viz., that the countries paying the lowest wages worked the longest hours and produced the dearest goods. Positive proof was wanting to establish the relative parts, known only from general trade facts. To make any headway, it was necessary to take the question out of the hazy atmosphere which had surrounded it, and to give it positive shape and form under the bright glare of facts. To do this effectively, all the leading industries had to be investigated and reviewed, and their comparative status and cost of production given.

If only a few industries had been treated by way of example, the supposition would have been justified that equally important industries would not be able to stand the ordeal of tariff reduction.

The Cost of Production.

Labor is the chief element of cost in the product. Whether it be the unassisted hand labor of domestic industry, the factory work of Continental Europe, with its inferior organization and machinery, or the more highly developed industry of England, brought to an all-pervading system of highest perfection in America, labor is the chief element of cost. In the former processes the labor is all expressed in the pay to the worker; in the latter the cost of machinery, of buildings, of superintendence and management, go into the cost as additionals. They are expressed either as direct labor items, as "general labor" expense, or as interest charges in the general expense charge on the product. The value of buildings and machinery expresses the labor put into their construction, and the annual charge for interest and depreciation is not less legitimately a labor charge because the outlay was made before direct production could take place. It is labor stored up in buildings, machinery, fixtures, etc.

In making comparisons I have taken this into full consideration. I must confess that I was more than surprised to find that, in all the leading industries, the general views expressed in my book, "The Industrial Situation" (published 1885), were verified to the fullest extent by these specific comparisons. Whatever detractors may have said, not one of them was able to show that the figures were incorrect. Other inquiries undertaken since the first publication of my reports have given fullest corroboration. I can, therefore, well challenge contradiction when I say that the figures prove beyond peradventure that barring slight exceptions, our labor is as cheap in all leading articles, which supply the necessaries of life, the clothing, implements, etc., of our people, as the labor of any other nation. The fact must be reassuring to those who think that we cannot return to such a tariff as we had before the war without injury to the working people engaged in those trades, or without necessitating a reduction of their present money wages. I purposely say money wages, because we have frequently told the workingman that a reduction of his wages under a lower tariff would be equalized by a reduced cost of living. The cost of living will, undoubtedly, be reduced by tariff reform, but the rate of wages need not be reduced on account of the labor cost of the product. Proof has been ample. It will be more assuring when we present it in the close phalanx of parallel columns in this summing up of the results of our inquiry.

COST OF LABOR IN THE LEADING ARTICLES OF MANUFACTURING INDUSTRIES REVIEWED IN THE PRECEDING CHAPTERS.

	AMERICA.	ENGLAND.	OTHER COUNTRIES.
	Cents.	Cents.	Cents.
BROWN STONEWARE:			
Butter Pots—½-gallon, per 100.......	71.3	109	
" 1 " "	100	158	
" 2 " "	162	293	
" 3 " "	245	450	
" 5 " "	553	730	
" 6 " "	666	1,200	
FLINT GLASS:			
Bottles –16-ounce, per 100	88	91	
" 2 " "	42	58	
Decanters, 1 quart "	375	450	
Pitchers, 1 quart "	400	475	
Goblets "	130	127	
Tumblers "	95	80	
Finger bowls "	125	146	
Bituminous coal, gross ton............	86 *	79†	79 to 89‡ (Ger.)
" " (Penn., 1890)	64	..	
" " (Connellsv.)	33	(Durham) 51	
Coke-making " "	32	" 24	
Iron ore " (Lake Sup.)	119	(Staffordshire) 146	
Cheaper ores " (Cumberl'd)	19	(Cleveland) 30	
Pig iron " (East'n Pa.)	125	(Middlesboro') 73 to 96	
" " (Pittsburgh)	158	..	
Bessemer steel rails " (East'n Pa.)	250 to 304	(Middlesboro') 307	
Cotton yarn, No. 20, per 100 pounds...	45	50	
" No. 40 " " ...	98	100	
Weaving print cloths " yards.....	40	48 to 51	
4-4 Sheeting " "	45	50	
Worsted yarn, 2-40 " pounds...	1,153	950	
6-4 WORSTED CLOTH:			
Weaving per yard........	24.4	10.8	
Dyeing and finishing "	4.1	4.7	
6-4 WOOLEN DRESS GOODS:			
Yarn pound.....................	4.8	4	
Weaving "	9.6	7.6	
Finishing "	2.6	4	
6-4 cheviot yarn, pound.............	3.9	4	
Weaving	7	4.4	
Carpets, yard.......................	4 to 5.25	4.5	
Silk throwing, pound................	32 to 37½	40	
Weaving wages, yard.................	7	8.9§	6 (Ger.)
Total, yard	18	13.9§	15.25 (Lyons.)
Ladies' boots, pair.................	35	64	57 to 61 (Ger.)
			71 (Austria).

* General for U. S. Census, 1880.   † North Staffordshire.
‡ Westphalia and Rhenish Prussia.   § Hand-looms, Zürich.

I leave out here Trenton white earthenware, as laboring under exceptionally disadvantageous conditions, backwardness and poor management, according to the manufacturers own contention. On the other hand, I leave out the kinds manufactured on the old plan in Europe and by the most advanced methods in America, as in naïl, rivet, and chain making.

I take only such manufactures as are conducted on the same methods, and there we find only in the weaving of worsteds and in some classes of woolens that the labor cost in America is above the English cost. But even here, as explained previously, owing to the different keeping of accounts and the lower general cost in American methods, the difference in the final cost is much smaller than given in the above labor differences, and practically disappears in a number of instances. The most gratifying part is that even in silks we have reduced the cost differences to so small a point that here also the period of tutelage may be declared at an end. In all other branches named in the above exhibit—and they comprise the most important branches of national activity—our labor is as cheap as that of the cheapest producers of Europe, and in a great number of them cheaper.

While we have been anxiously debating the best means of providing protection for our home industries, while the relative heights of protective tariffs were the only debatable ground for parties to divide on, the economic forces, fully dwelt upon in these pages, have actually accomplished what the most sanguine would have set down as one of the great aims to be striven for. America has practically worked out industrial independence, and can fairly claim release from the interfering barriers of oppressive laws. She can take up the contest with other nations, and only wants free materials to take a commanding position in foreign markets. We have shown that, under natural conditions, she can do this very well, but never under the artificial conditions of the McKinley tariff and hybrid reciprocity treaties, with their necessarily barren results and implied end, the reimposition of taxes on her own people by executive order in retaliation, if nations should remain obdurate, and not find this reciprocity as advantageous as Mr. Blaine would have them believe. In trade, as in private life, the Golden Rule works best.

Our industries, not less than our commerce, depend for their healthful growth upon an exchange of commodities and products with other nations. From our position, as illustrated, it can easily be seen that, if the ideal of our present school of protectionists could be reached by cutting ourselves off from all intercourse with foreign nations, and actual prohibition of imports could be secured, barbarization would follow. The first to suffer and decline would be our manufacturing industries. Nor does it require complete exclusion; barbarization will be proportionate to the ratio of exclusion dealt out.

Our industries are supplemented in a sense by those of Europe. What their higher cultivation of the arts enables Europeans to produce better and finer than we are capable of, does not all interfere with our work, but forces our manufacturers to put their best energies forward to attain, by improved means of production, results which shall gradually conquer the markets of America. It is only by this stimulation that we have reached the position of the present day. Great as the progress has been, we still are wanting very much in the essentials; how much, is seen from the importations constantly going on, no matter how high we place the tariff.

People will keep buying what they want, so long as they are led by their tastes and possess the means for gratifying them.

Economic and Sociological Deductions.

Gratifying as the results of the inquiry, as indexed in these tables, must be to national pride from an industrial point of view, the lessons to be deduced from the humanitarian point are of greater importance yet. The great social questions will be brought nearer a solution, and the labor question will lose its asperity, when we know that higher remuneration, better living, shorter hours, and lighter toil are the results of the most improved methods which have fructified labor so that it scatters abundance now in every direction. It barely needs asserting that no effort of the social reformer could dispel poverty were the products wanting with which to feed and clothe the masses, and for which the commercial mind, ever on the scent for a profit, is always perfecting the machinery of distribution.

That the higher earnings of our working classes are due to the freer operation of all the causes and influences referred to in the course of this discussion, and not possibly to an artificial cause like the tariff, is apparent from the inquiry into the cost of production. The fact that labor cost, generally speaking, is on a par, while the earnings are considerably (from 50 to 200 per cent.) above the earnings of the working classes of Europe, leaves room for but one interpretation—the greater productiveness of our labor and the consequent greater well-being of our working classes. Labor owes nothing to paternalism in legislation; it owes everything to the removal of the trammels put upon free exertion by impertinent and obstructive laws.

Conclusions.

An elucidation of all the economic problems touched upon would lead beyond the range set up for this treatise. It was intended to give the proof that the causes which are at work in building up a nation's prosperity are different from those usually assumed. To do this effectively I had to leave the trodden path of argument and confine myself strictly to the statement of the facts of commercial and industrial life—to use a vulgar phrase, "the knock-down argument," which speaks for itself. Still, it would not be doing justice to the subject to leave off without pointing out some glaring defects in the old views, which have led to much mistaken and ill-advised legislation. Our labor theories are still based on the wage fund theory, which has caused and still is causing much misery and strife. It has fortified itself so firmly in the thoughts of the age, that the *London Times* but expressed the views of a large portion of the possessing classes on both sides of the Atlantic when it said in an editorial not very long ago: "The clear profits of business is the fund on which the employer and the workman must depend for their respective shares. If the workman has more, the employer must have so much less, and there seems good evidence that of late years the workman has been receiving more than his former recognized share." Hence the converse: the smaller the sum paid in wages the greater are the profits.

It is evident that, so long as this is accepted as axiomatic, labor and capital will be constantly fighting a relentless war for the bigger slice. The recognition of the truth that labor and capital both derive their remuneration from the product, and that an increase in the productiveness of labor affords both labor and capital increased remuneration, gives at once a different aspect to the question. The old view resulted in material and intellectual repression of the working classes, and the new view must result in their material and intellectual advancement.

Once recognize the fact that, after all, man is the great wealth-producing machine, the source of all wealth, then all our efforts will be directed to the elevation of this machine to the highest potentiality.

What is labor? Physical and muscular exertion. It becomes economically valuable by intellectual guidance. The greater the intellectual force and physical power introduced by the laborer, co-operating with equally well-developed auxiliary and surrounding conditions, the greater must be the sum of the products created. But to this we must add the further and most important fact, that labor, be it ever so intelligently conducted, will always remain physical exertion. This is to say that labor is an expenditure of vital force. Unless this is replaced by wholesome nutrition (air, light, sanitation, and even cheerful surroundings, are part of wholesome nutrition), the frame will work itself out, and labor will become economically of smaller and smaller value.

Another fact of vital importance is the time during which the human frame is capable of its best exertion. In going over the contentions, not of fifty years ago, but of the present day, we find the assertion, by the defenders of long hours in factories, that the last hour is the one that gives the profit. This is not borne out by the facts. It is found by all who employ machinery that the work of the last hour is the least satisfactory, and the work of the first hours the best and most copious. I frequently found that after working extra hours many of my help came late the next morning or stayed away a day; others showed a lack of spirits and less efficiency. The spirit was wanting, the frame was tired. I gave it up after repeated experiments, and reaped better results with regular hours and premiums for any quantity beyond the daily averages of output. A little encouragement and consideration for help does wonders. We are all human and of one kind. But to Guildenstern the flute is a stick with holes and stops, to Hamlet an instrument out of which to draw harmonious sounds.

Close attention to speeded machinery is a much greater nervous strain than was required by the humdrum of old routine and hand work. I have the statement of one of the largest dye works in Zurich (mostly hand work, of course), to the same effect. The works employ some 450 hands. They formerly worked thirteen hours, with two hours for meals. The senior partner had hard work to obtain the consent of the other members of the firm to a reduction of the hours to twelve a day, or ten working hours. They figured out to him that it would entail a loss of 15,000 f. a year. The reduction of hours was introduced, more as a trial than a determined policy. But after the first year it was found that not only was no loss sustained, but, on the contrary, the results were more satisfactory than those of the preceding year. The facts are not so astonishing as men's obstinate resistance to their application. The concrete thrusts itself under everybody's eyes. In the abstract we continue the time-worn argument.

In England we hear the constant iteration that they cannot compete with Germany on account of the sixty-six hours and more of the German working week and the fifty-four hours of the English week. The establishment by international agreement of a uniform working day is mooted by influential voices in trade and manufacture, and discussed by statesmen in congresses and by cabinet ministers. To them it is the same whether labor is well conditioned or half starved; whether it has the old, slow, hand-tool method or is supplied with all the improved machinery and outfit which modern science has put at its disposal. A day's labor is a day's labor. The cheaper you get it and the more hours you can crowd into the day, the better off you are. Learned works are written on the subject, and still the facts point so strongly in the opposite direction that it is difficult to understand that there should be a difference of opinion. The opposition of Germany and of Austria to the reduction of their hours to the English standard of fifty-four hours, is based on substantial grounds. The length of the working day is an index of the productive ability of a nation. The application of the most improved methods to production (implying a better paid and better conditioned laborer) makes a shortening of hours practicable and even necessary, because of both the physiological fact stated above and the economic necessity. Production must go hand in hand with consumption. If, by the too rapid introduction of labor-saving devices, production runs ahead of demand, it must adapt itself to the altered condition by shortening the working time. But this is a self-adjusting process. The legislature can do no more than enact what the genius of the nation has wrought out in advance. The legislative enactment is the caption of a chapter in the economic history of the nation. But it follows from all this, that what is one man's meat is another man's poison. The means, methods, and general conditions under which labor exerts itself in the different countries also determine the hours of work. It would, indeed, be a dear price to pay for all the great advance by the parallel destruction of all the dear old landmarks, if the profits were only on the side of capital; if labor in England, and still more in the United States, should toil the same long hours and at the same low rates as in the more backward countries. But the great advances made in the economy of production in the highest developed industrial states have led directly to the short working day, to the material, intellectual, and political advancement and emancipation of the laborer, and hence are the cheering and elevating signs of a great and bright future.

That this is not a mere figure of speech, but based on all the collected facts of industrial life, we can show by an industry now conducted on the same principle by all nations, who have gone beyond the barbaric stage; that is to say, all nations west of the Vistula and the Carpathian mountains.

The Cotton Industry.

The average for weekly earnings from two factories shows the extremely low figures of 3½ florins ($1.54) for one situated in Eastern Bohemia, and of 5 florins ($2.20) for one in Western Bohemia. This is 26 cents and 36 cents, respectively, as the average day earnings of men and women. The working day averages 12½ hours net. In Switzerland I found 11 hours, with 3f. (58 cents) to 3f. 50c. (68 cents) for men and 2f. (39 cents) to 2f. 50c. (48 cents) for women. In Germany the hours are not fixed by law, but are matter of agreement between workers and employers. In textile factories they are assumed to be about 11 to 12 working hours. I accept the former, with 2 to 3 marks (48 to 73 cents) for men and 1½ to 2 marks (36 to 48 cents) for women, varying in the different parts of the country.* In Rouen, at Mr.

---

* The municipal authorities of Berlin collected in July, 1881, from the trade guilds and from the different benefit societies of workingmen the status of labor and wages. The information is interesting, as it gives the working time ruling in the different trades in connection with the

Pouyer-Quertier's mill, I found the hours to be from 5 A.M.
to 7.30 P.M., with 2½ hours for meals—12 working hours.

weekly wages. The Berlin returns allow us to judge of the conditions in other parts of the empire. I will insert here the statement, as published, of working hours and average wages of some 50 trades. It will be seen that the statements in the different parts of this book in regard to German working time and wages are fully sustained by this list:

MALES.	Daily Hours.	Average Weekly Wages in Marks.
Shoemakers..	13 to 17	12 to 15
Basters and adjusters (frequently all day Sundays)......	13 to 14	18
Tailors (half a day Sundays).............................	13	12
Ladies' cloak tailors (frequent Sunday work)............	11	18
Tanners (no Sunday work).................................	12 to 13	18
Barbers (regular Sunday work, with board and lodging).	14	9
Wigmakers (regular Sunday time of 10 hours)..........	14	19
Masons (at piece-work, 21 marks; frequent Sunday work)	12 to 13	19½
Roofers..	12	22
Slaters (over hours highly paid).........................	12	30
Stonecutters..	10	24
Hand and factory workers (frequent Sunday labor; 18 marks at piece-work)	12	13½
Sculptors and terra cotta workers........................	9 to 10	18 to 27
Painters (in winter 12 M.)................................	11	18
Potters...	12 to 13	15 to 19
Beltmakers and leather workers..........................	12	15
Coppersmiths (piece-work, 27 marks)....................	11 to 12	18
Needle-makers..	10 to 12	16 to 17
Filecutters...	11	18
Tinsmiths (the half of Sunday)...........................	12 to 13	18
Locksmiths..	13	10 to 15
Blacksmiths...	13	18
Machine and ironworkers................................	11½ to 12	12 to 15
Surgical instruments......................................	10	18
Machinists and opticians (piece-work, 18 marks)........	12	15
Soapmakers...	12	15
Silk ribbon weavers (half a day Sunday)................	10	12 to 15
Weavers...	14	12
Cloth shearers..	11 to 12	13½
Passementerie..	10	16½
Ropemakers...	6 to 7	15
Saddlers and harness makers............................	10 to 12	12 to 21
Upholsterers..	12	15 to 21
Cabinet-makers...	13	15 to 20
Coopers...	13	15 to 18
Brushmakers..	12 to 13	18
Combmakers..	12 to 13	14
Varnishers..	13	18
Gilders..	12	16
Bakers (with board and lodging).........................	unlimited	10
Confectioners (with board and lodging).................	unlimited	11 to 12
Butchers (Sunday work; with board and lodging)......	15 to 17	6 to 10
Brewers (½ Sunday time; free lodging).................	15	22
FEMALES.		
Silk weavers..	14	8 to 9
Spoolers..	14	7
Hosiery hands...	12 to 13	7½

Men's earnings were 3f. to 3.50f. (57 to 68 cents), and women's earnings, 2f. (39 cents). England's working time is an average of 9 hours a day, and the earnings of men would average about 4s., and of women from 2½ to 3s.

That cheap labor and long hours do not produce cheap goods is attested by the fact that all these nations defend themselves against the results of England's high pay and short hours by the familiar expedient of a high protective tariff. Now, if this "cheap labor," at the rate of pay it receives now, were to procure the same conveniences for which an English man and woman lay out their wages at free-trade prices (that is to say, obtain more commodities for the same unit of money), it would have to work the following numbers of hours against England's standard of 9 hours.* The wages of men and women are included in the table:

	Average Day Wages. Cents.	Present Hours.	Necessary Hours.
Germany	48 to 60	11	15¾ to 19¾
Switzerland	54	11	18
France	54	12	19¼
Western Bohemia	36	12¼	30
Eastern Bohemia	.26	12¼	41¼
England	86	9	9

I have here taken for comparison wages of adult, efficient workers only. The work is all carried on by the countries here represented on the same basis, nominally the same, at least. The differences in the employment of machinery, etc., have been the subject-matter of these chapters, and are supposed to be familiar to the reader. Yet it is all machine work, driven by steam power, and conducted in factories under the best intellectual management which

---

* Five days of 10 hours and half a day on Saturday.

the countries afford. But how world-wide the differences in the results!

If we extend this test to the workers in house industries and compare their earnings, working time, and labor results with the most advanced countries, then the results are startling indeed. The poor house-weavers of Eastern Bohemia (in the Giant Mountains district) do not earn more than 2.20 florins (92 cents) in the week, according to an inquiry undertaken in 1884. All members of the household co-operate. The children do the spooling. The wife relieves the husband at the loom. The work goes on for 16 or 18 hours a day. The intellectual standard of these poor people is about the lowest in all Europe. Intellectually dwarfed, physically starved. They would have to work 96 hours to accomplish what England accomplishes in 9 hours, and America in a smaller number yet.

But when we bring the old methods into comparison with the results of self-acting machinery in pinmaking or screwmaking, or even in the hand-fed machinery work of nailmaking, we see at its brightest the great lesson that all the benefits which labor has realized are the results of its greater productiveness and of the forces which have co-operated to bring about this greater productiveness.

The nailmaker in the Black Country of England, earning 2s. in 14 hours' work, would have to work 126 hours to earn the $4.50 or $5 of a Pittsburgh nailer—the result of 10 hours' work. And still at his 2s. a day he does not turn out the work as cheaply by a great deal as this remarkable combination of intellectual and mechanical force does under the American labor system.

Such conditions as we have depicted here, the substratum upon which labor rests and acts in the countries farthest backward, has been the state under which labor existed a hundred years ago in the more forward countries. The average earnings of an expert hand weaver were 10s. a week * (40 cents a day); the quartern loaf (4 pounds) was 11d. to a shilling (22 to 24 cents). Working hours unlimited. Hold this against an average of 4s. a day for expert male weavers, and bread at 4½d. the 4-pound loaf, and you have in a concise form the results which the introduction of the most improved methods in the economy of production has wrought in the condition of the working classes. That nothing at all equal to the present elevated standard of life of American and English working people could have been realized without the improvements and scientific methods in the economy of production is self-evident. Without an increased product no increase of consumables, hence nothing to divide. But it is equally evident that the material causes of well-being could not have been set in motion, or become operative factors without the assistance of the ethical forces which have created a new basis for an entire reconstruction of social conditions, as seen from our examples. Improvement has always taken its rise in the West. The oppression and depression of the working classes increase in an easterly direction. A hopeless acceptance of their

---

* The following quotations from Sir Frederic Eden represent the daily earnings in 1787. Outdoor laborers, 1s.; threshers, 1s.; laborers near towns, 1s. 4d. Manufacturing wool : scribblers, 1s. 3d.; shearers, 1s. 6d.; weavers, 1s. 6d. to 2s.; women spinners, 7d. (spinning much reduced through introduction of machinery—formerly, 1s. to 1s. 2d. reduced to 5d.; women in good health can only earn 2s. 6d. per week, some with family not more than 1s.). Coventry, ribbon weavers, 8s. to 12s. a week, children winders, 2s. to 3s. Kendall, woolen weavers, 10s. a week; calico weavers, 9s.

The introduction of machinery, begun in about 1780, was strenuously opposed by the workpeople. The result, however, was the same as illustrated elsewhere, a rise in the earnings of the working classes so engaged.

poor, miserable lot, as of the inevitable, characterizes these laborers. They would hardly have an understanding of the pitying sympathy which one cannot help feeling for them. Yet the starting point for improvement cannot be gained where hope does not light the way. As seen in our examples, the application of improved methods does not help much where this stimulus is absent.

In Berlin, even, I found this narrow-minded begrudging of a workingman's higher earnings. In piece work they reduce the pay of the greater output which brings higher earnings than the general rate. Hence the workingmen take good care not to produce more than is necessary to give that rate. The manufacturers returned to the day rate, as I was told by working people in Berlin, because the masters found that the men made too much money under the piece-rate system introduced in the flush times after the war. This characterizes the matter very well, and the economic results make it apparent enough that the mechanical improvements and scientific achievements of the age, open and free to all, are inoperative if they are not met by a population under responsive conditions. Given the starting point of free development and free play of forces, everything follows as by self-acting process. The endeavor of man to improve his condition is powerful enough to carry society, meaning essentially the working classes, to that stage of well-being which is the dream of our age, and the striving for which has given to the world so many finely-elaborated systems of social reform. But it has been shown that freedom from restraint and security under the law are all the guarantees required for securing the conditions under which the self-acting process of constant improvement takes place, and under which man can always be expected to exercise his fullest energy.

The Cause of Progress and Prosperity.

There is no royal road to prosperity. We can reach it only by hard and arduous toiling on the long and winding road of progress. The forces leading forward have been most powerful in the second half of our century, and the world has received the most astonishing results of the concentration of the highest intellectual forces on production, including the distributing branch. We have shown throughout this discussion what debt we owe to the scientist who quietly and unostentatiously has led to all these triumphs in the struggle of man with nature without even knowing to what beneficent results his discoveries would lead, in the clothing and the feeding of the wretched and the poor, the 90 per cent. of the nations. If abundance reigns where poverty and a mild species of starvation have been signifying the conditions, we owe it to him and to the leading minds engaged in commercial and industrial pursuits. But a tearing down of the landmarks, an entire upheaval of society was required to make the advent of this new era of progress and prosperity possible. The keenest minds are now engaged in the sciences, in production and distribution. They leave in contemptuous disregard the employments which in former times were alone considered proper for the most gifted as well as for the select of birth and fortune. Politics and war have lost their attraction, and the love of gain and of distinction in the fields of industry and commerce is the master passion of the age. Whether for praise or for blame, the fact exists. The keenest minds are all engaged in the work of production and distribution, and thus, though only intent on gain and personal distinction, they lead on in the evolution of industrial progress to that reign of plenty which is the necessary condition of the great social improvement so ardently looked for by the lovers of mankind, and never attainable by any other method than the chase after "filthy lucre." The builder and projector of a railroad, the inventor of a new machine, the discoverer of a new process by which nature is made to yield her jealously guarded treasures, the calculating and designing merchant and manufacturer—they all aim at money-making and furthering their own private ends, even by the destruction of their neighbors. Consciously or unconsciously, this is their aim. In the fierce competition of commercial life, the destruction of the neighbor is only paraphrased by the milder term of "trying to undersell him" by the hundred and one different methods in which push, energy, consolidation, etc., stand only in a general way as expressions of means by which the end is reached. A new method or an invention destroys even more completely than all the combinations of commercial energy. And still the scientist who plans them, who evolves them from his retort or his pencil, is as guileless as a new-born babe, and would be horror-struck at the heart-burning among men, the havoc and desolation among brick and mortar, machinery and ledger accounts, which his inventions and discoveries create. Yet, whatever the impulse and the aim, the result is the same: society reaps the benefit and, as has been shown with sufficient clearness, I trust, these greedy, self-seeking individuals are all working for one end—to reduce the cost of bread a penny or so, of clothing and the rest of the necessaries of life in like manner. And all engaged in the struggle for reducing the cost of living, be the motives never so selfish, are the real benefactors of their race. In no country has this concentration of the greatest mental energy on the subject of production—vulgarly speaking, "money-making"—been so exhaustive and complete as in

America. The reason is obvious. In no other country have the prejudices which hamper enterprise been so completely extirpated. A hundred years ago, or even more recently, the gentleman "who did not soil his hands by work or gainful occupations" was very fairly distributed over the Republic. He has disappeared. In England, shop-keeping England, he rules society, and his baneful influence prostrates energy and drives enterprising young men, scions of the nobility as well as of the middle classes, to these shores, where they can work in the field, the mill, the mine, as the slaves of the poor and the makers of their own fortunes. I need not speak of the Continent, where social prejudices increase in the ratio of the decrease of personal liberty. So it is, after all, the seed which was sown a little more than a hundred years ago in America and shortly thereafter in the nursery garden of great ideas, Paris, which bears all this luscious fruit. Much rank vegetation may be in the undergrowth. But what if there be? We shall learn by and by to get rid of noxious weeds and keep the wholesome species. Without political freedom and the destruction of the trammels which held down the old social structure, no progress is possible. The measure of progress and prosperity is the most complete where all the old restraints have been most radically removed and thrown into history's old lumber-yard. The middle ages of metaphysical abstraction and hazy speculation are only beginning to make room for the new era of practical creation. The old notions of social distinction are only now giving way to the much higher ideal and type of man, the maker of his own fortune. The great fortunes are frequently connected in America with the grimy hand and the sweating brow of the original canal digger and the mill-hand who owns them. If every drummer boy in France carried the marshal's baton in his knapsack, every laborer in America has a million in prospect. The one possibility made Napoleon's army invincible; the other gives America the industrial leadership of the world. Hope leads the imagination and makes man dare in the face of all difficulties. While under limitation of his freedom he would be but an indolent tool, he becomes an eager creator under conditions made possible by a Constitution which makes everybody free to become the creator of his own destiny.

With the right of suffrage in his hands, the American workingman is the state. He cannot blame his rulers, the tools of his own creation, for whatever impediments may prevent his reaping a fuller share of the fruit of his labor. If he permits the taxing power to be exercised in the interest of capital, under the false pretense of protection to him, while piece wages are less than in Europe, he has no one to blame but himself. If he permits taxes to be squandered on bounties and other unjustifiable expenditures, no scapegoat can be interposed on whom he may lay the responsibility. He chooses the law-makers, who would not dare to vote for any measure that is not supposed popular with the "masses." In fact, it is not unjust to say that the legislators are too eager to suppress their own better judgment and follow the popular drift. Education and enlightenment are the necessary adjuncts of universal suffrage, because they make political power the source of real blessings in the workingman's hand. All danger from misuse disappears with the insight into the connection of causes and effects. The fruits of civilization are safely lodged in the hands of those who are able to appreciate their advantages. They will see to it that the wealth accumulating from the annual production shall not all be turned into the hands of a few men favored by protection, but that the means shall be found to supply the

THE ECONOMY OF HIGH WAGES. 405

educational facilities which will eventually make labor independent, so that the hand that works and the brain which designs and guides shall become members of the same body. This is the natural tendency of economic forces not interfered with by law. Capital's share in the product becomes smaller and smaller with the increase of capital. Capital without labor to employ it would sink away and disappear. As capital grows, more labor must be employed. Capital competes with capital, and the share of profit becomes smaller, the demand for labor increasing constantly. Wages, however, are not affected by the shrinkage of profits.

It is evident that no gulf separates the laborer from the *Ultima Thule*, the full enjoyment of the fruits of his work, that he cannot bridge by his own intellectual advancement.

ADDENDA TO PART II., CHAPTER VI., RELATING TO COTTON HOSIERY.

The fine laid plans of the subtlest of minds are often frustrated by the fact that the minds of all men are wiser than the mind of any one man or of a combination of men. Applied to commerce it follows, from this, that no sooner is a law enacted obstructive to trade than the minds interested go to work to circumvent it. This is the easier with American tariff laws on account of the general ignorance of the lawmakers of the commonest industrial and trade facts. The very artifices and the complicated character of the law, designed to hinder importations, lead to it. Cotton hosiery shows the full bearing of this. The chief aim was here, as in most of the tariff increases, directed against the low-priced goods. The duty is graded according to value, as follows:

1. On value of not above 60 cents per dozen pair, 20 cents per dozen pair and 20 per cent. *ad valorem.* 2. Above 60 cents and not above $2.00 per dozen pair, 50 cents per dozen and 30 per cent. *ad valorem.* 3. Above $2.00 and not above $4.00 per dozen pair, 75 cents per dozen pair and 40 per cent. *ad valorem.* 4. Above $4.00 per dozen pair, $1.00 per dozen pair and 40 per cent. *ad valorem.*

The action was not so much directed against the range of prices covered by class I. Few goods were ever imported costing "not above" 60 cents the dozen. Most of the imports to be prevented by the new law would fall under the second class. Large importations of men's half hose would come in at 65 to 72 cents. On this price range, the duties would now be at 65 cents cost: 50 cents per dozen and 30 per cent., equal 69½ cents or 107 per cent; at 75 cents cost: equal 66⅔ cents or 92½ per cent. If the same goods would fall under classification I., they would pay 20 cents per dozen and 20 per cent. *ad valorem*, or something under 50 per cent. In order to be able to reduce the duty to the lower basis, the Chemnitz manufacturers were helped by the law itself in part, which makes packing charges, cartons, etc., dutiable, the same as the goods, by virtue of the administrative McKinley act. By shipping the goods without boxes, having the cartons made here; by sending them in the gray and having them dyed in America, whenever practicable; by economical changes in Chemnitz, reduction in the dyeing cost, which is done by outside dyers, who made a very high rate of profit heretofore (the work is distributed, a house-industry chiefly), etc., the foreign manufacturers were enabled to so far reduce the cost that they can bring in goods which otherwise would go into class II., under the lower range of duties, and so frustrate the part of the law intended for their exclusion. Very vexatious this. Short of absolute prohibition no device seems to be workable when it comes to the test.

INDEX.

Acreage and product, 150-152.
Adulteration in wool fabrics, 308, 340.
Advanced position of labor, causes of, 392-405.
Advantages, natural, and science, 139-144.
Agriculture in America cannot be protected, why, 6.
Agriculture, comparative results of, 122-125, 138-147.
Agriculture depressed by protection, 7.
Agriculture, lessons from progressing, 152.
Agriculture, results in, and institutions, 111-133.
Agriculture and soil, 110.
Aluminum, price reductions illustrated in, 87.
American and Berlin methods, 370-373.
American and English rates of wages, 199, 200, 211, 214-218, 226, 227, 237-240, 276, 280, 315, 348, 374.
American scientific methods, 86-103, 136-138.
American system, differences in, 56-66, 85, 398.
Arms and ammunition, 229-231.

Ancient art objects, 76-80.
Art and industries, 71-80.
Automatic appliances and machinery, 94-107, 224-232.

Backwardness and low wages, 64-66.
Boots and shoes, comparative cost of labor in, 373, 374.

Calico printing compared, 247-249.
Chemistry in Europe and in America, 88.
Cloaks, Berlin manufacturing system, 360-362.
Coal mining, cost of labor compared in, 24, 25, 209-211.
Coking, cost of labor compared in, 215.
Conclusions, 391-405.
Consumable quantities compared, 163-166.
Consumption and production, 60-64.
Color and taste, 248.
Cost of labor and wages, 31-34, 215.
Cotton, Egyptian, 14.
" manufacturing, 233-242.
" manufacturing, time and wages, ratio to output in, 397.
Cotton raising, comparative results in, 147.

Cotton spinning, 36, 237.
Cotton velvets, duties on, 250-253.
" " not feasible to manufacture here, 254, 255.
Cultivation and ownership, 132, 133.
Cut glass industry in America, 202.

Disingenuous methods, 334, 338, 350, 373.
Distribution and production, 60.
Division of labor in ready-made clothing, etc., 368-374.
Dress goods, cost of labor compared in, 330.
Dyeing, cost of, 277, 316, 331, 336.

Errors and misconceptions regarding wages, 63-66.
Economy and science, 92, 93.
Eden, Frederic, conditions described by, 155. 399.
Education, art and industrial, 69.
" industrial, in France, 68.
Education and production, 68.
England, art industries in, 69-72.
" helped by American tariff, 232, 242.
Equipment of labor and wages, 102.
Evolution, industrial, 58-64.
Exports in cotton goods, 248, 378.
Exporters handicapped, 232, 242, 376-378.

Finishing of dry goods, 249, 250.
Flanders and France, agriculture contrasted in, 133.
Flax raising, why futile in America, 258-261.
Floating labor no pressure on wages, 28.

Food and wages, 108.
Foreign labor and wages, 29, 30.
" trade, 248, 250, 375, 376.
France, art and industrial education in, 68.
Freedom and oppression, results in agriculture, 118-133.
Free raw material, 5.
Fuel saving in iron-making, 92.
" saving in steamships, results of, 105.

German workingmen, living of, 167-171.
Germany, house-industries of, 50-53, 156.
Germany, backwardness and low wages, 64-66.
Glass manufacturing, 194-207.

Hand looms, 50-57, 157.
High wages, benefit of, to industries, 61-64.
High wages, general effect of, 173, 374.
Holland's early freedom, effect of, 119-122.
Home manufactures supplemented by foreign imports, 389.
Hosiery, cost of production of, 255-257.
Hours and product, 392-397.
House industries, 50-55, 156.

Ignorance and poverty, 109.
" working classes kept in, 67.
Imitating American methods, 232.
Improvements in machinery and methods, 24, 36, 37.
Industrial art in Europe, 68-80.

INDEX. 411

Industrial and art education deficient in America, 84.
Industrial art museums, 74–80.
" decline in wool manufacturing, 308, 309, 321.
Industrial differences, 12, 55, 56, 389.
Industries not helped by high tariff duties, 232, 233, 248, 254, 257, 263, 267, 285, 293.
Inefficiency and high tariffs, 184.
Ingrain carpets, comparative cost of, 348.
Ireland. industries of, 41–47.
Iron prices, 96, 217.

Japanese art, 71.

Kitchen gardening, 149.
Knit goods, duties on, 344.
" " comparative cost of labor, 345, 346.

Labor, comparative cost of, 25, 192, 196, 209, 211, 214, 215, 216, 217, 218, 226, 227, 237, 240, 241, 276, 277, 279, 280, 315, 317, 318, 330–340, 348, 353–356, 372, 374, 387.
Labor, cost of, 20–27, 387.
" and nutrition, 392.
" productiveness of, 20–22, 39.
" saving, 107, 186.
" and the tariff, 18.
Laveleye E. de, agriculture in Lombardy, 128.
Lavergne L. de, land in England and in France, 110.
Leading articles, comparative cost of labor in, 387.
Legislative ignorance in the tariff, 11.
Linen, failure to manufacture, 263.
Loading of silks, the, 273.

Lombardy, early institutions of, cause of progress, 126–129.
Lombardy, irrigation, 126–129.
" superior agriculture, rise in, 126–130.
Low standard of living, 52–395.
Long hours, detrimental effect of, 392–397.

Machinery, 93–100, 229.
Manufacturers' demand for tariff reform, 5.
Manuring, 112, 113.
Master-craftsmen, 75.
McKinley tariff opposed to industrial progress, 12.
Metallurgic progress, 92–98.
Metal industries, injurious effect of tariff on, 222.
Metal manufactures, exports of, 232.
Method of inquiry, 310, 313.
Methods, persistence of, 55–66.
Monopolies and tariffs, 202–206, 220, 325.

Nail making in England and in America, 225, 226.

Ore mining, comparative labor cost of iron, 214.
Ownership of land by cultivator, 118–133.

Peasant industries, 40–48.
Pig-iron making, comparative cost of labor in, 216.
Pile-fabrics, duties on, 344.
Pin-making, illustrating progress by methods in, 99.
Plate-glass, expansion of industry, 206.

Ploughs, reduction in America, 97.
Plush and velvet industry in silk, 284–291.
Plush and velvet, excessive rates of duties, 285, 290.
Poland, cause of downfall of, 118.
" primitive agriculture of, 116–118.
Poverty and home-market, 44, 46.
" and ignorance, 109.
Pottery in America and in England, 175–192.
Pottery, labor-saving appliances in, 186.
Prices of commodities, 155, 159–173.
Price reductions and science, 87–102.
Price relations in pottery, 182.
Print cloth, labor cost, comparison in, 240, 241.
Print cloth, manufacturing cost, comparison in, 245.
Print cloth, profits, 245.
Producers, relative positions of, to tariffs, 4.
Product and raw material, 13.
Product, increasing, of soil, 147–152.
Production, comparative cost of, 25, 192, 209, 211, 214, 215, 216, 217, 218, 226, 227, 237, 240, 241, 276, 277, 279, 280, 315, 318, 330–340, 348, 353, 356, 374.
Productiveness of labor depending on wages, 39.
Product, the net, progressive increase of, 139–150.
Profitableness of high farming, 139–150.
Progress and prosperity, the causes of, 401–405.

Progress measured by consumption, 160–171.
Protection by distance, 360–362.
" claims exaggerated, 177–190.
Pulp and paper making, economies in, 89.

Raw material, 9, 13–16.
" " differences in, 13–17.
Ready-made clothing industries, 355–369.
Reciprocity treaties, why illusory, 379–382.
Republican methods of controversion, 243, 244.
Ricardo, David, theory on wages, 19.
Rise in wages and declining cost, 31–34, 64–66.
Russia, primitive agriculture of, 114–116.

Scarcity removed by science, 135–137.
Science and agriculture, 134–152.
Science and prices, 87–102, 280.
Science in production, 85, 269.
Sectionalism in the tariff, 223.
Selling values in pottery compared, 183, 189.
Senatorial pettifogging, 244.
Sheep raising and agriculture, 298–301.
Shoddy and wool cheviots, comparison of manufacturing cost, 340.
Shoddy and wool substitutes in American woolen industry, 307–309.
Shrinkage of wools, 303–306, 313.

INDEX.

Silk, comparison of manufacturing cost, 280.
Silk, dyeing, 277.
" industry, the, 269-290.
" throwing, 275, 276.
" domestic industry, 50-55.
" weaving, 50-55, 278, 279.
Sizing of cotton, 241, 248, 357.
Skill in industry, 82.
Skill and wages, 27.
Spare culture, 148.
Specific duties, 4.
Spinning, 36, 238.
Standard of living compared, 154-165.
Statistical vagaries criticised, 311-314.
Steamship building, 106, 107.
" the, as a scientific achievement, 103-105.
Steel rails, comparison of cost of labor in, 218, 219.
Steel rails, profit in, 220, 221.
" reduction of cost in, 93, 94.
Stoneware, brown, comparative rates of wages in, 192.
Survival of obsolete methods, 29, 224, 226.
Sweating system, the, 363-368.

Tariff, the democratic policy, 5.
" differences in European and American protective, 8.
Tariff rates, increase of, in cotton embroidery, handkerchiefs, and lace, 267.
Tariff rates, increase in cotton hosiery, 257.
Tariff rates, increase in cotton velvet, 251.
Tariff rates, increase in glass and glassware, 195.
Tariff rates, increase in Italian cloth and cotton warp dress goods, 323-326.
Tariff rates, increase in knit fabrics, 346.
Tariff rates, increase in linen, 262.
Tariff rates, increase of, in pile fabrics, 344.
Tariff rates, increase of, in pottery, 181.
Tariff rates, increase of, in silk plush and velvet, 284, 285.
Tariff rates, increase of, in woolens and worsteds, 323-326.
Tariff, preventive of exports, 378.
" to prevent revenue, 382.
Taste and value, 70-74, 246.
Technical education, 82, 83, 249.
Textile industries, the, 234.
Tin plate industry, the, 233.
Tool machinery, 224, 229-232.
Training, 82.
Trenton pottery manufacturers, 179-190.
Truck farming, 137-146.
Truck stores in the Pennsylvania coal regions, 211.
Trusts and the tariff, 202, 205, 206, 213, 220.

Wages and consumption, 6, 158-178.
Wages, comparative rate of, in coal mining, 25, 209, 211.
Wages, comparative rate of, in coke-making, 215.
Wages, comparative rate of, in glass ware, 196-200.
Wages, comparative rate of, in ingrain carpets, 348.

Wages, comparative rate of, in ladies' button boots, 374.
Wages, comparative rate of, in nails, spikes, rivets, 226, 227.
Wages, comparative rate of, in ore mining, 214.
Wages, comparative rate of, in pig-iron making, 216, 217.
Wages, comparative rate of, in print cloth, 237, 240.
Wages, comparative rate of, in sheetings, 241.
Wages, comparative rate of, in silk manufacturing, 276, 277, 279.
Wages, comparative rate of, in steel rails, 218.
Wages, comparative rate of, in woolens, 330-340.
Wages, comparative rate of, in worsted coatings, 315-318.
Wages and efficiency, 26, 27.
Wage earners and the tariff, 9.
Wages, cause of high, 31, 34.
" highest in unprotected industries, 10.

Wages, low, an industrial detriment, 35.
Wages, high, result in low cost of production, 32, 34, 215.
Wage theory, 18.
War tariff, the, 3.
Wool, different kinds of, 15, 16.
Wool duty, the, 4, 295.
Woolens, comparative cost, positions of, in England and America, 353-356.
Wool duty and manufacture, 302-304, 332.
Wool prices, 295, 297.
Wool supply, 298.
Wool and woolens, 304-355.
Worsteds, comparative manufacturing cost of, 315-317.

Young, Arthur, Flanders and France, 131.
Young, Arthur, Lombardy, 127.
" " workingmen's position in England and France, 153, 154.

www.ingramcontent.com/pod-product-compliance
Lightning Source LLC
Chambersburg PA
CBHW051728300426
44115CB00007B/512